HISTORY

WESTMINSTER ASSEMBLY OF DIVINES

BY
William Maxwell Hetherington, D.D., LL.D.

Reprint edition April 1993
From the third edition 1856

Still Waters Revival Books

4710-37A Ave. Edmonton, AB Canada T6L 3T5
"PUBLISHING THE TRUE PEACE" (Isa. 52:7)

PRINTED IN THE UNITED STATES OF AMERICA

ISBN 0-921148-32-1

COMMEMORATIVE EDITION

PUBLISHED IN CONJUNCTION WITH THE

350th ANNIVERSARY OF THE CONVENING

OF THE WESTMINSTER ASSEMBLY

CELEBRATED BY THE NORTH AMERICAN

PRESBYTERIAN AND REFORMED COUNCIL

LONDON, ENGLAND

SEPTEMBER 21-27, 1993

Sponsors For This Commemorative Edition:

*Christian Education and Publications Committee of the
Presbyterian Church in America*

*Administrative Committee of the
Presbyterian Church in America*

The Associate Reformed Presbyterian Church

Greenville Presbyterian Theological Seminary (SC)

Knox Theological Seminary (FL)

Westminster Theological Seminary (PA)

Covenant Presbyterian Church, Oak Ridge, TN

PREFACE.

In common with all true Presbyterians, I have often regretted the want of a History of the Westminster Assembly of Divines, by whose labours were produced the Confession of Faith, the Directory of Public Worship, the Form of Church Government, and the Catechisms, which have so long been held as the Standards of the Presbyterian Churches throughout the world. Especially in such a time as the present, when all distinctive Presbyterian principles are not only called in question, but also misrepresented and condemned, such a want has become absolutely unendurable, unless Presbyterians are willing to permit their Church to perish under a load of unanswered, yet easily refuted, calumny. And as the best refutation of calumny is the plain and direct statement of truth, it is by that process that I have endeavoured to vindicate the principles and the character of the Presbyterian Church.

When contemplating the subject, there were two not very reconcilable ideas before my mind. The one was, to restrict the Work to such a size as might keep it within the reach of all Presbyterians, even those whose means were more limited than their inclinations, but who equally needed and desired

information ; the other was, to give details sufficiently minute
and conclusive to place the whole matter fully and fairly before the mind of the reader, that he might be able to form an
accurate judgment respecting the character and proceedings
of the Westminster Assembly, and also of the Church and
people of Scotland, who were so intimately connected with it.
How far these conflicting purposes have been reconciled it is
for others to judge ; this, however, I may be permitted to say,
that no pains have been spared in the endeavour to ascertain
the truth in even the most minute points which required investigation ; almost every book or pamphlet of any importance written at the time, or by men whose course of inquiries
has led them to traverse that period, having been carefully
read.   I had, indeed, entertained the design of giving a complete list of all the productions, in book or pamphlet form,
which have been consulted or perused ; but, in honest sincerity, I confess that I shrunk from doing so, lest it might
seem too like mere ostentation.   For a similar reason, but one
or two references to authorities, in each instance, have been
given, when it would have been equally easy to have produced half a dozen ; and I have chiefly referred to original
authorities, rather than to those which may be got in the common histories of the period ; for there can be little use in quot-
ing Hume, and Brodie, and Laing, and Godwin, and D'Israeli,
when we have before us the original authorities on which
their statements are founded.   By adopting this method, I
have also avoided the necessity of encumbering my Work with
digressive corrections of the erroneous or distorted views generally given by these historians, in their accounts of the Westminster Assembly, and of the conduct of the Presbyterians.

Inquiries have been frequently made respecting the manuscript of the Westminster Assembly's proceedings, kept by

the scribes or clerks of the Assembly; but that important document appears to be irrecoverably lost. One account states that it was burned in the great fire of London, in the year 1666. It was long thought that a copy of it had been taken, and was preserved in the library of Sion College; and some aver that this was actually the case, and that it too was destroyed in the fire which burned the House of Commons in 1834, having been placed there, along with other manuscript records relating to the Church of Scotland, during the inquiries of the Committee on Patronage.

We are informed by Baillie, that many members of the Assembly employed themselves in taking copious notes, during the course of the discussions in which they were engaged. It might have been expected that several of these manuscript note-books would have been still extant, by comparing which, the loss of the Assembly's own record might have been in a great measure supplied. None, however, have been published, except Lightfoot's Journal, and Baillie's Letters, and Gillespie's Notes; which are accordingly the most minute and authentic accounts that can now be obtained. The edition of Baillie to which I have referred, is that admirable one recently published under the care of David Laing, Esq. To that gentleman, to the Librarians of the Advocates' and the Theological Libraries, to the Rev. Dr Cunningham, the Rev. Dr M'Crie, the Rev. Dr Goold, the late Rev. Samuel Martin of Bathgate, and the Rev. Robert Craig of Rothesay, I take this opportunity of expressing my grateful thanks for the access which they so readily gave me to their literary stores.

Dr Thomas Goodwin, one of the leading Independent divines, wrote fifteen volumes of notes or journals of the Assembly's proceedings, as we are informed in a memoir of his life by his son, three only of which are still preserved in

Dr Williams' Library, London. It was my intention to have consulted these, but I found it impracticable at the time. There are in the Advocates' Library, Edinburgh, two manuscript volumes of notes by Gillespie, one in quarto, the other in octavo; both of which I have been courteously permitted to peruse. They seem to be transcripts from the original, and of the two the octavo is the more complete. They both begin February 2, 1644; the quarto ends May 22, and the octavo, October 25, the same year. Their chief value consists in the complete corroboration which they furnish to the printed accounts of Lightfoot and Baillie,—as will be seen from an extract inserted in the Appendix; but they would be well worthy of publication in any collected edition of Gillespie's works—as has recently been done.

In tracing the controversies by which both Church and kingdom were agitated during the deliberations of the Westminster Assembly, it has been my endeavour to avoid, as much as possible, giving a controversial aspect to my own production. My duty was, to relate faithfully what was said, written, and done, by the eminent men of that period; and, in discharging that duty, I have often felt it expedient to transcribe their own language, as the most impartial way of recording their sentiments; and when occasionally stating my own opinions, I have striven to do so as fairly and impartially as may well be expected from one who does not hesitate to acknowledge that he feels deeply and warmly interested in every thing that relates to Presbyterian principles and character. Certainly I have no wish to misrepresent either the opinions or the practice of any body of sincere Christians,— least of all would I censure harshly the errors into which pious and earnest-hearted men were driven by Prelatic persecution, or into which they fell in the sudden revulsion produced by its overthrow, and in the excitement arising from unwonted religious liberty. Let me trust that Evangelical Dissenters will give credit to the sincerity of the feelings which I thus avow. There is no pleasure in recording the errors of the good, and the follies of the wise; but there may be much advantage, if we are thereby taught to shun the error and the folly, and to imitate only the goodness and the wisdom.

The plan of compression within the narrowest practicable limits, which I have adopted, has prevented me from recording many particulars of much interest and importance; but should time and health be spared me, I may at some future period resume the task, and attempt to produce a work on the subject at once more minute and more comprehensive. In the meantime, if my present Work shall be found to have vindicated the character of that truly venerable body of Presbyterian divines from the unjust aspersions by which it has been so long assailed, and to have rendered the principles which they held, and the objects which they sought to accomplish, more clear and intelligible than they have hitherto been, I shall be amply recompensed,—especially if, in pointing out the errors into which contending parties fell, and the way in which these errors and contentions might have been avoided, I shall have succeeded to any degree in directing the minds of all sincere Christians to contemplate the necessity and the practicability of realising now the great idea of a general Evangelical Union, far more extensive and complete than could have been either hoped for or attained at the period of the Westminster Assembly.

Torphichen Manse,
May 1843.

PREFATORY NOTE TO THE THIRD EDITION.

In preparing a new edition of the History of the Westminster Assembly, I have both given it a careful revision, for the purpose of correcting inaccuracies and inserting such further information as renewed inquiries had afforded; and in an additional chapter I have furnished an outline of the theological productions of that learned and venerable body, thereby supplying what had been complained of as defective,—the proof that their labours were not merely controversial. I have also enlarged the Appendix, by giving brief biographical sketches of the Scottish Commissioners to the Assembly; and a note on Philip Nye, the leading Independent divine, investigating the question how far he is entitled to be regarded as the man who first proclaimed the great principle of religious liberty. And I venture to entertain the hope, that these additions, amounting in all to about fifty pages, will be found to have increased the value of the work, and to have rendered it somewhat more worthy of that public favour with which it has already, in previous editions, been honoured.

Edinburgh, *May* 1856.

TABLE OF CONTENTS.

CHAPTER I.

INTRODUCTORY.

CHAPTER II.

MEETING OF THE WESTMINSTER ASSEMBLY.

CHAPTER III.

THE INDEPENDENT CONTROVERSY.

CHAPTER IV.

THE ERASTIAN CONTROVERSY.

CHAPTER V.

CONCLUSION OF THE WESTMINSTER ASSEMBLY.

CHAPTER VI.

THEOLOGICAL PRODUCTIONS OF THE WESTMINSTER ASSEMBLY.

APPENDIX.

HISTORY

OF

THE WESTMINSTER ASSEMBLY.

CHAPTER I.

INTRODUCTORY.

Quarrel between Henry VIII. and the Pope—Henry assumes the Supremacy of the Church of England—Overthrow of the Monastic System, and partial Reformation—Six Articles—Death of Henry—Accession of Edward VI.—Progress of Reformation—Homilies—Liturgy—Book of Ordination—Hooper's Opposition to the Ceremonies—Articles—Death of Edward—Accession of Mary—Restoration of Popery—Persecution—Frankfort—Puritans—Death of Mary, and Accession of Elizabeth—Revived Supremacy—Check to Reformation—Ceremonies — Convocation of 1562, with which all Reformation ceased—General view of the Puritan Controversy—Harsh conduct of Parker—The Puritans begin to form a separate Body—Their Opinions—Imprisoned—Parliament attempt to interfere—The Puritans associate for mutual Instruction—Form a Presbytery—The Queen and Grindal—Rise of the Brownists—Whitgift—Increased Severity—Bancroft's *jure divino* Prelacy—Martin Mar-Prelate Tracts—Sabbath Controversy—Death of Elizabeth, and Accession of James—Hampton Court Conference—Opinion of the Judges on the Power of the High Commission—Rise of the Independents—The Book of Sports—Resistance to Political Tyranny—Combination—Death of James, and Accession of Charles—Contests with Parliament—Laud—Contest with Scotland—The Long Parliament—Impeachment of Strafford and Laud—Smectymnuus—The Army Plot — Incident — Irish Massacre — Remonstrance — Protestation of the Bishops—Abolition of the Hierarchy—Intercourse with Scotland—Ordinance calling an Assembly of Divines—Summary.

THE remark has frequently been made, accompanied with expressions of surprise and regret, that no separate historical

B

account of the Westminster Assembly of Divines has yet been written. Every person who has directed his attention to the events of the seventeenth century, whether with regard to their civil or their religious aspect, has felt that it was impossible fully to understand either the one or the other line of study, without taking into view the character of the Westminster Assembly, the purpose for which it met, and the result of its deliberations. Yet, notwithstanding this universally felt necessity, the subject has never received an adequate investigation, and consequently still remains in such obscurity as renders it exposed to every kind of misrepresentation. Some have regarded it as comparatively an isolated event, not very influential on those around it, and serving chiefly to display, in a combined form, the characters of the men and measures of those times; others have viewed it as the abortive attempt of a parcel of narrow-minded and yet ambitious fanatics, serving to reveal their dangerous pretensions, and then, by its failure, exposing them to deserved ridicule. The mere student of civil history will doubtless see little in it to attract his notice, engrossed, as his attention will be, by the schemes of politicians and the din of arms; while, on the other hand, the mere theologian will generally be little disposed to regard any thing about it, except its productions. But the man who penetrates a little deeper into the nature of those unrevealed but powerful influences which move a nation's mind, and mould its destinies, will be ready to direct his attention more profoundly to the objects and deliberations of an assembly which met at a moment so critical, and was composed of the great master-minds of the age; and the theologian who has learned to view religion as the vital principle of human nature, equally in nations and in the individual man, will not easily admit the weak idea, that such an assembly could have been an isolated event, but will be disposed earnestly to inquire what led to its meeting, and what important consequences followed. And although the subject has not hitherto been investigated with such a view, it may, we trust, be possible to prove, that it was the most important event in the century in which it occurred ; and that it has exerted, and in all probability will yet exert, a far more wide and permanent influence upon both the civil and the religious history of mankind than has generally been even imagined.

Intimately connected as the Westminster Assembly was both with the civil and the religious history of the two kingdoms of England and Scotland, it will be absolutely necessary to give a preliminary outline of the leading events in both countries, from the time of the Reformation till the meeting of the Assembly, in order that a clear conception may be obtained of the cause of its meeting, the circumstances in which it met, and the object which it was intended to accomplish. We shall then be in a fit condition to investigate the proceedings of the Assembly itself, to understand their true character, to mark their direct bearing, and to trace their more remote results.

The circumstances that led to the disagreement between Henry VIII. and the pope are so well known, that it is unnecessary to do more than merely allude to them. Whether Henry actually began to entertain conscientious scruples respecting the lawfulness of his marriage with Katherine of Arragon, his brother Arthur's widow, before he came enamoured of Anne Boleyn, or whether his incipient affection for that lady induced him to devise a method of being released from his wife, is an inquiry of no great moment in itself, except as to its bearing on the character of the monarch. Suffice it to state, that the king consulted the Archbishop of Canterbury, and required him to procure the opinions of the bishops of England on the subject. All, with the exception of Fisher, Bishop of Rochester, declared that in their judgment it was an unlawful marriage. But as a dispensation had been obtained from the pope, before the marriage took place, it

became necessary to procure a papal recognition of the intended divorce; which was a matter of no little difficulty,
both because such a measure would seem to invalidate a
previous papal bull, to the discredit of the doctrine of infallibility, and because there would arise a serious question respecting the legitimacy of the Princess Mary, and offence
might be taken by the King of Spain. All these dangers
were clearly seen by Cardinal Wolsey; who, accordingly,
without venturing directly to oppose the king's desires, contrived to cause delays, to procure evasive answers, and to
protract the proceedings by every method which fear of the
issue could prompt and deep craft could devise. At length
Cranmer, till then a comparatively unknown man, suggested,
that, instead of a long and fruitless negotiation at Rome, it
would be better to consult all the learned men and universities
of Christendom, to ascertain whether the marriage were unlawful in itself, by virtue of any divine precept; for if that
were proved, then it would follow, that the pope's dispensation could be of no force to make that lawful which God has
declared unlawful.* When the king heard of this suggestion,
he immediately adopted it, sent for Cranmer, received him into
favour, and placed such confidence in his honour, integrity,
and judgment, that it was never afterwards thoroughly shaken,
either by the artifices of enemies, or the varying moods of the
capricious sovereign himself.

Cranmer prosecuted the scheme which he had suggested
so successfully, that he procured, both from the English universities, and from nearly all the learned men in Europe,
answers to the effect, that the king's marriage was contrary
to the law of God. These answers were laid before the
Parliament, which met in January 1531, and assented to by
both Houses, as also by the Convocation of the Clergy,
which was met at the same time. Still the pope had not
consented, and the hostility between him and Henry was

* Burnet's History of the Reformation, vol. i. p. 125.

necessarily increased by what had taken place regarding the proposed divorce. Henry was not disposed to pause now, till he should have secured his power over the clergy; and as they were all implicated in some of Wolsey's proceedings, which had been declared to have involved him in a *præmunire*, they were held to be amenable to all its penalties. Their danger rendered them submissive, and in the convocation at Canterbury, a petition was agreed upon to be offered to the king, in which he was styled, " The Protector and Supreme Head of the Church and the Clergy of England." Gratified with this title, the king granted a pardon to the clergy; but did not, as they had probably expected, permit it to remain an empty title. In May 1532, he informed the House of Commons that he had learned that all the prelates, at their consecration, swore an oath quite contrary to that which they swore to the crown—so that it seemed they were the pope's subjects rather than his; referring it to their care to take such order in it that the king might not be deluded. The prorogation of the Parliament prevented the immediate collision between the civil and the ecclesiastical powers, which the investigation of that point would have caused; but it was now abundantly evident on what the king had bent his mind. The question respecting the pope's supremacy was now the subject of inquiry and discussion throughout the kingdom; and at length it was formally brought before Parliament, and on the 20th of March 1534-5, a bill was passed, abolishing papal supremacy in England, and declaring the king to be the Supreme Head of the Church of England; and in the following June, a circular letter was sent by the king, not only to all the bishops, but also to all the justices of the peace, requiring the universal promulgation of the decree respecting the abolition of the pope's supremacy and the recognition of his own; and empowering the civil functionaries to ascertain whether the clergy did their duty sincerely.*

* Burnet's Hist. Ref., vol. iii. p. 144.

So delighted was King Henry with his title of Supreme Head of the Church, that he caused it to be enacted that it should be for ever joined to the other titles of the crown, and be reckoned one of them ; and even caused a seal to be cut for public use in his new ecclesiastical office ; and when directing a visitation of the whole clergy of England, dated the 18th of September 1535, added these words—"Under our seal, that we use in ecclesiastical matters, which we have ordered to be hereunto appended." *

It will be at once seen, that the title of Supreme Head of the Church, and the power in ecclesiastical matters which arose from it, were claimed by Henry, not as the necessary means for promoting reformation, nor from any religious conviction that the pope's assumption of it was in itself sinful ; but solely from the desire of rescuing himself from any control, and for the purpose of possessing, in his own person, the most full and absolute power that could be imagined. And it rendered it at once a matter of utter impossibility for the Church of England to prosecute its own reformation according to the deliberate judgment of its most enlightened members, whatever might be their opinion of the requirements of the Word of God. To this fatal dogma of the king's supremacy and headship of the Church of England may be directly traced nearly all the corruptions of that Church, and nearly all the subsequent civil calamities of the British Isles. For it would not be difficult to prove, that there can be no security for either civil or religious liberty in any country where the supreme civil and ecclesiastical jurisdictions are both possessed by the same ruling power. It matters little whether the ruling power be ecclesiastical, holding the civil subordinate to it, as does the Papacy ; or civil, holding the ecclesiastical subordinate, as in the case of Henry and his successors ; for in either case the result is a despotism, under which the people must sink into utter de-

* Burnet's Hist. Ref., vol. iii. p. 151.

gradation, or against which they are provoked, from time to time, to rise in all the dangerous fierceness of revolutionary convulsion. But it is enough merely to suggest this view at present; it will demand more particular examination in future stages of our inquiries.

Almost the first public use made by the king of his acknowledged supremacy in religion, was to send Cranmer, now Archbishop of Canterbury, on a visitation of the monasteries throughout the kingdom. It was no difficult matter to convict these popish institutions of such crimes and abominations as are not fit to be mentioned, " equal," says Burnet, " to any that were in Sodom;" so that their suppression was but the sweeping away of a great moral nuisance, too loathsome any longer to be endured. It served, at the same time, as a measure by which the king's coffers were replenished, some of his favourites enriched, and the better part of the nation gratified by the removal of a system of enormities which had been long regarded with extreme detestation. About the same time, it was resolved that the Bible should be translated into English, and published for the instruction of the community; though this was strenuously resisted by a large proportion of the clergy, and carried only by the influence of Cranmer and the queen. The fall of the queen, which took place soon after, threatened to retard the progress of reformation, and the pope attempted a reconciliation with the king. But Henry had no inclination to subject himself again to papal control; and, following Cranmer's advice, he proceeded to make further changes. In the year 1536, the Convocation were induced to agree to certain articles of religion, which were accordingly promulgated on the royal authority. In these articles, the standards of faith were declared to be,—the Bible, the Apostolic, Nicene, and Athanasian Creeds, and the decrees of the first four general Councils, without regard to tradition or the decrees of the Church; and the doctrine of justification was declared to " signify remission of sins, and acceptation into the favour of God, that is to say, a perfect renovation in Christ;" but auricular confession was held to be, necessary, the corporal presence of Christ in the sacrament was maintained, doing reverence to images and praying to saints were approved of, and various other corruptions and mere ceremonial observances were left untouched.* This limited reformation gave little satisfaction to any, one party thinking it too much, and the other too little; yet it tended to encourage those who wished reform, with the hope that what was thus begun would be gradually and thoroughly accomplished.

[1539.] In the year 1538, the English translation of the Bible was published, and injunctions were given to all the clergy to procure these Bibles, one for each church, and to encourage all persons to peruse them; condemning, at the same time, the worship of images, and permitting the prayers to saints to be omitted. But while the Reformers were rejoicing in this apparently rapid progress of the good work, their hopes were suddenly cast to the ground and their prospects darkened. The very next year, the king, on the pretext of putting an end to controversies in religion, required a committee to be appointed for the purpose of drawing up articles of agreement, to which all might consent. The committee could not agree, and the subject was brought before the House of Lords by the Duke of Norfolk, who named six articles for discussion. Notwithstanding the opposition of Cranmer, these articles were passed, and all the kingdom commanded to receive them, the penalty of opposition being imprisonment, forfeiture of property, or death as heretics. They contained the following tenets :—The real presence in the sacrament, communion in one kind only, the celibacy of the priesthood, that vows of chastity made by either sex should be observed, that private masses should be continued, and that auricular confession was necessary, and should be

* Burnet's Hist. Ref., vol. i. pp. 333-338.

retained in the Church.* By this act it was rendered abundantly evident, that little of Popery had been removed but the name; or rather, that England had obtained, instead of an ecclesiastical, a royal pope. Yet, with remarkable inconsistency, or at least want of penetration, the king very soon after consented to an act permitting private persons to purchase Bibles, and keep them in their own possession. The short-sighted despot did not perceive that the private use of the Scriptures would soon teach his people the right of private judgment also in matters of religion, which all his boasted supremacy would not long be able to control.

The fall of Cromwell, caused in a great measure by the intrigues of the popish party, allowed them to regain considerable ascendency, and retarded the progress of reformation, though it still continued slowly to gain ground. An attempt was made by the popish bishops to procure the suppression of the Bible, on the ostensible ground of its being an inaccurate translation. This, however, they did not obtain; but an act was made "about religion," the effect of which was to empower the king to confirm, rescind, or change any act, or any provision in any act, that treated of religion. A more complete and arbitrary supremacy in all matters of religion, than was now possessed by Henry, it is almost impossible to imagine. And the effect was correspondent to the cause; for the king, guided alone by his own fierce and capricious will, was almost equally hostile to both parties, popish and reforming, inflicting the extreme penalty of death upon either with indiscriminate severity. But the death of the king rescued the nation from intolerable oppression, and gave opportunity for the more earnest and successful prosecution of the great work of reformation under his young and amiable successor.

[1547.] No sooner had a suitable arrangement of civil affairs been effected by the regency, than Cranmer, supported by the Protector Somerset, and countenanced by the young

* Burnet's Hist. Ref., vol. i. pp. 400, 401.

king, Edward VI., resumed the important duty of prosecuting the reformation of the Church. By an act of the preceding reign, the proclamation of the king, or of his counsellors if under age, was of sufficient authority to enable them
to proceed, as if by act of Parliament, in cases not otherwise
provided for, so as not to encroach on the just liberties of the
subject, or to interfere with other acts or proclamations.
They accordingly sent out visitors over England, which was
for that purpose divided into six circuits. The duty of those
visitors was to inquire into all Church matters, to redress all
wrongs, and remove all abuses, and particularly to ascertain
the sufficiency or insufficiency of the clergy throughout the
country. Along with these visitors, they sent the most eminent preachers that could be found, to communicate sound
and full instruction in the true principles of religion to both
clergy and people. And to remedy the deplorable ignorance
which everywhere prevailed among the clergy, some were
appointed to compile homilies, explanatory of the most important doctrines and duties of Christianity. Several of
these homilies contain very clear and forcible statements and
elucidations of sacred truth, others are less valuable, and
some are not a little erroneous in several respects. They
were, however, well fitted to meet the necessities of an
ignorant clergy and an uninstructed people; but it could
scarcely have been dreamed by Cranmer, that the method
devised by him for the remedy of a disease would be retained
for its perpetuation,—that because he provided sermons and
prayers for those who could neither preach nor pray, *that*
would come to be regarded as a precedent of force enough to
prevent learned and pious men from preparing sermons and
prayers for themselves.

[1548.] The next reforming step was an act permitting
the communion to be received in both kinds. Then followed
another, prohibiting private masses. A catechism was soon
afterwards prepared by Cranmer. And proceeding to investi-

gate the offices, or ritual of the Church, it was at length determined that a new Liturgy should be prepared, as the best method of getting quit of the superstitions by which that in present use was disfigured. This Liturgy was confirmed by act of Parliament, in the year 1548–9, and its use commanded on the ultimate penalty of imprisonment for life.* About the same time, there were several severe proceedings against Anabaptists and other sectaries, one of whom, Joan of Kent, was condemned to the stake ; but the mild and gentle young king could not be induced to sign the warrant for her execution without the urgent persuasions of Cranmer himself, who, in this instance, as also in those of Lambert, and Anne Askew, in the preceding reign, forgot the spirit of that gentle and gracious religion of which he was so eminent a teacher and reformer.†

[1550–1.] The Book of Ordinations was next made and ratified, which had a strong tendency to give a character of fixed rigidity to the Church of England. The evil consequence of undue strictness in matters of mere form and ceremony was soon apparent, when Hooper refused to be consecrated as a bishop in the episcopal vestments. This simple-minded and sincere Reformer condemned these vestments as human inventions, brought in by tradition or custom, and not suitable to the simplicity of the Christian religion.‡ Few impartial persons will doubt that he was perfectly in the right, both in point of fact and in propriety of feeling ; for no one can deny the human origin of such matters, and few will regard them as conferring dignity on the gospel, so glorious in its divine simplicity. But he was to learn one direct consequence of the sovereign's supremacy, namely, that there was to be an order of the clergy decked with courtly adornments, and in that respect at least "conformed to the world," contrary to the apostolic precept. A great and wide-

---

* Burnet's Hist. Ref., vol. ii. pp. 116, 127.　　† Ibid., vol. ii. p. 179.
‡ Ibid., vol. ii. p. 245, *et seq.*

spread controversy arose on this subject. Correspondence was held with foreign churches and divines, with the view of ascertaining their opinion respecting the lawfulness of obeying the civil magistrate's order to use such vestments in the worship of God. Various opinions were given, many of the best and wisest men being extremely grieved that dangerous disputes should arise about matters not in their own nature of vital importance. Bucer recommended compliance; but wished these vestments disused, as connected with superstition, and a more complete reformation established. At length a compromise was effected. Hooper was required to wear the episcopal vestments when he was consecrated, and when he preached before the king, or in a cathedral; but was permitted to lay them aside on other occasions. This slight matter was a sufficient indication, that the reformation was to be stopped whenever it had reached as far as the king and court thought proper; and that those who wished for further reformation, and aimed at again realising primitive simplicity and purity, would be constrained to pause, and painfully to submit to what they could not remedy. It might have been regarded as of little consequence what vestments were worn in public worship; but it was a matter of grave and serious import to find, that conscientious feelings in affairs of religion were to be overborne by the dictate of the civil magistrate. From this time forward there began to be a party in England who longed for a more complete reformation than had been or could be obtained, although it was not till a considerably later period that this party attracted public attention under a distinctive name.

[1552.] In the year 1552, the alterations which had been made in the Book of Common Prayer by the reformers during the course of the preceding year, were ratified by act of Parliament, and ordered to be universally employed, under the penalties by which the previous Liturgy had been enforced. In the same year the Articles of Religion were prepared, chiefly by Cranmer and Ridley, and published by the king's authority, a short time before his lamented death.* A book was also drawn up for giving rules to the ecclesiastical courts in all matters of government and discipline; but this was never ratified, as the king's decease took place before it was fully prepared. This was, perhaps, the greatest misfortune that befell the Church of England in consequence of the premature death of Edward, as it was thereby left totally without government or discipline, such as, though limited by the acknowledged regal supremacy, might yet have been, in the first instance, administered by its own courts. Hence it became impossible for the Church of England to exercise any direct influence in checking immorality, reforming abuses, or even in preserving its own most sacred ordinances from profanation. Even Burnet laments its want of the power to exercise discipline, and suggests the desirableness that the power of excommunication might yet be brought into the Church.† Such, however, was the inevitable consequence of making the king the Supreme Head of the Church, rendering it necessarily impossible for the Church to reform itself beyond what he or his state advisers might choose to permit.

[1553.] The truth of this was immediately made apparent on the accession of Queen Mary, in the year 1553. An early act of her sovereignty was the issuing of a proclamation, in which she declared her adherence to the religion that she had professed from her infancy, disclaiming the intention of compelling her subjects, till public order should be taken in the matter by common consent; and, in the meantime, straitly charging that none should preach, or expound Scripture, or print any books or plays, without her special license. The deprived popish bishops were speedily restored to their sees, and the reformed bishops, some sent to prison at once, and others thrust out of the House of Lords, because they refused to reverence the mass at its opening. The laws passed

* Burnet's Hist. Ref., vol. iii. pp. 308, 310. † Ibid., vol. ii. p. 326.

by King Edward concerning religion were repealed; and a negotiation commenced for procuring a reconciliation with the pope. The mass was everywhere resumed, the laws against heresy revived, and every step taken for bringing the nation once more under the degrading thraldom of Popery, with all possible expedition. All this was done directly by the authority of the Queen, as Supreme Head of the Church of England; for this title she took care to retain and enforce at the commencement of her reign, though it was afterwards disused. Indeed, she could not so readily have accomplished her purpose without the power which this title was admitted to confer; so fatally was it productive of evil, so soon had it ceased to be available for good, even when held by the pious Edward.

But it is quite unnecessary to relate the events that successively followed, and to sketch even the outlines of the fierce persecution which characterised the reign of a queen so well known by the fearfully emphatic title of "The Bloody Mary." Life alone was wanting to her to have completely overthrown the Reformation in England, and to have placed again the kingdom beneath the Romish yoke. And it deserves to be carefully remarked, that this dread consummation was so nearly accomplished almost entirely by two conjunct influences—by the queen's ecclesiastical supremacy, and by the wealth and consequent power of the prelates. The tendency of the latter element had been foreseen by some, as appears from a letter written to the Protector Somerset by Sir Philip Hobby; in which, after suggesting the wisdom of appointing the godly bishops an honest and competent living, and taking from them the rest of those worldly possessions and dignities which tend to prevent the right discharge of their office, he adds, "The Papists say, They doubt not but my lords the bishops, being a great number of stout and well learned men, will well enough weigh against their adversaries, and maintain still their whole estate; which coming to pass, they have good hope that in time these princely pillars will well enough resist this fury, and bring all things again into the old order." * This shrewd prediction was well-nigh fulfilled in "Bloody Mary's" days; an approximation was made towards it again under the management of Laud; and it is possible that a similar peril may once more arise.

Reference has been already made to the opposition which Hooper offered to the episcopal vestments, and other unimportant and superstitious ceremonies, as probably exhibiting the very origin of what afterwards became the great Puritan party in England. Another event must also be mentioned, which certainly very much increased, and has by many been thought to have first caused, that unpropitious schism. During the persecution in the reign of Mary, many Protestants, both lay and clerical, sought safety by flight to the Continent. Of these a considerable body took up their residence at Frankfort, while others went to Strasburg, Zurich, and Basle. The Frankfort exiles at first entered into communion with a congregation of French Protestants, on the agreement that they should subscribe the French Confession of Faith, and not insist upon retaining the forms and ceremonies of the English Liturgy. For a time all went on in peace and harmony, under three pastors, chosen by the congregation, of whom John Knox was one; but the English having invited some of their countrymen at Strasburg and Zurich to come and join them, they replied, that they could not do so unless they would conform strictly and entirely to the religious service appointed by King Edward. The Frankfort congregation refused to do so; stating, that if the Strasburgh divines had no other views but to reduce the congregation to King Edward's form, and to establish Popish ceremonies, they had better stay away. The Frankfort brethren consulted Calvin, and other leading continental reformers, who all censured the English Liturgy, thought it more becoming godly ministers

* Burnet's Hist. Ref., vol. iii., p. 280.

of Christ to aim at something better and purer, and expressed surprise that they were so fond of "Popish dregs." The controversy might probably have gone no further, but for the inopportune arrival at Frankfort of Dr Cox, who had been tutor to King Edward, and possessed great influence among his countrymen. He at once broke through the whole previous agreement, interrupted the usual service, by answering aloud after the minister, and, by private intriguing, got the majority to consent to his aggressive innovations. The injured party applied to the magistrates, who gave order that the original agreement should be observed, threatening to shut up the place of worship if this command were disobeyed. With a baseness which has few equals, Cox and his party went privately to the magistrates, and accused Knox of treason against the Emperor of Germany, his son Philip, and Queen Mary of England; founding this charge on some expressions in his small treatise, entitled "Admonition to England." The magistrates were in great perplexity; for though they utterly disapproved of the conduct of Cox and the informers, they were afraid to offend the emperor's council. In this dilemma they advised John Knox to withdraw from Frankfort, for his own safety, and for the sake of peace. He consented, and withdrew amidst the complaints and tears of his attached friends. Following up his disgraceful victory, Cox falsely represented to the magistrates that the English Liturgy was now universally acceptable to the congregation, and procured an order for its unlimited use. He then abrogated the code of discipline, procured the appointment of a bishop, and rejoiced in having now "the face of an English Church." Thus, by intolerance, treachery, and despotism, they succeeded in overthrowing a Church whose scriptural simplicity and purity they might have rejoiced to imitate, and in setting up human inventions, in which pride and selfishness might glory; giving, likewise, an ominous intimation of the spirit likely to prevail in such a Church as theirs, should it regain the ascendency, and become established in England. For in this instance they had not to plead, as in the case of Hooper, respect for the civil authority by which vestments and ceremonies were enjoined, the Frankfort magistrates having actually discountenanced them ; but it was with them as it ever is when man mingles his own devices with God's appointments,—to his own vain fancies he clings with desperate and fierce tenacity, while he lays hold weakly and loosely on the unchanging laws and principles of divine revelation.*

[1558.] Elizabeth, upon her accession to the throne, found herself in a situation of considerable difficulty,—threatened with foreign wars, and her subjects divided, anxious, and alarmed on the all-important subject of religion. Her wisest counsellors advised her first to settle the relations of the country with foreign states, and then to proceed with what religious reformation might be necessary. There was also another reason for this course : Elizabeth, on her accession to the throne, sent intimation of that event to the pope, and waited an answer from Rome before declaring her purposes with regard to religion. That answer declared her illegitimate, and commanded her to abandon the throne, and submit to the will of the Roman pontiff. This insolence determined her to the support of the Protestant cause. To prevent disputes in the meantime, a proclamation was issued, prohibiting all preaching, and requiring that nothing should be done in public worship but the reading of the Gospel and Epistle for the day, the Lord's Prayer, the Creed, and the Ten Commandments, till proper arrangements should be made and further instructions given. Parliament met in January 1559. and proceeded with alacrity to the discharge of its duties. The Act of Supremacy, which had fallen into abeyance during the latter period of Mary's reign, was re-enacted, restoring to the Crown complete supremacy in all causes, civil and

* M'Crie's Life of Knox, pp. 86, 87; Neale's History of the Puritans, vol. i. pp. 76–82.

ecclesiastical, as it had been in the times of Henry VIII. and Edward VI.* To this bill several others were annexed, reviving various acts of the reign of Henry, and repealing those of Mary; so that, by this one enactment, the external policy of the Church was restored to almost the very same condition in which it had been at the death of King Edward. One proviso in this act, added for the purpose of enabling the queen to execute her supremacy, empowered such persons as should be commissioned by her majesty to reform and order ecclesiastical matters. This gave rise to the Court of High Commission, by which afterwards so many acts of cruelty and despotism were perpetrated, both in England and in Scotland; especially in the latter country, when Prelacy was forced upon it by the treacherous tyranny of King James.

Some of the reformed divines were next appointed to revise King Edward's Liturgy, and to see whether any such changes could be made in it as would tend to render it more likely to include some whose opinions were yet short of a thorough reformation. In particular, it was proposed to have the language of the communion service so modified that it might not necessarily exclude the belief of the corporal presence. After several alterations, all leaning rather to Popery than to Protestantism, had been made, the revised Book of Common Prayer was ratified by act of Parliament, and uniformity in worship according to it enjoined. The Popish bishops refused to take the oath of supremacy, and were, in consequence, deprived of their offices and powers. This enabled the queen

* In the queen's injunctions, subsequently issued, an explanation was given of the oath of supremacy; in which her majesty declared that she did not pretend to any authority for the ministering of divine service in the Church, and that all that she claimed was that which at all times belonged to the imperial crown of England;—that she had the sovereignty and rule over all manner of persons, under God, so that no foreign power had rule over them. If the oath of supremacy had implied no more than the plain meaning of these words, it would scarcely have been disputed by any; but it would have been ineffectual for the purpose for which it was intended, and it would not have sanctioned much that was done under its authority.

to supply their places with men better affected to reformation; which was accordingly done, though not without difficulty, the very best men being reluctant to undertake situations of such responsibility, and many being decidedly opposed to the ceremonies, rites, and vestments which were required, and which they regarded as remnants of superstition, and inconsistent with Christian simplicity.

The reforming divines soon became aware that in these points they had to encounter her majesty's opposition. The queen was naturally vain, and therefore fond of pomp and magnificence in every thing; nor did her reverence for religion teach her to abstain from presuming to seek the gratification of her personal tastes and prejudices in matters too sacred for mortal creature to tamper with. It was with great difficulty that they prevailed with her to insert in her injunctions a command for the removal of all images out of churches; but they could not induce her to abandon the use of a crucifix in her own chapel.

The controversy concerning vestments, and rites, and ceremonies continued, with increased asperity, on both sides. All the court divines, as they may be termed, headed by Archbishop Parker, supported the queen's desire for retaining as much show and pomp in religious matters as might be possible; while Jewell, Grindal, Sampson, Fox the martyrologist, and all the most distinguished for piety and liberal-mindedness, did their utmost to procure a more complete reformation; and for this purpose maintained a close correspondence with the most eminent of the continental reformers.* Jewell, in particular, exerted himself to the utmost against these vain frivolities. " Some," said he, " were so much set on the matter of the habits, as if the Christian reli-

* The leading men of the first race of Puritans were, Bishops Jewell, Grindal, Horn, Sandys, Pilkington, Parkhurst, and Guest; also Miles Coverdale, Fox, Dr Humphreys, Mr Sampson, and many others of scarcely inferior reputation. Even Parker at first opposed the episcopal vestments, and was consecrated without them.

gion consisted in garments; but we," added he, "are not called
to the consultations concerning that scenical apparel; he could
set no value on these fopperies. Some were crying up a golden
mediocrity; he was afraid it would prove a leaden one." * In
short, it is not too much to say, that all the best, wisest, and
most pious and learned divines of the Church of England—
all the true reformers—longed and strove for a more complete
reformation, lamented that it continued but a half-reformed
Church, and were the real forefathers of the Puritans.†

In the beginning of the year 1562, a meeting of the Convocation was held, in which the subject of further reformation was vigorously discussed on both sides. Some alterations
were made in the articles of religion, originally drawn up in
King Edward's reign. These were at first forty-two in
number; but by remitting some and combining others, they
were reduced to the thirty-nine which have ever since
formed the standard of faith in the Church of England. It
cannot be said that they were in all respects improved by
these alterations, as any one may see by comparing them.
But when it was proposed that there should be some alterations in the Prayer-Book, a very warm debate ensued. Six
alterations were proposed, to the following purport:—The
abrogation of all holidays, except Sabbaths, and those relating to Christ,—that in prayer the minister should turn his
face to the people, so that they might hear and be edified,—
that the ceremony of the cross in baptism might be omitted,
—that the sick and aged might not be compelled to kneel at
the communion,—that the partial use of the surplice might
be sufficient,—and that the use of organs be laid aside. ‡
The main argument used against these proposed improvements was, that they were contrary to the Book of Common
Prayer, which was ratified by act of Parliament, so that no

* Burnet's Hist. Ref., vol. iii. p. 424.
† In proof of this, see Life of Knox, Note R.
‡ Burnet, vol. iii. p. 443.

alteration of any thing contained in that book could be permitted. When the vote came to be taken on these propositions, forty-three voted for them, and thirty-five against; but when the proxies were counted, the balance was turned; the final state of the vote being fifty-eight for, and fifty-nine against. Thus it was determined, by the majority of a single vote, and that the proxy of an absent person, who did not hear the reasoning, that the Prayer-Book should remain unimproved, that there should be no further reformation, that there should be no relief granted to those whose conscience felt aggrieved by the admixture of human inventions in the worship of God, so that the Church of England was thenceforth to remain, like one of her own grand cathedrals, a stately mass of petrified religion.

A Book of Discipline was also prepared by the same Convocation. Whether it was the reformation of the ecclesiastical laws proposed formerly by Cranmer, does not appear; but it did not receive the approbation of the House of Lords, and sunk into complete oblivion. Perhaps the reason why it received so little countenance in high quarters, is explained in a letter from Cox, now Bishop of Ely, to Gualter of Zurich: " When I consider the sins that do everywhere abound, and the neglect and contempt of the Word of God, I am struck with horror, and tremble to think what God will do with us. We have some discipline among us with relation to men's lives, such as it is; but if any man would go about to persuade our nobility to submit their necks to that yoke, he may as well venture to pull the hair out of a lion's beard."* Several other points tending towards reformation were also proposed, but in vain; nothing more could be accomplished; so that it may be fairly said, that with the Convocation of 1562 ended the reformation of the Church of England, before much more than half its work had been done. And it will be admitted by all who are sufficiently

* Burnet's Hist. Ref., vol. iii. p. 464.

acquainted with the condition of the people throughout the country districts of the kingdom, that the reformation proper of the English nation is yet to begin.

From the time of the Convocation in 1562, the disagreement between the court divines and those who wished for further reformation, became gradually more and more decided. It may be expedient briefly to examine the views entertained by these two great opposing parties. The main question on which they were divided may be thus stated: Whether it were lawful and expedient to retain in the external aspect of religion a close resemblance to what had prevailed in the times of Popery, or not? The court divines argued, that this process would lead the people more easily to the reception of the real doctrinal changes, when they saw outward appearances so little altered, so that this method seemed to be recommended by expediency. The reformers replied, that this tended to perpetuate in the people their inclination to their former superstitions, led them to think there was, after all, little difference between the reformed and the papal Churches, and consequently, that if it made them quit Popery the more readily at present, it would leave them at least equally ready to return to it should an opportunity offer; and for this reason they thought it best to leave as few traces of Popery remaining as possible. It was urged, by the court party, that every sovereign had authority to correct all abuses of doctrine and worship within his own dominions: this, they asserted, was the true meaning of the Act of Supremacy, and consequently the source of the reformation in England. The true reformers admitted the Act of Supremacy, in the sense of the queen's explanation given in the injunctions; but could not admit that the conscience and the religion of the whole nation were subject to the arbitrary disposal of the sovereign. The court party recognised the Church of Rome as a true Church, though corrupt in some points of doctrine and government; and this view it was thought necessary to maintain, for without this the English bishops could not trace their succession from the apostles. But the decided reformers affirmed the pope to be antichrist, and the Church of Rome to be no true Church; nor would they risk the validity of their ordinations on the idea of a succession through such a channel. Neither party denied that the Bible was a perfect rule of faith; but the court party did not admit it to be a standard of Church government and discipline, asserting that it had been left to the judgment of the civil magistrate in Christian countries, to accommodate the government of the Church to the policy of the state. The reformers maintained the Scriptures to be the standard of Church government and discipline, as well as doctrine; to the extent, at the very least, that nothing should be imposed as necessary which was not expressly contained in, or derived from, them by necessary consequence; adding, that if any discretionary power in minor matters were necessary, it must be vested, not in the civil magistrate, but in the spiritual office-bearers of the Church itself. The court reformers held that the practice of the primitive Church for the four or five earliest centuries was a proper standard of Church government and discipline, even better suited to the dignity of a national establishment than the times of the apostles; and that, therefore, nothing more was needed than merely to remove the more modern innovations of Popery. The true reformers wished to keep close to the Scripture model, and to admit neither office-bearers, ceremonies, nor ordinances, but such as were therein appointed or sanctioned. The court party affirmed, that things in their own nature indifferent, such as rites, ceremonies, and vestments, might be appointed and made necessary by the command of the civil magistrate; and that then it was the bounden duty of all subjects to obey. But the reformers maintained, that what Christ had left indifferent no human laws ought to make necessary; and besides, that such rites and ceremonies as had been abused to idolatry, and tended to lead men back to Popery and superstition, were no longer indifferent, but were to be rejected as unlawful. Finally, the court party held that there must be a standard of uniformity, which standard was the queen's supremacy, and the laws of the land. The reformers regarded the Bible as the only standard, but thought compliance was due to the decrees of provincial and national synods, which might be approved and enforced by civil authority. In this point, the view entertained by the reformers might have been carried to the extent of oppression; but it never could have been very direct and immediate, and was subject to so many checks, that it amounted to little more than a remote possibility. At the same time, it is perfectly evident that the true principles of religious liberty and toleration were not understood by either party; and it may be fairly questioned, whether, even in the present day, these principles are rightly understood.

Such is a brief outline of the direct cause of the conflict between the court party of the English reformers, and their brethren who desired a more complete reformation, and of the leading arguments used on both sides. It cannot fail to strike every attentive reader, that precisely the same conflict is again renewed, both in England and Scotland, and in all its leading principles. So close indeed is the resemblance, that it is difficult to peruse the writings of those times without insensibly beginning to think we are reading some of the controversial works of the present day. And, perhaps, in order to arrive at a full understanding of the real nature and bearing of the present controversies, no better plan could be devised than to prosecute a careful study of the writings of the court divines, and the Puritans of the Elizabethan age.

But to resume. It seems to have been expected by the court party that the proceedings of the Convocation, and the acts of Parliament, injunctions, and proclamations, would speedily produce an entire conformity. In this expectation they were disappointed. The regular parochial clergy, both in town and country, not only disliked the vestments themselves, but perceived that, in general, the people bore towards these relics of a persecuting and oppressive system at least an equal aversion. Some, indeed, wore them occasionally, in obedience to the law, but more frequently officiated without them; and although the bishops, most of whom, though at first opposed, had become reconciled to the " scenic apparel," cited such persons into their courts, and admonished them, yet this had little effect, as they had not yet proceeded to suspension and deprivation. At length, information of these irregularities was given to the queen. Her majesty was highly displeased, especially on the ground that so little regard was paid to her laws, and gave strict command to the Archbishop of Canterbury, " to take effectual methods that an exact order and uniformity be maintained in all external rites and ceremonies, as by law and good usages are provided for."*

This severe and peremptory command immediately roused the bishops to activity, and, in particular, stimulated Archbishop Parker to such a degree of fierce and unrelenting sternness, as seemed completely contrary to all his former life and character. He did his utmost to urge forward Grindal, Bishop of London, to compel the ministers within his diocese to conform, though he well knew that the opinions of that pious prelate were not only averse from every thing like oppression, but were opposed, in particular, to the sacerdotal vestments. Parker framed some articles to enforce the habits, and requested the queen to give them the authority of her sanction. But the pride of Elizabeth could not endure that a subject should frame articles to enforce her decrees, and, instead of ratifying them, she issued a proclamation, requiring immediate uniformity in the habits, on pain of prohibition from preaching, and deprivation from office.

And now the storm burst forth in earnest. The whole

* Strype's Life of Parker, p. 155.

ministers of London were summoned to Lambeth, and the
question put to them, Whether they would conform to the
apparel established by law, and subscribe their admission on
the spot? Those who should refuse were to be suspended
immediately, and after three months deprived of their livings. Threats, persuasions, and the dread of poverty, induced sixty-one out of one hundred to subscribe ; thirty-
seven absolutely refused, and were immediately suspended,—
and those thirty-seven, as their oppressor admitted, were the
best and ablest preachers in the city.* Many churches were
at once shut up, the ruling party disregarding the loss of religious privileges to the congregations, in their zeal to enforce
conformity in matters which they themselves admitted to be
in their own nature indifferent. After a short interval,
many of the most pious and able men were ejected from the
churches, and cast upon the world in a state of utter destitution, even forbid to preach to others that Gospel which had
been to their own souls glad tidings of great joy. Surely it
had been a strange and a portentous thing to see such men
as Miles Coverdale, the translator of the Bible, in his feeble
but most venerable age, and Fox, the martyrologist, whose
writings had done so much for the overthrow of Popery, and
the support of the reformed faith, driven from their homes
and weeping flocks, and exposed to reproach and poverty,
because they would not consent to disfigure their persons
with the gaudy vestments characteristic of Romish superstition. In vain did the oppressed Puritans,—for we may now
fairly use that distinctive appellation,—apply to the Earl of
Leicester, the Earl of Bedford, and such other noblemen as
were known to be favourable to them, imploring these distinguished men to do their utmost to procure some mitigation
of such oppressive measures. No mitigation could be obtained. To conform or to suffer were the only alternatives ;
and they nobly chose the latter rather than violate conscience.

* Strype's Life of Parker, p. 215.

These severe measures adopted by the court party, and prosecuted with such unrelenting rigour against their better brethren, attracted the attention of the reformed churches in other countries. The continental divines wrote frequently to England on the subject, but without effect. The Church of Scotland, which had been reformed and re-organized on a truly scriptural model, by the blessing of God on the strenuous exertions of John Knox, also addressed an earnest and affectionate remonstrance to the English prelates, imploring them to treat their faithful and suffering brethren with greater tenderness, disapproving, at the same time, of their preposterous attachment to the superstitious trappings of Rome.* But all was in vain : brotherly kindness and Christian charity must equally be sacrificed to gratify the queen's taste for idle pageantry, and to cover the mean and self-condemned compliance of her courtly prelates. The ejected Puritan ministers found extreme difficulty in obtaining opportunities for preaching ; and some remained entirely silent. Many pamphlets, were, however, written by them, which tended to keep alive and spread their opinions, and which were eagerly read by the people. This drew from the Star Chamber a decree, strictly prohibiting the publication of all such writings, under heavy penalties.

[1566.] Thus, commanded to conform even against the dictates of conscience, ejected from their churches and forbidden to preach anywhere else, and deprived of the liberty of the press, the Puritans were driven to that extreme point where endurance ceases and active resistance begins. Accordingly, they met, and gravely and solemnly deliberated, Whether it were not now both lawful and necessary to separate from the Established Church ? After much earnest consultation, they came to the solemn and important conclusion, That since they could not have the word of God preached, nor the sacraments administered, without " idolatrous gear,"

* M'Crie's Life of Knox, p. 295.

as they termed the vestments and ceremonies, and since there had been a separate congregation in London, and another in Geneva, in Queen Mary's time, in which there was a book and order of preaching, administration of sacraments and discipline, free from the superstitions of the English service, it was their duty, in the present circumstances, to separate from the public churches, and to assemble, as they had opportunity, in private houses or elsewhere, to worship God in a manner that might not offend against the light of their consciences.* This most important event took place in the summer of the year 1566, and from that time onward the Puritan party may be regarded as forming a body distinct from the Church of England, although they were the true successors of the first and greatest reforming fathers of that Church.

It would be a great mistake to suppose, that the only subject in dispute between the Puritans and their antagonists was that respecting clerical vestments. That formed, indeed, a very prominent point in the controversy, because it was so apparent, and so easily brought under the terms of a royal proclamation. But there were many, and these still more important matters, which they wished to have reformed. Of these, the most prominent were the following. They regarded the assumed superiority of bishops over presbyters, as a higher order, and the claim, on their part, of the sole right of ordination, discipline, and government, as unscriptural in itself, and tending both to secularize them, and to produce an intolerable despotism. Along with this, they complained of the whole array of cathedral office-bearers as of the same character, and equally unwarranted. They lamented the want of discipline, in consequence of which it was impossible to maintain the purity of the most sacred ordinances. Regarding set forms of prayer as properly intended to meet the necessities of a time of ignorance, they

* Strype's Life of Parker, p. 241.

did not dispute their lawfulness, while they wished a greater
liberty in prayer, where such help was not required; and
they disapproved also of too many repetitions, of responses,
and of several exceptionable expressions, particularly in the
marriage and funeral services. They disapproved of the
reading of the apocryphal books in the church; and while
they regarded the homilies as in themselves valuable, they
held that no man should be ordained to the ministry who
was not himself able to preach, and to expound the Scriptures. While they complained of pluralities, non-residence,
and an unpreaching clergy, they viewed these as caused
chiefly by patronage exercised by the queen, bishops, and
lay-patrons, and held that it ought to be abolished, and
ministers to be appointed by the election of the people.
They condemned, on the one hand, the keeping of church-
festivals and saints' days, and on the other, the open and
flagrant violation of the Lord's day, as equally contrary to
Scripture. Cathedral worship, chanted prayers, and instrumental music, they also condemned, as tending rather to
amuse than to edify. And they declared their great reluctance to comply with certain rites and ceremonies which were
strictly enjoined, and which they regarded as superstitious or
unmeaning, such as the sign of the cross in baptism, baptism by midwives, the exclusion of parents and the employment of godfathers and godmothers, the rite of confirmation,
kneeling at the communion, as implying transubstantiation,
bowing at the name of Jesus, the ring in marriage, and certain foolish words used in the ceremony, and the wearing of
the surplice and other ceremonies used in divine service.

When so many, and such important topics were all equally
in dispute, and not the slightest redress could be obtained,
but conformity in every particular was enforced with the most
oppressive and unrelaxing rigour, it was not strange that the
persecuted Puritans should determine to separate themselves
from a Church which they regarded as but half reformed,

and which sternly refused to advance to a more pure and
perfect reformation, according, not to the will of princes, but
to the Word of God. And the time may come, when the
Church of England will bitterly bewail the insane conduct of
those who, in that reforming period, took up and pursued a
course which crushed the life-spring out of its heart, and
swathed up the cold and paralyzed remains, to lie in state, a
decent but a dead formality.

[1567.] The chief leaders of the separation, according to
Fuller, were the Rev. Messrs Colman, Button, Halingham,
Benson, White, Rowland, and Hawkins, all of whom held
benefices within the diocese of London. No sooner was the
queen informed that the Puritans had begun to form separate
assemblies for worship, than she commanded her commissioners to take effectual measures to keep the laity to their
parish churches; and to let them know, that if they frequented conventicles, or broke the ecclesiastical laws, they
should, for the first offence, be deprived of the freedom of
the city, and then abide what further punishment she would
direct. But the requirements of conscience are stronger
than a sovereign's threats. They continued to hold their
private meetings; and, on the 19th of June 1567, they
agreed to have a sermon preached and the communion dis-
pensed at Plumbers' Hall, which they engaged for that day.*
The day came, and they assembled to worship the God of
peace, but their peaceful worship was rudely interrupted by
the entrance of the armed officers of the civil power, who
seized upon the chief, dispersed the rest, and dragged their
victims to prison. Next day they were brought before the
Bishop of London, and the chief magistrate of the city,
charged with the heinous offence of forsaking the Church
which persecuted them, and setting up separate assemblies
for worship. They defended their conduct ably; but because they would not yield, they were, to the number of

---

* Strype's Life of Grindal, pp. 115, and 135, 136.

twenty-four men and seven women, sent to Bridewell, where they endured the hardships of more than a year's imprisonment.

[1571.] A parliament was held in 1571, in which there were some attempts made to procure a further reformation. One member, Mr Strickland, proposed to bring in a bill for that purpose, asserting that the Prayer-Book, with some superstitious remains of Popery in the Church, might be altered without any danger to religion. Her majesty was so displeased, that she sent for him to the council, reproved him sharply, and forbade his attendance in Parliament; but this caused such an alarm in the House of Commons, as a dangerous invasion of their privileges, that she found it convenient to remove her prohibition. An act was passed, ratifying the Thirty-nine Articles, which had been framed by the Convocation of 1562; and one clause in that act admitted the validity of ordination by presbyters alone, without a bishop.* This clause was greatly disliked by the bishops, and has been repeatedly condemned by their successors, but remains still unrepealed. The House of Commons were desirous also that articles of discipline should be framed and enacted; but when this was discountenanced by the bishops, they presented an address to the queen, representing the grievous injuries sustained by the Church and kingdom for want of true and efficient discipline, supplicating her majesty that proper laws might be provided and enacted for the reformation of these abuses. But the queen dissolved the Parliament without answering this supplication.

Although little was done in the Parliament to relieve the

* In none of the MS. copies of the Thirty-nine Articles, either as passed by the Convocation of 1562, or as ratified by the Parliament of 1571, is the clause in the 20th article to be found, by which the Church of England claims the power " to decree rites and ceremonies." It must have been surreptitiously introduced afterwards by some of the Prelatic party, without civil or ecclesiastical authority.—See *Historical and Critical Essays on the Thirty-nine Articles*, pp. 277-279.

oppressed Puritans, some steps were taken by the Convocation which tended to increase their oppression. A canon of discipline was framed, empowering the bishops to call in all their licenses for preaching, and to issue new licenses to those only whose qualifications gained their approbation; and among the qualifications specified, subscription to all the points of which the Puritans complained was particularly mentioned. These canons were not sanctioned by royal authority; but the bishops, knowing well the queen's inclinations, did not hesitate to enforce them with great rigour. Numbers of the Puritan divines were immediately deprived of their licenses to preach, because they refused to subscribe canons not yet legalized; and it became apparent that a formidable crisis was at hand.

At the very time that the bishops were thus silencing the persons whom they themselves admitted to be the best preachers in the kingdom, the state of religion throughout the country was truly deplorable. Of this Strype, no Puritan, presents the following outline :—" The churchmen heaped up many benefices upon themselves, and resided upon none, neglecting their cures; many of them alienated their lands, made unreasonable leases, and wastes of their woods; granted reversions and advowsons to their wives and children, or to others for their use. Churches ran greatly into dilapidations and decays; and were kept nasty and filthy, and indecent for God's worship. Among the laity there was little devotion. The Lord's day greatly profaned, and little observed. The common prayers not frequented. Some lived without any service of God at all. Many were mere heathens and atheists. The queen's own court an harbour for epicures and atheists, and a kind of lawless place, because it stood in no parish. Which things made good men fear some sad judgments impending over the nation."*

Perceiving that there was no prospect whatever of any

* Strype's Life of Parker, p. 395.

further reformation in religious matters proceeding from either the sovereign or the convocation, and lamenting the wretched ignorance and immorality which prevailed in the kingdom, the Puritans now resolved to exert themselves to the utmost of their means and opportunities for their own instruction, and that of their perishing countrymen. And as Dr Scambler, Bishop of Peterborough, was less intolerant than many of his order, the ministers within his diocese, particularly those of Northampton, with his approbation and that of the mayor of the town, formed an association for promoting the purity of worship and the maintenance of discipline. The regulations of this association were very temperate, involving no departure from any of the established modes of worship, nor any rigid disciplinary arrangements. And as they were aware of the extreme inability to preach instructively, which characterised very many of the clergy, they endeavoured also to provide a remedy for this evil. For this purpose they instituted what they termed " prophe-syings," taking the designation from 1 Cor. xiv. 31, " Ye may all prophesy one by one, that all may learn, and all may be comforted." In these prophesyings one presided, and a text previously selected was explained by one of the minis-ters to whom it had been assigned. After his exposition, each in turn gave his view of the passage ; and the whole exercise was summed up by the president or moderator for the day, who concluded by exhorting all to persevere in the dis-charge of their sacred duties.* This scheme, it is evident, was admirably calculated to increase the scriptural know-ledge, and promote the usefulness of the clergymen who en-gaged in it; and it deserved the cordial approbation of all who were desirous to promote the religious welfare of the community. But it was regarded with jealousy by the bishops, and ere long encountered the keen hostility of Elizabeth herself.

* Strype's Life of Grindal, pp. 175, 176.

D

[1572.] When the Parliament met in 1572, an attempt
was made by the House of Commons to mitigate the sufferings of the Puritans, and they passed two bills for that purpose.   This gave such offence to the queen, that she sharply
reproved them for interfering in such matters, and commanded them to deliver up the bills.   One of the members
boldly complained of this conduct, as trenching upon the
liberty of Parliament, and for his boldness was sent to the
Tower.   The Puritans, who had reason to expect some countenance from the Parliament, prepared a full statement of
their grievances and their desires, in a treatise entitled, " An
Admonition to the Parliament."   But while the Parliament
was not permitted to grant any redress, the authors of the
Admonition were cast into prison, and treated with great
severity.   Whitgift was appointed to answer the Admonition,
and Cartwright answered Whitgift, which led to a lengthened
controversy between these learned and able men.   Each, and
still more eagerly the partizans of each, claimed the victory ;
but the controversy did not terminate with the writings of
these antagonists, nor is it yet terminated.   It is waged in
the present day with equal keenness, and not inferior ability ;
it may be added, with no novelty in its leading principles,
and very little in its arguments.   Cartwright maintained,
that the Scriptures were not only the sole standard of doctrine, but also of discipline and government, and that the
Church of Christ in all ages was to be regulated by them.
Whitgift held, that the Scriptures were a rule of faith; but
not designed to be a standard of discipline and government,
—that this was changeable, and might be adapted to the
civil government of any country,—and that the times of
the apostles could not be the best model, but rather the
first four centuries of the Church, during which she had
reached a matured developement.   In what do these views
essentially differ from the advocates and opponents of Patris-
tic theology in the present day ?   Till men agree in some

leading principles by which any great controversy must be ruled, it is vain to expect that it can ever be brought to a satisfactory conclusion; yet those who appeal to Scripture authority alone, must surely be held to be following the most proper and authoritative method in discussions of that nature.

All hope of legislative assistance in prosecuting further reformation being cut off by the queen's arbitrary procedure, the Puritans resolved to take another step, still more daring and decisive than any on which they had previously ventured. Several of the ministers of London and its vicinity met together and determined to form themselves into a presbytery, to be held at Wandsworth, a village on the banks of the Thames, about five miles from the city. On the 20th of November 1572, about fifteen ministers met, eleven elders were chosen to form members of the body; their offices were described in a register, entitled, " The Orders of Wandsworth ;" and this was the first fully constituted Presbyterian Church in England.* The intelligence of this event soon reached the bishops; the Court of High Commission took alarm; the queen issued a proclamation for enforcing the Act of Uniformity; but the Presbytery of Wandsworth for a time eluded the fury of their enemies, and other presbyteries were formed in neighbouring counties.

There was now little possibility of reconciliation between the High Church and the Puritan parties; for the unbending determination of the former not to grant the slightest relief to the sufferings of their brethren, nor the least accommodation to their aggrieved consciences, had driven them from mere nonconformity into the adoption of a different form of Church polity, possessing in itself the elements of perpetuity and growth. Puritanism had thenceforward not only a vital principle, but also systematic organization, enabling it to live on, and increase in spite of any amount of persecution; for

* Neal, vol. i. p. 198; Collier, vol. ii. p. 541.

a system dies not with the individuals that held it, but draws into itself the fresh life of succeeding generations.

Having thus traced the rise of Puritanism, and seen its systematic organization, it will not be necessary to follow its progress so minutely in what remains of this introductory outline. We shall content ourselves with touching briefly on the main events which mark the growing development of the leading principles characteristic of the two contending parties.

The sufferings of the Puritans continued unabated during the remainder of the life of Archbishop Parker; many of them being silenced, imprisoned, banished, and otherwise oppressed by that relentless prelate. In vain did the House of Commons, and several influential noblemen, repeatedly interpose in their behalf; they were detested by the queen, and Parker was ready to gratify her majesty without scruple, and to any extent. In particular, he strove to suppress the " prophesyings," declaring that they were nests of Puritanism; and by his complaints he succeeded in directing against them the vengeance of the despotic sovereign. He did not, however, live to direct the storm which he had raised, but died in May 1576, and was succeeded by Grindal.

Grindal, aware of the opposition to the exercises or prophesyings which had been raised by his predecessor, attempted to regulate them so that no offence might be taken, or at least that they might be the more easily defended. But the queen had formed her resolution, from which she could not be moved by the most respectful and elaborate arguments, and the most humble entreaties of the afflicted archbishop. She " declared herself offended at the numbers of preachers, and also at the exercises, and warned him to redress both, urging that it was *good for the Church to have few preachers, and that three or four might suffice for a county ;* and that the reading of the homilies to the people was enough. In short, she required him to do these two things,—to abridge the number of preachers, and to put down the religious exercises."* This peremptory command both grieved and alarmed Grindal, who knew the excessive ignorance which prevailed both among the preachers and the people, and was anxious to promote whatever tended to the increase of religious knowledge and purity. He wrote to her majesty a long and earnest letter, entering fully into the subject, pleading the importance of preaching as the divinely appointed method of communicating religious instruction to the people, —showing how admirably these exercises were fitted to improve the ministers who joined in them, and consequently to qualify them for the discharge of their chief function ; and after imploring her not to suppress so valuable an institution, and stating his readiness to resign his office if that were her pleasure, declared that he could not, without offence to the majesty of God, send out injunctions for suppressing the exercises. To this solemn appeal the queen's answer was— an order for the imprisonment of Grindal in his house, and his suspension from his function for six months; and an immediate suppression of the prophesyings by the authority of a royal proclamation. Such were the fruits of the Crown's ecclesiastical supremacy, when possessed by a despotic monarch. It may be added, that Grindal had the firmness to maintain his integrity for eight years, during which his suspension continued, and his archiepiscopal functions were generally performed by a commission ; but at length he yielded so far as to suppress the exercises within his own jurisdiction, though he would not issue injunctions to that effect to the bishops. Unhappily it was not necessary ; they were in general but too ready to obey the arbitrary commands of their haughty and despotic sovereign.

[1580.] A few years afterwards another development of regal and prelatic tyranny appeared, in an act passed by the Parliament of 1580, prohibiting the publication of books or

* Strype's Life of Grindal, p. 221.

pamphlets assailing the opinions of the Prelates, and defending those of the Puritans. In the same session of Parliament another act was passed, one portion of which empowered the infliction of heavy fines and imprisonment upon those who absented themselves from " church, chapel, or other place where common prayer is said, according to the Act of Uniformity." The apparatus of persecution was now nearly complete ; and the pernicious character of the Crown's ecclesiastical supremacy was sufficiently evident in at least its main aspect, although it subsequently reached a far more terrible degree of persecuting intolerance. These harsh and oppressive measures had, however, as might have been expected, an effect the very reverse of that which their authors intended. Some of timid and wavering minds might be terrified and subdued; but the bolder and more high-principled men became only the more determined in proportion to the severity and intolerance of the treatment which they had to encounter. In their indignation they began to entertain feelings and opinions from which they would have shrunk, had they not been driven to extremities. Ceasing to complain of Popish vestments and ceremonies, and to supplicate a further reformation, some began to question whether the Church of England ought to be regarded as a true Church, and her ministers true Christian ministers. They not only renounced communion with her in her forms of prayer and her ceremonies, but also in the dispensation of word and ordinance.

The leader of these men of extreme views was Robert Brown, a person who held a charge in the diocese of Norwich, whose family connections gave him considerable influence, and procured him protection, he being nearly related to Lord Treasurer Cecil. Brown appears to have been a man of hot and impetuous temper; rash and variable, except when opposed, and then headstrong and overbearing. Throwing himself headlong into the Puritan controversy, he traversed the country from place to place, pouring out the most fierce and bitter invectives against the whole Prelatic party, and also against all who could not concur with him in the rude violence of his mode of warfare. After repeated imprisonments, and many attempts to form a new party, he at last partially succeeded in collecting a small body of like-minded adherents ; but was soon afterwards compelled to leave the kingdom, and to withdraw to Holland with a por-tion of his followers. There he formed a Church according to his own fancy ; but it was soon torn to pieces with inter-nal dissension, and Brown returned again to England, and exhibiting one of those recoils by no means rare with men of vehement temperament, he renounced his principles of separation, conformed to that worship which he had so vio-lently assailed, and became rector of a parish in Northampton-shire. The remainder of his life was by no means distin-guished by correctness of deportment, or purity of manners ; and at length he terminated his unhonoured days in the county jail, in the eighty-first year of his age.* From this person the first form of what has since been termed the In-dependent, or Congregational system of Church government, appears to have had its origin, the great majority of the Puritans either retaining their connection with the Church of England in a species of constrained half-conformity, or associating on the Presbyterian model. Brown not only re-nounced communion with the Church of England, but also with all others of the reformed Churches who would not adopt the model which he had constructed. The main prin-ciples of that model were, that every church ought to be con-fined within a single congregation ; that its government should be the most complete democracy ; and that there was no distinction in point of order between the office-bearers and the ordinary members, so that a vote of the congrega-tion was enough to constitute any man an office-bearer, and

* Neal, vol. i. pp. 245-247 ; Fuller, vol. iii. pp. 61-65.

to entitle him to preach and to administer the sacraments.
Those who adopted these opinions, and formed Congregational
Churches on the same model, were at first termed Brownists,
and were regarded by the main body of the Puritans with
nearly as much dislike as they were by the Prelatists.

In stating that the Independent, or Congregational system
of Church government may be said to have originated with
Robert Brown, it is not meant that those who at present adhere to that form of ecclesiastical polity are Brownists, as
that term was applied at first; but merely that Brown appears to have been the first who actually, in the formation of
a Church, embodied that idea, and that too in a much more
rigid and repulsive form than it subsequently assumed, when
again taken up and reconstructed by wiser and better men.
But it is of importance to mark beginnings, especially when
these teach lessons of great practical value. One of these
may be here very easily learned. The extreme pertinacity
with which the queen and her obsequious servants the bishops
strove to enforce entire conformity, produced an antagonist
principle, whose very essence was direct antipathy to their
eager wish, rendering it for ever impossible that their purpose
could be accomplished. Another remark may be made: the
system devised by Brown was, in its first appearance, altogether as intolerant, both in principle and in practice, as that
of its opponent, Prelacy; but in the stern strife which afterwards ensued between these equally intolerant antagonists,
they so far neutralized each other, as to give occasion to the
gradual, though even yet incomplete, development of the
great principle of religious toleration,—a principle utterly unknown to any party at the time, even while its rainbow-form
was beginning to bend its gentle radiance across the thunder-
gloom of their contention.

[1583.] The death of Archbishop Grindal gave the queen
an opportunity of promoting to that influential station which
he had held, a person more according to her own mind,

who would feel no compunction in proceeding to extremities against the Puritans. Her choice was easily made. Whitgift had already distinguished himself by his controversial writings against Cartwright, and was well prepared to enforce by power what he had failed to accomplish by argument. Scarcely was Whitgift placed in his seat of power, when he began to show how that power would be used. He drew up and published three articles, requiring that none be permitted to preach, or execute any part of the ecclesiastical function, unless he should subscribe them. These articles were to the following effect:—1st, The queen's supremacy over all persons, and in all causes, civil and ecclesiastical. 2d, That the Book of Common Prayer and of Ordination contained nothing contrary to the Word of God ; and that they will use it, and no other. 3d, Implicit subscription of the Thirty-nine Articles.* The Puritans would readily have acknowledged the queen's supremacy over all persons, and in all causes civil, but not in causes ecclesiastical; the *second* article they could not subscribe ; the *third* they were ready to subscribe with little difficulty. But they were all rigidly enforced; and in a short time several hundred of the best ministers in England were suspended for not subscribing. Not thinking even this sufficient, Whitgift applied to the queen to institute a new High Commission, that he might be enabled to wield a direct and irresistible power. She readily consented, and even gave to it an additional element of despotism, empowering the commissioners to impose an oath *ex officio*,—by means of which persons accused were bound, on their oath, to answer questions against themselves, and thus become their own accusers, or to be punished, by fine or imprisonment, for refusing to take such an oath, or to criminate themselves. The prelatic inquisition was now complete in its apparatus, and Whitgift was well qualified to act as the grand inquisitor.

* Neal, vol. i. pp. 260-263; Fuller, vol. iii. p. 68.

[1584.] The work of oppression went on now rapidly.
Mercy to preachers or people there was none. Elizabeth's
wisest statesmen stood aghast, when they beheld the deso-
lating effect of Whitgift's measures; but they interposed in
vain. Cecil, Burleigh, and Walsingham, had less influence
with the queen than Whitgift; because their advice was but
accordant with the dictates of prudence and Christianity,—
his with those of vanity and despotism. When Parliament
met, the House of Commons attempted to stem the tide of
persecution; and having received several petitions from the
Puritans, they prepared various bills to abridge the power of
the bishops, to reform abuses, and to promote discipline. But,
with considerable dexterity, Whitgift suggested to the queen,
that if the Parliament were to pass any such measures, they
could not be repealed by any other authority; whereas, whatsoever she should herself, or by the convocation, enact, her
own authority could at any time repeal.* Elizabeth welcomed
the suggestion. She reprimanded the Commons for interfering with ecclesiastical matters, which was touching her prerogative, and they were compelled to yield.

[1586.] The Puritans, thus driven from all legislative
remedy, yet regarded it as their duty, in their character of
Christian teachers, to exert themselves to the utmost for their
own improvement, and for the instruction and reformation of
the ignorant and neglected people. They accordingly formed
a Book of Discipline, for their own direction in the discharge
of their ministerial and pastoral duties; and this book was
subscribed by above five hundred of the most eminently pious
and faithful ministers in the kingdom.† This body was far
too numerous and important to be easily or wantonly crushed;
and yet, as Neal informs us, it constituted, in reality, but a
small portion of those over whom the terrors of suspension at
that period hung, amounting to not less than a third part of
the ministers of England.

* Life of Whitgift, p. 198.   † Neal, vol. i. pp. 314, 315.

[1588.] A new principle was now promulgated, for the support of prelatic power, of a more formidable nature than any that had hitherto appeared, and destined to produce the most disastrous results. Dr Bancroft, the archbishop's chaplain, in a sermon which he preached at Paul's Cross, January 12, 1588, maintained that bishops were a distinct order from priests or presbyters, and had authority over them *jure divino*, and directly from God.* This bold assertion created an immense ferment throughout the kingdom. The Puritans saw well, that, if acted upon, this principle would increase their oppression to an incalculable degree, inasmuch as it must subject them to an accusation of heresy, in addition to that of resistance to the queen's supremacy. The greater part of even the Prelatic party themselves were startled with the novelty of the doctrine; for none of the English reformers had ever regarded the order of bishops as any thing else but a human institution, appointed for the more orderly government of the Church, and they were not prepared at once to condemn as heretical all Churches where that institution did not exist. Whitgift himself, perceiving the use which might be made of such a tenet, said, that the Doctor's sermon had done much good,—though, for his own part, he rather wished than believed it to be true. On the other hand, the legal assertors of the queen's supremacy assailed this theory, as subversive of her majesty's prerogative; for, as they reasoned, if the bishops are not under-governors to her majesty of the clergy, but superior governors over their brethren, by God's ordinance, it will then follow that her majesty is not supreme governor over her clergy. Bancroft answered, that this inference was not a necessary consequence of his doctrine; because the sovereign's authority may, and very often does, corroborate that which is primarily from the law of God. This evasive reply seems to have satisfied the queen, aided,

* Life of Whitgift, p. 292; Collier, vol. ii. p. 609; Neal, vol i. pp. 321-323.

perhaps, by her own knowledge of its direct purpose, and of the character of her bishops, who longed for the extirpation of Puritanism, but had no desire to encounter her leonine wrath. The terrific power of this despotic principle did not, indeed, appear till after the lapse of two generations,—when, wielded by Laud, it convulsed the kingdom, and overthrew the monarchy. Its portentous reappearance in modern times may well excite alarm; embodying, as it does, the very essence of despotism, civil and religious, and possessing an energy that nothing human can control without a struggle, wide, wasting, and deadly,—too fearful even to be imagined.

[1589.] The struggle assumed a less serious aspect for a short time, in consequence of the publication of the famous Martin Mar-Prelate Tracts. Some of the Puritan party had procured a printing-press,—the liberty of the press having been taken away previously,—and commenced a series of pamphlets, containing attacks of wit, ridicule, mockery, and keen vituperation, against the bishops and their supporters. Many of these tracts displayed very considerable power of sarcasm and invective; and as they were written intentionally for the mass of the nation, they were composed in a style not merely plain, but affectedly rude and vulgar. They were not, however, to be despised. Amidst much coarse vituperation, they contained statements of facts which could not be disputed, set forth with such home-thrusting vigour, as caused every direct and strong-aimed blow to tell upon the assailed prelates. Great was the indignation and dismay of the bishops and their friends, and every exertion was made to detect and seize the hidden armoury of this unseen assailant. For a considerable time these efforts were unsuccessful, and the Prelatic party were constrained to attempt their own defence in literary warfare. But although they displayed considerable talent and activity in this attempt, they were not able to match their unknown antagonists, whose writings produced a deep and wide-spread impression on the public mind. At length the

Martin Mar-Prelate press was seized, with several unfinished tracts, and that aspect of the struggle terminated, but not till the Prelatic cause had sustained very considerable injury.

In the year 1591 the Parliament again met, and the House of Commons once more attempted to rescue the suffering Puritans, by instituting an inquiry into the conduct of the High Commission, in imposing oaths and subscriptions not sanctioned by law. The queen was highly incensed, commanded them not to meddle with matters of state or causes ecclesiastical, and threw several of the members, and even the attorney-general, into prison. The Parliament, with a tameness unworthy of the spirit of free-born Englishmen, not merely yielded, but passed an act for the suppression of conventicles, by which was meant all religious meetings, except such as the queen and the bishops were pleased to permit, on pain of perpetual banishment. The principle of this act was of the most despotic nature, converting any difference from the religion of the sovereign into a crime against the State, and rendering the mere want of conformity equivalent to a proof of direct opposition. Great numbers were subjected to the most grievous sufferings through this enactment. Some went into voluntary exile, to escape the horrors of imprisonment; some endured a lengthened captivity, and then were banished; and some, chiefly of the Brownists, were condemned to death, and on the scaffold declared their loyalty to their sovereign, while they ceased not to testify against the tyranny of the prelates.

[1595.] The controversy between the High Churchmen and the Puritans obtained the full development of all its main principles in the year 1595. At this time Dr Bound published a treatise on the Sabbath; in which he maintained its perpetual sanctity, as a day of rest equally from business and recreation, that it might be devoted wholly to the worship of God.* All the Puritans assented to this doctrine, while

* Fuller, vol. iii. pp. 143-146.

the Prelatists accused it as both an undue restraint of Christian liberty and an improper exalting of the Sabbath above the other festivals appointed by the Church. About the same time, a controversy arose in Cambridge respecting those doctrinal points which form the leading distinctions between the Arminian and the Calvinistic systems of theology. Till this period there had existed no doubt in the minds of any of the English divines that the Thirty-nine Articles were decidedly and intentionally Calvinistic. Indeed they could have no other opinion ; because they were perfectly aware how much influence the writings of Calvin exercised over the minds of those by whom these Articles were framed. After the controversy had prevailed in the university a short time, an appeal was made to Whitgift, who, with the aid of other learned divines, prepared nine propositions, commonly called the Lambeth Articles, to which all the scholars in the university were strictly enjoined to conform their judgments.* These Lambeth Articles were more strictly Calvinistic than Calvin himself would have desired ; and certainly prove that, in its early period, the Church of England was any thing but Arminian, whatever it may have since become. But though Whitgift was himself still a thorough Calvinist, considerable numbers of the Prelatic party were veering towards Arminianism ; so that, partly on that account, and partly on account of their more strict observance of the Sabbath sanctity, the Puritans were now led to a more important field of conflict than that on which they had hitherto striven against their antagonists ; and instead of contending about vestments and ceremonies, they now strove respecting great and important doctrines, and began to be termed Doctrinal Puritans. This led to two directly opposite results. It caused the Prelatists to swerve more and more widely from those doctrines which the Puritans maintained ; and it impelled the Puritans to prosecute a profound study of those points, which had

* Fuller, vol. iii. pp. 147-150.

thus become the elements of controversy. This may account for the remarkable power and accuracy with which the Puritan divines of that and the succeeding generation state and explain the most solemn and profound truths of the Christian revelation.

At length what may be termed a cessation of hostilities ensued. The queen was now evidently sinking under the infirmities of age, and both parties began to speculate upon the probable measures which might be adopted by her successor, James VI. of Scotland. The Puritans hoped that his Presbyterian education might predispose him to be favourable to their views ; and the Prelatic party were unwilling to exasperate, by continued severity, those who might possibly, ere long, be the ruling body in the Church. Both parties paused, at least in action ; but there is no reason to suppose that their feelings of mutual jealousy and dislike were abated. Nor was it consistent with the usual policy, or king-craft of James, to declare his sentiments and intentions, but rather to hold out plausible grounds of expectation to both parties,— thereby to secure the support of both, or at least to disarm the direct hostility of either.

[1603.] Queen Elizabeth died on the 24th day of March 1603, in the seventieth year of her age, and forty-fifth of her reign. In the following month, James left his native land, commencing his journey to London to take possession of the English throne, to which he was now the direct heir. On his progress southward, the Puritan ministers availed themselves of the opportunity to lay before him what is commonly termed the *Millenary Petition*. This name it did not receive because it was signed by one thousand ministers, for the actual number was seven hundred and fifty ; but because, in the preamble, it is said by the petitioners, "That they, to the number of more than a thousand ministers, groaned under the burden of human rites and ceremonies, and cast themselves at his majesty's feet for relief." That their num-

ber was not overstated is evident from the fact, that the petition was subscribed by the ministers of no more than twenty-
five counties, chiefly those of the northern, westland, and
midland parts of the kingdom ; so that probably not more
than one-half of the Puritan ministers had an opportunity of
signing their millenary petition.*

On the other hand, the Prelatic party were at least equally
strenuous in their endeavours to secure his majesty's favour;
and, as might be expected from their practised courtier-arts
and ready obsequiousness, were more successful.　But as
James had given a friendly reception to both parties, and as
he was vain of his own acquirements in theology, and of his
skill in polemical discussions, which he wished to exhibit to
his new subjects, he thought proper to appoint a conference
between the two parties, to be conducted in his own presence,
as final judge in all such matters.　This gave occasion to the
famous Hampton Court Conference, an account of which
was afterwards published by Dr Barlow, dean of Chester,
one of the disputants on the Prelatic side.　The Puritans
complained that Barlow gave a partial account of this conference, representing the Prelatic arguments in the best
manner of which they could admit, and weakening and
abridging those of the opposite party.　Even from the outline given by Fuller and Collier this is evident; and yet
so futile are the arguments of the king and the prelates, that
one is ashamed to read them, as reproduced by their own
historians.　In Barlow's own treatise, which is now lying
before me, the mean and abject servility of manner, and the
gross and fulsome flattery of language, employed by the prelates towards James, are such as to cause the cheek of every
person of generous and manly nature to burn with indignant
scorn.　A very brief account of this conference is all that can
be given here.

* Fuller, vol. iii. p. 172; Collier, vol. ii. p. 672; Neal, vol. i. pp. 371,
392.

The place appointed for this conference was the drawing-room at Hampton Court. On the High Church side the disputants were—the Archbishop of Canterbury, Whitgift; bishops,—Bancroft of London, Matthew of Durham, Bilson of Winchester, Babington of Worcester, Rudd of St David's, Watson of Chichester, Robinson of Carlisle, and Dove of Peterborough; deans,—Andrews of the Chapel, Overal of St Paul's, Barlow of Chester, and Bridges of Salisbury; and Dr Field and Dr King. On the part of the Puritans there were only four ministers,—Dr Reynolds and Dr Sparks, professors of divinity in Oxford; and Mr Chadderton and Mr Knewstubbs of Cambridge. The first day was a conference between the king and the prelates, in which his majesty praised the Church of England, and expressed his wish for satisfaction on a few points in the Prayer-Book, respecting excommunication, and about providing ministers for Ireland. By this an opportunity was given to the king and the prelates to form a mutual understanding before they encountered their opponents. On the second day, Dr Reynolds stated, in the name of the Puritans, and in the briefest possible form, the points on which the controversy chiefly turned, humbly requesting,—" 1. That the doctrine of the Church might be preserved in purity, according to God's Word. 2. That good pastors might be planted in all churches, to preach the same. 3. That the Church government might be sincerely ministered, according to God's Word. 4. That the Book of Common Prayer might be fitted to more increase of piety." *

Had these points been fairly discussed, the whole controversy might have been investigated, and some approximation might have been made towards an agreement, or at least a pacific arrangement, between the contending parties. But the king interrupted, reviled, and stormed; the courtiers laughed and mocked; and the prelates, by insinuations, in-

* Hampton Court Conference, p. 23.

E

terruptions, flatteries addressed to the king, and sneers
directed against the Puritans, succeeded in preventing such a
discussion as would have brought out the great principles
of the controversy, and in assisting to overbear the Puritans
with insult and ridicule. The king repeated his favourite
maxim,—" No bishop, no king;" and, at the close of the
day, asked Dr Reynolds if he had any thing else to offer.
He, perceiving the futility of continuing such a discussion,
answered, " No more, please your majesty." " Then," said
the king, " if this be all your party have to say, I will make
them conform, or I will harrie (spoil) them out of the land,
or else do worse."

The greater part of the third day's conference was occupied by the king and the prelates in matters relating to the
High Commission, the oath *ex officio,* and the slight alterations proposed in the Prayer-Book. Of all these the king
expressed his approbation ; and then the Puritan divines
were again called in to this mock conference. They now
knew that no alterations such as they had desired would be
obtained ; and, therefore, they contented themselves with
supplicating some concessions in point of conformity, in behalf of those ministers who could not in conscience submit to
the rites and ceremonies of the Church. The king sternly
declared that they must conform, and that quickly too, or
they should hear of it. Thus ended the Hampton Court
Conference, " which," says Dr Warner, " convinced the
Puritans that they were mistaken in depending on the king's
protection ; which convinced the king that they were not to
be won by a few insignificant concessions ; and which, if it
did not convince the privy council and the bishops that they
had got a Solomon for their king, yet they spoke of him as
though it did." * Even this does not fully express the extravagant strain of adulation in which they spoke. The
Archbishop of Canterbury (Whitgift) "said that undoubtedly

* Ecclesiastical History, vol. iii. p. 482.

his majesty spake by the special assistance of God's Spirit." Bancroft, Bishop of London, "upon his knee protested, that his heart melted within him with joy, and made haste to acknowledge to Almighty God the singular mercy we have received at his hands, in giving us such a king, as since Christ his time the like he thought hath not been." * Little wonder that the vain and pedantic monarch was delighted with his bishops.

[1604.] In the Convocation which met in 1604, Bancroft presided, Whitgift having died a short time previously. Soon after they met, Bancroft laid before them a Book of Canons, collected out of the articles, injunctions, and synodical acts passed in the reigns of Edward and Elizabeth, to the number of one hundred and forty-one. To these canons both Houses of Convocation assented, and they were ratified by the king's letters patent, but not confirmed by act of Parliament, so that, though binding on the clergy, they have not the force of statute laws. Of these canons, about three dozen are expressly directed against the Puritan opinions, rendering their junction with the Church impossible without sacrifice of conscience; and one of them requires that no person be ordained, or suffered to preach or catechise, unless he first subscribe willingly, and *ex animo*, the three articles already mentioned as Whitgift's articles.

Bancroft was promoted to the archbishopric of Canterbury, vacant by Whitgift's decease, and immediately proved how well qualified he was to discharge the function of grand inquisitor. He enforced subscription to canons and articles with the utmost rigour, silencing or deposing those Puritan ministers who refused to comply. Considerable numbers were thus reduced to the greatest distress, and some were driven into foreign countries to escape from persecution in their own. And that the archbishop's persecuting zeal might obtain as full a sanction as could be given to it by a partial

* Hampton Court Conference, pp. 93, 94.

and one-sided process, the king summoned the twelve judges to the Star-Chamber, and, in answer to three interrogative propositions, obtained as their legal opinion, That the king, having the supreme ecclesiastical power, could, without Parliament, make orders and constitutions for Church government; that the High Commission might enforce them, *ex officio*, without libel; and *that subjects might not frame petitions for relief without being guilty of an offence finable at discretion, and very near to treason and felony.**

This strange opinion ascribed to the king power in ecclesiastical matters of the most arbitrary and despotic kind, without limitation or redress; and as the enforcement of it necessarily required the exercise of civil power in the infliction of punishment, it deprived one large class of subjects of all liberty, civil and sacred, and if allowed in one class, might naturally introduce an equal exercise of despotism over every other. This may be regarded as perhaps the first distinct intimation to the kingdom at large of the peril in which civil liberty was placed by the arbitrary proceedings of the sovereign and the prelates in religious affairs; and it is not undeserving of notice, that it was founded on the opinion of civil judges, who, in their interpretation of law, were the subverters of the constitution, and the destroyers of both civil and religious liberty.

By means of the authority thus acquired, the prelates urged on their persecuting career with double eagerness and severity; and the Puritans became, in consequence, so much the more determined in their adherence to their principles. Not merely suffering, but calumny of the grossest kind, was their portion; and ambitious churchmen found that the readiest road to preferment in the Church was to pour forth violent invectives and dark aspersions against the detested Puritans. As an answer to these reproaches, and to vindicate their character, the Puritans published a treatise entitled " English

* Neal, vol. i. pp. 416, 417.

Puritanism," which Dr Ames (better known by his Latinised name, Amesius) translated into Latin for the information of foreign Churches. It contains a very full and impartial statement of the peculiar opinions of the much calumniated Puritans; and ought to be enough to vindicate them in the judgment of every candid and intelligent person.

[1610.] The violent proceedings of the Prelatic party, and the dangerous nature of the principles avowed by them, began to arouse the kingdom to a sense of the danger to which all liberty was exposed; and the Parliament prepared to interpose, and to seek redress of grievances which were becoming intolerable. But the king met all their remonstrances and petitions for redress with the most lofty assertions of his royal prerogative, in the exercise of which he held himself to be accountable to God alone, affirming it to be sedition in a subject to dispute what a king might do in the height of his power. The Parliament repeated the assertion of their own rights, accused the High Commission of illegal and tyrannical conduct, and advocated a more mild and merciful course of procedure towards the Puritans. Offended with the awakening spirit of freedom thus displayed, the king, by the advice of Bancroft, dissolved the Parliament, resolving to govern, if possible, without Parliaments in future. This arbitrary conduct on the part of James aroused, in the mind of England, a deep and vigilant jealousy with regard to their sovereign's intentions, which rested not till, in the reign of his son, it broke forth in its strength, and overthrew the monarchy.

[1616.] When the Puritans found, not only no hope of redress, but a constantly increasing severity of treatment, many of them, as has been stated, fled to the Continent, and there continued to discharge their sacred duties as they could find opportunity. Embittered somewhat by the persecution which they had suffered, and constrained to minister in congregations not united in any common body, several of them began to adopt the opinions at first taught by Brown, to the extent, at least, of regarding the Congregational or Independent as the best system of Church government, though not, like him, to the extent of denying the lawfulness of any other. Of these Mr Henry Jacob was one, who, having fled to Holland, became acquainted with Mr Robinson, pastor of a Congregational church at Leyden, and embraced his system. Returning to England in the year 1616, Mr Jacob imparted his views to several others of the suffering Puritans, who, considering that there was now no prospect of a thorough national reformation, resolved to separate themselves entirely from the Church of England, to unite in Church fellowship, and to maintain the ordinances of Christ in what they had come to regard as the purest form. They met, and in the most solemn manner declared their faith, pledged themselves in a mutual covenant to each other and to God, to walk together in all his ordinances, as he had already revealed, or should further reveal them, chose Mr Jacob to be their pastor, elected deacons, and thus formed the first congregation of English Independents. Such and so small was the beginning of a body which afterwards became so powerful, and influenced so strongly the movements of the revolutionary period.*

[1618.] The strongly contrasted tendencies of the two contending parties, Prelatists and Puritans, were rendered very apparent in the year 1618, by the publication of the king's Book of Sports. This book was drawn up by Bishop Moreton, at the king's direction, and dated from Greenwich, May 24, 1618.† The pretext for producing such a book was, that the strictness of the Puritans in keeping the Sabbath-day alienated the people, and left them exposed to the temptations of the Jesuits, who took occasion to seduce them back to Popery. To prevent this his majesty proposed, not that the people should be more carefully instructed in religion, but that, after divine service, they should be indulged in such recreations as dancing, archery, leaping, May-games, Whitsun-

* Neal, vol. i. pp. 461, 462.   † Fuller, vol. iii. pp. 270-273.

ales, morrice-dances, setting up of May-poles, and such like amusements. That the people should meditate on their religious duties, and prepare to practise the instructions given them in God's Word, did not seem to his majesty at all a desirable matter,—it might have led them to favour Puritanism. Queen Elizabeth disapproved of preaching, lest it should teach the people to think, and perhaps to inquire into matters of State. King James aimed at the same result by making their only leisure day, when they might possibly attempt the dangerous practice of cultivating their minds, a day of mere recreation. The reason is obvious. Thinking men cannot be slaves; and both these sovereigns were desirous of establishing a complete despotism. Religious men must think, and think solemnly and loftily; therefore, to prevent this, religion must give place to giddy mirth, and God's hallowed day must be profaned by every kind of idle recreation. And what must be said of the High Church party, who lent their aid in this fearful desecration and despotic scheme? Were they the friends of pure and holy religion, of rational improvement, of public freedom?

This Book of Sports, however, was at first ordered to be read merely in the parish churches of Lancashire; but one author asserts that it would have been speedily extended over the kingdom, but for the decisive refusal of Abbot, who had recently succeeded Bancroft in the archbishopric of Canterbury. But though a partial enforcement of this desecrating production was all that it could, at that time, obtain, its promulgation gave serious ground of dissatisfaction and dread to all the more decidedly pious persons in the kingdom, both Puritans and Churchmen, and tended not a little to confirm the growing jealousy of High Church measures.

The "king-craft," of which James considered himself so great a master, was perpetually leading him astray, and involving him in dangerous political errors, which, blending with the religious struggles that had so long prevailed, both increased the numbers and gave intensity to the feelings of those who regarded with jealousy the arbitrary measures of the Court. In one of his wise speeches the king gave a large explanation of his views with regard to Puritanism; from which it appeared, that he considered all to be Puritans who dared to oppose his absolute prerogative, and to maintain the rights and liberties established by law.* At the same time he discountenanced that system of theology generally termed Calvinism, though he had previously professed to hold it, and had sent divines to the Synod of Dort, where the opposite system, Arminianism, was condemned. But perceiving that the Puritans were Calvinists, he turned the sunshine of his favour towards those of the clergy who had begun to support Arminian tenets. In this manner he most unwisely brought about a combination of two false and dangerous principles on the one side, and of two true and salutary principles on the other;—the combination of despotism in the State and unsound theology in the Church, against the combination of political liberty and religious purity. The alliances formed on both sides were natural, for there is a strong and essential relationship between the component elements of each; and yet this very combination was the cause of many peculiarities in the struggle which afterwards arose, and of the various aspects which it wore, as the one or the other, political or religious, obtained the ascendency.

The combination thus begun in theory was soon forced into actual existence, when, in 1620, the king, offended with the Parliament for mentioning the subject of grievances instead of bestowing money, commanded them to forbear intermeddling with his government; and upon their recording in their journals a remonstrance and protestation in defence of their ancient and undoubted rights and privileges, he, in a storm of fury, tore out the protestation with his own hand, dissolved the Parliament, and issued a proclamation forbidding his

* Rapin, vol. ii. pp. 192, 193.

subjects to talk of State affairs.* This was despotism undisguised, and the heart of England understood and felt it. The element of resistance to political tyranny began to work in the minds of men, many of whom had but little regarded the sufferings of the Puritans under an equal tyranny of an ecclesiastical kind. But the storm was delayed, partly by the natural timidity of James, who was incapable of boldly executing what he tyrannically conceived, and partly also in consequence of his death, and the pause which naturally ensued at the commencement of a new reign, till its principles should be ascertained.

[1625.] Charles I., at his ascension to the throne in 1625, found the kingdom in a truly deplorable condition,—on the point of being convulsed with internal dissension, despised by foreign countries, and its treasury totally exhausted. It would have required a wise and prudent king, and sage and able counsellors, to have rescued the nation from such imminent and formidable perils. But Charles was narrow-minded and obstinate, impatient of advice except when it coincided with his own notions, bigoted in religious matters, entertaining the most despotic ideas of his royal prerogative, and so full of dissimulation, that neither his word nor the most solemn treaties could bind him, as subsequent events amply proved ; and his most trusted counsellors were his father's recent courtier-race of sycophants and oppressors. His marriage to Henrietta, daughter of the French king, and a zealous Papist, caused an additional ground of jealousy, lest persons of that religious persuasion should obtain undue and pernicious influence ; and many events tended to strengthen that apprehension. Instead of relaxing the severe and persecuting measures under which the Puritans had so long groaned, Charles, instigated by Laud, Bishop of London, afterwards Archbishop of Canterbury, continued to oppress that body of excellent men with increasing severity.

* Rapin, vol. ii. p. 212.

A contest arose between Charles and his first Parliament, chiefly on account of their remonstrances respecting the dangerous increase of Popery, and their determination to proceed with the impeachment of his favourite, the profligate Duke of Buckingham. To stop these measures, the king suddenly dissolved the Parliament ; and as he had not obtained the supplies which he desired, he proceeded to raise money by forced loans, ship-money, and other arbitrary and illegal exactions.* These violent encroachments upon liberty and property increased the spirit of disaffection which was already strong, compelling all who valued freedom to perceive that some decided stand must be made, unless they were prepared to sink into the degradation of utter slavery.

[1628.] During the interval which elapsed before the calling of the next Parliament, the clergy were employed to inculcate with all possible earnestness the doctrines of passive obedience and non-resistance, and to prove that the absolute submission of subjects to the royal will and pleasure, was authoritatively taught in the Holy Scriptures. Eagerly did the courtly divines comply with these directions, vieing with each other who should most strenuously promote the cause of despotism. In this glorious strife Sibthorp and Manwaring were peculiarly distinguished, broadly asserting that the king is not bound to observe the laws of the realm,—that the authority of Parliament is not necessary for the imposing of taxes,—and that those who refuse obedience transgress the laws of God, insult the king's supreme authority, and are guilty of impiety, disloyalty, and rebellion. When the Parliament again met in 1628, they proceeded against Manwaring for inculcating tenets destructive of the laws and liberties of the kingdom, and sentenced him to fine and imprisonment till he should make his submission. He submitted accordingly ; but the king soon afterwards rewarded his services in the cause of tyranny, by raising him first to a

* Rushworth, vol. i. p. 192; Whitelocke, p. 2.

deanery, and subsequently to the bishopric of St David's. The other advocates of passive obedience also received promotion; and the nation was constrained to perceive what were the principles by which the king intended to govern. The controversy between High Churchmen and Puritans, which had so long divided the kingdom, was thus forced to assume the character of one in defence of civil liberty. For it was clearly seen, that the High Church party, who had all along enjoyed exclusively the favour of the reigning monarch, were willing to procure and perpetuate that favour by supporting the royal prerogative in its most arbitrary pretensions, sacrificing without scruple equally the rights of conscience and the civil liberties of the kingdom.

The contest continued in both its converging lines. On the one hand, the king strove to obtain supplies without redressing grievances, employing already that dissimulation which afterwards caused his ruin, and assenting to a bill, or petition of right, the provisions of which he never fulfilled. On the other, Laud, who, on the death of Buckingham, obtained an undivided ascendency over Charles, prohibited doctrinal controversy respecting the Arminian tenets, and commanded the suppression of afternoon lectures, which were generally conducted by those Puritan divines who could not conform to the reading of the Liturgy in the forenoon service. This cunning prelate was well aware, that controversy on important doctrinal subjects cultivates the power of thought, and that lecturing cultivates knowledge; he knew also, that men who have been trained to think, and whose minds have acquired a store of sound religious knowledge, are incapable of becoming the slaves of either tyranny or superstition. And as the full development of his measures required the people of England to become superstitious slaves, it was necessary to suppress every thing which had a counteracting tendency. The same sort of instinctive perception of the readiest method of promoting mental and moral degradation

led Laud to persuade the king to revive the Book of Sports.
This was accordingly done in the year 1633, in the name of
that sovereign whom the Church of England still delights to
style " The Martyr," though it would not be easy to tell of
what cause he was the martyr, unless it were of prelatic
profanity, superstition, and despotism. It was not over one
county that the Book of Sports was now to be set up, in
opposition to the Word of God ; the bishops were directed to
enforce the publication of it from the pulpit through all the
parish churches of their respective dioceses. This caused
great distress of mind to all the pious clergymen. Some
refused to read it, and were suspended in consequence; others
read it, and immediately after having done so, read also the
Fourth Commandment, " Remember the Sabbath-day to keep
it holy ; " adding, " This is the law of God, the other is the
injunction of man." And notwithstanding the employment
of both power and guile, the people generally refused to turn
God's appointed times of holy rest into periods of heathen
saturnalia.

In the meantime, the tide of political conflict was advancing broad and deep. And as it had been caused at first by
the course of persecution on account of religion, when the
Parliament sought from time to time to interpose in behalf
of the suffering Puritans, it continued to retain its religious
character. Very strong and earnest language was used by
several of the leading members of the House of Commons,
condemning equally the Arminian doctrines and the tyrannical proceedings of the Prelatic party ; and with similar
directness and energy did they assail the illegal methods
adopted by the king to raise money, and the oppressive conduct of the persons employed in that service. The king
finding the Commons determined to defend their religious
and civil liberties, and to refuse subsidies till the grievances
of which they complained should be redressed, sent them
orders to adjourn. This arbitrary command they refused to

obey, till they should have prepared a remonstrance against the levying of tonnage and poundage, and, accordingly, pro- ceeded to frame their remonstrance and protestation. This document declared, in substance, that whosoever should introduce innovations in religion, or advise taking of tonnage and poundage not yet granted by Parliament, or submit to such illegal impositions, should be held as betrayers of, and enemies to, the liberties of England.* The Speaker refused to put these propositions to the vote, and attempted to leave the chair; but he was forced back to it, and held there till they were read and carried by acclamation. The Commons then adjourned; and four of the leading members, Eliot, Hollis, Valentine, and Cariton, were committed to the Tower, where Eliot was detained till he died, the others being released upon payment of heavy fines. Charles having now learned that the Parliament would not submit to be made a passive instrument in his hands to accomplish what he might please, determined to assume the whole powers of the Legis- lature, disregarding the form, as well as violating the spirit of the constitution, and realising the absolute despotism so fervently advocated by his sycophantic clergy. He ventured even to avow his desperate intention by a proclamation, in which he forbade the very mention of another Parliament. He had yet to learn, that to shut up a strong feeling in the heart, is to increase its suppressed strength, and to give it entire possession of the inner being.

As if for the very purpose of imparting additional intensity to the growing indignation of the kingdom, Laud, now Arch- bishop of Canterbury, proceeded with equal eagerness in imposing fresh ceremonies of the most absurd character upon the Church, and in the infliction of excessive cruelties upon the Puritans. These Popish ceremonies drove numbers into nonconformity; and the barbarities perpetrated upon those who dared to complain or to refuse compliance, provoked the

* Rushworth, vol. i. p. 659, et seq.

nation almost beyond endurance. Alexander Leighton was condemned to have his ears cut off, and his nose slit, to be branded on the cheek, to stand in that condition in the pillory, and then to be cast into prison till he should pay a fine utterly beyond his means,—a sentence equivalent to perpetual imprisonment.   Burton, Bastwick,* and Prynne suffered similar cruelties.   And great numbers were reduced to entire destitution, because they dared to write or speak against Laud's popish ceremonies, or against the prelatic system of Church government.   Numbers forsook the country, and retired some to the Netherlands, others to the settlements recently formed in America.   Never, probably, was there a period in which the principles of religious and civil liberty, and the feelings of human nature, were more shocked and outraged.   But a course of crime is also a course of infatuation.   At the very time when the cruel tortures of these wronged and oppressed sufferers were awakening the most intense sympathy in the nation, the king adopted a measure which roused a corresponding degree of political indignation. Finding it difficult to procure supplies as readily as his necessities required, he devised the plan of assessing not only the maritime, but also the inland counties for sums of money, for the ostensible purpose of building ships of war. This tax, as even Clarendon admits, was intended not only for the support of the navy, but " for a spring and magazine that should have no bottom, and for an everlasting supply for all occasions."   This was clearly perceived, and immediately opposed by the bold and wise assertors of national liberty. The celebrated Hampden refused to pay his share of the tax, and determined to bring the legality of levying such an impost to a public trial.   About the close of the year 1639, the cause was tried before the twelve judges in the Exchequer Chamber.   The judges hesitated.   They perceived clearly

* In passing sentence on Bastwick, the bishops denied that they held their jurisdiction from the king.—*Whitelocke*, p. 22.

that the law was in favour of Hampden; but they held their situations during the royal pleasure, and seven decided that the tax was legal, while one doubted, and four condemned it.* His majesty gained the decision; but Hampden and freedom gained the cause, in the strong feeling which was roused throughout the entire kingdom.

Another act of infatuation speedily followed. For a time the suffering Puritans alone had sought refuge from oppression in a voluntary exile; but now the defenders of civil liberty began to adopt the same course. At length even Hampden, and his cousin, Oliver Cromwell, discouraged with their long and hitherto fruitless struggle, resolved also to seek in the New World that liberty which seemed to have forsaken its ancient English home.† But an order was published, forbidding any to leave the kingdom without permission from the privy council. They remained, returned to the field of danger and of duty, and resumed a contest which presented now no medium between complete freedom and absolute slavery,—no retreat, no cessation, no alternative but victory or death. Thus, by this act of despotic infatuation, Charles gave to his most formidable antagonists the terrible energies of desperate necessity, and sealed his own dark and hapless doom.

There was still another element introduced about this time, as if to render the dreadful combination perfect for evil. Although Laud did not attempt to deny the king's supremacy in all matters ecclesiastical, yet the principle first promulgated by Bancroft—the divine authority of the episcopal order— had taken possession of his narrow and restless mind, and impelled him to endeavour partially to realize it, though its full and ultimate bearing lay far beyond his reach even to imagine. He not only drew the half of the chancery business into the hands of persons nominated to their offices by the prelates, but also prevailed upon the king to allow the bishops

* Whitelocke, p. 24.   † Neal, vol. i. p. 618.

to hold their ecclesiastical courts in their own names, and by their own seals, without the king's letters patent under the Great Seal. This was a direct infringement of the royal prerogative; and to this he succeeded in adding another as glaring, namely, the power of the bishops to frame new articles of visitation, without the king's authority, and to administer an oath of inquiry concerning them.* In this manner the prelates became possessed of extensive jurisdiction, both civil and ecclesiastical, not only independent of Crown and Parliament, but based upon the assumption of a divine right, which rendered them entirely irresponsible, and beyond the control of human law. Had not the spirit of liberty, civil and religious, been at that time vigilant and strong, these prelatic usurpations must have soon reduced England to a state of the most abject slavery. And although the fearful recoil caused the death of both the wily prelate and the misled king, it is greatly to be feared that the Laudean principle is not yet dead, though it has long been dormant, —that it may yet awake in portentous strength,—and that it may put forth a power, and give rise to a struggle, of tremendous magnitude, before it be itself destroyed.

At length the king reached the turning point of his wild and reckless course. Instigated by his evil genius, Laud, he strove to impose upon the Presbyterian Church and people of Scotland the whole mass of prelatic rites and ceremonies, for the sake of which he had already driven England to the extreme point of endurance. But that point had been long previously reached in Scotland, and the attempt provoked an instantaneous and determined resistance. A large portion of the nobility, nearly all the middle classes, the whole of the ministers, and almost the entire body of the people, united in a solemn national covenant in defence of their religious liberties, resolved to peril life, and all that life holds dearest, rather than submit to the threatened violation of

* Neal, vol. i. pp. 584, 585.

conscience. The king raised an army to subdue them by force, but shrunk from the perilous encounter, and framed an evasive truce. This abortive attempt exhausted his treasury, and compelled him reluctantly to call a Parliament, from which he hoped to procure supplies. The Parliament met on the 13th of April 1640, after an interval of twelve years ; but the spirit of liberty was now stronger in the bosom of its members than it had formerly been, and still less disposed to prostrate itself before the royal prerogative. His majesty demanded supplies, and promised then to grant time to take their grievances into consideration. The Commons began with applying for the redress of grievances, and refused to proceed with the grant of a subsidy till these should be redressed. Disappointed and enraged, the king dissolved the Parliament, and threw the leading members into prison. But as his need of money was urgent, he commenced exacting it more oppressively than ever, by forced loans, by ship-money, by granting monopolies, and by every artifice which want could suggest and tyranny employ. And, as if conscious that Episcopacy was the cause of the sovereign's distress, the Convocation which met at the same time, continued sitting after the dissolution of the Parliament, contrary to law and custom, and granted a considerable sum of money to his majesty, to enable him to prosecute the " Episcopal war." This appeared a dangerous precedent, fraught with peril to the liberties of the kingdom, since, on the one hand, the king could augment the revenues of the clergy, and on the other, they could replenish his coffers, be his purposes what they might, without legislative authority, and thereby give him the means of completing his despotic encroachments. Seventeen canons were also published by this Convocation, in the sixth of which all clergymen are required to take an oath, expressing approbation of the doctrine, discipline, and government of the Church of England, one clause of which says, " Nor will I ever give my consent

F

to alter the government of this Church, by archbishops, bishops, deans, archdeacons, &c., as it stands now established."* From this clause it obtained the name of "*the et cetera oath,*" and became an additional element of strife between the Prelatists and the Puritans, driving many ministers into the latter body, because they could not consent to swear adherence to they knew not what.

Charles having again obtained a sufficient sum of money to enable him to maintain an army, broke off all pacific relations with his Scottish subjects, and marched northwards to subdue them by force. But they were not unprepared for such an event. The long course of intriguing dissimulation which they had detected and baffled, during the previous stages of their transactions with his majesty, had led them to the conclusion, that he would observe the terms of the most solemn treaty no longer than till he could violate them with safety. They had therefore retained their military officers in pay, and were in a condition to raise an army at a moment's notice. There had been also begun a private correspondence between them and the leading English patriots; and they had received assurance, that if they should advance into England itself, they would be welcomed as deliverers. They accordingly crossed the border, defeated a strong party which opposed their passage of the Tyne at Newburn, took possession of Newcastle, and advanced into England. Alarmed with their progress, and finding it impossible to raise and maintain a sufficient force to resist them, in the disaffected state of his English subjects, the king appointed commissioners to treat with the Scots at Ripon. This led to a cessation of hostilities for two months, commencing October the 26th, during which the Scottish army were to be maintained at his majesty's expense; the remaining negotiations for peace were transferred from Ripon to London.

It had again become necessary to call a Parliament, for the

* Neal, vol. i. p. 630.

adjustment of the important matters in dispute; and great exertions were made on both sides in the election of members. But the heart of England was now fairly warmed, and its strong spirit roused. By far the majority of the elections were decided in favour of the defenders of liberty; and as all knew that the crisis had come, all were thoroughly prepared for the struggle. In that Parliament was collected not only the flower of living Englishmen, but it may be fearlessly said, that no age or nation has ever produced men of greater eminence, in abilities and character, than were the leaders of that celebrated assembly. To mention the names of Pym, Hampden, Cromwell, Selden, is to mention men of almost unequalled distinction, in sagacity, patriotism, strength of mind, and extent of learning; and those who held but a secondary position, were, nevertheless, men who were possessed of talents and energy enough to have earned high renown in any period less prodigal of human power. Such was that House of Commons, afterwards so famous under the name of the Long Parliament.

Scarcely had this Parliament met, on the 3d of November 1640, when ample proof was given that its members were fully aware of the great task they had to perform. They appointed four committees to conduct with rapidity the important matters before them: for religious grievances,—for the affairs of Scotland and Ireland,—for civil grievances,— concerning Popery and Popish plots. In these committees affairs were prepared for full discussion in the House, so that there might be neither loss of time nor mismanagement.* And as religious grievances had long been felt, and had led to the greater part of the civil oppression which had roused the kingdom, the Parliament took these immediately into consideration. The canons of the late Convocation were declared to be illegal, and not binding; and sharp animadversions were made respecting Laud, as their chief author.

* Whitlocke, p. 36.

This led to the framing of an impeachment against him, as engaged in the treasonable design of subverting the religion and laws of his country. The complaint of the Scottish commissioners against Laud, as the real author of all the commotions which had taken place in Scotland, formed a large and heavy portion of the charge which led to the impeachment of the unfortunate archbishop. An accusation, consisting of fourteen articles, was drawn up, presented to the House of Lords, and the charge being sustained, he was committed to the Tower.

About the same time, or rather a few days before it, the Earl of Strafford, Lord Lieutenant of Ireland, was also impeached, and committed to the Tower. The letters and despatches which passed between Laud and Strafford clearly prove that they were the prime instigators of all the tyrannical measures which had characterised the government of Charles for the preceding twelve years,—at which time Strafford (then Mr Wentworth) deserted the patriotic party, and, like all apostates, became the most bitter enemy of the cause which he had forsaken. The very term employed by Laud, as distinctive of himself and his measures—" Thorough — shows clearly the character of the keen, relentless spirit and despotic temper which filled his narrow mind. And the haughty, dark, and arrogant nature of Strafford,—conscious of great abilities, full of ambitious designs, and utterly unscrupulous with regard to the measures by which they should be carried into effect,—rendered him in every respect a dangerous man, particularly as the confidential adviser and favourite minister of a monarch who himself aimed at despotism. It was not strange that the Commons of England thought it necessary to remove such men from his majesty's councils, as a preliminary step towards the recovery of the nation's liberties. The result of these impeachments is well known; but as several important transactions intervened, these must first be narrated.

Redress was granted to several of those who had suffered under prelatic tyranny. Prynne, Burton, and Bastwick were released from their imprisonment in the Channel Islands, and conducted through London in a sort of triumphal procession. Alexander Leighton was also released from prison, and appointed keeper of Lambeth Palace. Several bishops and other clerical dignitaries were accused of illegal and oppressive conduct, and felt some portion of the weight of retributive justice. And so strong was the indignation which, long suppressed, now burst forth with proportionally greater vehemence, that some difficulty was experienced in restraining the people from inflicting upon their oppressors what Bacon terms "wild justice."

The flood-gates were now opened, the popular mind began to rush forth, and it required both great strength and great dexterity to guide it into a safe channel. It had been part of the Laudean policy to prevent all public discussion respecting the high pretensions of Prelacy; but freedom of discussion was now procured, and the press began to pour forth treatises of every kind and size, in which not only were the abuses of Prelacy fully stated, but also the Prelatic form of Church government itself was strenuously assailed. Bishop Hall wrote in defence of Episcopacy, and was answered by a celebrated treatise, under the title of "Smectymnuus," a word formed from the initial letters of the names of its authors, —Stephen Marshall, Edmund Calamy, Thomas Young, Matthew Newcomen, and William Spurstowe. Even the mighty Milton employed his pen in this keen literary warfare; and it is no rash matter to assert, that in learning, talent, genius, and strength of argument, the Puritan writers immeasurably surpassed their antagonists, and produced an impression on the public mind so deep and strong that it decided the controversy, so far as Prelatic Church government was concerned, even at its beginning.

Along with the literary warfare, another method of assault,

not less formidable, was employed. Petitions were poured
into the House of Commons from every part of the country,
signed by almost incredible numbers, against the hierarchy ;
some desiring its reformation, others praying that the whole
system might be destroyed. Of the latter kind, that which
attracted chief attention was one from the city of London,
signed by about fifteen thousand persons, and generally termed
" The Root and Branch Petition," on account of an expression which occurs in its prayer, viz., " That the said government, with all its dependencies, roots and branches, may be
abolished." Counter-petitions were also brought forward in
defence of the hierarchy, scarcely, if at all, less numerous.
Debates arose in consequence, and very strong language was
employed by several members, condemnatory of the oppres--
sive conduct of the hierarchy. Bills were also introduced,
chiefly with the view of taking away legislative authority
from the bishops, by relieving them from the discharge of
civil duties in the Upper House ; but the House of Lords
rejected these measures, and, after a protracted struggle,
there seemed to be no prospect of getting that grievance
remedied.

A difficulty of a legal nature occurred in the trial of
Strafford. Although his accusation specified matters of
the most arbitrary and oppressive character, yet it was not
clear that they fell within the express terms of statute-defini-
tion of high treason. The charge was therefore so altered as
to enable the Commons to proceed with a bill of attainder,
which passed that House, and was brought before the Lords.
There seemed to be great probability that it would be lost in
that House, when an event occurred which changed the
whole aspect of affairs, so far as that was pacific. A plot
was formed by some leading officers in the army and the
courtiers, to bring the army to London, in order to overawe
the Parliament, rescue Strafford, and take possession of the
metropolis. This plot was discovered, traced out, publicly

stated to Parliament by Mr Pym, on the 2d May 1641, and immediately the conspirators absconded,—some even seeking safety by fleeing to France.* The effect was like a lightning-flash,—sudden and fatal. It revealed to the community their own peril, and the nature of the measures which the king was capable of pursuing ; and thus it drove them to the conclusion that his word or treaty could not be trusted, and that the only method of securing their own safety consisted in depriving him of all power to injure them. Numerous and tumultuary mobs assembled around the Houses of Parliament, rending the air with cries of "Justice ! Justice !" In this state of public agitation the peers passed the bill of attainder.

Another important measure passed at the same perilous moment. The king was anxious that the Scottish army should return to Scotland, being well aware that its presence in England was a source of great strength to the patriots, paralyzing, at the same time, his own military preparations. He repeatedly urged Parliament to relieve the country from the oppressive burden of maintaining these two armies, the Scottish and his own. The House of Commons had already borrowed large sums for the payment of the current expenses; and a still larger sum would be required for the completion of the transaction. But when the plot against the Parliament was detected, the citizens of London, who had hitherto advanced the necessary supplies on Parliamentary security, refused to contribute any more on a security which appeared to be so precarious. Public credit being thus overthrown, the only expedient for its recovery which presented itself was, to secure the continuation of the Parliament till these troubles should terminate. A bill was framed for this purpose, enacting, "That this present Parliament shall not be adjourned, prorogued, or dissolved, without their own consent." This bill passed both Houses with very slight opposition, and

* Whitelocke, p. 43.

received the royal assent by commission, along with the bill
of attainder against the Earl of Strafford.* It would seem
that the detection of the plot against the Parliament had
completely stunned the king and his advisers, so that, in their
guilty confusion, they were incapable of perceiving the vast
import of such a concession, which rendered the Parliament
completely independent of, and co-ordinate with, the king
during its own pleasure.

Yet another step was taken, of scarcely less importance.
Mr Pym moved, that both Houses might join in some bond
of defence, for the security of their liberties and of the Protestant religion. A protestation was accordingly framed,
almost identical in principle with the National Covenant of
Scotland, though somewhat different in form, and less minute
in detail.†

The protestation was as follows :—" I, A. B., do, in the
presence of Almighty God, promise, vow, and protest to
maintain and defend, as far as lawfully I may, with my life,
power, and estate, the true Reformed Protestant Religion,
expressed in the doctrine of the Church of England, against
all Popery and Popish innovation within this realm, contrary
to the said doctrine ; and according to the duty of my allegiance, I will maintain and defend his majesty's royal person,
honour, and estate : Also the power and privileges of Parliament, the lawful rights and liberties of the subjects, and
every person that shall make this protestation, in whatsoever
he shall do in the lawful pursuance of the same ; and to my
power, as far as lawfully I may, I will oppose, and by all
good ways and means endeavour to bring condign punishment on all such as shall by force, practice, counsels, plots,
conspiracies, or otherwise, do any thing to the contrary in
the present protestation contained : And further, that I shall,
in all just and honourable ways, endeavour to preserve the

* Whitelocke, p. 43.
† Ibid. ; Rushworth, vol. iv. p. 241.

union and peace betwixt the three kingdoms of England, Scotland, and Ireland; and neither for hope, fear, or any other respects, shall relinquish this promise, vow, and protestation."

This protestation was subscribed by the whole House of Commons on the 3d of May, and next day by all the Peers present in Parliament, except two; it was then printed, and sent to every part of the kingdom, to be taken by the whole nation; and when it was opposed, the Commons passed a resolution, declaring, "That whosoever would not take the protestation was unfit to bear office in the Church or Commonwealth." To this course of procedure the king offered no opposition; and let it be observed, that the English House of Commons acted a much more arbitrary part, in the enforcing of this protestation, than had been done in Scotland with regard to the National Covenant: and as this took place more than two full years before the Solemn League and Covenant between the two kingdoms was even thought of, and was done by a House of Commons all nominally Episcopalians, it proves that it is directly contrary to fact and truth, to ascribe the severe measures of the Long Parliament to Presbyterian intolerance.

Events of great moment now followed each other with startling rapidity. A bill was passed abolishing the Court of High Commission; and another, putting an end to the Star-Chamber. Both these bills were signed by the king; and thus the main engines of oppression were destroyed. Acquiring fresh confidence by success, the House of Commons resumed their proceedings against the bishops, and actually prepared articles of impeachment. The king, perceiving that he was waging an unsuccessful warfare, changed his course, and suddenly intimated to the Parliament that he intended to pay a visit to Scotland, to complete the pacification with that country. The long-pending treaty was concluded and ratified, and his majesty journeyed to his native country with

such expedition as to show that some important measures
were in his mind. The leading Parliamentary politicians
penetrated his design,—which indeed was sufficiently apparent. He had felt the strength of that support which the
presence in England of the Scottish army gave to the patriotic
party ; and he justly imagined, that if he could not only
detach the Scots from the English Parliament, but gain them
to himself, he would then be able to reduce his refractory
subjects to his own terms. The king's absence necessarily
led to the adjournment of the Parliament; but its chief committees continued to meet, and a small committee was formed
to accompany his majesty to Scotland.* The secret purpose
of this committee was, to give to the leading Scottish statesmen such private information as should put them on their
guard against the arts of royal dissimulation which might be
practised. For this the Scottish leaders were already prepared by their own painful experience, and although the
king exerted himself to the utmost to give satisfaction to
them, and bestowed honours on the chief of the Covenanters,
yet he could not remove their suspicions,—still less induce
them to pledge themselves for the support of his intentions.

Not only were his majesty's expectations disappointed, but
additional cause was given to his people to watch all his
movements with increasing jealousy. Before the king's
arrival in Scotland, the Earl of Montrose had been detected
forming a conspiracy to betray the Covenanters, even while
acting as one of their commissioners at Ripon. For this,
and other similar matters, he had been imprisoned in Edinburgh Castle. Even in his confinement he found means of
corresponding with his associates, and, through them, with
the king ; and a plot was formed, of which there is strong
reason to believe the king to have been aware, to seize Argyle
and Hamilton, and either put them to death, or hurry them

---

* The committee were, the Earl of Bedford, Lord Howard, Sir Philip
Stapleton, Sir William Armyne, Mr Hampden, and Mr Fiennes.

on board a frigate which lay in Leith roads, and having thus struck terror into the Covenanters, to put the army into the hands of the king, at the head of which his majesty might return and overpower his refractory Parliament in England.* The discovery of this plot excited a sudden and strong commotion; but the king endeavoured to cause it to be regarded as entirely a groundless alarm, and redoubled his efforts to give all possible satisfaction to the Covenanters. This event, known by the name of "The Incident," sunk deep into men's minds, and led them to entertain the belief, that the king was capable of conniving at any measure, however dark and bloody, provided that it could promote his progress towards absolute despotism. The fearful outburst of Popish fury, termed the Irish Massacre, taking place at the same time, gave to all these suspicions the most dark and dreadful aspect, and filled the heart of both England and Scotland with intense horror and alarm. And although it may be difficult to prove that Charles directly instigated the Irish Papists to this insurrection, or anticipated the terrific deeds that were done, yet it would be still more difficult to acquit him of knowing that it was intended, and of conniving at it, with the expectation of turning it to his own advantage, by means of the armed forces which would be placed under his command.†

Such was the state of matters, and such the agitated temper of the kingdom, when Charles returned to London, again to resume his contest with the Parliament, now roused to a pitch of almost desperate determination. A committee had been appointed, a considerable time before, "to draw out of all the grievances of the nation such a remonstrance as might be a faithful and lively representation to his majesty of the

* Baillie's Letters, vol. i. p. 392; Brodie's British Empire, vol. iii. pp. 150-155.

† The perusal of "A Declaration of the Commons," &c., July 25, 1642, would prove to any impartial reader that there was such a plot between the queen and the Irish Papists, and that the king knew of it.

deplorable state of the kingdom. This remonstrance, consisting of two hundred and six articles,* was read in the House of Commons on the 22d of November 1641. It had to encounter a very strong opposition; and after a debate which lasted from three in the afternoon till three in the morning, it was carried by a majority of 11, the votes being 159 to 148. Within a few days after the remonstrance had been presented to his majesty, and before he had returned an answer, it was printed and dispersed all over the kingdom. By this step, certainly defective in courtesy, the Parliament fairly took their ground, threw themselves and their cause upon the principle and intelligence of the kingdom, and thenceforward the struggle was one between the sovereign and the nation.

The trial of the bishops, who had been impeached as authors of the nation's grievances, came next. The bishops attempted to stay the proceedings by entering a demurrer. Great and dangerous tumults arose in consequence of the position taken by the prelates; and they, alarmed, and considering themselves exposed to personal danger, determined to abstain from going to the House of Lords, and drew up a protestation against whatsoever should be done by Parliament in their absence, as null, and of no effect.† Their greatest enemies could not have suggested to them a more self-destructive course. They were immediately accused of acting in a manner destructive of Parliaments, and assuming a negative voice in the Legislature, possessed by the king alone; and a new impeachment being framed on this ground, ten of them were sent to the Tower.

[1642.] These proceedings exasperated the king to such a degree, that he immediately resolved to retaliate; and sent the attorney-general to the House of Commons to impeach of high treason five of the leading members, namely, Lord

* Rushworth, vol. iv. pp. 438-451; Whitelocke, p. 49.
† Whitelocke, p. 51.

Kimbolton, Sir Arthur Hazelrigge, Denzill Hollis, John Pym, John Hampden, and William Stroud. The Commons not having ordered them into custody, the king himself went to the House next day (January 4th) to seize them, attended by a crowd of armed men. They had received notice of his intention and withdrawn, so that when he placed himself in the Speaker's chair, and looked around him he perceived that this violent and unconstitutional attempt was abortive.* The most intense excitement arose, Parliament adjourned for a week, the citizens of London protected the five members, and offered to raise the trained bands for the protection of Parliament itself. In vain did the king attempt to overawe them by fortifying Whitehall, and placing artillerymen in the Tower. They were equally resolute, and prepared to bear back force by force if necessary. In this great moment, when every measure was surcharged with peril, the king's infatuation again prevailed; and instead of remaining either to amend his error, or to confront the danger, he forsook Whitehall on the 10th of January, removing first to Hampton Court, then to Windsor, and soon afterwards to York, leaving all the elements of strife, which his despotic proceedings had aroused, to combine and rush onward in a torrent of irresistible might.

Very soon after his majesty's departure from London, the bill to remove the bishops from the House of Lords, that they might not " be entangled with secular jurisdiction," was again brought forward, passed by a large majority on the 6th of February, and on the 14th of the same month obtained the royal signature by commission.

But the intentions of the king soon began to display their hostile aspect too evidently to be any longer misunderstood. From York he made a rapid movement upon Hull, at the head of a considerable body of cavalry, on the 23d of April, for the purpose of seizing upon that important town, and

* Whitelocke, p. 50.

taking possession of its magazines. Sir John Hotham refused to admit him with more than twelve attendants, having
been appointed to his situation as governor by the Parliament, to whom he was responsible for its custody; and the
king, in his disappointment and anger, declared him a
traitor.* Several manifestoes passed between the king and
the Parliament, both on account of this event, and with
regard to the command of the militia; but the progress of
negotiation, instead of producing an agreement rendered the
breach wider and wider, preparatory for an entire disruption.
Considerable numbers of both Houses forsook the Parliament
and joined the king; an army was formed, and Hull was
invested in regular form.   To meet this hostile movement,
the two Houses, on the 12th of July, resolved that an army
should be raised for the defence of the king and Parliament,
and gave the command to the Earl of Essex.   On the 9th of
August, the king proclaimed Essex and his adherents traitors;
and also declared both Houses guilty of high treason, forbidding all his subjects to yield obedience to them.   The Parliament, on the other hand, proclaimed all who should join
the king's army traitors against the Parliament and the kingdom.   In another proclamation, the king summoned all his
faithful subjects to repair to him at Nottingham, where, on
the 22d day of August 1642, he caused his standard to be
erected in a field adjoining the castle wall.   Few complied
with this warlike summons; but the standard was erected
amid the gathering gloom and the rising gusts of a commencing tempest, which, ere evening, increased to a perfect
hurricane, and dashed to the earth the royal banner,† as if
ominous of the fierce storm of civil war then bursting on the
land, and the disgrace and ruin that awaited the royal cause.
    It had for some time been clearly perceived by the Parlia-
ment that war was inevitable, especially after the king's
attempt upon Hull; and they accordingly began to make all

* Rushworth, vol. iv. p. 567.   † Clarendon, vol. ii. p. 720.

necessary preparations. The friendly countenance and support of Scotland was of the utmost importance, and this, therefore, they resolved to secure. Twice had the Council of Scotland attempted to mediate between the king and the Parliament, first in the beginning of the year, and again in May; but though the Parliament accepted their mediation, it was rejected by the king in a peremptory tone, commanding them to be content with their own settlement, and not to intermeddle with the affairs of another nation. The English Parliament, understanding that the General Assembly was to meet in Edinburgh about the end of July, addressed a letter to that body, stating the perilous aspect of affairs, and expressing their desire to avoid a civil war, and yet to promote reformation in both Church and State. The Assembly's answer, dated 3d August, expresses sympathy with the sufferings and dangers of England, recommends unity of religion, " That in all his majesty's dominions there might be one Confession of Faith, one Directory of Worship, one public Catechism, and one form of Church government," accusing the prelatical hierarchy of being the great impediment against obtaining that desirable result. A letter from a number of English divines was addressed to the same Assembly, in which, after expressing gratitude for previous advices, they state, " That the desire of the most godly and considerable part amongst us is, that the Presbyterian government, which hath just and evident foundation, both in the Word of God and religious reason, may be established amongst us, and that (according to your intimation) we may agree in one Confession of Faith, one Directory of Worship, one public Catechism and form of government."* From these expressions it is evident that both the English Parliament and the Puritan divines were perfectly aware of the views entertained by the Scottish Parliament and Assembly ; and yet did not hesitate to seek assistance, and to assent to the idea of a uni-

* Acts of Assembly, 1642.

formity in religious worship, which Scotland regarded as an indispensable condition.

Nor does it appear that the English Parliament entertained any reluctance to procure Scottish aid on such terms. For, in the month of September, a bill was passed through the House of Commons, and on the 10th of that month through the House 'of Lords, entitled " An Act for the utter abolishing and taking away of all archbishops, bishops, their chancellors and commissaries," &c.,—ordaining, that after the 5th of November 1643, there shall be no archbishop, &c., including the whole array of dignitaries and cathedral functionaries, and that all their titles, jurisdictions, and offices, " shall cease, determine, and become absolutely void;" that their possessions should return to the king ; that the property of cathedrals should be vested in trustees, who should give a stipend to their late possessors, and out of the remainder support preaching ministers, both in towns, and through the country where required."* Thus was the English hierarchy overthrown by a Parliament which even Clarendon admits to have been composed of men favourably disposed to Episcopacy ; and this overthrow took place at a time when the Parliament had not resolved to what form of Church government a legal ratification should be given, a whole year being allowed to elapse before the act of abolition should take effect, to allow ample time for the deliberations of an assembly of divines which they intended to call together for that purpose. And so far was the Scottish General Assembly from attempting to force England to adopt the Presbyterian form of Church government, that they abstained from framing a Confession of Faith and Directory for themselves, till it should be seen what England would do, that the matter might not be foreclosed, but the Church of Scotland left at liberty to adopt the same general system, if it should prove such as to gain their approbation. Even at an earlier period,

* Neal, vol. ii. pp. 150, 151.

in the very commencement of the negotiations between the English Parliament and the Scottish Church and people, the latter had strongly advocated a uniformity of religious worship in the three kingdoms, and at the same time had as strongly disclaimed the idea of presuming to dictate to England in so grave and important a matter. Yet this accusation is constantly urged against the Church of Scotland by her adversaries, in ignorance, it may be hoped, of the real facts of the case; although it is not denied that the Scottish Church naturally cherished the expectation that any thorough religious reform in England would produce a Church more resembling the other Protestant Churches than it had been under its wealthy and political hierarchy.

The sword was now unsheathed; and for a period the more harmless war of negotiations and manifestoes was abandoned, and a sterner conflict waged. Several battles were fought, some with doubtful success, and in others to the disadvantage of the Parliament. When the approach of winter led to a partial cessation of hostilities, proposals were again made for peace, and commissioners were sent from the Parliament to Oxford to endeavour to frame a treaty. The Scottish Council sent commissioners also. And hopes were for some time entertained, that the king would consent to such terms as might restore peace to the kingdom without the absolute surrender of its liberties. But it was discovered that his majesty was busily engaged in framing a double plot;—one part of which had for its object the seizure of London; the other, that Montrose should raise the Highlands of Scotland, while the Irish army should invade the western parts of that kingdom, and, having subdued the Covenanters, march to the assistance of the king against his English Parliament. The discovery of these plots, the contumelious treatment sustained by the Scottish commissioners, and the manifest duplicity of the king himself, caused the treaty to be broken off, and both parties prepared to resume the conflict in the field. Again the king's troops were repeatedly successful, and the Parliament were constrained to make redoubled exertions to maintain their ground. For the same reason, they were the more anxious to enter into a close treaty with Scotland, and appointed commissioners to attend the Scottish Convention of Estates, and General Assembly, which were to meet in the beginning of August 1643.

Before that period the Parliament had been endeavouring to advance in what they felt to be of primary importance,— the reformation of religion. By the act of September 10, 1642, it had been ordained that the prelatic form of Church government should be abolished from and after the 5th of November 1643; and it had also been determined that an assembly of divines should be held, to complete the necessary reformation. In the meantime, enactments were passed for the better observance of the Lord's Day,—the suppression of the " Book of Sports,"—the keeping of monthly fasts and lectures,—the removal of all superstitious monuments and ornaments out of churches,—and for the trial of scandalous and inefficient ministers, as well as for granting some support to those of the Puritan ministers who had been ejected in former times for nonconformity, or had recently suffered from the ravages of the king's army. One of the articles in the grand remonstrance of December 1641, had expressed the desire of the Parliament that there might be " a general synod of the most grave, pious, learned, and judicious divines of this island, assisted with some from foreign parts professing the same religion with us, who may consider of all things necessary for the peace and good government of the Church ; and to represent the result of their consultations, to be allowed and confirmed, and to receive the stamp of authority." During the treaty of Oxford, a bill of the same purport was presented, and rejected by his majesty. And when at length convinced that the king would make no concessions in behalf of civil and religious liberty, the Parliament resolved that they would delay no longer, but turn the bill into an Ordinance, and convene the Assembly by their own authority. This important Ordinance is dated June 12, 1643, and is as follows:—

"An Ordinance of the Lords and Commons in Parliament, for the calling of an Assembly of learned and godly Divines, and others, to be consulted with by the Parliament, for the settling of the Government and Liturgy of the Church of England, and for vindicating and clearing of the Doctrine of the said Church from false aspersions and interpretations.

"Whereas, amongst the infinite blessings of Almighty God upon this nation, none is, or can be, more dear unto us than the purity of our religion ; and for that, as yet many things remain, in the Liturgy, discipline, and government of the Church, which do necessarily require a further and more perfect reformation than yet hath been attained : And whereas it hath been declared and resolved by the Lords and Commons assembled in Parliament, that the present Church government, by archbishops, bishops, their chancellors, commissaries, deans, deans and chapters, archdeacons, and other ecclesiastical officers, depending upon the hierarchy, is evil, and justly offensive and burdensome to the kingdom, a great impediment to reformation and growth of religion, and very prejudicial to the state and government of this kingdom ; and that therefore they are resolved that the same shall be taken away, and that such a government shall be settled in the Church as may be most agreeable to God's Holy Word, and most apt to procure and preserve the peace of the Church at home, and nearer agreement with the Church of Scotland and other reformed Churches abroad : And for the better effecting hereof, and for the vindicating and clearing of the doctrine of the Church of England from all false calumnies and aspersions, it is thought fit and necessary to call an Assembly of learned, godly, and judicious divines, to consult and advise of such matters and things, touching the premises, as shall be proposed unto them by both or either of the Houses of Parliament, and to give their advice and counsel therein to both or either of the said Houses, when, and as often as, they shall be thereunto required :

"Be it therefore ordained, by the Lords and Commons in this present Parliament assembled, that all and every the persons hereafter in this ordinance named, that is to say," [Here follow the names] " and such other persons as shall be nominated and appointed by both

Houses of Parliament, or as many of them as shall not be letted by sickness, or other necessary impediment, shall meet and assemble, and are hereby required and enjoined, upon summons signed by the clerks of both Houses of Parliament, left at their several respective dwellings, to meet and assemble at Westminster, in the chapel called King Henry the Seventh's Chapel, on the first day of July, in the year of our Lord one thousand six hundred and forty-three; and after the first meeting, being at least of the number of forty, shall from time to time sit, and be removed from place to place; and also, that the said Assembly shall be dissolved in such manner as by both Houses of Parliament shall be directed. And the said persons, or so many of them as shall be so assembled or sit, shall have power and authority, and are hereby likewise enjoined, from time to time during this present Parliament, or until further order be taken by both the said Houses, to confer and treat among themselves of such matters and things, touching and concerning the Liturgy, discipline, and government of the Church of England, or the vindicating and clearing of the doctrine of the same from all false aspersions and misconstructions, as shall be proposed to them by both or either of the said Houses of Parliament, and no other; and to deliver their opinions and advices of or touching the matters aforesaid, as shall be most agreeable to the Word of God, to both or either of the said Houses, from time to time, in such manner and sort as by both or either of the said Houses of Parliament shall be required, and the same not to divulge, by printing, writing, or otherwise, without the consent of both or either House of Parliament.

" And be it further ordained, by the authority aforesaid, that William Twisse, Doctor in Divinity, shall sit in the chair, as pro-locutor of the said Assembly; and if he happen to die, or be letted by sickness, or other necessary impediment, then such other person to be appointed in his place as shall be agreed on by both the said Houses of Parliament. And in case any difference of opinion shall happen amongst any of the said persons so assembled, touching any of the matters that shall be proposed to them, as aforesaid, that then they shall represent the same, together with the reasons thereof, to both or either the said Houses respectively, to the end such further direction may be given therein as shall be requisite in that behalf. And be it further ordained, by the authority aforesaid, that for the charges and expense of the said divines, and every of them, in attending the said service, there shall be allowed unto every of them that shall so attend the sum of four shillings for every day, at the charges of the Commonwealth, at such time, and in such manner, as by both Houses of Parliament shall be appointed. And be it further ordained, that all and every the said divines, so as aforesaid required and enjoined to meet and assemble, shall be freed and acquitted of and from every offence, forfeiture, penalty, loss, or damage, which shall or may arise or grow by reason of any non-residence or absence of them, or any of them, from his or their, or any of their, church, churches, or cures, for or in respect of the said attendance upon the said service, any law or statute of non-residence, or other law or statute enjoining their attendance upon their respective ministries or charges, to the contrary thereof notwithstanding. And if any of the persons before named shall happen to die before the said Assembly shall be dissolved by order of both Houses of Parliament, then such other person or persons shall be nominated and placed in the room and stead of such person or persons so dying, as by both the said Houses shall be thought fit and agreed upon : And every such person or persons so to be named, shall have the like power and authority, freedom and acquittal, to all intents and purposes, and also all such wages and allowances for the said service, during the time of his or their attendance, as to any other of the said persons in this ordinance named is by this ordinance limited and appointed. Provided always, that this ordinance, or any thing therein contained, shall not give unto the persons aforesaid, or any of them, nor shall they in this Assembly assume to exercise, any jurisdiction, power, or authority ecclesiastical whatsoever, or any other power than is herein particularly expressed." *

Such was the Ordinance calling together the famous Westminster Assembly of Divines ; and while that Ordinance is immediately before the reader, it may be expedient to direct his attention to some of its peculiarities. About nine months had elapsed since the passing of the bill for abolishing the hierarchical form of Church government, during all which period there was no form of Church government in England at all. It was impossible, therefore, that the Assembly could meet in any ordinary form, either as a Convocation, according to the Prelatic system ; or by the votes of the ministers, according to the Presbyterian system ; but it was of necessity

* Rushworth, vol. v. pp. 337-339.

called by the Parliament, who nominated all the members themselves, for the purpose of obtaining their advice respecting the further reformation which should take place, and the organised form which should be assumed by the Church of England. For though the Prelatic system had been abolished, yet the Parliament did not imagine that the Church had therefore ceased to exist, as the language of the Ordinance proves. Let it be observed also, that one object in view by the Parliament in calling this Assembly, was for the express purpose of procuring a " nearer agreement with the Church of Scotland, and other reformed Churches abroad ;" so that, as there were no other kinds of national Churches but the Episcopalian and the Presbyterian, it must have been the intention of the English Parliament to bring their Church nearer to the Presbyterian system, if not to adopt that system entirely. It is therefore equally calumnious and absurd to accuse the Church of Scotland of attempting to constrain the English Parliament in its intended ecclesiastical reform, for the purpose of getting the Presbyterian polity introduced. The Parliament had to choose,—to retain the Prelatic system, with all the tyranny and oppression which had become absolutely intolerable,—to adopt the Presbyterian, to which the Puritan ministers were already predisposed,—or to have no national Church at all, with the imminent peril of national anarchy. And let this also be observed, that the long intermixture of civil and ecclesiastical jurisdictions in England, while it had given to the Parliament a very just dread of permitting ecclesiastical persons to possess civil jurisdiction, had both familiarised them with the idea, contained in the sovereign's ecclesiastical supremacy, of a blended jurisdiction, and had driven them to entertain the conviction that civil rulers ought to rule in ecclesiastical causes equally as in their own peculiar province. Even the fact that there was at the time no legal form of Church government in the kingdom, and that consequently there could be no assembly of divines without being called by Parliament, led to the infusion of an Erastian taint into the very calling together of that Assembly, and the framing of the regulations limiting and directing its deliberations.

Having now arrived at the actual calling of the Westminster Assembly of Divines, it may be expedient, before proceeding to relate its deliberations, to give a very brief outline of the leading topics contained in the history and character of the Church of Scotland, so far as it is necessary that these should be known, in order to obtain a full understanding of the subject.

The Reformation in Scotland began and was carried on in a manner the direct reverse of that which took place in England. In the latter country it began in royal caprice or passion,—was at the first rendered subservient to the arbitrary will of a despotic monarch, through the pernicious element of his ecclesiastical supremacy,—was checked and turned awry by that element, and in the struggle between those who wished a further and more complete reformation and the courtly and prelatic rulers of the Church, it ended in a civil and religious despotism too heavy and cruel to be any longer endured. In Scotland it was entirely an ecclesiastical movement from the very beginning. Patrick Hamilton, the noble and youthful friend of Luther and Melancthon, learned the doctrines of the reformed faith, and taught them to his countrymen, till his testimony was sealed with the blood of martyrdom. Wishart gave an additional impulse to the sacred cause, equally by his teaching and his death. Several of the Popish priesthood were converted, and aided in converting others. John Knox caught up the same testimony; and though, by the commanding power of his genius, and the unconquerable energy of his character, he caused the voice of religious reformation to be heard throughout the kingdom equally by prince and peasant, in the palace and the cottage,

still it was simply and essentially a religious reformation,
taking its form and impress directly from the Word of God
alone, and encountering at every step the formidable opposition of civil powers and political intrigues, instead of receiving from them its bias and its external aspect. Believing
that God's Word contained the only authoritative direction
for doing God's work, the Scottish reformers made their sole
appeal "to the law and to the testimony;" and though they
respected the great continental reformers, they sought the
principles of doctrine, discipline, and Church government,
from no foreign model, but from the Holy Scriptures alone.
Thus it was that the Church of Scotland framed its Confession of Faith and its First Book of Discipline, and met in its
first General Assembly for its own government, seven years
before it had even received the sanction of the Legislature.
Its first General Assembly was held in 1560,—the first act of
Parliament recognising it as the National Church was passed
in 1567. From its origin it had to encounter the world's
opposition; in its growth it received little or nothing of a
worldly intermixture; and when it reached somewhat of
matured form, it still stood opposed to the world's corrupting
influence.

But a few years elapsed till the rapacity and the overbearing force of the nobility began to pillage and assail the
Scottish Church; and where direct power could not prevail,
fraud and dissimulation were employed. The first attempt
against the free Presbyterian Church of Scotland, was that of
Regent Morton, who devised the well known scheme of
tulchan bishops, that by their instrumentality he might at
once seize its revenues and corrupt its courts. When King
James assumed the reins of government he followed a similar
course, with less energy, but greater cunning, and with unwearied pertinacity. His theory of government was absolute
despotism; and he had sagacity enough to perceive, that
where the civil and ecclesiastical jurisdictions were distinct,

his theory could not possibly be realized. And as the Church of Scotland was equally opposed to either aspect of his theory, refusing to intermeddle with civil affairs herself, and refusing to permit civil rulers to intermeddle with matters of a spiritual character, the wily tyrant saw the necessity of subverting the Presbyterian form of Church government, and establishing Prelacy in its stead ; well aware that he would easily acquire an influence over titled and wealthy clergy at Court, which he could never obtain over a free General Assembly. But neither force nor treachery could succeed till after he ascended the English throne ; when, by means of the combined power of English wealth and English influence, he so far changed the government of the Scottish Church as to procure the appointment of bishops, the half submission to certain rites and ceremonies, and the partial suppression of General Assemblies. Still a considerable portion of the nobility, the greater part of the ministers, and by far the majority of the people, remained Presbyterians in principle, and bore an insurmountable dislike to Prelacy. James had foresight enough to see that it would be hazardous to proceed farther ; and refused to comply with the solicitations of Laud, who was eager to impose the whole of his beloved Episcopalian forms on the Church of Scotland.

When Charles I. ascended the throne, he found England in a state of discontent swelling towards insurrection, in consequence of the long course of tyranny, civil and religious, which it had uneasily endured. Unfortunately for him and for the kingdom, he had imbibed all his father's despotic notions of the absolute and irresponsible nature of the royal prerogative ; and to little less than his father's dissimulation and insincerity, he added far greater strength of mind, and strength, or rather obstinacy of purpose. Yielding himself entirely to the counsels of Laud, and of his beautiful but imperious and relentless queen, he not only refused to mitigate the sufferings of the English Puritans, but resolved to

complete what his father had begun, and to bring the Scottish
Church into an entire conformity with that of England. A
Book of Canons, and a Liturgy, were framed by the Scottish
bishops, chiefly by Maxwell, bishop of Ross, revised by Laud,
and sent to Scotland to be at once adopted and used, without
even the formality of having them laid before any Scottish
civil or ecclesiastical court. The free spirit of Scotland was
roused by this mingled insult and tyranny. At first a sudden
tumult broke out, and rendered the scheme abortive; and
then followed a wide, deep, and steady determination to
wrench asunder the despotic yoke of Prelacy, and to restore
to Scotland, in all its original purity and freedom, her own
dearly purchased and beloved Presbyterian Church. Pledging
themselves in a sacred National Covenant, the noblest, the
wisest, and the best of Scotland's sons and daughters prepared
to encounter every peril, and to sacrifice all that life holds
dear, rather than yield up their most precious birthright and
inheritance,—their religious liberty. Provoked to see so bold
and firm a front of resistance shown to his despotic designs
in the poorest and least populous part of his dominions,
Charles raised an army and marched against his hitherto un-
conquered Scottish subjects. He was met on the border by
an equal array of that high-hearted and intelligent class of
men, the Scottish peasantry, who have no parallel in any land,
trained as they are from infancy to know, to love, and to fear
God, and fearing Him, to have no other fear. The king
could, in bitterness, mock their poverty, but he shrunk from
the encounter with men who knew better how to die in what
they believed to be the cause of sacred truth and liberty, than
how to yield. He framed an evasive peace, and returned to
England, purposing to conciliate the Parliament so far that
he might obtain the means of overwhelming Scotland by a
new army too mighty for that small kingdom to resist.

But the English Parliament had, with deep interest,
marked the power of high principles in the triumph of the

Scottish people; and refused to gratify their despotic sovereign, perceiving well that the overthrow of that free country would be speedily followed by the loss of their own remaining liberties. A secret, but a constant intercourse, was begun and carried on between the English Parliament and the Scottish Covenanters, for their mutual support in defending their civil and religious liberties against the aggressions of the king. And when Charles again raised an army for the prosecution of the *bellum Episcopale*, the "Episcopal war," the Scottish Covenanters no longer acted only on the defensive, but boldly entered England, declaring, at the same time, their pacific intentions, their friendship towards England, their loyalty to the king, and their desire only to procure the removal from his majesty's councils of those persons who were plotting the overthrow of religious and civil liberty in both countries. Charles again was constrained to recoil from their firm front, and to recommence a treaty of pacification, first at Ripon, and then at London. The Scottish commissioners experienced the most friendly treatment in London; and the preaching of the ministers, who were empowered to treat for the Church, while in the metropolis, attracted crowds, and appears to have produced a deep and favourable impression respecting both themselves and their cause, as even the bitter and contumelious language of Clarendon sufficiently proves.

The king perceiving that the presence of the Scottish commissioners in London tended to confirm their intimacy and influence with the Parliament, at length hastily concluded the treaty of pacification, and set out for Scotland, with the avowed intention of completely terminating all the necessary transactions with the civil and ecclesiastical authorities of that kingdom; but, as afterwards appeared, with the deep design of maturing the embryo plots of Scottish conspirators, and the intended insurrection of the Irish Papists. The intrigues of Montrose, the dark event termed "The Incident," the sudden outburst of the Irish Massacre, and the king's attempt, after his return, to seize the five members of the English Parliament, have all been already related briefly, and need not be here retraced. Suffice it to say, that, while considered separately, they were sufficiently startling, when viewed in the light of the king's previous conduct, and as they occurred in the order of time, they gave to all who valued religious and civil liberty in both England and Scotland a fearful impression of the terrible deeds which the king could do or sanction for the recovery of his shaken power, and the establishing of his desired absolute despotism. They saw with deep regret, that they had to deal with a sovereign who regarded treaties but as a species of diplomatic warfare, in which parties strive to overreach each other, and by whom the most solemn stipulations would be observed no longer than till his safety would permit, or his interest induce, him to break them. It became, therefore, imperatively necessary for the English Parliament and the Scottish Covenanters, that is, the Scottish nation, to enter into some common bond of union, by means of which they might prevent the danger of being deceived, divided, and overpowered by their unscrupulous antagonist, and both countries reduced to slavery and degradation.

In devising this common bond, there was some difference of opinion between the English Parliament and the Scottish Covenanters, though a difference rather of accident than of essence, arising out of the different points of view from which they contemplated the common object. In England, the long course of oppression pursued by Elizabeth, James, and Charles, fell chiefly on the Puritans, who never, at any time, had formed a majority in the nation ; and it was not till spiritual despotism began to produce civil tyranny, as it always does, that England fairly awoke. For that reason the main aspect of the struggle in England was one in behalf of civil liberty ; and, consequently, what they chiefly wished to form with Scotland was a civil league. On the other hand, the contest had from the first, in Scotland, been of a religious character, the king attempting to overthrow the religious liberties of the vast majority, and to place a religious despotism in the hands of a very small minority. And although civil liberty was also assailed inevitably, yet the primary and main object of attack was religion ; so that when the people of Scotland united to defend their sacred rights and privileges, their bond was almost entirely of a religious character, as is proved from the tenor of the National Covenant. And as it had been by means of English influence that the Church of Scotland had been overpowered, the statesmen and divines of Scotland were fully convinced that they could not safely enter into any close alliance with England, unless their great enemy Prelacy were first abolished, and that no secure and lasting intimacy could be maintained between the two countries if there were not at least a close approximation towards uniformity in religious worship, discipline, and government. This idea the Scottish commissioners strenuously, yet most delicately, pressed upon the notice of the English Parliament so early as the beginning of the year 1641 ; and in this they were supported by nearly all the Puritan ministers, those only excepted who had adopted the Congregationar system. What Scotland chiefly wished, therefore, was to enter into a religious covenant with the English Parliament. This, then, was the difference produced by these different circumstances. England wished for a *civil league* with Scotland for the preservation of their mutual civil liberties, but was willing that it should have also a *religious* aspect and influence. Scotland desired a *religious covenant* for the preservation of their mutual religious liberties, but was willing that it should have also a *civil* aspect and influence. And neither country wished to dictate to the other in either subject, but to leave national inclinations and peculiarities untouched. It is evident, that in these circumstances a union could be formed; but it is as evident, that in directness and sacredness of purpose, the superiority was on the side of Scotland; and also, that hers must be the greatest danger, from the certainty that thus leagued together she must share the fortunes of her mightier neighbour.

If the reader has at all attended to the facts stated, and the principles evolved in the preceding introductory pages, he must have perceived their extreme importance in themselves, and also the light which they throw on the subject to which he is now to direct his concentrated attention. In the earliest ages of Christianity, the civil power everywhere was hostile, because it was pagan, that is, idolatrous. When the civil power became avowedly Christian, it did so at a time when all the principles of Popery were already in existence, and wanted but a favourable opportunity for obtaining ascendency. This opportunity was furnished by the ignorance of the barbarian overthrowers of the Roman empire; and thus Popery arose into full power. One of its distinctive features was its assumption of supremacy in all matters, both civil and ecclesiastical. The fatal effect of this blending of jurisdictions was not at once apparent; but it led to absolute despotism and its counterpart, absolute slavery. At the Reformation, an attempt was generally made to separate the two jurisdictions, the civil and the ecclesiastical; but the importance of the idea was not fully appreciated, and the attempt was but partially successful.

In England, in particular, the sovereign, seizing upon the power formerly possessed by the pope, assumed both jurisdictions, and became head of the Church as well as head of the State. The pernicious consequences were soon apparent, —in the unsteady and fluctuating progress of religious reformation,—in the new forms of persecution,—in the complete stop put to further advancement in purity and truth,—and in the rapid growth of despotism, civil and religious.

These consequences advanced steadily, though with varying rapidity, during the reigns of Elizabeth, James, and Charles I., till they produced the absolute necessity of resistance, unless men were willing to submit to the entire loss of natural, national, and religious liberty. For though we have but touched the main points of the events of those reigns, it must be evident to every intelligent person, that there was not a single thing in which a human being could claim liberty to act, as a man, as a responsible and free agent, and as a member of the Christian Church, which was not directly and violently assailed by the prelates, under the authority of the sovereign's ecclesiastical supremacy. And as man can never be entitled to denude himself, or to suffer others to wrest from him his essential characteristics of a responsible and religious being, it had become a sacred duty to assert and defend his natural, national, and religious rights and responsibilities.

Further, when Prelacy, at first avowedly a human invention, arrogated a divine right, it assumed an aspect that could no longer be endured. Men may, in certain circumstances, abstain from asserting their natural rights; but when an attempt is made to abolish these rights even in God's name, it becomes a duty which they owe to God himself, to prevent the perpetration of a grievous wrong, so wrought as to involve a violation of His glorious and holy character and attributes. It was, therefore, a holy deed, to resist that form of prelatic tyranny; for it was a vindication of the King Eternal from a despotism usurped as if by his authority.

And let it be well observed, that the awfully pernicious character here ascribed to the assumed divine right of Prelacy, cannot be charged against Presbytery, when it, too, claims to be of divine right. Because, while it asserts that Christ, the only supreme Head and King of the Church, has appointed a government and office-bearers in his spiritual kingdom, it recognises equally the religious rights and responsibilities of the people, the free subjects of that kingdom, whose right to liberty of conscience is also a divine right. Nor can it ever become a Popery, by usurping civil authority, and exercising a spiritual and civil despotism; because it owns and teaches the divine right of the civil magistrate in his own department as also and equally an ordinance of God. But upon this subject it is needless to dwell at present; it will come more fully before us as we proceed in tracing the discussions of the Westminster Assembly.

CHAPTER II.

First Meeting of the Assembly of Divines at Westminster—List of Names
—Regulations—Order of Procedure—A Fast—The Thirty-Nine Articles
Revised—Commissioners sent to the Scottish Convention of Estates
and General Assembly—Discussions concerning a Treaty between the
Kingdoms—The SOLEMN LEAGUE AND COVENANT prepared and assented to—Taken in England and in Scotland—Remarks—Parties composing
the Westminster Assembly—Episcopalians—Puritans or English Presbyterians — Independents or Congregationalists — Characters of the
Leaders of that Party—Erastians—The leading supporters of that Party
—The Scottish Commissioners—Their Characters—Sectarians throughout the Country—Cause of so many Sects—Prelatic Tyranny and
Neglect of Instruction—Connection and intercourse between the Sectarians and the Independents in the Assembly—The misapplication of
the term Toleration—Remarks.

THE ordinance of the Parliament calling the Assembly of
Divines to meet at Westminster, on the 1st day of July 1643,
was issued, as has been stated, on the 12th of June, in the
same year. On the 22d of June, his majesty, by a proclamation, forbade their meeting for the purposes mentioned in
the parliamentary ordinance; declared that no acts done by
them ought to be received by his subjects; and threatened,
that if they should meet, he would proceed against them with
the utmost severity of the law. This was so far unpropitious,
even to his own cause, as it tended to prevent the greater
part of the Episcopalian divines who had been summoned,
from attending. The Scottish Convention of Estates met in
June, but came to no definite resolution; and public matters

H

were postponed till it should be more clearly known what terms would be proposed by the King and the Parliament, the Covenanters being unwilling directly to interpose, if that could be avoided.

The following is the list of names contained in the ordinance by which the Assembly was called ; amounting to one hundred and fifty-one in all, namely, ten Lords and twenty Commoners, as lay assessors, and one hundred and twenty-one Divines :—

LORDS.

Algernon, Earl of Northumberland.
William, Earl of Bedford.
Philip, Earl of Pembroke and Montgomery.
William, Earl of Salisbury.
Henry, Earl of Holland.
Edward, Earl of Manchester.
William, Viscount Say and Sele.
Edward, Viscount Conway.
Philip, Lord Wharton.
Edward, Lord Howard of Escrick.

COMMONERS.

John Selden, Esq.
Francis Rouse, Esq.
Edmund Prideaux, Esq.
Sir Henry Vane, Senior.
John Glynn, Esq., Recorder of London.
John Whyte, Esq.
Bulstrode Whitelocke, Esq.
Humphry Salloway, Esq.
Mr Serjeant Wild.
Oliver St John, Esq., Solicitor.
Sir Benjamin Rudyard.
John Pym, Esq.
Sir John Clotworthy.
John Maynard, Esq.
Sir Henry Vane, Junior.
William Pierpoint, Esq.
William Wheeler, Esq.
Sir Thomas Barrington.
Sir John Evelyn.
Walter Young, Esq.

DIVINES.

Herbert Palmer, B.D., of Ashwell.
Oliver Bowles, B D., of Sutton.
Henry Wilkinson, B.D., of Maddesden.
Thomas Valentine, B.D., of Chalfent Giles.
William Twisse, D.D., of Newbury.
William Reyner, of Egham.
Hannibal Gammon, of Maugan.
Jasper Hicks, of Lawrick.
Joshua Hoyle, D.D., of Dublin.
William Bridge, of Yarmouth.
Thomas Wincop, D.D., of Elesworth.
Thomas Goodwin, D.D., of London.
John Ley, of Budworth.
Thomas Case, of London.
John Pyne, of Bereferrars.
Francis Whidden, of Moreton.
Richard Love, D.D., of Ekington.
William Gouge, D.D., of Blackfriars.
Ralph Brownrigg, D.D., Bishop of Exeter.
Samuel Ward, D.D., Master of Sydney College, Cambridge.
John White, of Dorchester.
Edward Peale, of Compton.
Stephen Marshall, B.D., of Finchingfield.
Obadiah Sedgewick, B.D., of Coggeshall.
Thomas Carter, of Oxford.
Peter Clarke, of Carnaby or Kirby.
William Mew, B.D., of Essington.
Richard Capel, of Pitchcombe.
Theodore Backhurst, of Overton Wetsville.
Philip Nye, of Kimbolton.
Brocket Smith, D.D., of Barkway.
Cornelius Burgess, D.D., of Watford.
John Green, of Pencombe.
Stanley Gower, of Brampton.
Francis Taylor, of Yalding.
Thomas Wilson, of Otham.
Anthony Tuckney, D.D., of Boston.
Thomas Coleman, of Bliton.
Charles Herle, of Winwick.
Richard Herrick, of Manchester.
Richard Clayton, of Showell.
George Gipps, of Ayleston.
Calibute Downing, D.D., of Hackney.
Jeremiah Burroughs, of Stepney.
Edmund Calamy, B.D., of Aldermanbury.
George Walker, B.D., of London.
Joseph Caryl, of Lincoln's Inn, London.

Lazarus Seaman, B.D , of London.
John Harris, D.D., Warden of Winchester College.
George Morley, D.D., of Minden Hall.
Edward Reynolds, D.D., of Brampton.
Thomas Hill, B.D., of Tickmarsh.
Robert Saunderson, D.D., of Boothby-Parnell.
John Foxcroft, of Gotham.
John Jackson, of Marsac.
William Carter, of London.
Thomas Thoroughgood, of Massingham.
John Arrowsmith, D.D., of Lynn.
Robert Harris, B.D., of Hanwell.
Robert Cross, B.D., of Lincoln College.
James Ussher, Archbishop of Armagh.
Matthias Styles, D.D., of Eastcheap, London.
Samuel Gibson, of Burleigh.
Jeremiah Whittaker, of Stretton.
Edmund Staunton, D.D., of Kingston.
Daniel Featley, D.D., of Lambeth.
Francis Coke, of Yoxhall.
John Lightfoot, D.D., of Ashley.
Edward Corbet, of Merton College, Oxford.
Samuel Hildersham, of Felton.
John Langley, of West-Tuderly, Gloucester.
Christopher Tisdale, of Uphurstbourne.
Thomas Young, of Stowmarket.
John Philips, of Wrentham.
Humphrey Chambers, B.D., of Claverton.
John Conant, B.D., of Lymington.
Henry Hall, B.D., of Norwich.
Henry Hatton.
Henry Scudder, of Colingbourne.
Thomas Bayley, B.D., of Manningford-Bruce.
Benjamin Pickering, of East Hoatly.
Henry Nye, of Clapham.
Arthur Sallaway, of Severn Stoake.

Sidrach Simpson, of London,
Anthony Burgess, of Sutton-Coldfield.
Richard Vines, of Calcot.
William Greenhill, of Stepney.
William Moreton, of Newcastle.
Richard Buckley.
Thomas Temple, D.D., of Battersey.
Josias Shute, B.D., Lombard Street.
William Nicholson, D.D., afterwards Bishop of Cloucester.
Thomas Gataker, B.D., of Rotherhithe.
James Welby, of Sylatten.
Christopher Pashly, D.D., of Hawarden.
Henry Tozer, B.D., of Oxford.
William Spurstow, D.D., of Hampden.
Francis Cheynel, D.D., of Petworth.
Edward Ellis, B.D., of Gilsfield.
John Hacket, D.D., of St Andrew's London.
Samuel de la Place, } French Congregations.
John de la March, }
Matthew Newcomen, of Dedham.
William Lyford, of Sherbourne.
William Carter, of Dynton.
William Lance, of Harrow.
Thomas Hodges, of Kensington.
Andrew Perne, of Wisby.
Thomas Westfield, D.D., Bishop of Bristol.
Henry Hammond, D.D., of Penshurst.
Nicholas Proffit, of Marlborough.
Peter Sterry, of London.
John Erle, of Bishopston.
John Gibbon, of Waltham.
Henry Painter, B.D., of Exeter.
Thomas Micklethwait, of Cherryburton.
John Wincop, D.D., of St Martin's in the Fields.
William Price, of St Paul's, Covent Garden.
Henry Wilkinson, B.D., of St Dunstan's.
Richard Holdsworth, D.D., of Cambridge.
William Dunning, of Godalston.

SCOTTISH MEMBERS.

Lay Assessors or Elders.

John, Lord Maitland. | Sir Archibald Johnston, of Warriston.

Ministers.

Alexander Henderson, of Edinburgh. | Samuel Rutherford, of St Andrews.
George Gillespie, of Edinburgh. | Robert Baillie, of Glasgow.

SCRIBES OR CLERKS.

Henry Roborough. | Adoniram Byfield. | John Wallis.

Of this list, about twenty-five never appeared at the Assembly, one or two having died about the time of the meeting of the Assembly, and others fearing the displeasure of the king, or having a preference for the prelatic system. In order to supply the deficiency thus caused, and also occasional diminution caused by death during the protracted sittings of the Assembly, the Parliament summoned about twenty-one additional members, who were termed the superadded divines. The following is a list of their names, as far as is known :—

Mr John Bond.	Daniel Cawdrey, of Great Billing.	Mr Strong, of Westminster.
Mr Boulton.		John Ward.
Richard Byfield.	Mr Johnson.	Thomas Ford.
Philip Delme.	Thos. Dillingham, of Dean.	John Drury.
William Goad.	John Maynard.	William Rathband, of Highgate.
Humphrey Hardwick.	William Newscore.	
Christopher Love.	John Strickland, B.D., of New Sarum.	Simeon Ashe, of St Bride's.
William Massam.		Mr Moore.

There were thus in whole, thirty-two lay assessors, including those from Scotland; and one hundred and forty-two divines, including the four Scottish commissioners. But of these only sixty-nine were present the first day; and, generally, the attendance appears to have ranged between sixty and eighty. There are one hundred and two divines named in the common editions of the Confession of Faith; but several of those there named were not regular in their attendance. Not more than from a dozen to a score spoke frequently; many very learned and able men being contented to listen, to think, and to vote. The three scribes had no votes, being sufficiently employed in recording the propositions brought forward, the progress of the discussion, and the state of the vote when taken. Dr Twisse, of Newbury, was appointed prolocutor; and after his death he was succeeded by Mr Herle. Dr Burgess of Watford, and Mr White of Dorchester, were assessors to the prolocutor, to take the chair during his occasional absence.

It may serve to show the wish of the Parliament to act with fairness and impartiality, to state, that they named men of all shades of opinion in matters of Church government, in order that the whole subject might be fully discussed. In the original ordinance, four bishops were named, one of whom actually attended on the first day, and another excused his absence on the ground of necessary duty; of the others called, five became bishops afterwards; and about twenty-five declined attending, partly because it was not a regular convocation called by the king, and partly because the Solemn League and Covenant was expressly condemned by his majesty.

At length the appointed day came; and on Saturday, the 1st of July, the members of the two Houses of Parliament named in the ordinance, and many of the divines therein mentioned, and a vast congregation, met in the Abbey Church, Westminster. Dr Twisse, the appointed prolocutor of the Assembly, preached an elaborate sermon from the text, John xiv. 18 : " I will not leave you comfortless, 1 will come unto you." After sermon all the members present adjourned to Henry VII.'s Chapel ; and the roll of members being called, it appeared that there were sixty-nine clerical members present on that the first day of the Westminster Assembly. But as there had been no specific instructions given, nor any subject prepared for their immediate discussion, the Assembly adjourned till the following Thursday.

This very fact points out one peculiarity of the Westminster Assembly, to which allusion has been made. It was neither a Convocation, nor a Presbyterian Synod or General Assembly ; and it could not be either the one or the other, for the prelatic form of Church government had been abolished, and there was no other yet in existence. The true theory of the Westminster Assembly comprises two main elements ; —there was a Christian Church in England, but not organized ; and the civil power, avowing Christianity, had called an Assembly of Divines, for the purpose of consulting together respecting those points of government and discipline which require the sanction of civil authority for their full efficiency. Such an Assembly could have been called only by a Christian civil magistrate ; and only in a transition state of the Church, when disorganized, or not yet duly constituted. In such a state of matters, the problem to be solved was this : On what terms could a National Church be constituted, so as neither to encroach upon civil liberty, as the Papal and Prelatic Churches had done, nor to yield up those inherent spiritual rights, privileges, and liberties, which are essential to a Church of Christ? And, for that purpose, it was almost indifferent, whether the State should first mention the terms on which it would establish a National Church, or the Church specify the terms on which it would consent to be established; only, that the latter would have been the simpler and the purer method of making the arrangement. The former, however, was the plan adopted; and, for that reason, the statement of the propositions came from Parliament.

When the Assembly again met on the Thursday, the following instructions were laid before them, as general regulations, directed by the Lords and Commons in Parliament assembled:—1. That two assessors be joined to the prolocutor, to supply his place in case of absence or infirmity. 2. That scribes be appointed to set down all proceedings, and those to be divines, who are out of the Assembly, namely, Mr Henry Roborough, and Mr Adoniram Byfield. 3. Every member, at his first entry into the Assembly, shall make serious and solemn protestation, not to maintain any thing but what he believes to be truth and sincerity, when discovered to him. 4. No resolution to be given upon any question the same day wherein it is first propounded. 5. What any man undertakes to prove as necessary, he shall make good out of Scripture. 6. No man to proceed in any dispute after the prolocutor has enjoined him silence, unless the Assembly desire he may go on. 7. No man to be denied to enter his dissent from the Assembly, and his reasons for it, in any point, after it hath been first debated in the Assembly, and thence (if the dissenting party desire it) to be sent to the Houses of Parliament by the Assembly, not by any particular man or men, in a private way, when either House shall require. 8. All things agreed on, and prepared for the Parliament, to be openly read and allowed in the Assembly, and then offered as the judgment of the Assembly, if the major part assent;—provided that the opinion of any persons dissenting, and the reasons urged for it, be annexed thereunto, if the dissenters require it, together with the solutions, if any were given to the Assembly, to these reasons.*

To these general regulations the Assembly added some for their own guidance :—1. That every session begin and end with prayer. 2. That after the first prayer the names of the Assembly be called over, and those that are absent marked ; but if any member comes in afterwards, he shall have liberty to give in his name to the scribes. 3. That the appointed hour of meeting be ten in the morning ; the afternoon to be reserved for committees. 4. That three of the members of the Assembly be appointed weekly as chaplains, one to the House of Lords, another to the House of Commons, and a third to the Committee of both kingdoms.

It was also resolved, that every member of the Assembly, both Lords and Commons, as well as Divines, before his admission to sit and vote, should take the following vow or protestation : " I, ———, do seriously promise and vow, in the presence of Almighty God, that in this Assembly, whereof I am a member, I will maintain nothing in point of doctrine but what I believe to be most agreeable to the Word of God ; nor in point of discipline, but what I shall conceive to conduce most to the glory of God, and the good and peace of his Church." This protestation was appointed to be read afresh every Monday morning, that its solemn influence might be constantly felt.

In order that business might proceed regularly and expeditiously, the whole Assembly was cast into three equal committees ; the divines according to the order in which their names stood in the ordinance ; and the Lords and Commons into three corresponding divisions, according to their order also. Each committee chose for itself a chairman : the first chose

* Lightfoot's Works, vol. xiii. pp. 3, 4.

Dr Cornelius Burgess ; the second, Dr Staunton ; and the
third, Mr Gibbon. The account of the Assembly's order of
procedure given by Baillie is at once so graphic and so complete, that we cannot do better than extract the entire passage,
merely modernizing any peculiarities in spelling or obsolete
expressions :—

"The like of that Assembly I did never see ; and as we hear say, the
like was never in England, nor any where is shortly like to be. They
did sit in Henry the VII.'s Chapel, in the place of the Convocation ;
but since the weather grew cold, they did go to the Jerusalem Chamber,
a fair room in the Abbey of Westminster, about the size of the College
front-hall, but wider. At the one end, nearest the door, and along both
sides, are stages of seats, as in the new Assembly House at Edinburgh,
but not so high ; for there will be room but for five or six score. At
the uppermost end there is a chair set on a frame, a foot from the
earth, for the Mr Prolocutor, Dr Twisse. Before it, on the ground,
stand two chairs for the two Mr Assessors,' Dr Burgess and Mr White.
Before these two chairs, through the length of the room, stands a table,
at which sit the two scribes, Mr Byfield and Mr Roborough. The
house is all well hung (with tapestry), and has a good fire, which is
some dainties at London. Opposite the table, upon the prolocutor's
right hand, there are three or four ranks of benches. On the lowest
we five do sit. Upon the other, at our backs, the members of Parliament deputed to the Assembly. On the benches opposite us, on the
prolocutor's left hand, going from the upper end of the house to the
chimney, and at the other end of the house and back of the table, till
it come about to our seats, are four or five stages of benches, upon
which their divines sit as they please ; albeit commonly they keep the
same place. From the chimney to the door there are no seats, but a
void space for passage. The Lords of the Parliament used to sit on
chairs, in that void, about the fire. We meet every day of the week
but Saturday. We sit commonly from nine till one or two afternoon.
The prolocutor, at the beginning and end, has a short prayer. The
man, as the world knows, is very learned in the questions he has
studied, and very good, beloved of all, and highly esteemed ; but
merely bookish, not much, as it seems, acquainted with conceived
prayer, and among the unfittest of all the company for any action ;
so after the prayer he sits mute. It was the canny convoyance (skilful

management) of those who guide most matters for their own interest to plant such a man of purpose in the chair. The one assessor, our good friend Mr White, has keeped in of the gout since our coming; the other, Dr Burgess, a very active and sharp man, supplies, so far as is decent, the prolocutor's place. Ordinarily there will be present above three score of their divines. These are divided into three committees, in one of which every man is a member. No man is excluded who pleases to come to any of the three. Every committee, as the Parliament gives order in writing to take any purpose to consideration, takes a portion, and in their afternoon meeting prepares matters for the Assembly, sets down their minds in distinct propositions, backing their propositions with texts of Scripture. After the prayer, Mr Byfield, the scribe, reads the proposition and scriptures; whereupon the Assembly debates in a most grave and orderly way.

"No man is called up to speak; but whosoever stands up of his own accord, speaks so long as he will without interruption. If two or three stand up at once, then the divines confusedly call on his name whom they desire to hear first: on whom the loudest and maniest voices call, he speaks. No man speaks to any but to the prolocutor. They harangue long and very learnedlie. They study the questions well beforehand, and prepare their speeches; but withal the men are exceeding prompt and well spoken. I do marvel at the very accurate and extemporal replies that many of them usually make. When, upon every proposition by itself, and on every text of Scripture that is brought to confirm it, every man who will has said his whole mind, and the replies, duplies, and triplies are heard, then the most part call, ' To the question.' Byfield, the scribe, rises from the table, and comes to the prolocutor's chair, who, from the scribe's book, reads the proposition, and says, ' As many as are of opinion that the question is well stated in the proposition, let them say, Ay;' when ay is heard, he says, ' As many as think otherwise, say, No.' If the difference of ' Ayes' and ' Noes' be clear, as usually it is, then the question is ordered by the scribes, and they go on to debate the first scripture alleged for proof of the proposition. If the sound of Ay and No be near equal, then says the prolocutor, ' As many as say Ay, stand up;' while they stand, the scribe and others number them in their minds; when they sit down, the Noes are bidden stand, and they likewise are numbered. This way is clear enough, and saves a great deal of time, which we spend in reading our catalogue. When a question is once ordered, there is no more debate of that matter; but if a man will wander from the subject, he is quickly taken up by Mr Assessor, or many others, confusedly crying, 'Speak to order, to order.' No man contradicts another expressly by name, but most discreetly speaks to the prolocutor, and at most holds to general terms : 'The reverend brother who lately, or last, spoke, on this hand, on that side, above, or below.' I thought meet once for all to give you a taste of the outward form of their Assembly. They follow the way of their Parliament. Much of their way is good, and worthy of our imitation ; only their longsomeness is woful at this time, when their Church and kingdom lie under a most lamentable anarchy and confusion. They see the hurt of their length, but cannot get it helped ; for being to establish a new platform of worship and discipline to their nation for all time to come, they think they cannot be answerable, if solidly, and at leisure, they do not examine every point thereof." *

Having made these preliminary arrangements, the Parliament sent the Assembly an order to revise the Thirty-nine Articles, for the purpose of simplifying, clearing, and vindicating the doctrines therein contained. The discharge of this task was begun in the committees, and reported from time to time in the Assembly. On the first of these meetings to receive and consider reports, July 12th, "A letter," says Lightfoot, "came from Dr Brownrigge, Bishop of Exeter, to Dr Featly, or, in his absence, to Dr Gouge, which was openly read, wherein he excuseth his non-appearance in the Assembly, from the tie of the vice-chancellorship in the university that lay upon him." † The tenor of his excuse shows that he at least did not condemn the calling of the Assembly, nor thought his episcopal function of divine institution. Indeed there were many Episcopalians who had not embraced the high theory of Bancroft and Laud, otherwise none could have appeared in the Assembly at all ; and yet even Clarendon admits, that " about twenty of them were reverend and worthy persons, and episcopal in their judgments ; " ‡ and Fuller says, that " Dr Westfield (bishop of Bristol) and some few others seemed the only nonconformists among them for

---

* Baillie, vol ii. pp. 108, 109.   † Lightfoot, p. 5.   ‡ Clarendon.

their conformity, whose gowns and canonical habits differed from all the rest." * From this it appears that at least one bishop gave his presence to the meeting of that Assembly, which so many of his prelatic brethren since have termed impious and rebellious.

A new disaster having befallen the arms of the Parliament, in the defeat of Waller, the Assembly petitioned the Houses to appoint a fast throughout London, Westminster, and the suburbs; requesting that measures might be speedily adopted for promoting reformation, so that the divine wrath might be averted, and the wounds and miseries of the kingdom healed. This petition was granted; the 21st of July was set apart as a day of humiliation, fasting, and prayer. Mr Hill, Mr Spurstow, and Mr Vines, were appointed to preach before the Houses, and the day was observed with great solemnity within the specified boundaries. From this time forward, it was customary to appoint similar fasts, and public sermons before the Houses of Parliament; which sermons were printed by order of Parliament, frequently with prefaces before, or postscripts appended to them by their authors; and having been preserved, they form an admirable mass of information regarding the actual sentiments and state of feelings predominant in both the Parliament and Assembly, characterised by all the freshness and trembling earnestness, and intensity of hopes and fears, called forth by the varying vicissitudes of those eventful and fluctuating times.† The same circumstance proves, that on the part of the Parliament, the struggle in which they were engaged was by themselves regarded as to the full as much of a religious as of a political character; and that they were not ashamed to acknowledge that they looked to the favour and the protection of God for ultimate

---

* Fuller, vol. iii. p. 448.

† For the use of perhaps the most complete collection of these sermons extant, the author is indebted to the kindness and courtesy of the Rev. Mr Craig of Rothsay.

success in the perilous and important contest. It may be added, that however vehemently the king and his adherents asserted the divine source of the royal prerogative, we do not find that they attempted to hallow their cause, or to seek divine aid, by solemn religious acts ; but, on the contrary, that in order to draw the utmost possible breadth of distinction between themselves and the Puritans, they delighted to indulge to excess in every kind of licentiousness and immorality ; so that they frequently alienated those counties which were otherwise friendly to the royal cause, and drove the oppressed people into the ranks of the parliamentary armies, as the only way to rescue themselves and their families from the vicious brutalities of the proud and tyrannical cavaliers.

The Assembly continued to discuss the Thirty-nine Articles, and expended ten weeks in debating upon the first fifteen. But upon the arrival of the Scottish commissioners, or rather, soon after the signing of the Solemn League and Covenant, a new direction was given to the whole course of discussion ; so that it is unnecessary to trace that part of the proceedings which led to no practical result, and which, terminating abruptly and unfinished, cannot properly be said to form any part of the Assembly's actual proceedings. Let us rather direct attention to the formation of the Solemn League and Covenant itself.

When the English Parliament determined upon the abolition of the Prelatic hierarchy, they at the same time suggested the calling of an Assembly of Divines to deliberate respecting the new form to be established ; and they also applied to the Church of Scotland to send commissioners to the intended Assembly. The Scottish Church nominated some ministers and elders to be in readiness ; but the English Assembly not having been called till nearly a year had elapsed, serious doubts began to be entertained in Scotland respecting their sincerity, especially when no authorised person appeared at the Convention of Estates held on the 22d June, and prolonged during a fortnight. At length a messenger arrived, stating that the Assembly had met, and renewing their application for the presence of Scottish commissioners.* As the General Assembly was to meet on the 2d of August, and the Convention of Estates at the same time, the matter was deferred till then, that it might be fully and authoritatively arranged.

After several days of anxious expectation by the Scottish General Assembly, the English commissioners arrived on the 7th of August, and were received by a deputation of the Assembly on the following day. The English commissioners were, from the Lords, the Earl of Rutland and Lord Gray of Wark, the latter of whom declined the journey; from the Commons, Sir William Armyn, Sir Harry Vane the younger, Mr Hatcher, and Mr Darley; and from the Assembly of Divines, Mr Marshall and Mr Nye. They presented their commission, giving them ample powers to treat with the Scottish Convention and Assembly,—a Declaration of both the English Houses,—a letter from the Westminster Assembly, and a letter subscribed by above seventy of their divines, supplicating aid in their desperate condition. "This letter," says Baillie, "was so lamentable that it drew tears from many."† The leading statesmen and divines in Scotland immediately took these matters into serious and most anxious deliberation. All were of opinion that it was necessary to assist the English; but how that assistance should be given they could not so readily determine. At one time the prevalent idea was, that Scotland should interpose as a mediating power, without altogether taking part with the Parliament; but a more careful and full deliberation convinced them that this was impracticable. They had learned by sad

---

* Baillie, vol. ii. p. 80.
† Ibid., vol. ii. p. 89. All the documents referred to, with their answers, may be seen in the Acts of Assembly 1643.

experience that the king's most solemn treaties could not be depended on, when they had seen the treaty concluded at Dunse ordered to be burned by the hands of the hangman, and themselves denounced as rebels. And as the English Parliament had not hitherto exhibited any similar insincerity, there was no reason for equal distrust with regard to their declarations ; while the Scottish statesmen and ministers could not but perceive, that if the king should succeed in subjugating his English Parliament, he would then be able to assail Scotland with an irresistible force.

Still there was one difficult point. The English commissioners sought to enter into a civil league with Scotland, for the defence of the civil liberties of both countries. But as the entire spirit of the contest in which Scotland had been engaged was of a religious character, in defence of religious liberty, and had been conducted to a prosperous issue by the strength of a religious covenant into which the nation had entered, the Convention and Assembly insisted upon a religious covenant between the two kingdoms. To this the English commissioners at length assented, on the suggestion of Sir Harry Vane, that the two ideas might very properly be combined ; and hence the bond of union between the two countries was so framed as to embrace both subjects, and received the appropriate designation of THE SOLEMN LEAGUE AND COVENANT.

This important document was framed by the celebrated Alexander Henderson, moderator of the Assembly, and laid before the English commissioners. At first they startled somewhat at its terms, some of them wishing for a greater latitude of expression, to leave room for the introduction of the Independent or Congregational system. In this, too, a slight compromise was made, no specific plan for the reformation of religion in England and Ireland being stated, except that it should be " according to the Word of God, and the example of the best reformed Churches." With this mode of expressing the general principle all were satisfied ; and after receiving the approbation of the private committees, the Solemn League and Covenant was submitted to the General Assembly on the 17th of August 1643, passed unanimously,* amidst the applause of some, and the bursting tears of a deep, full, and sacred joy of others ; and in the afternoon, with the same cordial unanimity, passed the Convention of Estates. " This," says Baillie, " seems to be a new period and crisis of the most great affair which these hundred years has exercised these dominions." He was not mistaken ; it was indeed the commencement of a new period in the history of the Christian Church, though that period has not yet run its full round, nor reached its crisis,—a crisis which will shake and new-mould the world.

It is customary for a certain class of writers to say, that in the discussion respecting the Solemn League and Covenant, there was a contest of cunning between the English commissioners and the Scottish Covenanters, and that the superior subtlety of Sir Harry Vane enabled him to beguile the Scottish negotiators, who, in their blind attachment to their own Presbyterian system, could not conceive that any thing else was meant by the expression, " The best reformed Churches." This is but a weak invention of the enemy. In the beginning of the year 1641, the Scottish commissioners had both suggested the idea of a closer agreement between the Churches of England and Scotland, and disclaimed the presumption ot urging their system upon the mightier kingdom.† And in the ordinance summoning the Assembly, one object is said to be, to obtain " a nearer agreement with the Church of Scotland, and other reformed Churches abroad." Further, the Church of Scotland had delayed the framing of a Directory,

* The Lord High Commissioner, Sir Thomas Hope, declined assenting to the Covenant in his official capacity, but personally he gave his cordial concurrence.

† See Appendix.

very much that she might be the more at liberty to accommodate her procedure to what might be resolved upon by the English Assembly, when it should have accomplished its task. It would appear, therefore, that there was no craft nor overreaching on either side ; and that, so far as there was a compromise, it was one of candour and frankness, well understood by both parties, for the purpose of leaving matters open to a full and fair discussion.

When the Solemn League and Covenant had thus received the assent of the Scottish Convention of Estates and General Assembly, a copy of it was sent to the English Parliament and the Westminster Divines, for their consideration. Commissioners were appointed to attend that Assembly, partly elders and partly ministers. The elders were, the Earl of Cassilis, Lord Maitland, and Johnston of Warriston ; the ministers were, Messrs Henderson, Baillie, Gillespie, Rutherford, and Douglas ; but neither the Earl of Cassilis nor Mr Robert Douglas ever attended, so that the Scottish commissioners were six in all. When the document reached Westminster, several days were spent by the English divines in considering its various propositions, and some slight verbal alterations were made, for the sake of explanation,—particularly the specific statement of what is meant by Prelacy ; and at last it was agreed to by all except Dr Burgess, who continued to resist it and to refuse his assent for several days, till he incurred the serious displeasure of both Assembly and Parliament,—which he at last averted by yielding.*

Immediately after the rising of their own General Assembly, three of the Scottish commissioners, Lord Maitland, Alexander Henderson, and George Gillespie, set off for London ; the other three followed about a month afterwards. On the 15th

---

* The angry language of Dr Lightfoot is positively ludicrous :—"A wretch that ought to be branded to all posterity, who seeks, for some devilish ends, either of his own or others, or both, to hinder so great a good of the two nations."—*Lightfoot*, vol. xiii. p. 12.

of September the Scottish commissioners were received into the Westminster Assembly with great kindness and courtesy, and welcomed in three successive speeches, by the Prolocutor, by Dr Hoyle, and by Mr Case. Mr Henderson replied, expressing the deep sympathy felt by the kingdom and Church of Scotland for the sufferings of England, and the readiness with which they would to the utmost assist the good work of religious reformation thus begun. The Solemn League and Covenant was then read over clause by clause, and explanations given where it seemed of doubtful import, till the whole received the sanction of the Assembly. It was then appointed by the Parliament, and assented to by the Assembly, that the Covenant should be publicly taken by these bodies on the 25th of September. On that day, accordingly, the House of Commons, with the Assembly of Divines and the Scottish commissioners, met in the Church of St Margaret, Westminster; and the Rev. Mr White of Dorchester, one of the assessors, commenced the solemnity with prayer. Mr Nye then addressed the dignified and grave audience in a speech of an hour's duration, pointing out the Scripture authority of such covenants, and the advantage of which they had been productive to the Church of God in all ages. Mr Henderson followed in a speech considerably shorter, but of great dignity and power. Mr Nye then read it from the pulpit, slowly and aloud, pausing at the close of every article, while the whole audience of statesmen and divines arose, and, with their right hands held up to heaven, worshipped the great name of God, and gave their sacred pledge.* Then the members of the House of Commons subscribed the Covenant on one roll of parchment,† and the Assembly on another; and when this was done, the solemn scene was closed by prayer and praise

---

* Rushworth, vol. v. p. 475.

† This roll was subscribed by two hundred and twenty-eight members of the House of Commons, whose names may be seen in Rushworth, vol. v. pp. 480, 481. On that roll appears the name of Oliver Cromwell.

I

to that omniscient God to whom they had lifted up their hands and made their vows.

To complete in one view the account of this matter, the Covenant was taken by the House of Lords on the 15th of October, after sermon by Dr Temple, and an exhortation by Mr Coleman. It was taken also by the congregations in and around London on the following Lord's day. On the 9th of October the king issued a proclamation from Oxford, denouncing this document as " in truth nothing else but a traitorous and seditious combination against us and the established religion of this kingdom ;" straitly charging and commanding all his loving subjects, upon their allegiance, " that they presume not to take the said seditious and traitorous Covenant." * And at last an order was issued by the Parliament, in February 1644, commanding the Covenant to be taken throughout the kingdom of England by all persons above the age of eighteen years ; which order was accompanied by an exhortation prepared by the Assembly of Divines. In Scotland, as soon as information was received of what had taken place in London, the Committee of Estates ordered the Covenant to be subscribed by all ranks and conditions of people, on penalty of the confiscation of property, or such other punishment as his Majesty and the Parliament might resolve to inflict. This harsh command was intended to bear against that faction of the nobility who were known to have entered into a secret confederacy with the king; and its effect was, to drive some into flight, and all into more desperate opposition. But this, it will be observed, was the act of the civi not the ecclesiastical, authorities in Scotland ; and it proceeded mainly upon the principle, that the bond thus enforced was not only a religious covenant, but also a civil league. It was unfortunate that civil and religious matters should have been so blended, because whatever civil measures were adopted, or civil penalties were inflicted, were sure to be unfairly charged against

* Rushworth, vol. v. p. 482.

the religious element, instead of the civil, to which they truly owed their origin. But even this unpropitious circumstance was forced upon the Covenanters ; partly by the fact that the proceedings of the king were equally hostile to civil and to religious liberty, and partly by their unavoidable union with the English Parliament, in which the struggle was even more directly for civil than for religious liberty.

The importance of the Solemn League and Covenant, thus agreed upon and subscribed by the ruling constitutional authorities, civil and ecclesiastical, in both Scotland and England, renders it necessary that it should be presented to the reader in the body of the work, rather than in an appendix :—

" The Solemn League and Covenant, for reformation and defence of religion, the honour and happiness of the King, and the peace and safety of the three kingdoms of Scotland, England, and Ireland ; agreed upon by Commissioners from the Parliament and Assembly of Divines in England, with Commissioners of the Convention of Estates and General Assembly of the Church of Scotland ; approved by the General Assembly of the Church of Scotland, and by both Houses of Parliament, and the Assembly of Divines in England, and taken and subscribed by them anno 1643 ; and thereafter, by the said authority, taken and subscribed by all ranks in Scotland and England the same year ; and ratified by act of the Parliament of Scotland anno 1644. (And again renewed in Scotland, with an acknowledgment of sins and engagement to duties, by all ranks, anno 1648, and by Parliament, 1649 ; and taken and subscribed by King Charles II., at Spey, June 23, 1650 ; and at Scoon, January 1, 1651.)

" We, noblemen, barons, knights, gentlemen, citizens, burgesses, ministers of the Gospel, and commons of all sorts, in the kingdoms of Scotland, England, and Ireland, by the providence of God living under one king, and being of one reformed religion, having before our eyes the glory of God, and the advancement of the kingdom of our Lord and Saviour Jesus Christ, the honour and happiness of the king's majesty and his posterity, and the true public liberty, safety, and peace of the kingdom, wherein every one's private condition is in-

cluded : and calling to mind the treacherous and bloody plots, conspiracies, attempts, and practices of the enemies of God, against the
true religion and professors thereof in all places, especially in these
three kingdoms, ever since the reformation of religion ; and how
much their rage, power, and presumption, are of late, and at this time,
increased and exercised, whereof the deplorable state of the Church
and kingdom of Ireland, the distressed state of the Church and
kingdom of England, and the dangerous state of the Church and
kingdom of Scotland, are present and public testimonies : we have
now at last (after other means of supplication, remonstrance, protestation, and sufferings), for the preservation of ourselves and our
religion from utter ruin and destruction, according to the commend-
able practice of these kingdoms in former times, and the example
of God's people in other nations, after mature deliberation, resolved
and determined to enter into a Mutual and Solemn League and
Covenant, wherein we all subscribe, and each one of us for himself,
with our hands lifted up to the Most High God, do swear,—

" I. That we shall sincerely, really, and constantly, through the
grace of God, endeavour, in our several places and callings, the
preservation of the reformed religion in the Church of Scotland, in
doctrine, worship, discipline, and government, against our common
enemies ; the reformation of religion in the kingdoms of England
and Ireland, in doctrine, worship, discipline, and government, according to the Word of God, and the example of the best reformed
Churches ; and shall endeavour to bring the Churches of God in
the three kingdoms to the nearest conjunction and uniformity in
religion, Confession of Faith, Form of Church Government, Directory
for Worship and Catechising ; that we, and our posterity after us,
may, as brethren, live in faith and love, and the Lord may delight to
dwell in the midst of us.

" II. That we shall, in like manner, without respect of persons,
endeavour the extirpation of Popery, Prelacy (that is, Church government by archbishops, bishops, their chancellors and commissaries,
deans, deans and chapters, archdeacons, and all other ecclesiastical
officers depending on that hierarchy), superstition, heresy, schism,
profaneness, and whatsoever shall be found contrary to sound doctrine
and the power of godliness ; lest we partake in other men's sins, and
thereby be in danger to receive of their plagues ; and that the Lord
may be one, and his name one, in the three kingdoms.

" III. We shall, with the same sincerity, reality, and constancy, in our several vocations, endeavour, with our estates and lives, mutually to preserve the rights and privileges of the Parliaments, and the liberties of the kingdoms; and to preserve and defend the king's majesty's person and authority, in the preservation and defence of the true religion and liberties of the kingdoms; that the world may bear witness with our consciences of our loyalty, and that we have no thoughts or intentions to diminish his majesty's just power and greatness.

"IV. We shall also, with all faithfulness, endeavour the discovery of all such as have been or shall be incendiaries, malignants, or evil instruments, by hindering the reformation of religion, dividing the king from his people, or one of the kingdoms from another, or making any faction or parties among the people, contrary to this League and Covenant; that they may be brought to public trial, and receive condign punishment, as the degree of their offences shall require or deserve, or the supreme judicatories of both kingdoms respectively, or others having power from them for that effect, shall judge convenient.

"V. And whereas the happiness of a blessed peace between these kingdoms, denied in former times to our progenitors, is, by the good providence of GOD, granted unto us, and hath been lately concluded and settled by both Parliaments; we shall, each one of us, according to our place and interest, endeavour that they may remain conjoined in a firm peace and union to all posterity; and that justice may be done upon the wilful opposers thereof, in manner expressed in the precedent article.

"VI. We shall also, according to our places and callings, in this common cause of religion, liberty, and peace of the kingdoms, assist and defend all those that enter into this League and Covenant, in the maintaining and pursuing thereof; and shall not suffer ourselves, directly or indirectly, by whatsoever combination, persuasion, or terror, to be divided or withdrawn from this blessed union and conjunction, whether to make defection to the contrary part, or to give ourselves to a detestable indifferency or neutrality in this cause, which so much concerneth the glory of GOD, the good of the kingdom, and honour of the king; but shall, all the days of our lives, zealously and constantly continue therein against all opposition, and promote the same, according to our power, against all lets and impediments whatsoever; and what we are not able ourselves to suppress or overcome, we shall reveal and make known, that it may be timely prevented or removed: All which we shall do as in the sight of God.

"And, because these kingdoms are guilty of many sins and provocations against GOD, and his Son JESUS CHRIST, as is too manifest
by our present distresses and dangers, the fruits thereof; we profess and declare, before GOD and the world, our unfeigned desire
to be humbled for our own sins, and for the sins of these kingdoms;
especially that we have not, as we ought, valued the inestimable
benefit of the Gospel; that we have not laboured for the purity
and power thereof; and that we have not endeavoured to receive
Christ in our hearts, nor to walk worthy of him in our lives; which
are the causes of other sins and transgressions so much abounding
amongst us: and our true and unfeigned purpose, desire, and endeavour, for ourselves, and all others under our power and charge,
both in public and private, in all duties we owe to GOD and man,
to amend our lives, and each one to go before another in the example of a real reformation; that the Lord may turn away his wrath
and heavy indignation, and establish these Churches and kingdoms
in truth and peace. And this Covenant we make in the presence
of ALMIGHTY GOD, the Searcher of all hearts, with a true intention
to perform the same, as we shall answer at that great day, when
the secrets of all hearts shall be disclosed; most humbly beseeching the LORD to strengthen us by his HOLY SPIRIT for this end,
and to bless our desires and proceedings with such success, as may
be deliverance and safety to his people, and encouragement to other
Christian Churches, groaning under, or in danger of the yoke of
antichristian tyranny, to join in the same or like association and
covenant, to the glory of GOD, the enlargement of the kingdom of
JESUS CHRIST, and the peace and tranquillity of Christian kingdoms
and commonwealths."

It is difficult to conceive how any calm, unprejudiced,
thoughtful, and religious man can peruse the preceding very
solemn document, without feeling upon his mind an over-
awing sense of its sublimity and sacredness. The most
important of man's interests for time and for eternity are
included within its ample scope, and made the subjects of a
Solemn League with each other, and a sacred Covenant with
God. Religion, liberty, and peace, are the great elements of
human welfare, to the preservation of which it bound the
empire; and as those by whom it was framed knew well

that there can be no safety for these in a land where the mind of the community is dark with ignorance, warped by super- stition, misled by error, and degraded by tyranny, civil and ecclesiastical, they pledged themselves to seek the extirpation of these pernicious evils. Yet it was the evils themselves, and not the persons of those in whom those evils prevailed, that they sought to extirpate. Nor was there any inconsis- tency in declaring that they sought to promote the honour and happiness of the king, while thus uniting in a Covenant against that' double despotism which he strove to exercise. For no intelligent person will deny, that it is immeasurably more glorious for a monarch to be the king of freemen, than a tyrant over slaves; and that whatsoever promotes the true mental, moral, and religious greatness of a kingdom, promotes also its civil welfare, and elevates the true dignity of its sove- reign. This, the mind of Charles was not comprehensive enough to learn, nor wise enough to know, especially as he was misled by the prelatic faction, who, while seeking their own aggrandizement, led him to believe that they were zeal- ous only for his glory,—a glory the very essence of which was the utter annihilation of all liberty, civil and religious. And as this desperate and fatal prelatic policy was well known to the patriotic framers of the Solemn League and Covenant, they attached no direct blame to the king himself, but sought to rescue him from the evil influence of those by whose pernicious counsels he was misled. Aware, also, how often the wisest and best schemes are perverted and destroyed by the base intrigues of selfish and designing men, the Cove- nanters solemnly pledged themselves to each other and to God, not to suffer themselves to be divided or withdrawn from the constant and persevering prosecution of their great and sacred cause, till its triumph should be secured, or their own lives terminate. In this strong resolution were in- volved, a lofty singleness of purpose, deliberate determination, and not only self-denial,' but, if necessary, self-sacrifice, that

to the world a great example might be given for better times
to follow and to realise.

Such were the great principles of the Solemn League and
Covenant; and, while it is easy, very easy, to frame captious
objections against minor points and forms of expression, as is
very often done, we do not hesitate to say, that in our
opinion, no man who is able to understand its nature, and to
feel and appreciate its spirit and its aim, will deny it to be the
wisest, the sublimest, and the most sacred document ever
framed by uninspired men. But, as afterwards appeared, it
was premature; it far outwent the spirit of the time; it was
understood and valued but by few; and it was regarded by
all who could not understand it with the most intense and
bitter hatred, mingled and increased by fear. Let not, however, this admission be taken in its most unlimited sense.
If the Solemn League and Covenant was premature, that
detracts not from its real value; it only proves that it was
promulgated in ignorant and " evil times, with darkness and
with dangers compassed round." And let these questions be
asked and thoughtfully answered:—Has it perished amid
the strife of tongues? Has it sunk into oblivion, and ceased
to be a living element in the quick realms of thought? Are
there none by whom it is still regarded with sacred veneration?
Is it not true, that, at this very moment, there are many
minds of great power and energy, earnestly engaged in reviving its mighty principles, and fearlessly holding them forth
before the world's startled gaze? And if such be the case,
may it not be, that what two hundred years ago was premature, has now nearly reached the period of a full maturity,
and is on the point of raising up its sacred and majestic head,
" strong in the Lord and in the power of his might?"

Before proceeding to relate the discussions of the Westminster Assembly of Divines, thus finally constituted and
prepared for its duties, it may be expedient to give a brief

view of the parties, by the combination of which it was from the first composed, by whose jarring contentions its progress was retarded, and by whose divisions and mutual hostilities its labours were at length frustrated and prevented from obtaining their due result.

When the Parliament issued the ordinance for calling together an Assembly of Divines for consultation and advice, there was, it will be remembered, actually no legalised form of Church government in England, so far as depended on the Legislature. Even Charles himself had consented to the bill removing the prelates from the House of Lords ; and though the bill abolishing the hierarchy had not obtained the royal sanction, yet the greater part of the kingdom regarded it as conclusive on that point. The chief object of the Parliament, therefore, was to determine what form of Church government was to be established by law, in the room of that which had been abolished. And as their desire was to secure a form which should both be generally acceptable, and should also bear, at least, a close resemblance to the form most prevalent in other reformed Churches, they attempted to act impartially, and, in their ordinance, they selected some of each denomination, appointing Bishops, untitled Episcopalians, Puritans, and Independents. Several Episcopalians, and at least one Bishop, were present in the first meeting of the Assembly. But when the Solemn League and Covenant was proposed and taken, and when the king issued his condemnation of it, all the decided Episcopalians left, with the exception of Dr Featly. He remained a member of the Assembly for some time ; till, being detected corresponding with Archbishop Ussher, and revealing the proceedings of the Assembly, he was cut off from that venerable body, and committed to prison.* From that time forward there were no direct supporters of Prelacy in the Assembly, and the protracted controversial discussions which arose were on other subjects; on which ac-

* Neal, vol. ii. pp. 234, 235.

count we have nothing to do with the Episcopalian controversy, beyond what has been already stated in our preliminary pages.

There can be no doubt that the close alliance which the English Parliament sought with Scotland, and the ground taken by the Scottish Convention of Estates and General Assembly, in requiring not only an international league, but also a religious covenant, tended greatly to direct the mind of the English statesmen and divines towards the Presbyterian form of Church government, and exercised a powerful influence in the deliberations of the Westminster Assembly. But let it be also remembered, that in every one of the reformed continental Churches, either the Presbyterian form, or one very closely resembling it, had been adopted; and that the Puritans had already formed themselves into presbyteries, held presbyterial meetings, and endeavoured to exercise Presbyterian discipline, in the reception, suspension, and rejection of members. Both the example of other Churches, therefore, and their own already begun practice, had led them so far onward to the Presbyterian model, that they would almost inevitably have assumed it altogether apart from the influence of Scotland. In truth, that influence was exerted and felt almost solely in the way of instruction, from a Church already formed, to one in the process of formation; and none would have been more ready than the Scottish commissioners themselves to have repudiated the very idea of any other kind of influence. It may be said, therefore, with the most strict propriety, that the *native* aim and tendency of the Westminster Assembly was to establish the Presbyterian form of Church government in England, the great body of English Puritans having gradually become Presbyterians. There is reason to believe that both Pym and Hampden favoured the Presbyterian system; but their early and lamented death deprived that cause of their powerful support, and the House of Commons of their able and steady guidance. The chief promoters of Presbytery in the House of Commons were,

Sir William Waller, Sir Philip Stapleton, Sir John Clotworthy, Sir Benjamin Rudyard, Colonel Massey, Colonel Harley, Serjeant Maynard, Denzil Hollis, John Glynn, and a few more of less influential character.

The Independents, or Congregationalists, formed another party, few in point of number, but men of considerable talent and learning, of undoubted piety, of great pertinacity in adhering to their own opinions, and, we are constrained to say, well skilled in the artifices of intriguing policy. The origin of the Independent system has been already stated briefly in our introductory remarks, and will require little further elucidation. It was, according to the statement of its adherents, a medium between the Brownist and the Presbyterian systems. They did not, with the Brownists, condemn every other Church as too corrupt and antichristian for intercommunion,—for they professed to agree in doctrine both with the Church of England in its Articles, and with the other reformed Churches; but they held the entire power of government to belong to each separate congregation; and they practically admitted no Church censure but admonition,—for that cannot properly be called excommunication which consisted not in expelling from their body an obstinate and impenitent offender, but in withdrawing themselves from him. With regard to their boast of being the first advocates of toleration and liberty of conscience, that will come to be examined hereafter: this only need be said at present, that toleration is naturally the plea of the weaker party; that the term was then, has been since, and still is, much misunderstood and misused; and that wherever the Independents possessed power, as in New England, they showed themselves to be as intolerant as any of their opponents.

The leading Independents in the Westminster Assembly were, Dr Thomas Goodwin, Philip Nye, Jeremiah Burroughs, William Bridge, and Sidrach Simpson. These men had at first been silenced by the violent persecution of Laud and

Wren, and had then retired to Holland,—where they continued exercising their ministry among their expatriated countrymen for several years. Goodwin and Nye resided at Arnheim, where they were highly esteemed for their piety and talents. Bridge went to Rotterdam, where he became pastor of an English congregation, previously formed by the notorious Hugh Peters. Burroughs went also to Rotterdam, and became connected with the congregation then under the pastoral care of Bridge, in what was termed the different but co-ordinate office of teacher. Simpson subsequently joined himself to the two preceding brethren, having, according to their system, given an account of his faith. But though at first highly approving the order of the church under the care of Mr Bridge, he subsequently proposed some alterations which would, as he thought, promote its welfare,—particularly the revival of the prophesyings used by the old Puritans. This Mr Bridge opposed, and Mr Simpson withdrew from communion with him, and formed a church for himself.* The quarrel, however, did not so terminate. Mr Ward, another ejected Puritan, having about the same time retired to Holland, came to Rotterdam, and having joined Mr Bridge's church, was appointed his colleague in the pastoral office. He, too, wished for additional improvements; and as he did not retire, like Simpson, but continued the struggle, Bridge thought it necessary to depose him from the ministry,—which his superior influence in the congregation enabled him to accomplish. To prevent the evil consequences which might have resulted from these unhappy divisions, Goodwin and Nye came from Arnheim, instituted an investigation of the whole matter, and induced the two contending brethren and their adherents to acknowledge their mutual faults, and to be reconciled.† The reconciliation, however, appears to have

---

* Brook's Lives of the Puritans, vol. iii. p. 312.

† Brook, vol. ii. p. 454; Edward's Antapologia, pp. 115–117; Baillie's Dissuasive, pp. 75–77.

been but superficial, and to have required the interposition of the magistracy ere it could be even plausibly effected. Such divisions might have caused these divines to entertain some suspicion that the model of Church government which they had adopted was not altogether so perfect as they wished it to be thought; but so far as their subsequent conduct, as members of the Westminster Assembly, is concerned, this does not seem to have been the case in even the slightest degree. When the contest between the King and the Parliament had become so extreme that the Parliament declared its own continuation as permanent as it might itself think necessary, and began to threaten the abolition of the whole prelatic hierarchy, the above-named five Independent divines returned to England, prepared to assist in the long-sought reformation of religion, and to avail themselves of every opportunity which might occur to promote their favourite system. And admitting them to be conscientiously convinced of its superior excellency, they deserve no censure for desiring to see it universally received. In every such case, all that can be wished is, that each party should prosecute its purpose honourably and openly, in the fair field of frank and manly argument, with Christian candour and integrity; and not by factious opposition, or with the dark and insidious craft too characteristic of worldly politicians.

Of these five leading Independents, often termed " The Five Dissenting Brethren," Goodwin appears to have been the deepest theologian, and perhaps altogether the ablest man; Nye, the most acute and subtle, and the best skilled in holding intercourse with worldly politicians; Burroughs, the most gentle and pacific in temper and character; Bridge is said to have been a man of considerable attainments, and a very laborious student; and Simpson bears also a respectable character as a preacher, though not peculiarly distinguished in public debate. To these Baillie adds, as Independents, Joseph Caryl, William Carter (of London), John Philips,

and Peter Sterry,—naming nine, but saying that there were
" some ten or eleven." * Neal adds Anthony Burgess and
William Greenhill.† Some of the views of the Independents
were occasionally supported by Herle, Marshall, and Vines,
and some few others; but none of these men are to be included in the number of the decided Independents.

The third party in the Assembly were the Erastians; so
called from Erastus, a physician at Heidelberg, who wrote
on the subject of Church government, especially in respect of
excommunication, in the year 1568. His theory was,—
That the pastoral office is only persuasive, like that of a professor over his students, without any direct power; that
baptism, the Lord's supper, and all other gospel ordinances,
were free and open to all; and that the minister might state
and explain what were the proper qualifications, and might
dissuade the vicious and unqualified from the communion,
but had no power to refuse it, or to inflict any kind of censure.
The punishment of all offences, whether of a civil or a religious nature, belonged, according to this theory, exclusively
to the civil magistrate. The tendency of this theory was,
to destroy entirely all ecclesiastical and spiritual jurisdiction,
to deprive the Church of all power of government, and to
make it completely the mere "creature of the State." The
pretended advantage of this theory was, that it prevented the
existence of an *imperium in imperio*, or one government
within another, of a distinct and independent nature. But
the real disadvantage, in the most mitigated view that can be
taken, was, that it reproduced what may be termed a civil
Popedom, by combining civil and ecclesiastical jurisdiction,
and giving both into the possession of one irresponsible power,
—thereby destroying both civil and religious liberty, and
subjecting men to an absolute and irremediable despotism.
In another point of view, the Erastian theory assumes a still
darker and more formidable aspect. It necessarily denies

* Baillie, vol. ii. p. 110.   † Neal, vol. ii. pp. 275, 360.

the mediatorial sovereignty of the Lord Jesus Christ over his Church,—takes the power of the keys from his office-bearers and gives them to the civil magistrate,—destroys liberty of conscience, by making spiritual matters subject to the same coercive power as temporal affairs naturally and properly are ; and thus involves both State and Church in reciprocal and mutually destructive sin,—the State, in usurping a power which God has not given ; and the Church, in yielding what she is not at liberty to yield—the sacred crown-rights of the divine Redeemer, her only Head and King.

But as the Erastian controversy will come fully before us in the debates of the Assembly, it is unnecessary to enter upon it here. There were only two divines in the Assembly who advocated the Erastian theory ; and of these, one alone was decidedly and thoroughly Erastian. The divine to whom this unenviable pre-eminence must be assigned, was Thomas Coleman, minister at Bliton in Lincolnshire. He was aided generally, but not always, by Lightfoot, in the various discussions that arose involving Erastian opinions. Both of these divines were eminently distinguished by their attainments in Oriental literature, particularly in rabbinical lore; and their attachment to the study of Hebrew literature and customs led them to the conclusion, that the Christian Church was to be in every respect constituted according to the model of the Jewish Church : and having formed the opinion that there was but one jurisdiction in Israel, combining both civil and ecclesiastical, and that this was held by the Hebrew monarchs, they concluded that the same blended government ought to prevail under the Christian dispensation. Of the lay assessors in the Assembly the chief Erastians were, the learned Selden, Mr Whitelocke, and Mr St John ; but though Selden was the only one of them whose arguments were influential in the Assembly itself, yet nearly all the Parliament held sentiments decidedly Erastian, and having seized the power of Church government, were not disposed to yield it up, be the opinion of the assembled divines what it might. Hence, though the Erastian divines were only two, yet their opinions, supported by the whole civil authority in the kingdom, were almost sure to triumph in the end. This, in one point of view, was not strange. The kingdom had suffered so much severe and protracted injury from the usurped authority and power of the prelates, that the assertors of civil liberty almost instinctively shrunk from even the shadow of any kind of power in the hands of ecclesiastics. A little less passion and fear, and a little more judgment and discrimination, might have rescued them from this groundless apprehension ; and they might have perceived that freedom, both civil and ecclesiastical, would be best secured by the full and authoritative recognition of their respective jurisdictions, separate and independent. But indeed this is a truth which has yet to be learned by civil governments,—a truth unknown to ancient times, in which religion was either an engine of the State or the object of persecution,—a truth unknown during the period of papal ascendency, in which the Romish priesthood usurped dominion over civil governments, and exercised its tyranny alike over the persons and the conscience of mankind,—a truth first brought to light in the great religious reformation of the sixteenth century,—but not then, nor even yet, fully developed, rightly understood, and permitted to exercise its free and sacred supremacy. That it will finally assume its due dominion over the minds and actions of all bodies of men, both civil and ecclesiastical, we cannot doubt ; and then, but not till then, will the two dread counterpart elements of human degradation, tyranny and slavery, become alike impossible.

Into these three great parties, Presbyterian, Independent, and Erastian, was the Westminster Assembly of Divines divided, even when first it met ; and it was inevitable that a contest would be waged among them for the ascendency, ending most probably either in increased hostility and abso-

lute disruption, or in some mutual compromise, to which all
might assent, though perhaps with the cordial approbation of
none. The strength of these parties was more evenly balanced at first than might have been expected. The Puritans,
though all of them had received episcopal ordination, and
had been exercising their ministry in the Church of England,
under the hierarchy, were nearly all Presbyterians, or at least
quite willing to adopt that form of church government,
though many of them would have consented to a modified
Episcopacy on the Usserian model. Their influence in the
city of London was paramount, and throughout the country
was very considerable; and as they formed the most natural
connecting link with Scotland, they occupied a position of
very great importance. Although the Independents were
but a small minority in the Assembly, yet various circumstances combined to render them by no means a weak or insignificant party. They were supported in the House of
Peers by Lord Say and Sele, and frequently also by Lords
Brooke and Kimbolton,—the latter of whom is better known
by his subsequent title of Lord Manchester. Philip Nye, one
of the leading Independents, had been appointed to Kimbolton
by the influence of Lord Kimbolton, and continued to maintain a constant intercourse with him, both while he was acting as a legislator, and when leading the armies of the Parliament. It is even asserted by Palmer, in his " Nonconformist's Memorial," that Nye's advice was sought and followed in the nomination of the divines who were called to
the Assembly.* And when, further, it is borne in mind
that Oliver Cromwell was an Independent, and acted as
lieutenant-general under Lord Manchester, it will easily be
perceived that Nye's intercourse with the army was direct
and influential, and that thus the Five Dissenting Brethren
were able to employ a mighty political influence. Nor can
the Erastian party be justly termed feeble, though formed by

* Palmer's Nonconformist's Memorial, vol. i. p. 96.

K

not more than two divines, and a few of the lay assessors,
who were not always present; for both Coleman and Lightfoot were influential men, on account of their reputation for
learning, in which they were scarcely inferior to Selden himself, in the department of Hebrew literature. So high was
Selden's fame, that any cause might be deemed strong which
he supported; and Whitelocke and St John possessed so
much political influence in Parliament that they could not
fail to exercise great power in every matter which they promoted or opposed. But the main strength of the Erastian
theory consisted in the combination of three potent elements;
—the natural love of holding and exercising power, which is
common to all men and parties, tending to render the Parliament reluctant to relinquish that ecclesiastical supremacy
which they had with such difficulty wrested from the sovereign; their want of acquaintance with the true nature of
Presbyterian Church government, which led them to dread
that if allowed free scope it might prove as oppressive as
even the Prelatical, beneath whose weighty and galling yoke
the nation was still down-bent and bleeding; and the strong
instinctive antipathy which fallen human nature feels against
the spirituality and the power of vital godliness. It is easy
to perceive, that the theory which was supported by these
three elements in thorough and vigorous union, was one
which it would be no easy matter to encounter and defeat; or
rather, was one over which nothing but divine power could
possibly gain the victory.

The Scottish commissioners cannot with propriety be regarded as forming a party in the Westminster Assembly, as
they and the English Presbyterians were in all important
matters completely identified. Still it may be expedient to
give a very brief account of men who occupied a position so
important, and exercised for a time so great an influence on
the affairs of both kingdoms. Their names have been already
mentioned; and it has also been stated, that neither the Earl

of Cassilis nor the Rev. Robert Douglas ever attended the Westminster Assembly. Lord Maitland and Archibald Johnston of Warriston gave regular attendance, and took deep interest in the proceedings. At that time Lord Maitland appeared to be very zealous in the cause of religious reformation, and a thorough Presbyterian ; but, as afterwards appeared, his zeal was more of a political than of a religious character. After the restoration of Charles II., he conformed to Prelacy, became the chief adviser of that monarch in Scottish affairs, received the title of Duke of Lauderdale, and is too well known in Scottish history as a ruthless and bloody persecutor. Johnston of Warriston was in heart and soul a Covenanter on religious, not political principles; from which he never swerved. One only stain appears in his life, if stain it can be called,—his consenting to receive office under the government of Cromwell, after that remarkable man had reduced the three kingdoms to his sway, and when there was every reason to expect that his dominion would be lasting. Such being the case, Warriston had but to choose to serve his country under Cromwell, or not to serve it at all. He chose the former alternative ; and after the Restoration, was constrained to flee from Scotland to escape the mean vindictive hostility of the king. Having been at length seized by his pursuers, he was dragged back to his native country, that his enemies might satiate their malice by murdering the inch of life that existed in his aged and feeble form. He was a man of great strength and clearness of intellect, fervidly eloquent in speech, and of inflexible integrity.

The four Scottish divines were in every respect distinguished men, and would have been so regarded in any age or country. Alexander Henderson was, however, cheerfully admitted to be beyond comparison the most eminent. His learning was extensive rather than minute, corresponding to the character of his mind, of which the distinguishing elements were dignity and comprehensiveness. When called to quit the calm seclusion of the country parish where he had spent so many years, and to come to the rescue of the Church of Scotland in her hour of need, he at once proved himself able to conduct and control the complicated movements of an awakening empire. Statesmen sought his counsel ; but with equal propriety and disinterestedness he refused to concern himself with anything beyond what belonged to the Church, —although the very reverse has often been asserted by his prelatic calumniators. Though long and incessantly engaged in the most stirring events of a remarkably momentous period, his actions, his writings, his speeches, are all characterised by calmness and ease, without the slightest appearance of heat or agitation ;—resulting unquestionably from that aspect of character generally termed *greatness of mind ;* but which would in him be more properly characterised by describing it as a rare combination of intellectual power, moral dignity, and spiritual elevation. It was the condition of a mighty mind, enjoying the peace of God which passeth understanding,—a peace which the world had not given, and could not take away.

George Gillespie was one of that peculiar class of men who start like meteors into sudden splendour, shine with dazzling brilliancy, then suddenly set behind the tomb, leaving their compeers equally to admire and to deplore. When but in his twenty-fifth year, he published a book against what he termed the " English Popish Ceremonies," which Charles and Laud were attempting to force upon the Church of Scotland. This work, though the production of a youth, displayed an amount and accuracy of learning which would have done honour to any man of the most mature years and scholarship. In the Assembly of Divines, though much the youngest member there, he proved himself one of the most able and ready debaters, encountering, not only on equal terms, but often with triumphant success, each with his own weapons, the most learned, subtile, and profound of his antagonists. He must have been no common man who was ready on any emergency to meet, and frequently to foil, by their own acknowledgment, such men as Selden, Lightfoot, and Coleman, in the Erastian controversy; and Goodwin and Nye in their argument for Independency. But the excessive activity of his ardent and energetic mind wore out his frame; and he returned from his labours in the Westminster Assembly, to see once more the church and the land of his fathers, and to die.

Samuel Rutherford gained, and still holds, an extensive reputation by his religious works; but he was not less eminent in his own day as an acute and able controversialist. The characteristics of his mind were, clearness of intellect, warmth and earnestness of affection, and loftiness and spirituality of devotional feeling. He could and did write vigorously against the Independent system, and at the same time, love and esteem the men who held it. In his celebrated work, "Lex Rex," he not only entered the regions of constitutional jurists, but even produced a treatise unrivalled yet as an exposition of the true principles of civil and religious liberty. His "Religious Letters" have been long admired by all who could understand and feel what true religion is; though grovelling and impure minds have striven to blight their reputation by dwelling on occasional forms of expression, not necessarily unseemly in the homeliness of phrase used in familiar letters, and conveying nothing offensive according to the language of the times. His powers of debate were very considerable, being characterised by clearness of distinction in stating his opinions, and a close syllogistic style of reasoning; both the result of his remarkable precision of thought.

Robert Baillie, so well known by his "Letters and Journals," was a man of extensive and varied learning, both in languages and systematic theology. He rarely mingled in debate; but his sagacity was valuable in deliberation, and his great acquirements, studious habits, and ready use of his pen, rendered him an important member of such an Assembly.

The singular ease and readiness of Baillie in composition, enabled him to maintain what seems like a universal correspondence; and at the same time to present in a vivid, picturesque, and exquisitely natural style, the very form and impress of the period in which he lived, and the great events in which he bore a part. And when it was necessary to refute errors by exhibiting them in their real aspect, the vast reading and retentive memory of Baillie enabled him to produce what was needed with marvellous rapidity and correctness. Scarcely ever was any man more qualified to " catch the manners living as they rise," and at the same time to point out with instinctive sagacity what in them was wrong and dangerous.

Such were the Scottish commissioners; and it may easily be believed that they acted a very important and influential part in the Westminster Assembly of Divines.

But there was another party in England, though not represented in the Westminster Assembly, which exercised a commanding influence in the affairs of that momentous period. Perhaps it is not strictly correct to call that a party which was rather a vast mass of heterogeneous elements, without any principle of mutual coherence, except that of united resistance and hostility to every thing that possessed a previous and authorised existence. But the effect on the country was even more powerful for evil than it could have been had the numerous sects to whom we are referring been organised into a party; for in that case their strength could have been estimated, their demands brought forward in a definite form, what was right and reasonable granted, and what was manifestly wrong and unreasonable detected and exposed. Even before the meeting of the Long Parliament, there had sprung up a great number of sects, holding all various shades of opinion in religious matters, from such as were simply absurd, down to those that were licentiously wild and daringly blasphemous. It is almost impossible even to enumerate the

Sectarians that rushed prominently into public manifestation when the overthrow of the prelatic hierarchy and government rendered it safe for them to appear ; and it would be wrong to pollute our pages with a statement of their pernicious and horrible tenets.* These may be seen at large in Baillie's " Dissuasive from the Errors of the Times," " Edwards's Gangræna," " A Testimony to the Truth of Jesus Christ," by the London Ministers, and other similar works by Prynne, Bastwick, and others.

The question may be fairly and properly asked, How it happened that so many strange and dangerous sects appeared at that peculiar juncture ? Prelatic writers have been in the habit of asserting that it was in consequence of the overthrow of the Prelatic Church government, when people were left to follow the vagaries of their own unguided imagination, by which they were led into all the errors of enthusiastic frenzy and fanatical darkness. But this solution does not touch the essence of the inquiry, How came men to be so prone to follow these insane and dangerous errors ? In answer to this question there are at least two points to be carefully considered,—how had Prelacy *governed*, and how had Prelacy *taught*, the people of England ? It has been already shown, that from the very commencement of the Reformation in England, the principle of the king's supremacy in matters ecclesiastical—a principle essentially despotic, by its combination of civil and spiritual jurisdiction—had been the governing principle in the English Church. At first it showed its tyrannical tendency, by imposing ceremonies not warranted by the Word of God, and associated with Popery ; and by

---

* "John Lillburn related it unto me, and that in the presence of others, that returning from the wars to London, he met *forty* new sects, many of them dangerous ones, and some so pernicious, that howsoever, as he said, he was in his judgment for toleration of all religions, yet he professed he could scarce keep his hands off them, so blasphemous they were in their opinions."—*Bastwick's Second Part of Independency*, postscript, p. 37. Lillburn was himself a Leveller.

enforcing these without the slightest regard to tenderness of feeling, or liberty of conscience. Advancing on its despotic career, it interfered with the forms and the language of worship, prescribing to man after what manner, and in what terms, he was to address his Creator, without regard to that Creator's own commands. At length it reached its extreme limits, and presumed to exercise absolute control over the doctrines which Christ's ambassadors were to teach; thus rashly interfering not merely with man's approach to God, but also with God's message to man. This extreme point of spiritual despotism was reached, when the king and his prelates authoritatively commanded the Lord's-day to be violated, and forbade any other but the Arminian system of doctrine to be preached. Hence it appears that Prelatic Church government had proved itself to be a complete and oppressive despotism, increasing in severity as it increased in power. And let it be observed, that during its progress it had silenced or ejected great numbers of the ablest and best ministers throughout the kingdom, without scruple and without mercy. Such a course of tyranny could not fail to produce a strong reaction in a high-minded people like the English, causing them, in the violence of the revulsion and recoil, to regard every form of ecclesiastical government as inevitably tyrannical; just as the extreme of civil despotism tends to throw a nation at one bound into the extreme of republicanism. In this manner Prelatic tyranny was the very cause why so many sects sprung up, repudiating every kind of ecclesiastical government.

Again, with regard to how Prelacy had *taught* the people of England, there needs but little to be said; for it is a melancholy truth, that *teaching the people* seems never to have been regarded by the Church of England as necessarily any part of its duty. In a Church where a despotic monarch exercises the supremacy, this is not surprising; for it requires no great degree of penetration to perceive that an intelligent and truly religious people cannot be enslaved. This Elizabeth well knew, and therefore she disapproved of preaching ministers. For the same reason, what were termed "prophesyings," or meetings for mutual instruction, and also lecturings, were prohibited. And perhaps it would not be far from the truth were we to conjecture, that the reason why parochial schools were never instituted in England, is to be found in the same despotic principle which led the English kings and Church to wish the people to remain ignorant, that they might be the easier kept in a state of blind subjection. It will be remembered also, that whenever the Puritan ministers became what was thought troublesome, in their endeavours to teach their poor and ignorant countrymen, they were immediately silenced ; and, as toleration was then unknown, they were compelled to desist from their hallowed labours, on pain of imprisonment, exile, or death. Taking this view, which is the true one, it is mere mockery to say that Prelacy had ever even attempted to *teach* the people of England at all,—unless, indeed, we were to say that it had striven earnestly to teach them, that external rites and ceremonies of man's institution are more important than the Word of God, and that it was right to profane that day which God has commanded to be remembered and kept holy.

Such had been the *governing*, and such the *teaching* of Prelacy in England ; and it was not strange that men, groaning under oppression, and kept in utter darkness, should wrench asunder their fetters furiously, and should be dazzled when they rushed at once into unwonted light. It was not strange that they should hastily conclude that whatever was remotest from such a system was best ; and should therefore be eager to destroy that form of ecclesiastical government, and to resist the establishment of any other, lest it should prove equally despotic. Nor was it strange, that people strongly excited on the subject of religion, and uninstructed in its great leading truths and principles, should very readily adopt any and every theory which was boldly and plausibly promulgated. Thus it was easy for any man who possessed sufficient fluency of speech to impose upon an excited and ignorant people, to gain a number of adherents to his opinions, and to become the founder and leader of a sect. It has often been said by those who support Prelacy, not as of divine authority, but as a useful and suitable form of Church government, that it was devised for the purpose of producing and preserving uniformity in the Church. Unfortunate device! It never could have had a more full and authoritative sway than that which it enjoyed during the reigns of Elizabeth, James, and Charles I. ; and it produced the most complete anarchy, and gave rise to Sectarianism to the greatest extent, and in the most repulsive forms, that ever shocked the Christian world. It at once kept men in ignorance, and drove them to madness; and ever since it has appealed to their frantic conduct as a proof of its own calm excellence.

The truth of this view may be shown by a parallel, but a strongly contrasted instance. After the restoration of Charles II., the Presbyterian Church of Scotland was violently overthrown, and its adherents subjected to twenty-eight years of terrific and relentless persecution. Did the people of Scotland split into innumerable and extravagant sects, when thus deprived of their religious teachers, and oppressed with the most remorseless cruelty? They did not. One sect alone appeared, after the persecution had lasted twenty years, and in a parish where there had been a Prelatic incumbent all that time; it never mustered more than four men, and twenty-five or twenty-six women, and it perished within a few months. What caused this remarkable difference? One answer only can be given—The superiority of the Presbyterian system, which had so thoroughly instructed the people, that they could and did retain their calm and regulated consistency of doctrine and character in the midst of every maddening and delusive element; while, on the other hand, when the Prelatic government of England was broken up, its oppressed and ignorant people rushed headlong into the most wild, extravagant, and pernicious errors. This we believe to be the true explanation of the matter, though we are well aware that it will not be readily admitted by the admirers of Prelacy. But the truth must be stated, be offended who may ; and it will be well for Britain, and for Christendom, if, should a period of similar breaking up and reconstruction arrive, men will learn by the sad experience of the past, and never more presume, either to supersede God's institutions with man's inventions, or, in their violent recoil, refuse to submit themselves to what God has appointed, and has so often and so manifestly honoured and sanctioned with His blessing.

The pernicious effect of these multitudinous sects upon the proceedings of the Westminster Assembly, we shall have occasion hereafter to show. It will be enough here to suggest what will then be proved. Although the Independent party in the Assembly did not openly avow, or rather disclaimed, connection with the Sectarians that swarmed throughout the kingdom, yet they so far held intercourse with them, and occasionally defended them, as to secure their support, and thereby to render themselves in some measure the representatives of a large portion of the English community. For this purpose they strove to retard the progress of the Assembly, while they were mustering their adherents and concentrating their strength,—evidently expecting that they would eventually secure the establishment of their own system. In the Assembly and Parliament both, they had the aid of Sir Harry Vane the younger, one of the most subtle politicians of the age,—a man whose mind was full of theoretic and impracticable speculations, and whose restless activity of temperament kept him perpetually scheming or executing something new, —whose very constitution of mind was sectarian, because it was constructed in sections, without continuity or harmony. And in the Parliament and army they had the far more important support of Oliver Cromwell, with whom they held constant intercourse, and by whom there is every reason to believe they were employed and overreached. It is not meant, that the Independent members of Assembly were completely identified with the political Independents of the army; but there was so much of a community of feeling and interest between them, that it was not difficult for such a man as Cromwell to employ both of these parties in the promotion of his own designs.

What we have termed the political Independents of the army, were composed of sectarians of every possible shade of opinion; and from them, rather than from the religious Independents in the Assembly, arose the idea of *toleration*, of which so much use was subsequently made. As used by those military sectarians, the meaning of the term was, that any man might freely utter the ravings of his own heated fancy, and endeavour to proselytise others, be his opinions what they might,—even though manifestly subversive of all morality, all government, and all revelation. Such a toleration, for instance, as would include alike Antinomians and Anabaptists, though teaching that they were set free from and above the rules of moral duty so completely, that to indulge in the grossest licentiousness was in them no sin; and Levellers and Fifth-Monarchy Men, whose tenets went directly to the subversion of every kind of constituted government, and all distinctions in rank and property. This was what *they* meant by *toleration*,—and this was what the Puritans and Presbyterians condemned and wrote against with startled vehemence. And it is neither to the credit of the Independent divines of that period, nor of their subsequent admirers and followers, that they seem to countenance such a toleration, the real meaning of which was, civil, moral, and religious anarchy. It is, however, true, that out of the discussions which this claim of unbounded and licentious toleration raised, there was at length evolved the idea of religious toleration, such as is demanded by man's solemn and dread characteristic of personal responsibility, and consequent inalienable right to liberty of conscience. And let it be noted, that this great idea was fully admitted by those who reasoned and wrote most strongly against the "unbounded toleration" claimed by the Sectarians; although, in their opposition to that claim, they occasionally used language which might seem to condemn what in reality they both demanded for themselves and readily allowed to others.* It is usual for a certain class of writers to accuse the Presbyterians of wishing to seize and wield a tyranny as severe as that of Prelacy, against which they raised such loud complaints. Without undertaking to defend all that they said and did, this may be safely affirmed, that both the principles and the constitution of a rightly formed Presbyterian Church render the usurpation of power and the exercise of tyranny on its part wholly impossible. A Presbyterian Church in the process of formation, still trembling from the savage grasp of Prelacy, and surrounded by wild and fearful forms of sectarianism, as was its condition at the time of the Westminster Assembly, might act with some rashness and severity; a corrupt Presbyterian Church, such as was that of Scotland during the domination of Moderatism, might act despotically; but in its own nature, with its subordination of courts, and an equal or preponderating admixture of elders in them all, it can neither usurp clerical domination nor sink into jarring anarchy. In its purest state and its fullest exercise, it gives and preserves both civil and religious liberty,—both doctrinal truth and disciplinary purity,—both national instruction and national

* We shall have occasion, in a subsequent part of this work, to prove that the true idea of toleration, in its right moral and religious sense, was first taught and first exemplified by the Presbyterian Church of Scotland, next by the Puritans, and then adopted, but corrupted, by the Sectarians and Independents.

peace. On the other hand, Prelacy, in its most powerful and active state, has ever tended to destroy both civil and religious liberty; has checked doctrinal truth, and disregarded disciplinary purity; has never attempted to instruct the nation, but left it a prey to ignorance and error; and has, both in Scotland and England, inflicted the most cruel persecution, and given rise to bloody civil wars. This is a startling contrast, but not more startling than true. There is yet another point of contrast. During the past century Prelacy sunk into dormancy, and became mild and inoffensive: Presbytery sunk into dormancy, and became cruel and oppressive, as if agitated by wild dreams under that fierce incubus, Moderatism. Prelacy has awoke, and begins to mutter words of fearful import, indicating the return of its oppressive spirit: Presbytery has awoke, and has begun her hallowed work of instructing her own people, while she offers her cordial fellowship to all who love her Divine and only Head. The inference is obvious, and may be thus stated: When the vital spirit of Prelacy is inert, it becomes comparatively harmless: when the vital spirit of Presbytery is inert, or repressed, it becomes oppressive. Again, when the vital spirit of Prelacy is active, it becomes despotic and persecuting, intolerant and illiberal: when the vital spirit of Presbytery is active, it becomes gracious and compassionate, tolerant of every thing but sin, and generous to all who believe the truth and love the Saviour. Let the thoughtful reader say, which system is of human, and which of divine institution,—which shows a spirit of the earth, earthly, and which, of heavenly origin and character.

CHAPTER III.

THE INDEPENDENT CONTROVERSY, ANNO 1644.

The Assembly directed to begin the Subjects of Discipline, Directory of Worship, and Government—The Subject of Church-officers stated and Discussed—Pastor—Doctor—Ruling Elder—Deacon—Widow—Ordination of Ministers—Opposition of the Independents—Consent of the Congregation, or Election—Contest with the Parliament about Ordination—Directory for Public Worship—Propositions concerning Presbyterial Church Government—The Apologetical Narration by the Independents—Answers to it—The Antapologia—Views of the Independents—Keen and Protracted Debates—Excommunication—Selden and Gillespie—Nye—Attempt to Accommodate—The Power of Congregations—Suspension and Excommunication—Committee of Accommodation—Proceedings of that Committee—Suspended—Reasons of Dissent by the Independents—Answers by the Assembly—General Outline of these Reasons and Answers—The Independents Requested and Enjoined to State their own Model of Church Government—The Publication of a Copy of a Remonstrance—Assembly's Answer to it—The Committee of Accommodation Revived—Additional Papers Prepared—Ends without Effecting an Accommodation—Brief Summary of the Points of Disagreement between the Presbyterians and Independents—Political Intrigues—Errors of both Parties.

ABOUT a fortnight after the House of Commons had taken the Solemn League and Covenant, and while the Assembly of Divines were engaged in discussing the doctrinal tenets of the sixteenth of the Church of England's Thirty-nine Articles, on the 12th of October 1643, they received an order from both Houses of Parliament, requiring them to direct their deliberations to the important topics of discipline, and a directory of worship and government. The order was as follows:—

" Upon serious consideration of the present state and conjuncture of the affairs of this kingdom, the Lords and Commons assembled in Parliament do order, that the Assembly of Divines and others do forthwith confer and treat among themselves, of such a discipline and government as may be most agreeable to God's Holy Word, and most apt to procure and preserve the peace of the Church at home, and nearer agreement with the Church of Scotland, and other Reformed Churches abroad, to be settled in this Church in stead and place of the present Church government by archbishops, bishops, their chancellors, commissaries, deans, deans and chapters, archdeacons, and other ecclesiastical officers, depending upon the hierarchy, which is resolved to be taken away; and touching and concerning the Directory of Worship, or Liturgy, hereafter to be in the Church: and to deliver their opinions and advices of and touching the same to both or either House of Parliament with all the convenient speed they can."

By this order the attention of the Assembly was turned from any further examination of the Thirty-nine Articles, and fairly directed to the important task for the accomplishment of which they had been called together. Baillie informs us that Henderson did not entertain any sanguine expectations of their conformity to the Church of Scotland, till they should have experienced the advantage of the Scottish army's presence in England.* This proves that he was not overreached by the English commissioners in the framing of the Solemn League and Covenant, but was quite aware of the views and feelings which they entertained, although he cherished the hope that circumstances might lead to a better result.

After having made some preliminary arrangements, and prepared their own minds by keeping a solemn fast, the Assembly read the order from Parliament, pointing out the new field of deliberative discussion on which they were to enter. The first question that arose regarded the order of procedure, whether they should begin with government or discipline,

* Baillie, vol. ii. p. 104.

and it was agreed that they should begin with the subject of
Church government. This suggested another preliminary
point,—whether the Scriptures contain a rule for government.
Goodwin and the other Independents eagerly urged that this
question should be first of all debated and decided, he expressing his conviction that the Word of God did contain a rule.
Lightfoot opposed this course, and wished the Assembly first
of all to give a definition of the leading term of all their discussions, "*a Church.*" It is evident that this would have
been the most logical course, first to define a Church, then to
inquire into its government, and lastly to treat of discipline,
which is government in operation. But it was felt that this
course would bring forward first the very points on which the
greatest differences of opinion were known to exist; and
therefore it was judged prudent rather to adopt a less perfect
order of procedure, for the purpose of ascertaining first how
far all could agree, in the hope that then their differences
would either disappear, or be capable of being brought into
some general accommodation. It was accordingly resolved,
that since all admitted the existence of a Church, and of
Church government, however they might differ regarding
their nature and extent, these subjects should be left for the
present indefinite, and they should commence with the subject of office-bearers in the Church, or, to use their own term,
Church-officers.*

From this early, and comparatively slight discussion, it was
evident that both parties in the Assembly were keenly vigilant lest any thing should be done which might in any degree
prejudge their opinions; and consequently, that their debates would be eager, animated, and protracted, on every
controverted topic. But as the very object for which the
Assembly was called was to prepare a form of Church government, of discipline, and of worship for the nation, which was
intended to be final and lasting, it was judged right to give

* Lightfoot, p. 20.

L

to every portion of their great work the benefit of the most full and deliberate discussion, though at the expense of considerable delay.

Committees, according to the usual arrangement, had been appointed to prepare the subject of Church-officers for public discussion, and gave in their separate reports. That of the second committee began thus :—" In inquiring after the officers belonging to the Church of the New Testament, we first find that Christ, who is Priest, Prophet, King, and Head of the Church, hath fulness of power, and containeth all other offices, by way of eminency, in himself; and therefore hath many of their names attributed to him." To this sacred and comprehensive proposition they appended a number of Scripture proofs, in six divisions. The following names of Church-officers were mentioned as given in Scripture to Christ :—1. Apostle ; 2. Pastor ; 3. Bishop ; 4. Teacher ; 5. Minister, or Διάκονος ; but this last name was rejected by the Assembly, as not meaning a Church-officer in the passage where it is used. The report of the third committee was similar in character, ascribing, in Scripture terms, the government to Jesus Christ, who, being ascended far above all heavens, " hath given all officers necessary for the edification of his Church ; some whereof are extraordinary, some ordinary." Out of the scriptures referred to they found the following officers :—Apostles, Evangelists, Prophets, Pastors, Teachers, Bishops or Overseers, Presbyters or Elders, Deacons, and Widows.*

In the discussion which followed upon the reading of these reports, it is rather remarkable that the Erastians took no part ; although the full meaning of the main proposition,— that Christ contains all offices, by way of eminency, in himself, and has given all officers necessary for the edification of his Church,—seems to contain enough to preclude the Erastian theory. But we shall have occasion to show the

* Lightfoot, p. 23.

reason why they allowed this proposition to pass unchallenged. It did not, however, escape the opposition of the Independents. Mr Goodwin opposed it, as anticipating the Assembly's work, and concluding that Christ's influence into his Church is through his officers, whereas he questions whether it be conveyed that way or not. Again, when the kingly office of Christ was under discussion, Goodwin doubted whether the Scriptures prove that Christ is King, in regard of discipline in the Church. He questioned also whether the Headship of Christ should be specified, as being no office *in* the Church. All these objections were overruled, and the reports approved, as the basis of subsequent deliberations.

The four following questions were also reported by the third committee :—" 1. What officers are mentioned in the New Testament ? 2. What officers of these were *pro tempore*, and what permanent? 3. What names were common to divers officers, and what restrained ? 4. What the office of those standing officers ?" The general names of officers having been already stated, the debate arose on the second question,—" What officers were perpetual ?" The office of apostles was declared to be only *pro tempore*, and extraordinary, for the eight following reasons:—1'. They were immediately called by Christ ; 2. They had seen Christ; 3. Their commission was through the whole world ; 4. They were endued with the spirit of infallibility in delivering the truths of doctrine to the churches; 5. They only by special commission were set apart to be personal witnesses of Christ's resurrection ; 6. They had power to give the Holy Ghost ; 7. They were appointed to go through the world to settle churches, in a new form appointed by Christ; 8. They had the inspection and care of all the churches. Little opposition was made to these reasons, and that little was chiefly made by Mr Goodwin,—particularly respecting the power of the apostles to plant and settle churches ; he being afraid, apparently, that if he admitted this power, even in apostles, it might so far condemn the practice of the Independents, where ordinary believers formed themselves into churches, and appointed their own officers totally without the intervention or aid of any other church, or of any person previously ordained. Not a single voice was raised in behalf of the theory first started by Bancroft, and carried to its height by Laud,—that prelates are the successors of the apostles, and possess their office and its authority, in virtue of unbroken personal apostolic succession,—this extravagant absurdity being abandoned by all.

Another point respecting the apostleship was introduced, which led to considerable discussion, not on its own account, but because of its ultimate consequence :—That the apostles had the keys (that is, the power of government, doctrine, and discipline) immediately given to them. The importance of this point consisted in its bearing upon the Independent theory; as also, though not so directly, upon Erastianism. Lightfoot granted that the keys were universally held to mean the government of the Church; but that in his own opinion the keys were given to Peter only, to open the door of admission to the Gentiles; and that he regarded the power of the keys as merely the authority to declare doctrinal truths. In this view, as we shall have occasion to show, lay the germ of Lightfoot's Erastianism. The Independent brethren resisted the idea that the power of the keys was committed to the apostles in any sense implying official authority; it being one of their principles, that the Church, in their sense of that term, namely, ordinary believers, possessed all power and authority. Goodwin, Simpson, Burroughs, and Bridge, all engaged in this debate on the negative side; but the Assembly affirmed the proposition.

The next discussion arose respecting the office of pastor, which the report stated to be perpetual, and to consist in feeding the flock, and in the dispensation of sacraments. In the term "*feeding*" was included, to preach and teach, to convince, to reprove, to exhort, and to comfort. Mr Coleman questioned whether a pastor, in the Old Testament, meant the ecclesiastical officer in the Church, and not constantly the civil. This was supported by Lightfoot; and here also appeared the germ of their Erastianism. A long discussion followed on the question, Whether the public reading of the Scriptures be the pastor's office? some desiring to retain what was termed "a reader" in each congregation; but it was at length decided to belong to the pastor's office. The duty of catechising was also assigned to the pastor; and likewise that of praying when he preached, which had been prohibited by the bishops. It was also held, that it belongs to the pastor to take care of the poor, though not to supersede the deacon's office.

The next subject which occupied the Assembly's attention was the question, whether pastors and teachers, or doctors, formed one and the same office. The Independents maintained the divine institution of a doctor, as distinct from a pastor, in every congregation. It had been their own practice to have a doctor or teacher, as holding a somewhat subordinate position to that of the pastor,—one to which an ordinary member might readily aspire, forming a connecting link between the pastor and the people; and they were exceedingly desirous to persuade the Assembly to retain this distinction. On the other hand, this was one of the peculiarities of the Congregational system, different from what prevailed in all other Churches, and it was strenuously and even keenly resisted by the Assembly. At length Henderson interposed to procure an accommodation and agreement between the contending parties. It was at last concluded, that there are different gifts, and corresponding difference of exercises in ministers, though these may belong to the same person; that he who most excels in exposition may be termed a doctor; that such a person may be of great use chiefly in universities; and where there are several ministers in the same congregation, each may devote himself to that department in which he most excels; and that where there is but one, he must to his ability perform the whole work of the ministry. Henderson warned the Assembly that the eyes of all the Reformed Churches were upon them, earnestly watching whether their proceedings would be such as to promote or prevent the desired uniformity of all Protestant Christendom; entreating them not to be too minutely metaphysical and abstract in treating of such matters, but rather to direct their attention to leading and important topics, with the view of securing a general harmony, though smaller points should be allowed considerable freedom of interpretation.*

A still more important subject then came before the Assembly,—the subject of ruling elders; on the right understanding and decision of which depended the adoption or rejection of the distinctive principle of Presbyterian Church government. It was brought forward in the following terms:—" That besides those presbyters that both rule well and labour in the word and doctrine, there be other presbyters, who especially apply themselves to ruling, though they labour not in the word and doctrine." Aware that this order of Church-officers was almost a novelty in England, Henderson took an early part in the debate, showing that it had been used in the Reformed Churches at a very early period,— even before its institution at Geneva,—and that it had proved very beneficial to the Church of Scotland. Nearly the whole talent and learning of the Assembly were called into long and strenuous action by this discussion, which began on the 22d of November, and was not concluded till the 8th of December. The institution of ruling elder was opposed by Dr Temple, Dr Smith, Mr Gataker, Mr Vines, Mr Price, Mr Hall, Mr Lightfoot, Mr Coleman, Mr Palmer, and several others, besides the Independents,—of whom, however, Nye and Bridge opposed but partially. It was supported by Mr Marshall, Mr Calamy, Mr Young, Mr Seaman, Mr Walker,

* Lightfoot, pp. 53, 58; Baillie, vol. ii. p. 110.

Mr Newcomen, Mr Herle, Mr Whitaker, and the Scottish divines, of whom Rutherford and Gillespie particularly distinguished themselves. At length, having thoroughly exhausted their arguments, Henderson moved that a committee might be appointed to draw up a statement how far all parties were agreed, with the view of arriving at some fair accommodation ; and being supported by Goodwin, this motion was agreed to, and the debate terminated. The report of the committee contained these three propositions :—1. Christ hath instituted a government and governors ecclesiastical in the Church ; 2. Christ hath furnished some in his Church with gifts for government, and with commission to exercise the same when called thereunto ; 3. It is agreeable to, and warranted by, the Word of God, that some others beside the ministers of the Word, or Church-governors, should join with the ministers in the government of the Church." To these propositions were added the texts, Rom. xii. 7, 8, and 1 Cor. xii. 28. "Some liked the propositions," says Lightfoot, " but not the applying of the places of Scripture ; and of that mind was I myself,—for the proposition I understood of magistracy."* The first and second propositions were, however, affirmed without opposition, and the third with only the negative vote of Lightfoot himself ; the texts also were approved, with the additional opposition of Dr Temple.

The carrying of this question was justly regarded as of the utmost importance, as fixing the character of the Church to be established ; and it is matter of surprise that the opposition sunk so nearly to nothing. Even the accommodation by means of which these propositions were framed and carried, was somewhat of a perilous experiment; for it narrowly missed introducing the unsound principle of admitting into the arrangements of the Church what had no higher authority than considerations of expediency and prudence. For all were willing to have admitted the order of ruling elders

* Lightfoot, p. 76.

on these grounds ;* but this was decidedly rejected, especially by the Scottish divines, and by those of the Puritans
or English Presbyterians who fully understood the nature of
the controversy so long waged by their predecessors, against
admitting into a divine institution any thing of merely human
invention.

There was yet one point to be discussed respecting the
ruling elder. It had been decided that this officer is of divine
institution, but it remained to define in what his office consisted ; and this gave rise to another, and a very animated
debate. In the previous discussion respecting the office itself, considerable weight had been attached to the argument
drawn from the constitution of the Jewish Church, and from
the elders of the people in that institution ; and when preparing to define the office of an elder in the Christian Church,
reference was again made to the corresponding functionary
among the Jews; and the question arose, Whether the Hebrew
elders were chosen purposely for ecclesiastical business? Coleman first brought forward the inquiry, affirming that both the
elders and the seventy senators in the sanhedrim were civil
officers; Mr Calamy and Dr Burgess both held the reverse ;
and Mr Gillespie proved that the seventy were joined with
both Moses and Aaron at their institution,—that the elders
in other passages of Scripture are joined with the priests, and
in others with prophets, and in others are spoken of as distinct from the rulers.† Lightfoot somewhat differed from
Coleman, and also from Selden, who took part in this debate ; and, after a very learned and animated discussion, the
opinions of the Assembly being nearly balanced, the subject
was laid aside for a time, without any definite conclusion.

The office of deacon next engaged their attention. The
institution of this office was not denied, but several were of
opinion that it was of a temporary nature. This view was
entertained by few except the Erastians ; and when the As-

    * Baillie, vol. ii. p. 111.   † Lightfoot, p. 78.

sembly decided that the office of deacon was of a permanent nature, Lightfoot alone voted in the negative, though both Coleman and Selden had spoken against it. The opposition to the permanency of this office seems to have arisen chiefly from the fact, that there existed in England a civil poor-law, instituted in the reign of Elizabeth; which led some to oppose the deaconship as unnecessary, and others, as interfering with a civil arrangement. It was well suggested by Mr Vines, "That the provision of civil officers made by the civil State for the poor should rather slip into the office of a deacon, than the reverse, because the latter bears the badge of the Lord."

As the report concerning Church-officers had mentioned "widows," this was the last point to be discussed, whether widows were to be considered as deaconesses, and their office one of permanent continuation in the Church. Some of the Independents, and one or two others, were inclined to retain this office; but after some debate it was decided that the existence of such an office in the Church was not proved. With this discussion terminated the year 1643, in which the business of the Assembly had been chiefly of a preliminary character. It had, however, been solemnly decided, that Christ is so completely the Head of the Church, that all its offices are essentially in him, and from him are they all primarily and authoritatively derived; that of these offices some are extraordinary, and have ceased,—those, namely, of apostles, prophets, and evangelists; that pastors and doctors, or teachers, are essentially the same, and form the highest order of divinely appointed officers in the Church; that ruling elders are also of divine appointment, and are distinct from pastors; and that deacons are likewise of divine and permanent institution, though not entitled to preach or to rule, but to take charge of charitable and pecuniary concerns. And as considerable progress had thus been made, reasonable hopes might have been cherished that the business of the Assembly would continue

to proceed with as much celerity as was consistent with the
grave deliberation due to its vast importance.

But there were other elements of a less propitious nature at
work, some of which had already appeared, and others were
felt, though scarcely yet fully visible. On the 19th of October, soon after the Assembly had seriously begun its task, the
House of Commons intimated, through Dr Burgess, their
desire that two points should be decided upon as speedily
as possible, namely, an arrangement for the ordination of
ministers; and an arrangement for their institution and induction to vacant benefices.* The former of these points
could not be determined till the Assembly should have discussed the subject of Church-officers in general. But as the
latter was a subject of immediate and urgent importance, a
committee was appointed to determine in what manner trial
should be made of the qualifications of those who might apply for those vacant benefices. Twenty-one rules of examination were at length drawn up, in conformity with which every
applicant was to be tried, in order to ascertain his soundness
in doctrine and fitness for the situation. Application was
frequently made by ministers who had been cruelly plundered
by the king's army, and constrained to flee to London, both
for safety and to seek some kind of maintenance. The examination of such applicants proved to be a very delicate task,
as the king's army plundered alike the sound Puritans and
the erratic Sectarians,—so that persons of each character made
application to the Assembly. Sometimes the Sectarians,
knowing that no rule of ordination had yet been framed, procured ordination from other Sectarians, and attempted to
deceive the examinators; and when this was either not attempted, or found impracticable, they then endeavoured to
form a party among the citizens, and others who had flocked
to London, that from them they might derive a means of
subsistence. This led directly to a prodigious increase of

* Lightfoot, p. 24.

sectarianism in London, and tended to throw the whole city into a state of confusion and anarchy. To remedy this state of matters, the city ministers presented a supplication to the Assembly, lamenting their disturbed condition; requesting order to be taken for the ordination of ministers; stating the fearful increase of pernicious sects, and complaining of their restless endeavours to gather separate congregations; and requesting the Assembly to intercede with the Parliament for the redress of these grievances, and for the erection of a college at London, where the youth might be educated, as Oxford was in the possession of the king.* The Assembly answered, that it was not yet safe to meddle with the ordination of ministers; that they had applied to the Parliament for redress in the other matters; and desired information to be given respecting those who gather churches, that in this also they may seek redress. Mr Nye objected to the expression against gathering churches, and was sharply answered.† This apparently slight incident we have mentioned, because it indicates the line of policy which the Independent party were beginning to pursue, in connecting themselves with the mass of Sectarians throughout the kingdom, in which Nye performed so active a part, and of which he seems to have been the chief contriver.

[1644.] The year 1644 began with the introduction into the Assembly of subjects still more certain to produce disunion than any that had been previously discussed. The general subject of Church-officers had been so far determined; but the most important parts of this matter remained to be debated, namely, the method of appointing Church-officers, and the authority which they ought to possess, or, in other words, ordination and discipline. Well did the Assembly know that great diversity of opinion would arise on these two leading points, and gladly would they have avoided entering upon them till a subsequent period, had it been at all

* Lightfoot, p. 57; Baillie, vol. ii. p. 111. † Lightfoot, p. 62.

practicable. But the disturbed state of the country, increased
and aggravated by the want of religious ordinances and
government, rendered it imperatively necessary that some
steps should be taken for the remedy of so many and such
great national maladies. A commission had been appointed
in September 1643, for the purpose of inquiring into the
conduct of ministers throughout the country, and of removing
all such as were convicted of scandalous conduct, or proved
to be destitute of sufficient qualifications. On the 17th of
November, Parliament authorised the publication of a treatise, entitled, " The First Century of Scandalous and Malignant Priests ; or, a narration of the causes for which Parliament hath ordered the sequestration of the benefices of several
ministers complained of before them," &c. This was drawn
up by Mr White, M.P., the chairman of the commission ;
and it certainly proves that the ministers so sequestered were
utterly unworthy of the sacred office, or rather, that many of
them were unworthy of the name of men, though we cannot
pollute our pages by quotations.*   The reason of referring to
the subject, is to show the necessity thence arising for the ordination of other men to supply the benefices become vacant
by means of these sequestrations. However desirous, therefore, the Assembly were to postpone the consideration of a
subject, on which they were certain to disagree, till they should
have framed a Confession of Faith, and other matters, in
which entire unanimity was expected, they were constrained
reluctantly to proceed to doubtful disputations.

There is considerable difficulty in giving a direct and con-
tinuous view of the discussions on which we are now to enter,
in consequence of the contemporaneous, or rather intertwined
manner in which they arose and were conducted ; for instead of continuing steadily to prosecute one subject till
it was completed, and then passing on to another, there were
generally two or three subjects under deliberation at the same

* First Century, &c.

period, each being peculiarly intrusted to one or other of the committees in which they were prepared for public debate, and were successively laid aside and resumed according to their respective states of preparation. For example, on the 2d of January 1644, the two following subjects were both brought forward :—" Pastors and teachers have power to inquire and judge who are fit to be admitted to the sacraments, or kept from them ; as also who are to be excommunicated or absolved from that censure : " and, " The apostles had power to ordain officers in all churches, and to appoint evangelists to ordain." Notwithstanding the general terms employed, it was impossible to discuss these propositions without bringing forward the very points on which the greatest amount of division existed, namely, discipline and ordination ; and as they investigated every topic in a minute and scholastic manner, by a series of fine-drawn distinctions and syllogistic propositions previously prepared in the committees, it almost inevitably followed, that the business of the committees came before the Assembly on alternate days. In order to avoid the seeming confusion of such a mode of procedure, it will be expedient for us to trace each separate subject till its completion, instead of attempting to carry them forward contemporaneously, as the Assembly did.

It was in consequence of the method of treating every subject minutely, and as convenience served, that the proposition respecting the apostolic office was thus brought forward, long after its main elements had been defined, and its character as extraordinary and temporary admitted. When this part of the definition was stated, namely, " That the apostles had power to ordain officers in all churches, and to appoint evangelists to ordain ; " the Independents were afraid, that if this passed unquestioned, it might be held to have been already decided that the apostles alone had that power, and that they had so transmitted it by Church-officers that none others could ordain ; whereas they held that the Church itself, that

is, ordinary Church members assembled, possessed that power.
It was also disputed whether the term used, Acts xiv.
23, χειροτονία, meant ordination or election ; and on this point a
long debate took place, Gillespie, Vines, Simpson, and others,
holding that *election* was the proper meaning.* After some
further debate on the power of the apostles to appoint evangelists to ordain, the whole proposition received the sanction
of the Assembly.

On the 9th of January, the whole question of ordination
was fairly stated by Dr Temple, chairman of one of the committees, in the following series of interrogatory propositions:—
" 1. What ordination is ?   2. Whether necessarily to be continued ?   3. Who to ordain ?   4. What persons to be ordained, and how qualified ?   5. The manner how ? " To
these were appended the following answers for the Assembly's
consideration :—" 1. Ordination is the solemn setting apart
of a person to some public office in the Church.   2. It is
necessarily to be continued in the Church.   3. The apostles
ordained, evangelists did, preaching presbyters did : because
apostles and evangelists are officers extraordinary, and not to
continue in the Church ; and since, in Scripture, we find ordination in no other hands, we humbly conceive that the
preaching presbyters are only to ordain."   The first proposition was affirmed without much debate.   The second was
opposed chiefly because of the word " necessarily,". Mr Nye
questioning whether it were *necessitate finis*, or *necessitate pre-
cepti*,—a necessity for the accomplishment of the purpose, or
a necessity arising out of its being commanded.   Both sides
shrunk from the danger of division on this point; and having
changed the word " necessarily " into " always," the proposition was affirmed.   In the next proposition it was easily
admitted that apostles and evangelists ordained; but when
that passage, 1 Tim. iv. 14, was referred to, as proving that
preaching presbyters ordained, a very considerable debate

* Lightfoot, pp. 100–102; Baillie, vol. ii. p. 129.

arose, Lightfoot, in particular, asserting that it must mean, not ordination, but admission to be an elder ; and when it was affirmed by the Assembly, he and some others voted in the negative.*

This was, however, merely the beginning of the struggle. When the latter part of the proposition was brought forward for debate, " preaching presbyters were only to ordain," it was felt by all, that to this the Independents would not assent without some modification. Calamy, Gillespie, and Seaman, proposed, therefore, that a committee of Independents might be chosen, who should, in their own terms, state the question concerning ordination ; in the hope that, by having both views of the subject brought forward at once, it might be possible to fuse and blend them together, so as to prevent division. Their report was given in by Mr Nye, as follows: —" 1. Ordination, for the substance of it, is the solemnization of an officer's outward call ; in which the elders of the Church, in the name of Christ, and for the Church, do, by a visible sign, design the person, and ratify his separation to his office, with prayer for, and blessing upon his gifts in the ministration thereof. 2. That the power that gives the formal being to an officer, should be derived by Christ's institution from the power that is in elders as such, on the act of ordination,—as yet, we find not anywhere held forth in the Word." It will readily be supposed that the Assembly must have listened to such vague and unintelligible propositions with considerable amazement, not unmingled with displeasure, to find their courtesy requited by such studied ambiguity, certainly not calculated, and it could scarcely be thought intended, to promote agreement. They questioned the use of the word " elders," as obscure and ambiguous ; also the expression " for the Church," which Nye interpreted, *vice ecclesiae*, in the stead of the Church. " Other scrupulous and ambiguous passages," says Lightfoot, " were found ; which,

* Lightfoot, p. 113.

after a very long canvass upon them, were laid by, and our old proposition re-assumed."*

The conduct of the Independents, on this occasion, was both discreditable in itself, and led to very pernicious results. It was discreditable either to their candour or their talents, to produce propositions couched in such ambiguous language, much more calculated to perplex than to clear the subject; and as they were men of decided abilities, the accusation falls upon their character, and constrains us to regard them as uncandid and disingenuous. But finding that they had succeeded so ill in their attempt to deceive or confuse in this instance, they never again could be prevailed upon to state to the Assembly their own opinions in writing, though sufficiently pertinacious in retaining them, and supporting them by every kind of argument. The new course of tactics thus adopted proved the means of retarding the Assembly beyond measure, and ended at last in rendering all its prolonged toils comparatively abortive.

When the Assembly was on the point of resuming the consideration of its own propositions, Lord Manchester entered, bringing an order from the House of Lords, which required the Assembly to make haste and conclude the subject of ordination. A committee was appointed to prepare the matter for public discussion; and next day, 22d January, the two following propositions were reported:—"1. That in extraordinary cases something extraordinary may be done, until a settled order may be had; yet keeping as close as may be to the rule. 2. It is lawful, and according to the Word, that certain ministers of the city be desired to ordain ministers in the city and vicinity, *jure fraternitatis.*" A keen debate ensued, Coleman, Goodwin, and Nye opposing,— Vines, Seaman, Lightfoot, and others supporting the report. Nye, in particular, offered the most determined and pertinacious resistance to the clause "keeping as close to the rule as

---

* Lightfoot, p. 115.

may be." "Again," says Lightfoot, "he interposed, again, and again;"* but, in the end, the vote was carried in the affirmative. Every kind of scruple was started, every kind of objection brought forward by the Independents, aided by Selden, with whom they did not hesitate to make common cause in this matter. Nye even went so far as to argue that bishops might still ordain, rather than he would admit the case to be extraordinary, requiring a prompt remedial measure. In order, if possible, to end the tedious debate, it was proposed by Gillespie, that the question of a presbytery should be expressly declared as still left open; and Vines moved that the Independents should propose their own way for the supply of the present necessity. The Earl of Pembroke urged haste, as both Church and kingdom were on fire, and might be destroyed during such tedious delays; but Nye would not abate his opposition. After a keen and even stormy debate of fourteen days' duration, the subject was laid aside, in compliance with the request of Lord Say, who supported the Independents; and who suggested that it would really expedite the matter first to decide what ought to be the ordinary way and rule of ordination, to which any thing extraordinary could be then made to conform. The cause of the extreme obstinacy of the Independents in this discussion, was their fear that it would overrule two points which they held to be of vital importance, involving the very essence of their system, namely, the power of ordination by a single congregation; and the existence and powers of a presbytery. The Assembly repeatedly assured them that these subjects should not be regarded as in any respect decided; and Gillespie tendered four distinct arguments to show that it could not determine the question of a presbytery.†

The subject of ordination was again resumed on the 18th of March, partly with reference to the existing necessity, and partly as occurring in the course of discussion respecting the

* Lightfoot, p. 117.   † Ibid., p. 130.

M

calling and appointment of ministers. One additional element of some importance was now introduced, which led to another still more important;—the first was the necessity of designation to some particular place, to avoid disorder and irregularity; and the second, arising out of this, was, the consent of the congregation to which the pastor is to be ordained. The form of the proposition brought forward on this point was, "That he be recommended to that congregation to whom he is to be a minister, and have their consent, unless they can show just cause of exception against him." Gillespie proposed to add, "Or will petition for a man that they conceive may be more advantageous to them in his preaching, and more powerful upon their experience." Henderson wished this question to be debated: "The presbytery recommend one, and the people desire another; how shall it be determined?" Gillespie desired that this might hold: "In no case, in a settled church, a minister may be obtruded on a congregation." Rutherford said, "The Scriptures constantly give the choice of the pastor to the people. The act of electing is in the people; and the regulating and correcting of their choice is in the presbytery." Gillespie again resumed: "But if they cannot show just cause against him, what then is to be done? The people say, We see no error in him, in life and doctrine, but honour and reverence him; but we can better profit by another: what is to be done in this case?" He then moved that this proposition might be debated: "He that is to be ordained be not obtruded against the will of the congregation: for the prelates are for obtrusion, the separation for a popular voting; therefore let us go in a medium." At length the debate terminated by the passing of the following proposition:—"No man shall be ordained a minister of a particular congregation, if they can show any just cause of exception against him." *

* Lightfoot, pp. 230-233. The conduct and language of the Scottish divines in this debate prove clearly that they held the principle of election

In the beginning of April the Assembly completed the doctrinal part of ordination, and proceeded to frame a directory how it should be conducted. A committee was chosen to prepare it for debate, consisting of Messrs Palmer, Herle, Marshall, Tuckney, Seaman, Vines, Goodwin, Gataker, and the Scottish ministers. Their report was given in and ratified on the 19th of April, and next day laid before both Houses of Parliament. Although Parliament had repeatedly urged the Assembly to hasten forward the directory and rules for ordination, yet, when this had been done, the matter was allowed to remain inoperative, for want of the ratification of the Legislature, from the 20th of April, when it was received, till the 15th of August. Before it was returned, some rumours had been in circulation that considerable alterations had been made by the Parliament; and when it was actually produced before the Assembly, these were found to be more extensive than had even been apprehended. They had omitted the whole doctrinal part of ordination, and all the scriptural grounds for it; and they had chosen only the extraordinary way of ordination, and even in that part had struck out whatever might displease the Independents, the patrons, and the Erastians.* The Scottish commissioners would by no means consent to these alterations; and, in an address to the Grand Committee of Lords, Commons, and the Assembly, they expressly condemned them. This decided conduct, aided by a timely petition to both Houses from the city ministers, produced the desired effect;† and, on the 16th of September, the Assembly's directory for ordination was returned, restored to its original condition. On the 18th, a committee was appointed for the ordination of ministers, consisting of ten of

by the people to be the right one; and that the utmost modification of it to which they could consent was, that no man be intruded. They were, in short, what would now be termed " decided Non-Intrusionists," at the least; and their consent to a modified proposition was caused by their dread of the sectarian confusion then prevalent in England.

* Baillie, vol. ii. pp. 198 and 221.   † Rushworth, vol. v. p. 780.

the Assembly divines, and thirteen of those belonging to the city of London. This was ratified by both Houses on the 2d of October; and thus that long delayed point was concluded. *

As the discussions respecting the directory for public worship were not of such importance as those concerning government and discipline, and were first concluded, though not begun till after the other had continued for a considerable time, it will conduce to simplicity and clearness to give an outline of the former of these topics in the present place.

On the 21st of May 1644, Mr Rutherford moved for the speeding of the directory for public worship, to which no attention had hitherto been paid. In consequence of this motion, Mr Palmer, chairman of the committee appointed for that purpose, gave in a report on the 24th, which brought the subject fairly before the Assembly. Some little difference of opinion arose, whether any other person, except the minister, might read the Scriptures in the time of public worship; which terminated in the occasional permission of probationers. But when the subject of the dispensation of the Lord's supper came under discussion, it gave rise to a sharp and protracted debate, chiefly between the Independents and the Scottish commissioners. The Independents opposed the arrangement of the communicants, as seated at the communion table, it being the custom among them for the people to remain in their pews; while the Scottish members urgently defended the proposed method of seating themselves at the same table. Another disputed point was, with regard to the power of the minister to exclude ignorant or scandalous persons from communion. The debates on these points occupied the Assembly

* Rushworth, vol. v. p. 781. The names of the Assembly divines were, Drs Burgess and Gouge, Messrs Walker, Conant, Cawdry, Calamy, Chambers, Ley, Gower, and Roborough. The city ministers were, Messrs Downham, Dod, Clendon, Bourne, Roberts, Offspring, Crauford, Clarke, Billers, Cooke, Lee, Horton, and Jackson. A similar committee was also appointed for the county of Lancaster.—*Neal,* vol. ii. p. 273.

from the 10th of June to the 10th of July. The directory for the sacrament of baptism was also the subject of considerable debate, continued from the 11th of July to the 8th of August. The directory for the sanctification of the Sabbath was readily received ; and a committee was appointed to prepare a preface for the completed directory for public worship. This committee consisted of Messrs Goodwin, Nye, Bridge, Burgess, Reynolds, Vines, Marshall, and Dr Temple, together with the Scottish ministers. The appointment of so many of the Independents was for the purpose of avoiding any renewal of the protracted contentions in which they had so long held the Assembly, as we learn from Baillie. * This part of the Assembly's labours received the ratification of Parliament on the 22d of November 1644 ; with the exception of the directions for marriage and burial, which were finished on the 27th of the same month, and soon afterwards the whole received the full ratification of Parliament.

It will be remembered that the Assembly of Divines, when required by Parliament to prepare a new form of government and discipline, attempted at first to begin and proceed with their task in a manner strictly systematic and logical, commencing with Christ, the Divine Head of the Church, who possesses all power and all offices by way of eminency in Himself ; from that they proceeded to mention the various kinds of Church-officers who are named in the Scriptures, and to define the nature of their official powers and duties, intending to complete this part before undertaking any other. But they were turned aside from the systematic course of procedure, partly by the urgency of the Parliament's desire to obtain a directory for ordination to supply vacant charges; and partly by their own wish to avoid the discussion of controverted topics till they should have agreed on as many as possible. Even in these preliminary steps, however, they came into contact with several points which led to keen de-

* Baillie, vol. ii. p. 242.

bates between the Independent and the Presbyterian parties, proving but too plainly that a full agreement was scarcely to be expected. For a time the Scottish commissioners strove to act the part of peace-makers, and repeatedly moved to avoid disputable topics, and to direct their attention chiefly to those on which all might be united. As the subjects on which they were engaged advanced, this became impracticable, and all parties prepared for the struggle. On the 19th of January 1644, Dr Burgess reported from the first committee, who were to draw up the propositions concerning Presbytery in the following terms :—" 1. That the Scripture holdeth out a Presbytery in a Church, 1 Tim. iv. 14 ; Acts xv. 2, 4, 6. 2. That a Presbytery consisteth of ministers of the Word, and such other public officers as have been already voted to have a share in the government in the Church."*

The subject having been thus brought forward in the Assembly in the due order of procedure, the Scottish commissioners prepared a book containing an outline of the Presbyterial form of Church government, as it already existed in Scotland, and caused a copy of it to be given to each member of Assembly. They also prepared a paper containing a brief statement of the chief heads of Church government, which having been laid before the Grand Committee, was by them transmitted to the Assembly for their consideration. It was to the following effect :—" Assemblies are fourfold : 1. Elderships of particular congregations ; 2. Classical Presbyteries ; 3. Provincial Synods ; 4. National Assemblies. Elderships particular are warranted : 1. By Christ's institution, Matt. xviii. 17 ; 2. By the common light of nature ; 3. By unavoidable necessity. Classical Presbyteries are warrantable : 1. By Christ's institution, Matt. xviii. 17; 2. By the example of Apostolic Churches—instancing in the Church of Jerusalem, Antioch, Ephesus, Corinth, Rome,

* Lightfoot, p. 115.

&c."* These propositions were given to the committee which was intrusted with the preparation of all matters connected with Presbytery, as the proper channel through which they might again be brought forward in the Assembly ; not, however, without some opposition, both from the Independents and from Selden. This took place on the 25th of January ; and on the 27th of the same month, Lord Wharton reported from the House of Lords, that a person named Ogle, formerly a royalist officer, at that time a prisoner, had been detected holding correspondence with Lord Bristol, expressing his hope that a large party of the Parliament's adherents might be induced to join the king, "if the moderate Protestant and the fiery Independent could be brought to withstand the Presbyterian."† His lordship produced, at the same time, letters from the Earl of Bristol, encouraging the scheme of bringing in the Independents to the support of the royal cause. In this plot the Independents in the Assembly do not appear to have been directly implicated ; for Nye and Goodwin assisted in its detection, by obtaining permission to hold private intercourse with Ogle, and to seem to consent to his proposals, with the view of ascertaining their full extent and nature.‡ Although the Assembly Independents were vindicated from participation in this plot, yet a certain amount of suspicion rested on the party in general, which, together with the points of difference already stated, and those on the brink of being brought forward, seem to have induced them to adopt a course which proved exceedingly pernicious, so far as regarded the prospect of arriving at ultimate unanimity.

About the end of January, or the beginning of February 1644, they published a treatise, termed " An Apologetical Narration, humbly submitted to the Honourable Houses of Parliament, by Thomas Goodwin, Philip Nye, Sidrach Simpson, Jeremiah Burroughs, William Bridge." The date on

* Lightfoot, p. 119.   † Ibid., p. 126.   ‡ Baillie, vol. ii. p. 137.

the title-page is 1643; but the parliamentary year commenced on the 25th of March, according to the English
computation; and Baillie mentions this treatise as newly
published, in a letter dated the 18th of February 1644, he
dating the beginning of the year from January, as had been
the custom in Scotland from the year 1600. The language
of Baillie is very pointed respecting this production. "At
last," says he, " foreseeing they behoved ere long to come to
the point, they put out, in print, on a sudden, an Apologetical Narration of their way, which long had lain ready beside
them, wherein they petition the Parliament, in a most sly
and cunning way, for a toleration; and withal lend too bold
wipes to all the Reformed Churches, as imperfect yet in their
reformation, till their new model be embraced."* Baillie
further insinuates, that the appearance of the treatise was
" by some men intended to contribute to the very wicked
plot, at that same instant a-working, but shortly after discovered almost miraculously." If this conjecture be correct,
the intercourse of Nye and Goodwin with Ogle may have
been for the purpose of concealing their own connection with
the plot, rather than to aid in its complete detection. We
are not, however, desirous to fix upon them a larger amount
of criminality, as conducting dark and treacherous intrigues,
than can be maintained by the clearest and most irresistible
evidence, and therefore shall not at once adopt the suggestion
of Baillie.

The publication of this treatise, the " Apologetical Narration," by the Independents, tended greatly to prevent the probability of any amicable arrangement in which all parties
might agree. Till that time nothing had been done which
foreclosed the possible adjustment of at least all minor differences; and the Scottish divines, in particular, had striven to
avoid the premature determination of points disputed by the
Independents. But when they had thus carried the contro-

* Baillie, vol. ii. p. 130.

versy away from the Assembly to the Parliament, and had,
by publishing this work, laid it before the world, it became
almost morally impossible that any accommodated adjustment could take place, each party feeling bound in honour to
make out its own cause, and to adhere pertinaciously to the
views thus publicly declared. It may be remarked also, that
the Scottish commissioners had always caused their publications to be laid before the Assembly, so as to render them
fairly the subjects of discussion ; whereas the Independents
addressed their production to the Parliament, and published
it to the community, without formally giving copies to the
Assembly ; so that, whatever might be thought, the subject
could not, without violation of order and propriety, be taken
up and debated there. This, of course, led to the publication
of a series of answers, in which, as usual, each disputant
was more eager to confute his antagonist than to promote
peace and harmony. From that time forward the contest
between the Independents and the Presbyterians became one
of irreconcilable rivalry, to which the utter defeat of the one
or the other was the only possible termination. And historical truth compels us to say, that as this bitter warfare
was begun by the Independents, they are justly chargeable
with all the consequences of the fatal feud.

The " Apologetical Narration" is, in many points of view,
a remarkable production. Though it extends to no more
than thirty-one pages of small quarto, it contains a very
plausible account of the history of the five Independent
divines, the peculiar tenets of Church government which they
held, and their objections against the Presbyterian system ; so
expressed as both to convey a highly favourable view of themselves and their opinions to Parliament, and to the public,
and to serve as the vehicle of skilfully constructed adulation
to Parliament itself. The treatise begins by complaining of
the accusations which were generally urged "(though not expressly directed against us in particular, yet in the interpreta-

tion of the most reflecting on us)," by which they had been awakened and enforced to anticipate a little that discovery of themselves which otherwise they had resolved to have left to time and experience of their ways and spirits. They present themselves, therefore, " to the supreme judicatory of this kingdom ; which is, and hath been in all times, the most just and severe tribunal for guiltiness to appear before, much more to dare to appeal unto ; and yet, withal, the most sacred refuge and asylum for mistaken and misjudged innocence." They then mention that most of them had enjoyed stations in the ministry ten years before, which they had been constrained to abandon in consequence of the corruptions in the public worship and government of the Church. Having been compelled first to look at the *dark part*, as they term it, or the actually existing evils, which forced them to exile, they next began to inquire into and examine the *light part*, or the positive part of Church worship and government, as stated in the apostolic directions, and the examples of the primitive New Testament Churches. " In this inquiry," say they, " we looked upon the Word of Christ as impartially and unprejudicedly as men made of flesh and blood are like to do in any juncture of time that may fall out."—" We had no new commonwealths to rear, to frame church government unto (a hint for the Erastians), whereof any one piece might stand in the other's light, to cause the least variation by us from the primitive pattern ; we had no state ends or political interests to comply with ; no kingdoms in our eye to subdue unto our mould, which yet will be co-existent with the peace of any civil government on earth; no preferment of worldly respects to shape our opinions for : we had nothing else to do but simply and singly to consider how to worship God acceptably, and so most according to his Word." * These good men do not seem to have perceived that a precisely similar course of reasoning, in a closely similar condition, led to the erroneous

* Apologetical Narration, pp. 3, 4.

conclusions of the ascetic and monastic orders in the early ages of Christianity, nothing being more common than for men to spring from one extreme into that which is most directly and remotely opposite. And it will be observed that there is an allusion to the usual charge brought against the Scottish Covenanters, which it would have been more in accordance with the spirit of charity and peace not to have made.

They next proceed to point out the advantages which they enjoyed from the writings of the Nonconformists—the errors of the Separatists, or Brownists—the example of other Reformed Churches, and particularly the example of their expatriated countrymen in New England. As if to prove that they were not men of unaccommodating temper, and rigid sectarian spirit, they admit that even in the worst times of the Church of England, "multitudes of the assemblies and parochial congregations thereof were *the true churches and body of Christ, and the ministry thereof a true ministry*" (the *italics* are in the work itself) ; "and that they both had held, and would hold, communion with them as the churches of Christ." Mention is also made of the friendly terms in which they had lived with the National Presbyterian Church of Holland, as a further proof of their truly Christian fairness and liberality of spirit.

Having given this general view of their own feelings, they proceed to state briefly the way and practices of their churches, which, accordingly, we quote in their own words: " Our public worship was made of no other parts than the worship of all other Reformed Churches doth consist of: As public and solemn prayers for kings and all in authority, &c.,—the reading the Scriptures of the Old and New Testament, exposition of them as occasion was ; and constant preaching of the Word, the administration of the two sacraments, baptism to infants, and the Lord's supper, singing of psalms, collections for the poor, &c., every Lord's day. For officers and public rulers in the Church, we set up no other but the very same which the Reformed Churches judge necessary and sufficient, and as instituted by Christ and his apostles for the perpetual government of his Church; that is, pastors, teachers, ruling elders (with us not lay, but ecclesiastical persons separated to that service), and deacons. And for the matter of government and censures of the Church, we had not executed any other but what all acknowledge, namely, *admonition*, and *excommunication* upon obstinacy and impenitency (which we bless God we never exercised). This latter we judged should be put in execution for no other kind of sins than may evidently be presumed to be perpetrated against the party's known light. We had these three principles more especially in our eye to guide and steer our practice by: First, the supreme rule *without us* was the primitive pattern and example of the churches erected by the apostles. A second principle we carried along with us in all our resolutions was, not to make our present judgment and practice a binding law unto ourselves for the future, which we in like manner made continual profession of upon all occasions; which principle we wish were (next to that most supreme, namely, to be in all things guided by the perfect will of God) enacted as the most *sacred law* of all other, in the midst of all other laws and canons ecclesiastical in Christian States and Churches throughout the world. Thirdly, we are able to hold forth this true and just apology unto the world, that in the matters of greatest moment and controversy, all still chose to practise safely, and so as we had reason to judge that all sorts, or the most of all the churches, did acknowledge warrantable, although they make additaments thereunto."

In order to explain what they mean by these *additaments*, they proceed to say,—" For instance: whereas one great controversy of these times is about the *qualification of the members* of churches, and the promiscuous receiving and mixture of good and bad; therein we chose the better part, and to be sure, received in none but such as all the churches in the world, by the balance of the sanctuary, acknowledge faithful." With regard to Church government, after referring to the Presbyterian system at that time prevalent in all the Reformed Churches, except that of England, they say,—" We could not but judge it a safe and an allowed way, to retain the government of our several congregations for matters of discipline within themselves, to be exercised by their own elders, whereof we had (for the most part of the time we were abroad) three at least in each congregation, whom we were subject to; yet not claiming to ourselves an *independent power* in every congregation, to give account or be subject to none others, but only a full and entire power complete within ourselves, until we should be challenged to err grossly." To meet the objection, that such a system afforded no remedy for misconduct in any erring congregation, they state, that when one church gives offence to others, they ought to submit to trial and examination by those offended; and if the offending church should persist in their error, then the others are " to pronounce that heavy sentence against them, of withdrawing and renouncing all Christian communion with them until they do repent." This sentence of *non-communion*, as they term it, is what they meant by *excommunication ;* and as its efficiency was questioned, they say, in answer to such an objection : " And if the magistrate's power (to which we give as much, and, as we think, more than the principles of the Presbyterial government will suffer them to yield) do but assist and back the sentence of other churches denouncing this *non-communion* against churches miscarrying, according to the nature of the crime, as they judge meet, and as they would the sentence of churches excommunicating other churches in such cases, upon their own particular judgment of the cause; then, without all controversy, this, our way of Church proceeding, will be every way as effectual as their other can be supposed to be."

A short narrative is then given of the way in which they had succeeded in terminating a dispute which had occurred among them while in Holland; but strict truth constrains us to say, that their narrative is by no means of an impartial character; and as the whole facts of the case were well known to many of the Assembly divines, from their intercourse with the Netherlands, they could not fail to be displeased with this apologetic account of the affair. The relation goes on to suggest, in a tone of considerable self-complacency, that though the Reformed Churches had made considerable progress, yet it seemed likely that a much more perfect reformation might be obtained; manifestly implying that this would best be accomplished by following their model. Again complaining of the reproaches and calumnies which they had endured, they mention, as among them, " *That* proud and insolent title of *Independency* was affixed unto us, as our claim; the very sound of which conveys to all men's apprehensions the challenge of an exemption of all Churches from all subjection and dependence, or rather a trumpet of defiance against whatever power, spiritual or civil; which we do abhor and detest: Or else, the odious name of *Brownism*, together with all their opinions as they have stated and maintained them, must needs be owned by us; although upon the very first declaring our judgments in the chief and fundamental point of all *Church discipline*, and likewise since, it hath been acknowledged that we differ much from them. And we did then, and do here publicly profess, we believe the truth to lie and consist in a *middle way*, betwixt that which is falsely charged on us, *Brownism;* and that which is the contention of these times, the *authoritative Presbyterial government* in all the subordinations and proceedings of it." *

After a few more general declarations respecting their own "peaceable practices," and "constant forbearance" in the midst of many provocations, and their resolution to bear

* Apol. Nar., pp. 23, 24.

all "with a quiet and strong patience," they intimate their intention to decline further controversy, reserving the declaration and defence of their opinions to the Assembly. They declare also their full agreement with the Assembly in all points of doctrine that had yet been discussed; and their wish to yield in matters of discipline, in which alone they had yet differed, to the utmost latitude of their light and consciences. And finally, they conclude their Apologetical Narration, by beseeching the Parliament to regard them as men who, if they cannot be promoters, have no wish to be hinderers of further reformation; who differ less from the Reformed Churches and their brethren than they do from what themselves were three years past; who have long been exiles and are now sufferers of reproach; and who pursue no other design but a subsistence, be it the poorest and meanest, in their own land, with the enjoyment of the ordinances of Christ, and with the allowance of a latitude to some lesser differences with peaceableness, as not knowing where else with safety, health, and livelihood, to set their feet on earth.

The publication of this Apologetical Narrative operated instantaneously like a declaration of war. A number of answers almost immediately appeared, various in talent, learning, and power, but at least sufficiently keen and pointed. Even the calm, plausible, and stately tone of the Narrative, tended to provoke their antagonists to the use of undue asperity; for they regarded it as an attempt to recommend their own system, and disparage others, by means of careful concealments, plausible evasions, and alluring insinuations of its accommodating nature, skilfully contrasted with hints and suggestions of an unfavourable kind respecting the character and tendency of the Presbyterian form of Church government and discipline. For this reason many seemed to think that the Narration was not merely to be answered, but assailed with vehemence and indignation. In this, although the temptation was great, they certainly erred,

and erred grievously; both because such a method is not
likely to disarm hostility, or remove prejudice, and because
it seemed to prove that the charge of intolerance, so frequently urged against them, was but too well founded. Let
it, however, be observed, that none of the Scottish divines
entered warmly into this controversy, although the Independents had alluded to them in a manner sufficiently ungracious.
Baillie, indeed, speaks of them with considerable severity in
some parts of his letters; and the view which he gives of
their system in his "Dissuasive," is certainly not such as
would gratify its adherents; and Rutherford did not hesitate
to encounter them in fair argument, in several of his works,
but without any asperity of temper, or harshness of language.
They were answered by Mr Herle, in his treatise entitled
" The Independency upon Scripture of the Independency of
Churches;" and he also retained a dignified and Christian-
like calmness of spirit and manner. But other antagonists
kept no such terms. Dr Bastwick, Mr Vicars, and Mr
Edwards, assailed the Narration with not less keenness of
expression than strength of argument. Of these answers, the
most elaborate was that entitled " Antapologia; or, a Full
Answer to the Apologetical Narration; by Thomas Edwards,"
extending to 259 pages of small quarto, and embracing every
disputed or suggested topic. It will scarcely be denied, by
those who have carefully perused the Antapologia, that it
furnishes a very ample and strong, but most ungracious refutation of the main positions taken up by the authors of the
Apologetical Narration. No formal reply was returned by
the Independents to the Antapologia; but Mr Burroughs
sometime afterwards published a vindication of himself from
some of the charges that had been urged against him. To
that vindication we may have occasion to refer subsequently,
for another purpose.

Instead, therefore, of tracing the Antapologia, and extract-
ing its statements, it may be enough to advert to some of the

main points in which it answered the Narration. It is
proved clearly by facts, that the Independent brethren had
not been such silent and retiring men as they represented
themselves to have been; but that, on the contrary, they had
been very active in endeavouring to recommend and spread
their own views as widely as possible; that in reality all
their principles, of which they spoke as in a great measure
discovered by themselves, in their own study of the Scriptures, had been previously promulgated and acted upon by
others; that, in effect, their boasted theory of *non-communion*
had not been found adequate to the maintenance of peace
among them, and had but very imperfectly answered the end
in the case to which they referred as a practical instance of
its sufficiency; that they had not experienced any peculiar
hardships either before or during their exile; and that, since
their return, they had enjoyed comfort, influence, and honour,
at least equal to that which any of the Presbyterians had obtained. The insinuations against the Presbyterian system
were shown to be invidious and unfounded, and were very
sharply retorted against themselves and their course of procedure; and their practice in "gathering churches out of
churches," was shown to be contrary to their own declarations as members of the Westminster Assembly. It was
proved, also, that they maintained a more intimate intercourse with the Brownists and other Sectarians than they
were willing to admit; and were engaged in a series of intrigues which they were anxious to conceal. All these
points appear to be proved in the Antapologia by a strength
and minuteness of evidence which could not be set aside,
and which they did not attempt to meet. But there was so
much of a fiercely hostile spirit displayed by Edwards, that
his attack recoiled somewhat upon himself, and diminished
considerably the value of his production, while it furnished a
kind of excuse for his antagonists in abstaining from giving
a direct answer.

N

Such was the first direct outbreak of the controversy between the Independents and the Presbyterians,—a controversy greatly to be deplored, as having proved ultimately the main cause why the Westminster Assembly failed to accomplish all the good which had been expected from its important deliberations. Viewed as a theological controversy alone, it contained but few, and these not vitally important, elements. There was no disagreement between the two parties in matters of doctrine; they both admitted the same orders of office-bearers in the Church, though the Independents would have recognised more than the Presbyterians thought either necessary or commanded in the Scriptures; and they differed little in their opinions respecting the powers properly inherent in congregations. But the Independents refused to recognise the Presbyterian system of successive Church courts,—as presbyteries, synods, and assemblies,—possessing authoritative jurisdiction over those immediately beneath them, though they were willing to admit the advantage of synods, in cases of difficulty, to the opinions of which great respect would be due, but not subjection and necessary obedience. The point, however, on which the greatest disagreement existed, was that relating to the ideas which they attached to the term, Church. In their view, each company of believers, though not more than seven in number, forms a church, complete in itself, and in no respect subordinate to, or requiring the aid of, any other church. Such a church might, at its first formation, be entirely without pastors, elders, or church-officers of any kind; but having met together, and made a solemn declaration of faith, and entered into a mutual church-covenant, they immediately became possessed of such inherent powers as to entitle them to choose and ordain all necessary church-officers, without the presence or the intervention of any pastor previously ordained. Other pastors might indeed be present, but their presence was not necessary to the validity of the ordination conferred. In the same manner, the congregation of ordinary members might censure or depose their office-bearers, and choose and ordain new ones whenever they thought proper; and if the office-bearers did not readily submit and become private members again, the congregation were entitled to withdraw from communion with them altogether, and to reconstruct their system as at first. Against such proceedings no appeal could be taken to any other authority, each congregation possessing all power in itself, and being free to have recourse to the principle of non-communion in any case, though against the whole Christian Church. Even when thus stated, the difference between the Independent and the Presbyterian systems may be brought within a very narrow compass. The Presbyterians never denied that a company of true believers might be a true church, though destitute of pastors; nor that they might select the most grave and pious of their number, and set him solemnly apart to the office of the ministry, without the presence of any ordained pastor, if in circumstances where that could not be obtained. They admitted that the Church must possess in itself the power of all that is necessary to the continuation of its own existence. But they held, also, that Christ himself at first chose and appointed office-bearers, and gave to them authority to ordain others; that this was matter of precept, and to be regularly obeyed in every instance where that was possible, because it had been so commanded; while they regarded the Congregational mode as a matter of necessity, justifiable only in cases where without it the enjoyment of Christian ordinances could not be obtained. The error of the Independents consisted in adopting as the ordinary rule the *case of necessity*, instead of the *method of precept*; and in adhering so pertinaciously to this view as to condemn and refuse to admit into their communion all who could not agree with them.

It was a necessary consequence of this essential principle, that the Independents held the theory of admitting none to be members of their churches except those whom they be-

lieved to have been thoroughly and in the highest sense rege-
nerated, or, in the language of the time, " true saints," and
consequently, perfectly qualified to exercise rightly all the
high and sacred functions which they asserted to belong to
the congregation, as in itself a complete church. For the
same reason, they necessarily opposed the idea of a national
Church, in any other sense than as a series of congregational
churches, gathering together true believers as the wheat, and
leaving the chaff to its fearful fate. And following up this
theory, they regarded it as perfectly right to gather churches
of their own kind out of the congregations of other ministers,
—a process which necessarily gave great offence to those
whose congregations they thus divided and led away. Nor
was it at all strange that considerable numbers should be
willing to join a system which gave such irresponsible power
to ordinary Church members; and which, at the same time,
certainly tended to encourage the feeling of spiritual pride in
those who, in being admitted, were recognised as truly re-
generated persons. In one point of view they were, to a certain extent, right. It must always be desirable that Church
members should be real believers, and that Christian communion should be enjoyed by none but true believers; but it
must always be impossible for man, who cannot read the
heart, to avoid being deceived by the plausible language and
manners of skilful hypocrisy,—and therefore it was impossible
for the Congregational theory to be fully realized. And at
the same time, while assuming so much purity and reality in
its members, its want of the power either to inflict Church
censures or to appeal to higher authority, rendered it peculiarly unable to preserve that very purity in which it assumed
its superiority over other Churches to consist. Still further,
by placing the very essence of its system in congregational
power, it necessarily stood closely allied, in theory at least,
with all the multitudinous sects with which that period was
so prodigiously rife,—all of which were perfectly ready to

maintain the sole and uncontrollable power of separate congregations; and thus the Independents were in a manner compelled to become the head sectarian body, and to defend not only their own religious liberties, but also the liberty claimed by the most wild and monstrous sects to hold and to teach errors the most immoral and blasphemous,—of which they by no means approved, or rather, which they strongly condemned, but could not consistently oppose. They were thus led to advocate a toleration in theory which they never granted where their own power was predominant, as in New England,—and which, it may be added, they never would consent to grant to the Presbyterians, whom they would not admit to communion with them unless they were willing to abandon Presbyterianism, and become Congregationalists. But as the subject of toleration was scarcely suggested in the Apologetical Narration, we shall postpone the consideration of it till we reach the period when it became a leading element of controversy.

All the topics which have been stated above were known to the two parties of Presbyterians and Independents in the Assembly, before the publication of the Apologetical Narration, and several of them had casually become the subject of debate ; but there had been considerable forbearance on both sides, arising from a natural and laudable reluctance to anticipate a perhaps unavoidable contest. The Scottish divines, in particular, had repeatedly interposed to prevent any premature discussion of debatable subjects, and had recommended as much accommodation to the views of the Independents as was consistent with the maintenance of principle. And although the allusions to them in the Apologetical Narration were sufficiently ungracious and irritating, they were in no haste to show resentment ; being far more desirous to see the religious welfare of the community promoted and secured, than to vindicate their own character from groundless aspersions. But, nevertheless, the publication of that most ill-omened production caused an estrangement which was never fully removed, and led to a degree of keenness and obstinacy in all the subsequent deliberations of the Assembly, whenever disputed points arose, which tended greatly both to retard their proceedings and to obscure the prospect of ultimate and harmonious success in their great work. And having thus opened the subject of the Independent controversy, we shall now proceed to trace it, according to the course which circum- stances led it to pursue.

After some preliminary arrangements, in which it was agreed that the Independents should bring forward their ob- jections to the proposition of the committee, the subject was formally stated, on the 6th of February, in the following terms :—" The Scripture holdeth forth that many particular congregations may be under one presbyterial government." The Independent argument against this proposition was stated by Mr Goodwin, to this effect, as given by Lightfoot : —"If many elders put together make one presbytery classical, then every one of those elders is to be reputed as an elder to every one of those churches ; but the Word of God doth not warrant any such thing." In proof of the minor proposition he argued thus :—" The deacons are not to be officers to divers churches, therefore not the pastor ; the pastor is not to preach in divers churches, therefore not to rule ; the several congregations are not to give honour or maintenance to the pastor of another church ; one pastor was not chosen, ordained, and maintained by divers churches, therefore not to have power in them ; several offices are not to meet in one and the same person."* It will be observed that this argument opposed presbyterial government not on scriptural grounds, but on the supposed incongruities and inconveni- ences of the system ; and this was promptly and very easily met.

Mr Vines, in answer to the major proposition, replied, that " what belongs to the whole, as such, does not belong to

* Lightfoot, p. 132.

every part;" but the presbytery is an aggregate whole, and
so are the churches combined under this presbytery ; therefore
the relations borne by the presbytery to the church of its
bounds have respect to the aggregate whole, and do not interfere with the peculiar relations which the respective pastors
and congregations bear to each other. He illustrated his
argument by reference to the original government of the
Hebrew commonwealth, where the heads of the tribes
governed the whole community; but this did not alter the
relation between the head of each tribe and that particular
tribe ; and he showed that the Independent argument might
be retorted against their own system. Mr Marshall began by
proving the proposition of the committee :—That the whole
Church is but one body, and its members ought to act not as
distinct persons, but as joint-members ; that the office-bearers
were instituted by Christ, for the general good and edification, and also ought to act in unity : that members are bap-
tized not into one particular congregation, but into the general
body; and that this general body is cast into societies, which
are called by divines *instituted churches*. He further reasoned, that it appears from Scripture, that when so many
were converted in any city as to make a congregation, the
apostles appointed them elders ; that though they increased,
so as to form many congregations in that city, they continued
to be but one Church, as at Jerusalem ; that though not
specifically declared, yet it seemed probable that the several
pastors had their several charges : and that this pattern ought
to be followed. Mr Gillespie pursued a similar line of
argument ; gave an illustration from the representative
government of the States-General in the Netherlands ; and
added, that the power of government in a presbytery is not
power of order, but of jurisdiction, and that they govern not
as presbyters, but as a presbytery. Mr Seaman met the objections of Mr Goodwin, by proving that the inconveniences
alleged against the presbyterial government of churches

would, were they just, apply equally to civil government of
the representative kind; but no such inconveniences or incongruities were experienced : therefore the objections urged
by Mr Goodwin could not be well founded. He proved,
also, that a minister may stand in relation to more congregations than one, and that several offices may, without incon-
gruity, meet in one person : that a minister may do his duty
in one congregation and also in the presbytery, as a representative may to his own constituents and also to the general
administration ; and that the people may enjoy their full
rights under a presbyterial government, in the choice of their
pastor, as in civil matters they have their full rights in the
choice of their parliamentary representatives.*

Such is a fair outline of the arguments used on both sides
at the commencement of the main stem of the Independent
controversy. When Mr Goodwin replied, he admitted the
truth and applicability of the logical maxim, " What belongs
to the whole, as such, does not equally belong to each part;"
for the whole is a presbytery, but every member of it is not
a presbytery. Various attempts were made by him, and
also by others of the Independents, to escape from the force
of the argument, and to support their own proposition, but
without success. A slight change was given to the course of
debate by the reference which Mr Burroughs made to 1 Cor.
v. 4, in which church censure is spoken of as inflicted in the
presence of the church ; and this, he endeavoured to prove,
could not have taken place had it been the deed of a presbytery. A lengthened discussion arose on this point, in which
much minuteness of criticism and subtlety of argument were
displayed on both sides, till the topic was abandoned, as not
conclusive. During this debate, Mr Nye admitted that there
was a very close approximation between the two systems,
saying, that the Independents " held classical and synodical
meetings very useful and profitable, yea, possibly agreeable

* Lightfoot, pp. 132-134.

to the institution of Christ; but the question is this, Whether these meetings have the same power that *ecclesia prima*, or one single congregation, has?"* If he and his friends could have admitted one additional elementary principle, there might speedily have taken place a complete agreement,— namely, that the power of presbyteries, synods, and assemblies, is cumulative, not privative; that is, that it consists in the collected power of all the congregations of which it is composed, and in reality adds to the power of each, rather than takes away its proper power from any.

Becoming weary of this protracted discussion, several of the divines proposed that they should leave off these metaphysical disquisitions, and proceed to the consideration of those passages of Scripture which might be brought forward as direct proofs; but by the vote of the Assembly the Independents were allowed to continue bringing forward all their objections.† This we mention in order to show that the Assembly treated the Dissenting Brethren with extreme indulgence and toleration, and never attempted to run them down by the force of numbers and the authority of a vote, as they could have so easily done, and no doubt would have done, had they been the intolerant and overbearing bigots which they have been so generally and so unjustly called.

On the 14th of February the first committee reported, in confirmation of the proposition that many congregations may be under one presbytery, the following instances from Scripture:—1. The Church of Jerusalem; 2. The Church of Corinth; 3. Of Ephesus; 4. Of Antioch. Assuming that the existence of many congregations, and but one presbytery at Jerusalem, had been proved in a former debate, the other instances were proved by the following arguments: Corinth —from the time of Paul's abode there; from the different places of meeting, as Cenchrea, the house of Justus, and of Chloe, and the use of the word "churches," in the plural; and

---

* Lightfoot, p. 144. † Ibid., p. 147.

from the multitude of pastors,—1 Cor. i. 12, iv. 15: and that
these congregations were under one presbytery,—1 Cor. v.,
2 Cor. ii. Ephesus—from Paul's continuance there; the special
effect, and the reason of his stay given ; from the multitude
of pastors, termed "elders" and " overseers," or bishops; and
under one presbytery, which exercised jurisdiction,—Rev. ii.
1,2. Antioch—from a multitude of believers,—Acts xi. 21–26;
and from numbers of pastors and teachers,—Acts xiii. 1, xv.
35. The report concluded with this argument:—" Where
there were more believers than could meet in one place, and
more pastors than could be for one congregation, then there
were more congregations than one ; but it was so in these
Churches; and it was lawful for these to be under one presbyterial government: therefore it is so now."* These propositions were, as usual, laid aside till the objections already
stated by the Independents should have been fully debated.

The discussion respecting church censure and excommunication was again resumed, with reference to 1 Cor. v. ; and
Mr Goodwin argued that " discipline did not constitute a
church, nor is any note of a church." Selden doubted whether
the passage referred to had any thing to do with excommunication. This was answered very strongly by Mr Vines and
others ; and the Independents were requested to state clearly
their opinion on the subject. To this Goodwin answered,
" That the people cannot excommunicate; and that the people,
if need be, yet must have their vote." The inference was immediately drawn, that if the elders were outvoted the excommunication would be prevented, and thus the theory of the
Independents, of simple admonition or non-communion,
would alone be practicable. At last the Assembly decided,
that the argument of the Independents was not proved, and
did not conclude against the proposition.

The attention of the Assembly was next directed to Matt.
xviii. 15–17, by Mr Bridge, who endeavoured, in a very

* Lightfoot, p. 151.

elaborate argument, to prove that the church there mentioned was not a civil court, not a Jewish sanhedrim, not a presbytery or synod, not a national church, but a particular congregation only, and yet that it had the power of the highest censure, without appeal ; therefore every particular congregation, consisting of elders and brethren, should have entire and full power and jurisdiction within itself. Mr Marshall met the argument, point by point, in an answer equally full and elaborate ; assuming, as the basis of his reply, that the term " church " neither meant universal, national, nor provincial only, nor a single congregation only; but either, or all in turn, as the occasion might require. Mr Vines, Mr Gataker, Mr Goodwin, Mr Calamy, and others, took part in the debate, which was conducted with great skill and ability.

When the subject was resumed, another direction was given to the discussion by Selden, who produced a long and learned argument to prove that the passage of Scripture in question contained no authority for ecclesiastical jurisdiction. His object was, to guard against any conclusion of the Assembly, which might contradict the Erastian theory, and therefore he laboured to represent the whole as relating to the ordinary practice of the Jews in their common courts ; by whom, as he asserted, one sentence was excommunication, pronounced by the civil court. Herle and Marshall both attempted answers, but, says Lightfoot, " so as I confess gave me no satisfaction." Gillespie then came to the rescue, and, in a speech of astonishing power and acuteness, completely confuted Selden, even on his own chosen ground, and where his strength was greatest. He proved that the passage could not mean a civil court, because,—1. The nature of the offence and cause treated of is spiritual ; 2. The end is spiritual, for it is not restitution or satisfaction, but to gain the soul ; 3. The persons are spiritual, for Christ speaks to his apostles ; 4. The manner of proceeding is spiritual—all is done in the name of Christ ; 5. The censure is spiritual, for it is binding the soul; 6. Christ would not have sent his disciples for private spiritual injuries to civil courts; 7. The Church of the Jews had spiritual censures, and the expression, " Let him be as a heathen," imported prohibition from sacred things, for the heathen might not come into the temple; and the ceremonially unclean might not enter, much more the morally unclean.* This appears to have been the speech referred to by Wodrow, and of which there still exist many traditionary anecdotes, illustrative of the very extraordinary effect produced upon all that heard it. Selden himself is reported to have said, at its conclusion, " That young man, by this single speech, has swept away the labours of ten years of my life;"† and it is remarkable that Selden made no attempt to reply to Gillespie, though he answered some of the arguments used by others who spoke after him.

About the same time Mr Nye craftily endeavoured to excite the jealousy of the Parliament against presbyterial church government, but overreached himself. He had attempted to frame an argument against the power of presbyteries, on the assumption " That there is no power over another power, where there is no distinction in nature nor difference in operation;" but he was called to order, as not speaking to the question. On the following day, finding the Assembly full of the nobility and members of Parliament, he resumed the argument, persisting in his speech against the evident feeling of the House; and after he had attempted to show that the admission of a power over a power, in Church courts, would lead to an ecclesiastical government commensurate with that of the civil, he drew the inference, that it would be pernicious for a great commonwealth were so great a body to be permitted to grow up within it; in short, he attempted to alarm the Parliament, by the dread of that phantom of which so much has been heard, an *imperium in*

* Lightfoot, pp. 165-168.
† Wodrow's Analecta; M'Crie's Sketches, p. 300; Appendix.

imperio, or one government within another, as a formidable
and monstrous anomaly, dangerous to the peace of states and
kingdoms. This insidious attempt caused a great sensation ;
some proposed that he should be at once expelled, others
declared that his language was seditious ; and it was voted
that he had spoken against order—which was the highest
censure that the Assembly inflicted. Mr Marshall appealed to
all the parliamentary members present, whether the presbyterial government be more terrible to them than ten thousand or twenty thousand congregations, none in reference or
dependence to another. Warriston showed that the ecclesiastical and civil governments strengthened each other ; and
that one power over another in the Church no more tended
to produce confusion or injury than in civil matters, where
one court is subordinate to another, and yet but one State.
And Mr Whitelocke, M.P., followed a similar course of
illustration, and ended his remark by saying, " What a confusion it will prove to have congregations independent ! "
This debate, ending so very much the reverse of what Nye
expected, caused the Independents to abate their opposition
considerably ; and it was voted that their arguments had not
concluded against the proposition before the Assembly.*

The next subject was respecting the instance of the Church
at Jerusalem as proving that one presbytery was over many
congregations. Although considerable time was spent in
discussing this topic, it did not draw forth any great exhibition of learning or power, such as had been previously displayed. Almost the only idea of importance brought out in
this discussion was that suggested by Gillespie, namely, that
there could be no other principle whereby several congregations could be one church, but only government. Their
dwelling in one town made them a civil body, but not an
ecclesiastical ; their ecclesiastical union could not be but
in a presbytery, for they could not meet together in

* Lightfoot, pp. 168-170 ; Baillie, vol. ii. pp. 146, 147 ; Appendix, Nye.

one place : therefore it was only as forming a presbytery, and in respect to government, which is the function of a presbytery, that they could be one ecclesiastical body. Once more the Independents were staggered, and could not answer. Both Goodwin and Nye admitted that at least the keys of doctrine are in the hands of a synod or assembly ; and that as many men united have more moral power than one man, so many churches joining together must have more ecclesiastical power than one church. And in order to avail themselves of this renewed approximation, the Assembly, on the motion of Mr Henderson, proposed a committee for the purpose of attempting to obtain an accommodation with the Independents; and Messrs Seaman, Vines, Palmer, Marshall, Goodwin, Nye, Burroughs, and Bridge, together with the four Scottish divines, were named for the committee. On the 14th of March this committee reported that the Independents had agreed to the following propositions :— " 1. That there be a presbytery, or meeting of the elders of many neighbouring congregations, to consult upon such things as concern those congregations in matters ecclesiastical ; and such presbyteries are the ordinances of Christ, having his power and authority. 2. Such presbyteries have power, in cases that are to come before them, to declare and determine doctrinally what is agreeable to God's Word ; 'and this judgment of theirs is to be received with reverence and obligation, as Christ's ordinance. 3. They have power 'to require the elders of those congregations to give an account of any thing scandalous in doctrine or practice."* The Assembly agreed to the continuance of the committee, and granted them liberty to take into consideration any thing that might tend to accommodation, and to report when convenient. Thus, again, it appears that the Assembly was the very reverse of intolerant and overbearing.

Another report was brought forward from this committee

* Lightfoot, pp. 214, 215.

about a week afterwards, containing two additional propositions, forming five in all, as follow:—" 4. The churches
and elderships being offended, let them examine, admonish,
and, in case of obstinacy, declare them either disturbers of
the peace, or subverters of the faith, or otherwise, as the nature and degree of the offence shall require. 5. In case that
the particular church or eldership shall refuse to reform that
scandalous doctrine or practice, then that meeting of elders,
which is assembled from several churches and congregations,
shall acquaint their several congregations respectively, and
withdraw from them, and deny Church communion and fellowship with them."* The account given by Baillie, though
less minute, and not using the very language of the committee, expresses his view of the result even more strongly:
" We have agreed on five or six propositions, hoping, by
God's grace, to agree in more. They yield, that a presbytery, even as we take it, is an ordinance of God, which hath
power and authority from Christ to call the ministers and
elders, or any in their bounds, before them, to account for
any offence in life or doctrine, to try and examine the cause,
—to admonish and rebuke, and if they be obstinate, to declare them as heathens and publicans, and give them over to
the punishment of the magistrates; also doctrinally, to declare
the mind of God in all questions of religion, with such authority as obliges to receive their just sentences; and that they
will be members of such fixed presbyteries, keep the meetings, preach as it comes to their turn, and join in the discipline
after doctrine."† Surely but very little more was necessary
to have produced a complete agreement between the Presbyterians and the Independents, since the latter party had thus
assented to all that was essential to Presbyterian Church
government: but unhappily they seemed to dread, that by
uniting with the Presbyterians, they should lose their influence among the Sectaries, and in the army; and Nye in

* Lightfoot, p. 229.　　　　　† Baillie, vol. ii. p. 148.

particular was too deeply engaged in the political intrigues of Vane and Cromwell to be willing to relinquish that influence which rendered him a person of importance.*

On the 13th of March the discussion terminated in the affirmation of the propositions respecting Church government, so far as regarded the general statement, and the proofs from the instances of Jerusalem and Corinth, after having occupied the attention of the Assembly for thirty days passed in earnest and strenuous debate, during which all the arguments which profound learning and acute ingenuity could devise were brought forward and discussed with equal minuteness and ability. The subject was then referred to the committee, that all the points which had been decided might be systematically arranged, partly to be ready to be reported to the Parliament, and partly for the satisfaction of the Assembly itself, and for the sake of order. This report was produced on the 10th of April, the Assembly having been occupied in the interim with the subject of ordination, as already related. The propositions reported were the three following :—" 1. The Scripture doth hold out a presbytery in a church; 2. A presbytery consisteth of ministers of the Word, and such other public officers as are agreeable to and warranted by the Word of God, to be Church governors, to join with the ministers in the government of the Church; 3. The Scripture holds forth that many congregations may be under one presbyterial government. Proved by the instance of the Church at Jerusalem." The instance of the Church at Corinth was not given, as it had been adduced chiefly for the purpose of proving the power of Church censures. Though the Independents had assented to the essence of these propositions in the committee for accommodation, yet they vehemently opposed the sending of them to the Parliament for ratification; and the Assembly, on the motion of Mr Marshall, again consented to lay them aside for a time.†

* Appendix, Nye. † Lightfoot, p. 250.

The Assembly resumed the subject on the 16th of April, to prove Presbyterial government from the instance of the Church of Ephesus ; and after some debate, this instance was sustained as a proof of the main proposition. Another topic followed, which cost some discussion, namely, that so many visible saints as dwelt in one city were but one Church in regard of Church government. On this point, Rutherford was anxious to guard against any infringement of the due power in censure and government in particular congregations ; and in this he was supported by Henderson. This guard was necessary, in consequence of extreme views held by some English Presbyterian divines, who, in order, apparently, to keep as far as possible remote from the Independent system, opposed any power of censure or government in congregations, and denied the right or propriety of congregational elderships.* This is mentioned chiefly for the purpose of corroborating an idea which has been repeatedly suggested,— that instead of the Scottish commissioners being the direct instigators of the Westminster Assembly to aim at a rigid and unaccommodating form of Church government essentially intolerant and tyrannical, the very reverse is the truth ; for while they refused all compromise of fundamental principles, they were exceedingly desirous to remove every thing in minor matters to which their brethren could not readily assent, or from which they dreaded an interference with their own conscientious scruples.

Some difficulty was encountered in stating how Christians should be most conveniently and regularly formed into distinct congregations, so as best to obtain the benefit of pastoral instruction and superintendence. This the Assembly thought should be by the bounds of their dwellings,—that is, by the parochial system ; but the Independents opposed it, because it was contrary to their mode of " gathering churches," as it was termed. The proposition was however affirmed.

* Lightfoot, pp. 255, 256; Baillie, vol. ii. p. 177.

O

The subject of ruling elders was again resumed, on the 3d of May, after having been laid aside for a considerable time. At first it was proposed that there should be at least one ruling elder in every congregation ; but this was strenuously opposed by the Scottish commissioners, as in reality not forming a congregational eldership. It was at length decided, that in every congregation there should be, besides the minister, others to assist him in ruling, as elders; and some to take care for the poor, as deacons ; the number of each to be proportioned to the congregation.

Another topic then called forth a strenuous debate of five days' duration, namely, " That no single congregation, which may conveniently join together in an association, may assume unto itself all and sole power of ordination." Against this proposition the Independents mustered all their adherents, and put forth their whole strength, because it condemned the central principle of their system. When it came to the vote, "it was affirmed by twenty-seven, and denied by nineteen; and this business," adds Lightfoot, " had been managed with the most heat and confusion of any thing that had happened among us."* When the reasons to prove the general proposition were brought forward, another keen struggle took place, the first reason being carried by a majority of four votes, the second by a majority of five. †

The committee appointed to frame a summary of Church government, produced, instead of a report, a proposition to be debated, to the following effect :—" Concerning the ruling officers of particular congregations, they have power,—1. Authoritatively to call before them scandalous or suspected persons ; 2. To admonish or rebuke authoritatively; 3. To keep from the sacrament authoritatively ; 4. To excommunicate." The first topic was easily admitted, with a slight change on its terms ; as was also the second ; but the third led to a protracted and very learned debate, having been re-

* Lightfoot, p. 262.   † Ibid., p. 267.

cast into this form : " Authoritative suspension from the Lord's table of a person not yet cast out of the church, is agreeable to the Scripture."* This proposition was opposed by Coleman, Herle, Case, and particularly by Lightfoot, who attempted to prove his view by the instance of Judas; and this led to a discussion on that point, in which scarcely any agreed with Lightfoot's opinion. The chief advocates of suspending scandalous persons were Young, Calamy, Gillespie, Rutherford, Reynolds, Burgess, and Dr Hoyle. The Independents did not enter warmly into the discussion ; and Goodwin, after endeavouring to represent it as differing little from admonition, concluded by saying, that his judgment fell in with the proposition, only he liked not the authoritative doing of it. It was at length decided in the affirmative, none voting against it but Lightfoot. But though the proposition had thus obtained the sanction of the Assembly, it was afterwards opposed by the Parliament ; as, indeed, might have been expected, from the lax notions entertained generally by men of the world on all such subjects.

The subject of excommunication was not again resumed till the 16th of October, when two passages of Scripture were brought forward to prove it, namely, 1 Cor. v., and Matt. xviii. 17, 18. Both were admitted, and the proposition was further supported by this argument : " They that have authority to judge of and admit to the sacrament such as are to receive it, have authority to keep back such as shall be found unworthy." Against this Lightfoot alone voted in the negative ; and that chiefly because he was not convinced that there is suspension or excommunication, as a power belonging to the Church,—an opinion which sprung from his Erastianism. Thus terminated the debates on that much contested point, on the 25th of October, so far as the Assembly was concerned : the opinions of the Parliament will fall under our observation when we come to the Erastian controversy.

* Lightfoot, p. 268.

Affairs had now attained so much maturity that a crisis had become inevitable; for every point having been very fully debated between the Presbyterians and the Independents, they must either unite, or adopt some new course which should render union impossible. The Presbyterians had done every thing in their power to meet the scruples of the Dissenting Brethren, both by allowing them to bring forward every objection which they could devise, and to debate till all were thoroughly exhausted, and also by appointing a committee of their own number to confer with them, in the hope of avoiding a final disruption. But when the Dissenting Brethren could not persuade the Assembly to adopt their views in preference to its own, they renewed their intrigues with the Independents in the army, by whose influence they knew they would be supported. The state of political affairs was favourable to their schemes. Soon after the battle of Marston, in which the king's army sustained such a severe defeat, proposals were made for a treaty of peace, of which the Presbyterians in the Parliament were cordially desirous, if it could be obtained on terms sufficient to secure the liberties of the kingdom. But this was by no means what the Independents in both Parliament and army desired, consequently the scene of contest was removed from the tented field to the legislative assemblies; and this brought Oliver Cromwell to the House of Commons. This deep-minded and far-foreseeing man perceived clearly that were a peace concluded, and Church government established, his ambitious prospects must be completely destroyed; and with his usual sagacity, anticipating the unyielding obstinacy of the king, which would render any satisfactory pacific arrangement impossible, he set himself chiefly to prevent the settlement of the Church by means of a Presbyterian establishment. "This day" (13th September), says Baillie, "Cromwell has obtained an order of the House of Commons to refer to the committee of both kingdoms the accommodation or toleration of the Independents,—a high and unexpected order." In another passage, referring to the same event, Baillie adds, that " this was done without the least advertisement to any of us or of the Assembly." " This has much affected us. These men have retarded the Assembly these long twelve months. This is the fruit of their disservice, to obtain really an act of Parliament for their toleration, before we have got any thing for Presbytery either in Assembly or Parliament." *

The order from the House of Commons was produced in the Assembly on the 16th of September, in the following terms :—" That the committee of Lords and Commons appointed to treat with the commissioners of Scotland, and the committee of the Assembly, do take into consideration the differences of the opinions of the members of the Assembly in point of Church government, and to endeavour an union, if it be possible. And in case that cannot be done, to endeavour the finding out some way how far tender consciences, who cannot in all things submit to the same rule which shall be established, may be borne with according to the Word, and as may stand with the public peace ; that so the proceedings of the Assembly may not be so much retarded." † In compliance with this order, the committee met on the 20th of September, and appointed a sub-committee, consisting of Dr Temple, Messrs Marshall, Herle, Vines, Goodwin, and Nye, to consider of the differences of opinion in the Assembly, in point of Church government, and to report to the Grand Committee. These divines accordingly formed what was called the sub-committee of agreements ; and prepared several propositions concerning the government of particular congregations, ordination, &c., which they laid before the Grand Committee on the 11th of October. Having some additional propositions to frame respecting the jurisdiction of Presbyteries and Synods, they were adjourned, and appointed to meet again on the 15th of October, and then to produce a

* Baillie, vol. ii. pp. 226, 230.　　† Papers for Accommodation, p. 1.

completed report. When they met on the day appointed, their additional propositions were read; but when it was proposed to take them into consideration, it was objected, that it was not consistent with strict propriety to discuss objections against a proposed rule of Church government till that rule itself should have been completed by the Assembly and the Houses of Parliament. The proceedings of this Committee of Accommodation were therefore suspended by the House of Commons till their further pleasure, no real progress towards an agreement having been made.

Without relating minutely the proceedings of this committee, it may be enough to state, that in what was termed the preface of their report, they expressed their confidence that they would jointly agree in one Confession of Faith, and in one Directory of Public Worship, their only difference being in points of Church government. They framed nine propositions respecting the power of individual congregations, in six of which they were all agreed, with a slight and unimportant explanation. The points of the other three in which the Independents could not quite agree with the Presbyterians, respected the power of congregations to excommunicate members, or ordain elders by the sole authority of the people, seeking merely the *advice* of neighbouring ministers, but not subject to the control of a presbytery; and the parochial system, which the Independents opposed, as contrary to their theory of gathering churches out of other churches. To this system of the Independents the Presbyterians would not consent, as giving countenance to schism, and perpetuating strife and jealousy among both ministers and people. With regard to the jurisdiction of Presbyteries and Synods, the Independents could consent to nothing more than the advice of neighbouring ministers, to be respected, but not authoritative further than admonition; and in case of the offending congregation not submitting, withdrawing from it, and denying Church communion and fellowship, but without any actual power within the range of any particular congregation over any offending member, though the congregation itself might be admonished for not putting forth its own power to reform its own members. It is plain that the essential difference between the two parties remained undiminished; the Independents continued to maintain the sole power of congregations to exercise Church government, and to demand the privilege of gathering churches, or congregations, out of the congregations of the Presbyterians, with whom, nevertheless, they could continue to hold occasional communion. These points the Presbyterians regarded as utterly subversive of their whole system; and though they would have tolerated in practice, they could not consent to give it an avowed and legal sanction, regarding it as nationally impolitic, in a religious point of view sinful, and with regard to the Covenant, a violation of their oath, being virtually to sanction and legalize schism. Besides, they perceived clearly that this avowed and legal sanction to the Independent system would of necessity involve an equal permission to the wildest and most immoral and blasphemous Sectarians to frame separate congregations, and collect adherents, by every artifice, and to the ruin of both Church and kingdom.

Although no accommodation resulted from the deliberations of this committee, there is every reason to think that Cromwell and Nye obtained the end they had in view when it was proposed. The progress of both Parliament and Assembly towards the ratification of the propositions respecting Church government, was suspended, and time was obtained for adopting another course. Accordingly, on the 7th of November, the Independents began to talk of giving in to the Assembly their reasons of dissent from the Assembly's propositions respecting Church government. On the 14th of November these reasons were produced, and on the following day were read, and a committee of twenty appointed to take them into consideration. The most prominent persons of that committee were, Drs Temple and Hoyle, Messrs Marshall, Tuckney, Calamy, Palmer, Vines, Seaman, and Lightfoot; and their answers to the reasons of dissent were read in the Assembly on the 17th day of December, and continued on the following days till they had been fully heard, previous to their being transmitted to Parliament.

Thus terminated the deliberations of the Westminster Assembly, so far as regarded the proceedings of the year 1644. But as these proceedings had chiefly involved the controversy between the Presbyterians and the Independents; and as the points in which they differed had been all thoroughly debated in the Assembly in the course of the year 1644, and the contest had now assumed a literary character, in consequence of the production of written reasons of dissent, and written answers to those reasons, it seems expedient to complete our brief outline of this important controversy, though touching a little upon the events of subsequent years, before directing our attention to the Erastian controversy.

The Dissenting Brethren entered their dissent with reasons in writing, to be presented to the Honourable Houses by the Assembly, to the three following propositions, as the only points in which there existed direct and essential differences between them and the Presbyterians, namely,—" 1. *To the third proposition concerning presbyterial government*; 2. *To the propositions concerning subordination of assemblies*; 3. *To the proposition concerning the power of ordination, whether in a particular congregation, though it may associate with others.*"

The third proposition concerning Presbyterial Church government was as follows :—" The Scripture doth hold forth that many congregations may be under one presbyterial government. This is proved by instances : 1. Of the Church of Jerusalem, which consisted of more congregations than one, and all those congregations were under one presbyterial government; 2. Of the Church of Ephesus, in which there were more congregations than one, and where there were many elders over those congregations as one flock, though those many congregations were one Church, and under one presbyterial government." As this proposition, together with its subordinate details, and the Scripture texts on which the whole is founded, are stated fully in the Confession of Faith, and Directory, it cannot be necessary to occupy space by their insertion.

The Dissenting Brethren gave in reasons against the proposition itself, and also against the instances by which it was proved. Their argument against the proposition is in the following terms:—" If many congregations having all elders already *affixed* respectively unto them, may be under a presbyterial government, then all those elders must sustain a *special* relation of elders to all the people of those congregations as one Church, and to every one as a member thereof; but for a company of such elders already affixed to sustain such a relation, carries with it so great and manifold incongruities and inconsistencies with what the Scriptures speak of elders in their relation to a church committed to them, and likewise with the principles of the Reformed Churches themselves, as cannot be admitted: and therefore such a government may not be." The proposition thus stated is explained, defended, and enforced, in a treatise of forty pages, by the Dissenting Brethren, whose names, now increased to seven, are subscribed to it, namely, Thomas Goodwin, Philip Nye, Jeremiah Burroughs, Sidrach Simpson, William Bridge, William Greenhill, William Carter. It does not appear necessary to give any summary of the arguments brought forward by these brethren against the Assembly, or in illustration of their own negative proposition; because, from the proposition itself, every reader will see that their major proposition rests on an assumption which itself required to be both explained and proved; and that their minor proposition was merely a congeries of supposed incongruities and inconsistencies, which they asserted would follow, but which could not be proved to be necessary consequences, and had not followed in churches already under Presbyterian government.

The answer of the Assembly extended to eighty pages, which, in one point of view, was much more than enough; but aware that their task was not only to meet the argument of the Dissenting Brethren, but also to produce a defence of Presbyterian Church government, such as might be laid before the public, they entered fully into the subject, both meeting objections, and restating their own direct arguments. In this manner they produced an exceeding able treatise, exhibiting clearly and amply the grounds of Scripture and reason on which the Presbyterian Church government, in their opinion, rested; and certainly the Dissenting Brethren themselves, must have felt that they were more than answered, even allowing for their natural predilection for their own system. It is impossible to condense this able defence of Presbyterian Church government, so as to present it within the limits of the present work. This only can we state, that the Assembly's answer begins by proving the fallacy, and the pernicious consequences of that assumption on which the main argument of their opponents was based. They then showed that the argument of Independents was really directed against a proposition which the Assembly never held, and therefore that it was beside the question altogether. And then, returning to the subject as stated by the Dissenting Brethren, and, for the sake of argument, allowing it to be regarded as fairly put, they proceeded to meet and refute it point by point, in a very masterly manner, uniting extensive learning, acuteness of distinction, logical precision of thought, clear and energetic language, and a profound knowledge of Scripture, and veneration of its sacred truths, as the sole rule of guide in all matters of a religious nature.

The *second* subject against which the Independents entered their dissent with reasons was, The propositions concerning the subordination of assemblies. These propositions were three in number, but, as their dissent was directed chiefly against the third, the statement of it may be enough : "It is lawful and agreeable to the Word of God, that there be a subordination of congregational, classical, provincial, and national assemblies; that so appeals be made from the inferior to the superior respectively. Proved from Matthew xviii., which, holding forth the subordination of an offending brother to a particular church, it doth also, by a parity of reason, hold forth the subordination of a congregation to superior assemblies." The Dissenting Brethren introduce their argument in the following manner :—"Although we judge synods to be of great use, for the finding out and declaring of truth in difficult cases, and encouragement to walk in the truth; for the healing offences, and to give advice unto the magistrate in matters of religion; and although we give great honour and conscientious respect unto their determinations; yet seeing the proposition holds forth, not only an occasional, but a *standing* use of them, and that in subordination of one unto another, as juridical, ecclesiastical courts, and this in all cases, we humbly present these reasons against it :—1. All such subordinations of courts, having greater and lesser degrees of power, to which, in their order, causes are to be brought, must have the greatest and most express warrant and designment for them in the Word. Whence it is argued thus : Those courts that must have the most express warrant and designment for them in the Word, and have not, their power is to be suspected, and not erected in the Church of God; but these ought to have so, and have not : therefore their power is to be suspected, and not erected in the Church of God. 2. If there be such a subordination of synods in the Church of Christ, then there is no independency but in an œcumenical council. 3. That Church power which cannot show a constant divine rule for its variation, and subordination, and ultimate independency, is not of God, and so may not be ; but this variation of Church power into these subordinations, cannot show any such steady and constant rule for these things : therefore it may not be. 4. The government which necessarily produceth representations of spiritual power out of other representations, with a derived power therefrom, there is no warrant for ; but these subordinations of synods, provincial, national, œcumenical, for the government of the Church do so : therefore for them there is no warrant." To these they added some arguments against the instances from Acts xv., and Matt. xviii., which had been adduced by the Assembly.

In the reasonings of the Dissenting Brethren, it is somewhat curious to observe that they made use of both the Erastian and the Episcopalian arguments, as these seemed to serve their purpose ; as, for instance, the Erastian, " Why may not all other churches be governed as well as that of Geneva, without appeals, if the magistrate oversees them, and keeps each to their duties ? " * The Episcopalian argument is not so succinctly stated ; but it is an attempt to turn against the Presbyterians the argument used by them against the Episcopalians, of the want of an express institution of the subordination of office-bearers in the Church. And, in the course of their argument and illustrations, they made so many concessions, that it is rather difficult to conceive on what their final opposition rested. As, for instance, they admitted " that synods are an ordinance of God upon all occasions of difficulty ; that all the churches of a province may call a single congregation to account ; that they may examine and admonish, and, in case of obstinacy, may declare them to be subverters of the faith ; that they have authority to determine in controversies of faith ; that they may deny Church communion to an offending and obstinate congregation, and that this sentence of non-communion may be enforced by the authority of the civil magistrate ; and that they may call before them any person within their bounds, concerned in

* Reasons of the Dissenting Brethren, p. 124.

the ecclesiastical business before them, and may hear and determine such causes as orderly come before them."* Having made so many and such important concessions, the Independents might, with very little difficulty, have assented fully to the Assembly's propositions ; and probably would have done so, but for the influence of intriguing politicians, who dreaded nothing so much as an early and harmonious adjustment of all differences in the Assembly.

The answer of the Assembly began by laying open the essential point of difference, which consisted, not in a denial of synods, but of the standing use of them, and their subordination to one another, not the subordination of congregations to them. They then showed that the main argument of the Independents was not directed against the proposition of the Assembly, but against a peculiar construction of it by themselves, and that, too, a construction disclaimed by the Assembly. Then, as in their previous answer, they proceed to consider the reasonings of their opponents, sometimes proving that these are self-destructive, and confute their own theory, sometimes pointing out their fallacious character, and sometimes meeting them by a distinct and irresistible refutation of a strictly logical kind. In one instance, the mode of the Dissenting Brethren's argument is very strongly urged against themselves ; and since they demand " the greatest and most express warrant for the subordination of synods," they are asked to prove their own system, viz., the gathering of churches out of churches, the ordination and deposition of ministers by the people alone, the passing by one single congregation of the sentence of non-communion against all the churches in a province or a kingdom, which would surely require a warrant as great and express, or should teach them somewhat to abate in their demand.† In short, it is perfectly clear, in our apprehension, that both in point of conformity to the language and arrangements of Scripture, and

* Reasons and Answers, p. 138.   † Ibid., p. 147.

in point of distinctness and strength of logical reasoning, the answer of the Assembly is abundantly conclusive.

The *third* subject against which the Independents entered reasons of dissent in writing was, the proposition concerning the power of ordination. That proposition was in the following terms :—" It is very requisite, that no single congregation that can conveniently associate, do assume to itself all and sole power in ordination." Against this they offered these reasons : " Where there is a sufficient presbytery, all and sole power in ordination may be assumed, though association may be had ; but there may be a sufficient presbytery in a particular congregation : therefore a particular congregation may assume all and sole power in ordination. That which two apostles, being joined together, might do in a particular congregation, that ordinary elders may do in a particular congregation ; but Paul and Barnabas ordained elders in particular congregations, though they might associate : therefore ordinary elders may ordain in particular congregations." * The expansion of this argument served only to dilute it the more, and to make its fallacy apparent.

In their answer, the Assembly Divines seem almost to have been ashamed to analyze and expose the weak sophistry of the Dissenting Brethren's argument. " We expected," say they, " from our brethren, in a search for truth, not a contest for victory, arguments to prove, that every single congregation have the whole power of ordination within themselves, and that none but themselves may ordain for them ; but this they are pleased to decline." They then prove that the argument is illogical and vicious, containing more in the conclusion than in the premises, and yet not concluding against the proposition in debate ; and, entering into a more minute examination of it, they not merely refute it, but by availing themselves of the concessions made by the Independents in the course of their own illustrations, they completely over-

* Reasons of Dissent, pp. 190, 191.

throw the whole Congregational theory. For the Independents had admitted that association of congregations neither adds to nor diminishes the power of a presbytery, but is by way of accumulation, not privation; and this argument is itself an answer to all their own accusations against the Presbyterian system of Church government, on the ground of its depriving congregations of their due power, since the association of congregations, like that of elders, is by way of accumulation, not privation. It will be observed also, that there is in the argument of the Independents, a deceptive use of the word presbytery, which they employed to mean the elders of a particular congregation, whereas the proper sense of the term implies the collected ministers and elders of several contiguous congregations. The answer of such arguments was an easy task, and was very successfully accomplished.

These Reasons of Dissent, and the Answers by the Assembly, occupied the attention of that venerable body during the conclusion of the year 1644, and the early part of the year 1645; and when fully completed, both the reasons and the answers were submitted to the consideration of the Parliament. After remaining in possession of the Parliament for a considerable time, and when the discussions of the Assembly had terminated, an order was issued by the House of Lords, on the 24th of January 1648 (or 1647, according to their style), that these reasons and answers should be printed from the papers in the hands of Adoniram Byfield, one of the Assembly's scribes, after having been inspected by Messrs Goodwin and Whittaker, to secure their genuineness and authenticity; and they were published in the same year, under the title of " The Reasons presented by the Dissenting Brethren against certain Propositions concerning Presbyterial Government; together with the Answers of the Assembly of Divines to those Reasons of Dissent." In the year 1652, the same publication received a new title-page, and was called " The Grand Debate concerning Presbytery and Independency, by the Assembly of Divines convened at Westminster by authority of Parliament." This a careful examination of several copies of both dates and titles enables me to state with perfect certainty, not only the pages, but the verbal and literal errors being everywhere identical; and this is here mentioned in order to put it in the power of any person who may possess the volume to verify the preceding account, whether as here given, or as referred to by other authors under the title of "The Grand Debate."

About the time when these written discussions began to be interchanged, there was one remaining topic unsettled, on which some difference of opinion was entertained. The Assembly had unanimously agreed, that " excommunication is an ordinance of Christ;" but some difference of opinion existed respecting the body to which properly the power of excommunication belonged. A small committee was appointed for the purpose of attempting an accommodation between the Presbyterians and the Independents on this point; and on the 10th of January 1645, this committee gave in a report to which all assented, and it received the unanimous and glad sanction of the Assembly. Four days afterwards, the Independents requested that the whole directory of excommunication might be referred to a similar committee of accommodation; and this, too, the Assembly granted, in the hope of at last obtaining an amicable and harmonious arrangement. Yet, when the report of that committee had been produced, assented to by the Assembly, and voted to be transmitted to the Houses of Parliament, the Independents entered their dissent from it, as an accommodation " in any other sense than that each might interpret and use it according to their own peculiar views." * Against this procedure the Assembly complained, regarding it as a deceptive evasion, much more fitted to perpetuate disagreement than to promote accommodation, and lead to union.

* Answer to a Copy of a Remonstrance, p. 16.

The Assembly further complained, that the Dissenting Brethren never gave any definite statement of what they really wished, but merely opposed almost every proposition respecting Church government, and brought forward objections. At length one of the Independents, on the 11th of February 1645, said that they were willing to be formed into a committee to frame and report their judgment respecting the best model of Church government. This the Assembly gladly hailed, declaring that there was nothing which they more earnestly desired than to know the full mind and wish of the Dissenting Brethren. Immediately the Independents recoiled from their proposal, and declined being made a committee for that purpose. On the 21st of March they were urged to enter upon the task, and one of them read a paper containing seven propositions, but refused to give it to the scribe, would not reproduce it, and finally declined the discussion. Again, on the 4th of April, the Assembly resumed the suggestion, and notwithstanding the opposition of the Independents, resolved, " That the brethren of this Assembly that had formerly entered their dissent to the propositions about Presbyterial government, shall be a committee to bring in the whole frame of their judgment concerning Church government in a body, with their grounds and reasons." * Being thus in a manner constrained to prepare their own desired model, they first requested that it might be brought forward and debated part by part, as the subject of Presbyterial government had been. To this the Assembly objected, both because their own course of procedure had been that of necessity, not choice, and not, in their opinion, the best mode, and because there were not many points against which the Independents had dissented, so that the whole might most easily and conveniently be brought forward at once. The Independents then obtained permission to refrain from attending the ordinary committees, that they might have sufficient leisure

* Answer to a Copy of a Remonstrance, p. 19; Baillie, vol. iii. pp. 266, 267.

P

to prepare their own model of Church government. Long
and anxiously did the Assembly look for the promised model,
but in vain. Wearied at last with this protracted delay, on
the 22d of September they urged the Independents to make
all convenient speed, and requested them to give in a report
of what they had done within a fortnight if possible.

One fortnight passed, and no report was produced; another
ran its round, and still no report appeared. But, on the 22d
of October 1645, instead of the long expected model of Church
government, the Independents laid before the Assembly what
they termed a Remonstrance, stating the reasons why they
declined to bring forward their model of Church government.
This was soon afterwards published, without the authority of
either Assembly or Parliament, under the title of " A Copy
of a Remonstrance." The Assembly immediately prepared
an answer to this remonstrance ; and having laid it before the
Houses of Parliament, it was, after some delay, directed to
be printed, by an order of the House of Lords, bearing date
24th February 1646, (or, according to the parliamentary year,
1645.)* The answer of the Assembly is expressed in somewhat sharper terms than any of their preceding papers; which
is not surprising, considering the disingenuous and evasive
conduct of the Independent party; and it certainly exposes
their duplicity in a manner altogether unanswerable. The
conclusion of this paper is peculiarly significant: " Upon
which considerations we think, not that the brethren have
any cause to decline the bringing in of their model at this
time, but that they have some other cause than what they
pretend to, and that something lies behind the curtain which
doth not yet appear : possibly not any one of them is yet at
a point in his own judgment, nor resolved where to fix, they
having professed to keep as a reserve, liberty to alter and re-
tract; which, if their model were given in, they could not so
fairly and honourably do : or possibly they are not all fixed

* Baillie, vol. iii. p. 344.

in one and the same point : possibly they cannot agree among themselves, for it is easier to agree in dissenting than in affirming ; or possibly if they seven can agree, yet some other of their brethren in the city, to whom it may be the model was communicated, did not like it; or if so, yet possibly the brethren might foresee, that if this model should be published, there are some who at present are a strength to them, and expect shelter from them, who may disgust it: or, at least, they are resolved to wait a further opportunity to improve what they have prepared; it may be when the Assembly is dissolved, and so not in a capacity to answer them ; or when the Presbyterian government begins to be set up, when they promise to themselves there will be discontent among the people, and look upon that, it may be, as the most advantageous time of putting pen to paper. But whatever the cause be, we commit our cause to the Lord, who loves truth and simplicity, and will, we doubt not, discover it in due time."*

Almost simultaneous with the production of these papers, one effort more, a last effort, was made to prevent, if possible, a final disagreement between the Presbyterians and the Independents. The Committee of Accommodation, which had been in abeyance for nearly a year, was revived by an order of both Houses of Parliament, dated 6th November 1645. This committee met on the 17th of the same month, and resumed their now well-nigh hopeless task, to find some ground on which both parties could harmoniously unite. Several meetings were held, and several papers framed by each party, but no approximation towards union appeared, both retaining their peculiar views, with little, if any modification. The last meeting took place on the 9th of March 1646, when very long and elaborate answers were produced by the members of Assembly to the opinions, reasonings, and requests of the Dissenting Brethren. After that the committee met no more,

* Answer to a Copy of a Remonstrance, p. 24.

the controversy, so far as regarded debate and writing, terminated without any agreement; and the matter became a conflict of principle against intrigue and power. It is impossible to review this protracted controversy between the Presbyterians and the Independents without the deepest regret. From the very beginning it greatly hampered the proceedings of the Assembly, gave rise to excessively protracted discussions on almost every subject connected with Church government and discipline, exposed the unsettled affairs of both Church and State to all the perils of delay, and gave time to every hostile element to acquire matured strength, and every dangerous machination to obtain complete development. Yet the differences between the two contending parties do not appear to have been necessarily irreconcilable, had it not been for the perverting power of political influence. In point of doctrinal views of sacred truth and modes of public worship there existed no material disagreement between the Presbyterians and the Independents. In matters of discipline, the difference of opinion became narrowed to a single point, and even that point was at one time removed in the Committee of Accommodation, though it was again partially replaced by the Dissenting Brethren. The three propositions against which they gave in reasons of dissent, namely, concerning presbyterial government, the subordination of assemblies, and the power of ordination, were all capable of being reduced to one point also,—and that a point so minute as almost to disappear under discussion, and to require considerable dexterity in its maintainers to discover, and again bring it into prominent manifestation. For the admissions of the Independents at different times extended so far as to leave nothing in dispute, except the single link connecting their system with that of the Brownists, and the other Sectarians of the period,—the right of a congregation, or church, to use their own term, however few in regard to numbers, and even though devoid of a pastor and elders, to possess and to exercise all and sole power of ecclesiastical jurisdiction within itself, without regard to any and every other church in the world, and accountable to none for its procedure, be that what it might.

How the Independents contrived to reconcile this central principle with their repeated concessions respecting the authority of synods, as an ordinance of God, the sentences of which might be enforced by the civil magistrate, it is somewhat difficult to imagine. Nor did they, in point of practice, act according to this principle, or theory; for in the churches of New England, which were all constructed according to the Independent system, they did not hesitate to coerce and restrain, with great rigour and severity, those who presumed to differ from them in religious matters,—inflicting the sentences of imprisonment, banishment, and even perpetual slavery.* Yet had they acted according to their own theory, they ought to have passed no other sentence than that of non-communion, each little church of half a dozen having sole power in itself, and being independent of every other. But in New England, where their system had at first freedom to put forth its native tendencies, it was found to be absolutely incompatible with the peace and good order of society; and therefore, the very necessity and duty of self-preservation constrained the Independents of that country to make such alterations in their system as might save them from total disorganization. There is reason to believe, that the consciousness of these inherent defects in their system operated very powerfully in causing the Dissenting Brethren to make the numerous and important concessions which have been stated; and that they would have finally embraced the Presbyterian form of Church government, but for the existence of one or two most unfortunate and injurious preventing causes. They had become involved in the political movements of the period, chiefly through the intriguing character of Nye,

* Baillie, vol. ii. p. 183.

and the influence of Cromwell and Sir Harry Vane ; and the position which they occupied in the Assembly rendered them in a manner the representatives of the almost innumerable swarms of Sectarians with which the kingdom was rife.

Both of these causes operated so steadily in the same direction that they may be viewed as one, and the effect may be thereby the more clearly traced. The civil war between the King and the Parliament had not continued long till it began to become apparent that it would most probably end in a revolution, and a change of the form of civil government. Whether this had been foreseen from the first by Cromwell, and his own conduct guided by that anticipation, cannot be certainly known ; but this, at least, may be safely said, that such an idea would enable us to give a complete explanation of all the proceedings of that otherwise most mysterious man. Let it, then, be assumed that such was his aim and expectation. Nothing could have been more fatal to this prospect than an early and amicable settlement of a pure, free, and comprehensive system of Church government, whether that had been a modified Episcopacy on Ussher's model, or a Presbyterian form, similar to that of Scotland. In either case the life and sovereignty of the king would have been preserved, even in spite of his own characteristic obstinacy, and peace would have been restored to the country without an absolute revolution. It was therefore Cromwell's policy to prevent, by every possible means, an early settlement of the great religious questions by which the heart of the community was so deeply and powerfully stirred. For this purpose he maintained a secret but a close intercourse with Nye, and induced him and the other Dissenting Brethren to exert themselves to the utmost in retarding the progress of the Assembly. When that could no longer be accomplished by mere debate, then he devised the Committee of Accommodation, by means of which new methods of delay were employed. In the meantime, he availed himself of the rapid increase of Sectarians, encouraged their enthusiastic feelings, new-modelled the army, placing them in its ranks and himself at its head; then, having swept the loose and disorderly, though daring, cavaliers of Charles from the field, he was able to dissolve the Parliament, break up the Assembly, assume an absolute dictatorship in all matters, civil and religious, and become the chief of a republic or commonwealth.

Such, certainly, was the issue; and it will not be denied that the outline we have traced shows how all these events combined to lead as directly to the result as if they had been all preconcerted and prearranged in the powerful mind of one bold and far-forecasting man. It was easy for such a man to overreach the simple-minded, and to employ the crafty, for the promotion of his own purposes, leading them all the while to imagine that they could not possibly better secure the triumph of their peculiar designs; and it may be fairly supposed that Cromwell did deceive the Independent divines, and make use of them for the accomplishment of an object which they had never contemplated, and from the very thought of which they would have instantaneously recoiled. Yet so deeply was Nye implicated in the political intrigues of Cromwell, that, after the Restoration, it was debated for several hours in council, whether he should be excepted from the act of indemnity, and expiate his conduct by the forfeit of his life.* But whatever Nye might have known of Cromwell's secret schemes, and though his brethren were greatly led by him in the course which they followed, there is no reason to believe that they were fully aware of the object which he had in view, or would have approved it if they had. Certainly Goodwin, Burroughs, and Bridge, were men of too pure and spiritual a mould to have lent themselves consciously to the promotion of any merely political intrigue.†

* Palmer's Nonconformist's Memorial, vol. i. p. 96; Appendix, Nye.
† This I hold myself quite at liberty to state, from a careful perusal of the writings of these pious men; and especially from Goodwin's work " On

There was also evidently not a little of prejudice and jealousy on both sides. The Dissenting Brethren had suffered so much from prelatic despotism, that they entertained a perfect horror of all ecclesiastical jurisdiction, even to a most absurd extent, rendering them incapable of calm deliberation on the subject. And, on the other hand, the Presbyterians were so shocked with the blasphemous tenets and enormous immoralities of many of the Sectarians, that they were excited to use the language of intolerance, in their earnest desire to procure the suppression of those pernicious errors; and they were led also to regard with considerable distrust the requests of the Independents for toleration, in consequence of the position which they occupied, as in some measure the representatives of the Sectarians, whose wild and dangerous opinions and practices might, as they dreaded, be sanctioned under a general toleration. Neither party took a sufficiently comprehensive view of their own position and that of their opponents, and consequently both parties erred, and contributed to each other's final overthrow, when, at the Restoration, their common enemy was placed again in the possession of supreme power. Their treatment of each other was mutually destructive, and we cannot exculpate either party from blame, though we think the Independents were the more culpable. And it is but justice to state, that, of the Scottish commissioners, Baillie alone expressed himself with bitterness against the Independents; the rest making many an earnest attempt to allay hostility and promote harmony. But Baillie was himself tinged with prelatic feelings, and had a tendency to political intrigues; as became apparent when he joined the Resolutioners, in the contest which divided and overthrew the Church of Scotland.

the Constitution, Right, Order, and Government, of the Churches of Christ," in the fourth volume of his works; which seems to be the result of his attempt to frame a model of the Independent system of Church government, and which, with all its defects, shows much of a Christian spirit and temper.

Some very important lessons may be learned from the errors of the contending parties in the Westminster Assembly. Whenever divines intermeddle with political affairs, they become both the tools and the victims of diplomatic craft, and promote their own ruin. A Church totally disjoined from the State, and even incapable of junction with it, is not more, perhaps it is less, free from the dangers of political contamination and injury, than one already established, or treating about the terms of an establishment. Such was the fate of the Independents two hundred years ago, equally with that of the Presbyterians; and the Dissenters of both England and Scotland of the present day may admit, that they have received nothing but injury from their political connections, while a Church holding the Establishment principle, but maintaining spiritual freedom, will have to encounter the hostility of all political parties. If ever a thorough and cordial union of evangelical Christians be formed, it must be kept perfectly free from the perverting influence of secular considerations,—and especially from the intrigues of worldly politicians. Christian Churches will find it possible to agree exactly in proportion as they are pure and spiritual; and where that is not the case, any agreement will be but a deceitful truce or an armed neutrality,—incapable of producing a lasting peace, and liable at any moment to be changed into keen and implacable hostility.

CHAPTER IV.

THE ERASTIAN CONTROVERSY, 1645-6.

Erastians in the Assembly and in Parliament—Theories held by them—Beginning of the Controversy—Excommunication—Selden's Argument—Answered by Gillespie—Discussion on the Doctrinal Part of the Directory for Ordination—Whitelocke's Argument—Firmness and Triumph of the Assembly—Debate in Parliament on the subject of the *Jus Divinum*—Whitelocke—Suspending from the Sacrament—Debate in Parliament—Selden and Whitelocke—Remarks—Continued Struggle with the Parliament—Ordinance on Suspending from Communion, and Erastian element in it—Firm Conduct of the Assembly and the City Ministers—Ordinance for the Election of Ruling Elders and the Erection of Presbyteries, and Erastian element in it—Interposition of the Scottish Commissioners of Parliament—Haughty Conduct of the English Parliament—Boldness of the Assembly—Questions respecting the *Jus Divinum*—Main Proposition of the Assembly's Answer Destructive of the Erastian Principle—General Answer—Change in the Temper of Parliament, and One Point Yielded to the Assembly—Bearing of Political Events on the Parliament's Conduct—The King Surrendered—Vindication of Scotland's Conduct—First Meeting of the Synod of London—And of Lancashire—Last Votes of Parliament on the subject of Presbyterian Church Government—Discussion concerning the Confession of Faith—Vindication of it from the Charge of being Tainted with Erastianism—Ratified, with some Exceptions—The Literature of the Erastian Controversy.

THERE were in the Westminster Assembly, as has been already stated, three parties, the Presbyterians, the Independents, and the Erastians. In the preceding chapter our attention has been almost solely occupied with the Independent controversy; both because it actually óccurréd first in order of time, and because it seemed expedient to complete a general view of it before entering upon the consideration of Erastianism, although some discussions on that subject were intermingled with what more strictly related to the prior matter of debate. And in order to obtain a full view of the Erastian controversy, we must revert a little to its beginnings, some of which occurred at an early stage of the Assembly's deliberations, although the main struggle with the Erastians took place after that with the Independents had virtually terminated, so far at least as the Assembly was concerned.

It was somewhat ominous of evil, that the very calling of the Assembly was solely the deed of the civil power, and that their deliberations were limited to such matters as should be proposed to them by the Parliament. Yet, in the universal confusion into which both Church and State had been cast, this was unavoidable, and might not have led to any evil consequences, had the civil government been satisfied with the due exercise of their own powers in calling forth and putting into operation the remedial energies of the Church in its own sacred province. Nor was it strange, that men who had so recently suffered so much from prelatic tyranny should regard with alarm all ecclesiastical power whatever, and by the strength of a violent revulsion and rebound, should spring to the opposite conclusion, that there ought to be no power or jurisdiction, except that of the civil magistrate. Such appears to have been the predominant state of mind and feeling among the members of the Long Parliament in general, together with the peculiar opinions held by individuals, and caused by their diversities of studies or professional pursuits. " Most of the lawyers," says Baillie, " are strong Erastians, and would have all the Church government depend absolutely upon the Parliament." And of Selden, he says, " This man is the head of the Erastians; his glory is most in the Jewish learning; he avows everywhere that the Jewish State and Church were all one, and that so in England it must be, that the Parliament is the Church." * Lightfoot and Coleman, the only Erastian divines in the Assembly, adopted the same line of thought and argument with Selden, and reasoned from the blended polity, as they affirmed it to be, which prevailed among the Jews, in order to maintain that a similar arrangement should exist in Christian States, in which the civil magistrate, being a Christian, ought to possess and wield all jurisdiction both civil and ecclesiastical. The mere lawyers, on the other hand, maintained the Erastian theory on the weaker and more easily refuted argument, that unless the civil magistrate possessed all jurisdiction there would arise the intolerable anomaly of an *imperium in imperio*,—one independent government within another; which in their opinion would be fatal to all good government, and produce inextricable confusion.

The easy connection between this theory and that which had long prevailed in the Church of England, will be readily perceived. The ecclesiastical supremacy of the English monarchs was held to be similar to that which had been held by the Jewish kings, and by the Christian emperors; and it was with some plausibility argued, that these formed authoritative precedents for a Christian sovereign's possession and exercise of jurisdiction within the Church, in all matters of censure, although it gave no authority to interfere in the administration of ordinances, or in the ordination or deposition of ministers, which accordingly were left theoretically free, though practically they were subject to the most absolute control. For the same reason, no opposition was made by the Erastians to the great idea stated by the Westminster Assembly, that "Christ, who is prophet, priest, king, and head of the Church, hath fulness of power, and containeth all other offices by way of eminency in himself;" because they were prepared to hold, that in a Christian state, Christ had delegated the power of jurisdiction to the Christian civil magistrate, defending that

* Baillie, vol. ii. p. 266.

opinion by the analogy of the Jewish state and kings. The kind of arguments brought forward by them in support of this theory, and the counter arguments by which these were met, we must now proceed to state; which we shall endeavour to do with all possible impartiality.

It will be evident to every intelligent reader, that the ground taken by the learned and able Erastians of that period, while it was one of very considerable plausibility, led them to assail directly that element of Church government which involves the exercise of discipline, or Church censure; because, since the only authority which a Church can possess is over the conscience, the only way in which it can have, and exercise jurisdiction, is by spiritual censures directly affecting the conscience of delinquents; so that if a Church cannot inflict censures, it cannot possibly have a distinct and independent government of its own. The Erastians of the Parliament were aware that it would be absurd for them to call themselves a Church, in the strict sense of that term, and consequently, that it would be absurd to pretend that they could themselves admit and ordain ministers, a matter which manifestly belongs to the function of Church-officers; but they perceived that they might more plausibly and successfully assail the power of inflicting censures, and thereby overthrow Church government, on the ground that all jurisdiction belonged to the civil magistrate, even ecclesiastical jurisdiction, in Christian States, though they admitted that it might properly be held and exercised by the Church under a heathen government.

The first intimation of the controversy occurred on the 8th of January 1644, when the second committee gave in a report concerning the work of pastors, to the following effect:—— "Pastors and teachers have power to inquire and judge who are fit to be admitted to the sacraments, or kept from them; and also who are to be excommunicated or absolved from that censure." This proposition the Erastians could not permit to

pass unchallenged; and therefore Selden interposed, and
" desired that the business of excommunication might first be
looked upon, for that very much may be said to prove *that
there is no excommunication at all;* and for that, in this kingdom, ever since it was a kingdom, Christian excommunication
hath ever been by a temporal power; as in the pope's rule
here, his own excommunication could not be brought in
hither, but by permission of the secular power, otherwise it
was death to him that brought it; and excepting the case of
heresy and *concubitus illicitus,* the episcopacy never had power
to excommunicate." * This was sufficiently intelligible; but
though the Assembly perceived clearly the import of Selden's
remarks, it was not judged expedient to enter upon the subject precipitately; and therefore it was remitted to the second
committee to take the whole business of excommunication
and censures into consideration.

Although the Assembly did not wish to provoke an early
discussion with the Erastians, and especially were desirous to
have as many points ratified as might be possible, before a
final struggle on the essential elements of disagreement, still
it was not practicable to avoid coming into collision whenever
the controverted topics occurred in the course of debate. Thus
the question respecting excommunication again arose when
the Assembly were debating this proposition,—" Scripture
holdeth forth that many particular congregations may be
under one presbyterial government;" for the Independents
opposed that proposition on the ground, that it would destroy
the rights and powers of particular congregations in the important point of maintaining their own purity by excommunicating guilty members, since the Scripture rule, as they
argued, is " In the presence of the people," which cannot take
place if a presbytery excommunicate, and must therefore be
done by a single congregation. During the greater part of
the discussion which followed on this point, the Erastians

* Lightfoot, p. 106.

continued silent, and allowed the Independents to bring forward every argument which they could devise, being quite
willing that the Presbyterian system should be defeated if
possible by the Dissenting Brethren, whose own plan they
would themselves take care to nullify. But when the Independent arguments had been all heard and answered at great
length, Selden interposed, and brought forward his own view
in the following manner, as given by Lightfoot, who concurred with him, and whose report may be depended on as
stating the argument in its most favourable aspect.
    The passage of Scripture under discussion was 1 Cor. v.
4 : " In the name of our Lord Jesus, when ye are gathered
together, and my spirit, with the power of our Lord Jesus
Christ." " Mr Selden," says Lightfoot, " questioned whether
this place have any thing to do with excommunication ; and
that συναχθέντων ὑμῶν καὶ τοῦ ἐμοῦ πνεύματος, must be joined
together to this sense, ' seeing that you and my spirit are together ;' or, it may bear this, ' when my spirit and you shall
come together ;' or, 'howsoever you have not been humbled as
you ought, yet my spirit and you agreeing now at last.' And
so, Neh. iv, 8, συνηχθησαν is meant, and is of the same sense
with *convenire*, either *in loco* or *animo*. And he cited Faber.
Stapulensis, that takes the word from συναχθομαι, 'to mourn or
grieve.' *Ergo*, there being so many interpretations, it is not fit
to build upon. This epistle is written to the Church and to
the saints ; where the Church signifieth the governing body
of the Church. 2. The Jews had two kinds of sanhedrims,
the great and the less ; and, Numb. xxxv., the congregation
must judge the heedless murderer, which the Jews generally
understood of קטנה לנסת, and Lev. iv. 13, ' If the whole congregation have sinned,'—the Jews constantly understand this
of the great sanhedrim. And so might the presbytery here,
though ἐκκλησίας συναχθεισης had been the phrase. About
Jerusalem it was still called the Church, not only under
Judaism, but also under Christianity. 3. Ancient times,

indeed, have called excommunication 'giving up to Satan, and our own kingdom hath called the excommunicated person ' the devil's person ;' but for the first three hundred years most [none ?] of the Fathers take this place for excommunication ; and he also showed that P. Molinos proves that it meaneth no such thing. He queried whether this were the incestuous, he that is mentioned to be excommunicated hereafter, who is called 'the evil person to be taken away,' in the last verse, where many copies have *τα*, and not *τον πονηρον*." *

This argument produced little effect upon the Assembly, and after Mr Vines had answered it, the discussion with the Independents was resumed.

Having failed on this point, Selden prepared to put forth all the strength of his rabbinical lore in the discussion concerning the meaning of Matt. xviii. 15–18, which was brought forward to prove ecclesiastical jurisdiction, and also the subordination of Church courts, and successive appeals ending in excommunication. The Independents had admitted that the passage did prove jurisdiction and church censure, but laboured to limit the whole procedure within one congregation, so as to deny appeals to presbyteries. Selden again came forward, and again we shall give his argument as reported by Lightfoot :—

" Mr Selden confessed that he could not find any kind of jurisdiction in this chapter ; and he told a story of a Jesuit, Xavier, that turns the place in Persic, ' *Dic principi ecclesiae.*' Also, that all the Fathers in the first times do never apply this text to jurisdiction, before Rome Church grew high, namely, not in the first four centuries, unless it be in the forged book of Cyprian, *De Abusionibus Saeculi.* Then he offered these things : 1. To consider the time, place, and way of writing of this. Matthew's Gospel was first written, viz., about eight years after Christ's ascension ; so it is in an old copy of Greek used by Beza, and an Arabic. 2. It is conceived it was written in Hebrew, for the Hebrews, and as the Syrian ראלדי. Now, in the Hebrew text it is

* Lightfoot, pp. 153, 154.

עדה in these two editions we have, and belike in Matthew's; now in chapter xvi. it is קהל. Now, the Acts of the Apostles, which is the first place we find *ecclesia* in, was not written of fourteen years after this of Matthew. Now the course of admonition among the Jews was: They distinguished betwixt offences betwixt man and man, and betwixt man and God. Now he that had been offended by man was to go single and desire satisfaction ; and if he would not hearken, then take more company, and if אינו שומע, then לבים הגד. Now every one of the courts was called עדה. Excommunication among the Jews might be inflicted by any of twelve years old ; and so, by consequence, every court might do it ; but the synagogue did not use it, and ἀποσυνά- γωγος was not utterly outlawed from the synagogue, but some part of ordinary free conversation denied him. Now, עדה, קהל, *ecclesia*, &c., must be interpreted, according to tho occasion, for a ccrtain number, *secundum subjectam materiam*, as Deut. xxiii., ' An Ammonite may not enter בקהל : that is, of women; for the Jews understood it of marrying an Israelitish woman. He concluded that this place might very well mean a sanhedrim. Christ was in Capernaum now, when he spake this, where there was a sanhedrim. Now his speech is so Jewish, that it results to this, If an Israelite offend thee, tell the sanhedrim. To the objection, But what means, ' Let him be unto thee an heathen?' he answered, This indeed may be excommunication by the court ; or, by himself : ' If thy brother offend,' &c., after such and such admonition, sue him at the court, or else inform of him there ; if he will not obey the court, do thou excommunicate him." *

Such was the boasted argument of the man emphatically styled " the learned Selden." Its object was, to explain away the force of the term *ecclesia*, or " church," and to reduce the passage to a strictly Jewish application ; then, by allusions to some indefinite Hebrew customs, to resolve the matter into a mere application to a civil court, in cases where a private and friendly arrangement could not be effected'; reducing, at the same time, the meaning of the term " excommunication " into the act of one person merely declining to hold intercourse with another person from whom he had received offence. Yet the ostentatious display of minute rabbinical

* Lightfoot, pp. 165, 166.

Q

lore which he brought forward, seems to have somewhat staggered the Assembly, as appears from the inconclusive remarks of Herle and Marshall, as reported by Lightfoot. But Gillespie saw through the fallacious character of Selden's argument; and in a speech of singular ability and power completely refuted his learned antagonist, proving that the passage could not be interpreted or explained away to mean a mere reference to a civil court. By seven distinct arguments he proved that the whole subject was of a spiritual nature, not within the cognizance of civil courts; and he proved also, that the Church of the Jews had and exercised the power of spiritual censures. The effect of Gillespie's speech was so great as to astonish and confound Selden himself, who made no attempt to reply; and the result was, that the Assembly soon afterwards decided that the negative arguments of Selden and the Independents were not conclusive, and the proposition was affirmed.*

Closely connected with this subject was the proposition which asserted "that authoritative suspension from the Lord's table of a person not yet cast out of the Church, is agreeable to the Scripture;" and this point held the Assembly in debate from the 20th to the 24th of May 1644, when it was affirmed; the opposition being made chiefly by the Independents, while the Erastians reserved their strength for the Parliament, well knowing that their views would coincide with the notions of men of the world, and would not be subjected to such a narrow scrutiny there as in the Assembly. The subject will come before us again, when we come to treat of the Parliament's proceedings.

It was mentioned in the preceding chapter, that when the Assembly had completed the Directory for Ordination, the result was laid before the Parliament to receive its ratification, that it might have the authority of law; and that the Parliament allowed it to lie past for some time, and then

* See before, pp. 201, 202; also Appendix.

made considerable alterations upon it before returning it to the Assembly, which they did on the 15th of August 1644. These alterations were so many, and of such importance, striking out the doctrinal part of the Directory, that the Assembly refused to consent to them, and proceeded to debate afresh the topics so altered or struck out. Mr Whitelocke, a leading member of the Commons, entered into the debate; and passing from the direct point in hand, made a long, and certainly not a peculiarly able speech on the question, whether Presbyterial Church government be *jure divino,*—of divine institution. He admitted that Church government, in the abstract, is of divine institution, but held it doubtful whether any peculiar form, Episcopacy, Presbytery, or Independency, can claim that high authority; nor did he think it of any importance to determine the point, because no decision could alter its nature; if of divine institution, it would remain so, whether men affirmed it or not; and if not so, the authority of man could not elevate it to that height. He advised the Assembly, therefore, to be content with stating to the Parliament, " that the government of the Church by presbyteries is most agreeable to the Word of God, and most fit to be settled in this kingdom."* It is easy to see the tact of the politician in Whitelocke's suggestion, which, according to his own understanding of it, left it in the power of the civil government to establish any form of Church government of which they might approve, and to change it as they might think it expedient; while, if the strictest sense of the words were held, Presbyterians might very properly conclude that the Church government which is " most agreeable to the Word of God," must therefore be of divine institution.

But the Assembly were neither to be overawed nor deceived in this matter. Information of these alterations was communicated to the Scottish commissioners, before it was made known to the Assembly; the effect of which was, first

* Whitelocke, p. 95.

a private remonstrance to certain of the Parliament, and then a preparation for a strenuous struggle in the Assembly itself.* The Scottish commissioners further addressed the Grand Committee on the evils resulting from such a prolonged delay, in the conclusion of which they expressly condemned the Parliament's alterations, stating the reasons of their disapprobation. This bold course was seconded by a petition from the city ministers, on the 18th of September; and on the 2d of October the Parliament issued an ordinance, sanctioning the Assembly's Directory of Ordination, and appointing a committee of divines to ordain ministers in London. The difference between the conduct of the Assembly in this point, and the manner in which they acted towards the Independents, must strike every attentive and candid reader. Although highly disapproving of the pertinacious obstinacy with which the Dissenting Brethren clung to their own views, and threw every possible obstacle in the way of an early and satisfactory settlement of Church government, yet the Assembly continued to treat them as brethren, bore with their lengthened speeches and subtle distinctions, admitted many modifications of their own opinions, and did their utmost to procure an amicable adjustment of all differences, so far as the conscientious views of both parties could be reconciled. But when the Parliament attempted to exercise an Erastian supremacy, and to strike out what they believed to have the authoritative sanction of the Word of God, they refused to yield; and in this instance their firmness and energy were crowned with success. It was, no doubt, in the power of the Parliament to refuse to sanction the Directory of Ordination; but it was also in the power of the Assembly and the city ministers to refuse to ordain on Erastian principles : and the Parliament, aware that they could not, even plausibly, attempt to compel ministers to ordain, yielded the point, and reserved their Erastianism for the still undecided subject of Church censures.

* Baillie, vol. ii. p. 198.

The leading propositions respecting Church government having been nearly completed, several members of both Houses of Parliament attended the Assembly, 7th November 1644, and required them to hasten a report of what had been done " concerning the government of the Church ; and the rather, because they" (Parliament) " had been solicited by the Committee of the State of Scotland for it."* Dr Burgess and a select committee were directed to prepare all that had been voted by the Assembly, that it might be laid before Parliament in proper form with all convenient speed. This was done, read over in the Assembly, compared with the papers in the hands of the scribes, and a committee named to lay the whole before the House of Commons on the 15th of November. The account of what took place in the House of Commons, upon the presenting of this paper, is both curious and instructive, as an exhibition of political management. " The Assembly of Divines, as soon as the House of Commons were sate, and before they were full, came to the House and presented them with the Assembly's advice and opinion, *for the Presbyterian government to be settled ;* and an expression was in their advice, that the Presbyterian government was *jure divino.* Glyn and Whitelocke were then in the House, and few others but those who concurred in judgment with the Assembly, and had notice to be there early, thinking to pass this business before the House should be full. Glyn stood up and spoke an hour to the point of *jus divinum* and the *Presbyterian government ;* in which time the House filled apace : and then Whitelocke spoke to the same points, enlarging his discourse to a much longer time than ordinary, and purposely that the House might be full,—as it was before he had made an end. And then upon the question it was carried, to lay aside the point of *jus divinum ;* and herein Glyn and Whitelocke had thanks from divers, for preventing the surprisal of the House upon this great question."† Such

* Lightfoot, p. 323.   † Whitelocke, p. 106.

is the account given by Whitelocke, in a tone of evident self-
complacency, looking upon himself as having materially aided
in the achievement of a meritorious exploit. How far we are
to believe his suggestion respecting the crafty design of the
Assembly, to procure a ratification of their opinion concerning
the divine right of Presbyterian Church government in a
thinly attended House, composed chiefly of their friends, may
well be doubted, since the order for the Assembly's committee to lay their propositions before Parliament " to-morrow
morning " was publicly given, as Lightfoot states,—and of
course in the hearing of Lightfoot himself, who could easily
have notified the matter to his Erastian friends, so as to prepare them for the stratagem, had such a thing been intended.
In truth, the publicity of the direction renders the idea of
an intended stratagem on the part of the Assembly incredible ; while Whitelocke's account proves him to have
been sufficiently on his guard, whatever may have been the
case with others. And it will be observed, that the House
did not at that time positively reject, but merely " lay
aside," or postpone, the consideration of the claim of divine
right.*

[1645.] From about the close of the year 1644 till about
April 1645, the Assembly was chiefly engaged in the Independent controversy, receiving the written reasons of dissent,
and returning written answers to these reasons. During that
period the debates of the Assembly were of little importance,
and the Erastian controversy also remained in comparative
abeyance. Indeed the debates of the Assembly may be said
to have almost terminated with the close of 1644 ; for their
public deliberations after that time were chiefly occupied with
the framing of the Catechisms' and the Confession of Faith ;

---

* The account of this matter given by Neal is worse than inaccurate.
He says, " When the question was put, it was carried in the negative; "
whereas it was only "laid aside," not negatived. Neal thought it a victory over the Presbyterians,—hence his misrepresentation.

and although the very solemn and important nature of these subjects required mature study and great precision of language, which formed necessarily a work of considerable time, yet there existed so much harmony of doctrinal principles among them, that their discussions very seldom assumed the distinctive character of debate. The chief cause, probably, why the Erastian controversy was allowed to slumber during that period, was, that the parliamentary politicians were engaged in the treaty of Uxbridge with the king, and were exceedingly anxious to conclude a peace with his majesty, if possible, being apprehensive that the self-denying ordinance would be carried by the intrigues of Cromwell, and the sword be thereby wrested from their grasp. That ordinance, after a struggle of nearly three months, was at last ratified by both Houses, on the 3d of April 1645, and from that time the army was virtually independent of the Parliament, and ere long became its master, or rather, the tyrant of both Parliament and kingdom.

Mention has been already made of the disinclination of the Parliament to agree to the Assembly's proposition respecting the power of ministers to keep back from the Lord's table persons not yet cut off from the Church. This power the Erastians were reluctant to sanction ; and the Assembly was equally urgent that it should be fully sanctioned, both because they believed it to be necessary, to prevent that sacred ordinance from being profaned, and because one point strongly urged by the Independents, in defence of their separation, was the want of sufficient reformation in congregations. The subject was laid before the Parliament on the 6th of March 1645, by the Assembly, and on the 10th of the same month by the city ministers.* On the 21st the Parliament took the subject into consideration, and on the 25th some votes were passed respecting it, in some particular points. Again, on the 27th the Assembly gave to the House their advice con-

* Whitelocke, pp. 130, 131.

cerning not admitting scandalous and ignorant persons to the sacrament. Thus urged to what they had no mind to grant, the Parliament, on the 1st of April, emitted an order, "That the Assembly set down in particular what measure of understanding persons ought to have of the Trinity, and other points debated, before they be admitted to the sacrament." * The object of this order was evidently to engage the Assembly in a discussion which might occupy their attention for a considerable time, and perhaps involve so much confusion and disagreement of opinion as should render a definite answer impracticable. But the desire of the Assembly was not to be so evaded; and they experienced less difficulty in answering the question of the Parliament than Erastian lawyers had expected. Some additional votes respecting Church government were about the same time passed by the Parliament, the purport of which is thus stated by Baillie:—" They have passed a vote in the House of Commons, for appeals from Sessions to Presbyteries, from these to Synods, from these to national Assemblies, and from these to the Parliament. We mind to be silent for some time on this, lest we mar the erection of the ecclesiastical courts; but when we find it seasonable, we mind to make much ado before it go so. We are hopeful to make them declare, that they mean no other thing, by their appeals from the national Assembly to a Parliament, than a complaint of an injurious proceeding; which we did never deny." †

Repeated debates took place in Parliament respecting the demands of the Assembly, during the months of May, June, and July, though without arriving at any conclusion. On the 30th of July Coleman preached a sermon before the House of Commons, of the most perfectly Erastian character, to which we shall have occasion hereafter more particularly to refer. On the second day after, viz., on the 1st of August, the Assembly sent a deputation to the House, desiring " that

* Whitelocke, p. 134. † Baillie, vol. ii. p. 267.

a speedy course might be taken about those who should be thought not fit to be admitted to the sacrament, namely, the ignorant, scandalous, and profane : it being a thing that, if effected exactly to the rule, would much tend to the glory of God and the good of this whole kingdom." The Speaker answered, " That the House was in debate of the same business long before their coming, and that they would expedite it with as much conveniency as could be." * Not dismayed by this short answer, the Assembly, on the 8th, presented a petition, in which they " declared plainly their claim, *jure divino*, of power to suspend from the sacrament all such as they should judge to be scandalous or ignorant ;" † and on the 11th a petition of a similar nature was presented to the House of Lords. Parliament was thus constrained to take the subject into full consideration, for the purpose of giving a clear and decided deliverance concerning it; and an elaborate discussion took place on the 3d of September, in which the Erastians declared their opinions fully.

" The House fell into debate," says Whitelocke, " of the great business of the Church,—the points of excommunication and suspension from the sacrament. Selden declared his opinion, ' That for four thousand years there was no sign of any law to suspend persons from religious exercises. That under the Law every sinner was, *eo nomine*, to come to offer, as he was a sinner ; and no priest, or other authority, had to do with him, unless it might be made appear to them, whether another did repent or not,—which was hard to be done. Strangers were kept away from the passover, but these were Pagans, and such as were not of the Jewish religion. The question is not now for keeping away Pagans in times of Christianity, but Protestants from Protestant worship. No divine can show that there is any such command as this to suspend from the sacrament. If, after Christ suffered, the Jews had become Christians, the same ground upon which

* Whitelocke, p. 158.   † Ibid., p. 160.

they went as to their sacrifices would have been as to the
sacrament; and certainly no way nor command to keep any
one from partaking of it. No man is kept from the sacrament, *eo nomine*, because he is guilty of any sin, by the constitution of the Reformed Churches, or because he hath not
made satisfaction. Every man is a sinner, the difference is
only, the one is in private, and the other a sinner in public.
The one is as much against God as the other. *Dic Ecclesiae*
('Tell it to the Church'), in St Matthew, was to the courts
of law which then sat in Jerusalem. No man can show any
excommunication till the Popes Victor and Zephorinus, two
hundred years after Christ, first began to use it upon private
quarrels. Thereby (it appears) excommunication is but human
invention; it was taken from the heathens.'" *

Such was the argument of " the learned Selden ;" and very
probably the members of the House thought it very learned,
and fraught with sound theology. If it had been delivered
in the Assembly it would have been estimated by a different
standard, and subjected to a more searching scrutiny,—as had
been the case with arguments and assertions of a similar character in an instance already related.

The substance of Mr Whitelocke's speech was as follows :—

" The Assembly of Divines have petitioned and advised the House of
Commons, that in every presbytery, or Presbyterian congregation, the
pastors and ruling elders may have the power of excommunication, and
the power of suspending such as they shall judge ignorant or scandalous persons from the sacrament. By 'pastors' I suppose they mean
themselves, and others who are, or may be, preachers in the several
congregations, and would be ἐπίσκοποι, 'bishops,' or overseers of these
congregations. By 'ruling elders' I take their meaning to be, a select
number of such as in every one of these congregations shall be chosen
for the execution of the church government and discipline in them respectively. They may properly enough be called pastors, from our
Saviour's charge to his disciples, 'Feed my sheep ;' so that a pastor is
to feed those committed to his charge with spiritual food, as the shep-

* Whitelocke, p. 163; Rushworth, vol. vi. p. 203.

herd feeds his flock with temporal.   If so, how improper, then, will it
be for those who are to feed the flock, to desire the power to excommunicate any,—to keep them from food,—to suspend any from the
sacrament,—to drive them from feeding on the bread of life,—to forbid any to eat of that whereof Christ, the great Shepherd of our souls,
hath said, ' Take, eat,'—to forbid those to drink whom they shall judge
unworthy, when our Saviour himself said, 'Drink ye all of this.'   In
the Old Testament, ' Ho, every one that thirsteth,' &c., said the prophet; yet now his successors would be authorised to say to some persons, ' You do not thirst,' though they themselves say they do, and to
deny them milk and water, bread and wine, when they desire it.
Surely it is not proper for pastors, for feeders of flocks, to deny food
to any of their flock who shall desire it.   But some have said, that it
is the part of a good shepherd, if he see one of his sheep going astray
into a ground where the grass will bring the rot, to chase him out of
that pasture.   And they apply it to spiritual pastors suspending those
from the sacrament whom they fear, by the unworthy receiving of it,
may eat and drink their own damnation.   This may be a charitable
simile, but will hardly be found a full answer; for it is not the receiving of the sacrament, but the unworthiness of the receiver, that
brings destruction.   And whether he be unworthy or not, it is not in
the judgment of pastor, or of any other, but of the party only who is
the sinner; for none can know his heart but himself, and a commission
will scarce be produced for any other to be judge thereof.   The person
refused may say to the pastor in this case, ' Who made thee judge ? '
Besides, the authority desired is not only of *suspension*, but of *excommunication*,—which is a total driving or thundering away of the party
from all spiritual food whatsoever.   And if a shepherd shall chase away
his sheep from all pastures, that indeed will bring the hunger-rot upon
them.   The more sinful persons are, the more they have need of instruction; and where can they have it better than from the lips of the
learned and pious pastors, who ought to preserve knowledge.

  " But it hath been said that the ruling elders are to join with them ;
let us inquire who they are.   In some congregations in country vil-
lages, perhaps they may not be very learned themselves; yet the
authority to be given them is sufficiently great.   The word 'elders,'
among the Hebrews, signified the men of greatest power and dignity ;
the members of their great sanhedrim were styled elders ; so were
the princes of their tribes."   [Then, as if in rivalry of Selden, he
enlarged upon the use of a similar title among the Grecians, the

Phœnicians, the Tyrians, the Romans, the Spaniards, the Italians, the Saxons,—giving the etymology of Earl, Alderman, and Sir.] " And so they may allow the title of elders to the chief and select men of every presbytery. Yet if this power (excommunication and suspension) be allowed them, they may well challenge the title of elders in the highest signification. The power of the keys is a great power; the Romish Church will acknowledge it, and the foundation of their supremacy to be built upon it. Whatsoever they bind or loose upon earth to be bound or loosed in heaven, is a power which may claim the highest title imaginable. Although I can never presume that the reverend and pious learned gentlemen who aim at this power, can have the least supposition of any such effect by it, yet if any petitioners should sue you to be made judges or justices, I believe you would judge their petition the less modest, and them the less fit for such offices; but to this I make no application, and I hope none shall make any use of it. Power is thought fit to be given to suspend from the sacrament two sorts of persons,—the *ignorant* and the *scandalous.* I am sure that I am a very ignorant person; we are all more ignorant than we ought to be of the truth of Christ; even amongst the pastors and elders in some places, the most learned may in other places be adjudged ignorant. The more ignorant people are, the more some will blame their pastors, who ought to instruct them, and, by private conference, inform them, and rectify their understandings; and that is a good part of spiritual food. And to keep an ignorant person from the ordinances is no way to improve his knowledge. Scandalous persons are likewise to be suspended; and that is to be referred to the judgment of the pastor and ruling elders. Where a commission for them to execute this judicature is extant, will be hard to show. Both pastors, and elders, and people, are scandalous, in the general sense. We are all of us gross sinners, and our best performances are but scandalous, as to the true and sincere profession of the gospel of Christ. Those who are scandalous sinners ought to be admonished to forsake their evil ways, and to amend their lives; and where can they receive this admonition, and hope for more conviction of their consciences, than by hearing good sermons, and being admitted to be partakers of the holy ordinances; but to excommunicate them, deprives them wholly of the best means for their cure. The best excommunication is, for pastors, elders, and people, to excommunicate sin out of their own hearts and conversations,—to suspend themselves from all works of iniquity. This is a power which, put in execution, through the assistance of the Spirit of God, will prevent all disputes about excommunication and suspension from the sacrament. A man may be a good physician, though he never cut off a member from any of his patients; a body may be very sound, though no member of it was ever cut off; and surely a church may be a good church, though no member of it hath ever been cut off. I have heard here many complaints of the jurisdiction formerly exercised by the prelates, who were but a few; there will be, by the passing of this now desired, a great multiplication of spiritual men in government. Where the temporal sword (the magistracy) is sufficient for punishment of offences, there will be little need for this new discipline; nor will it be so easily granted."—" After a long debate," adds Whitelocke, in the Narrative part of his work, " the House referred this matter to a further consideration by the Grand Committee, to whom it was formerly referred." *

From the circumstance of the preceding speech being given at full length by both Whitelocke and Rushworth, it is evident that it must have been regarded by the Erastians of the Parliament as exhibiting the ablest statement and advocacy of their opinions. One thing, indeed, it proves very clearly, namely, that when civilians attempt to reason upon theological questions, they are in great peril of forfeiting their reputation either for candour and intelligence, or for clearness of thought and power of reasoning. It will be observed that Whitelocke deals very much in vague generalities, about the character and duties of pastors and elders, and the effect of suspending from the sacrament and excommunicating; and that he insinuates the danger of allowing such powers to be exercised by the Church courts, but carefully avoids making any specific applications. This method of stating his opinions left him at full liberty to use all the artifices of sophistry which he could command; and, accordingly, his whole speech is a tissue of sophistical plausibilities. As, for example, " The duty of a pastor is to feed his flock; therefore he can have no right to refuse food to any." But he should have proved that the only duty of a pastor is to feed; otherwise

* Whitelocke, pp. 163, 164; Rushworth, vol. vi. pp. 203–205.

his argument cannot prove that it may not be also a duty to refuse, for proper reasons. Again, "The unworthiness of the receiver alone brings destruction ; but none can judge of this but the sinner himself: therefore the pastor ought not to have power to refuse." True, the unworthiness of the receiver brings destruction ; but it is not true that none can be a judge of this but the sinner ; for his conduct may be so glaringly sinful, and he may be so recklessly impenitent, that every one may be able to judge him by his fruits, and may be constrained to shun him as incorrigibly wicked and impious. Once more, " All are ignorant and scandalous in the widest sense of these terms ; but the best way to remedy this is, to give them an opportunity of hearing good sermons, and to admit them to the holy ordinances." Certainly it may be a good way for instructing the ignorant, to bring such persons where they will hear good and sound instruction, and the Westminster divines never dreamt of preventing any from hearing sermons ; but admission to ordinances, that is, to the Lord's table, is a totally different matter, and instead of tending to instruct, might more probably tend to harden an impenitent sinner, and might lead him to regard himself as needing no further amendment.

But it cannot be necessary to detect all the fallacies of this much boasted speech ; that every sound and right-minded reader will do for himself. It has been inserted, however, for the purpose of giving a favourable specimen of the kind of arguments employed by the Parliamentary Erastians of that period ; which are essentially the same as those used by many Erastians in the present day, with, perhaps, this exception, that few modern Erastians can reason even so well, or have skill enough to enter so deeply into the subject.

The language of Baillie, in a letter written at this juncture, shows the strong anxiety entertained by the Assembly regarding this important subject, and gives also another proof of the temperate spirit and calm prudence of the Scottish commissioners. After mentioning the difficulty which the Assembly felt in enumerating all kinds of scandalous offences, on which account they required to have power to exclude all scandalous as well as some, he adds, " The general they would not grant, as including an arbitrary and unlimited power. Our advice (that of the Scottish commissioners) was, that they (the Assembly) would go on to set up their presbyteries and synods with so much power as they could get ; and after they were once settled, then they might strive to obtain their full due power. But the Assembly was of another mind ; and after divers fair papers, at last they framed a most zealous, clear, and peremptor one, wherein they held out plainly the Church's divine right to keep from the sacrament all who are scandalous ; and if they cannot obtain the free exercise of that power which Christ hath given them, they will lay down their charges, and rather choose all afflictions than to sin by profaning the holy table." * It was the presenting of this paper which gave occasion to the preceding speeches of Selden and Whitelocke. And although the Parliament were determined not to grant the full claim of the Assemby, yet they were not prepared at once to declare that determination, but still continued to keep the subject in a state of suspense, hoping, probably, that the divines would at last consent to accept some lower measure. While Parliament treated the Assembly with a considerable degree of guarded respect, they showed their temper more plainly to the city divines, a petition from whom, "for establishing Presbytery, as the discipline of Jesus Christ, they voted to be scandalous."† It might have puzzled those sage senators to have defined their own language, and showed in what respect such a petition was *scandalous;* but it was easy for them to apply harsh and ungracious epithets to a request which they were determined to refuse.

It has been already mentioned that the Parliament had required the Assembly to state " what measure of understand-

* Baillie, vol. iii. p. 307.   † Whitelocke, p. 159.

ing persons ought to have of the Trinity, and other points debated, before they be admitted to the sacrament;" and also, that they required an enumeration of such scandalous offences as deserved the censure of suspension from ordinances. To the former point the Assembly readily prepared an answer ; but they found the latter more difficult, both because the attempt to enumerate such offences suggested additional ones, and because the inevitable tendency of such an attempt was to present their whole system in its most repulsive aspect, and even to prevent themselves from having a discretionary power to mitigate its apparent severity. At length, however, on the 14th of October the Assembly presented their advice on these points to the Parliament, at the same time clearly declaring their earnest desire that the general principle should be affirmed, and the details left to be regulated according to the peculiarities of each specific case.* But the Parliament resolved to turn this paper of advice into an ordinance of both Houses ; and on the 15th voted, as a preliminary step, " that the presbytery should not suspend from the sacrament for any other offences than those particularly mentioned in the ordinance;" which, adds Whitelocke, displeased some who were earnest to give an arbitrary power to the presbytery.† Strange that this legislator could not perceive that Parliament was retaining a much more arbitrary power in its own possession,—a power which is absolute despotism, claiming to rule alike over person, property, and conscience.

On the 20th of October 1645, this important document passed both Houses, under the designation of " An Ordinance of the Lords and Commons assembled in Parliament, about Suspension from the Lord's Supper." ‡ The statement of the amount of religious knowledge which ought to be possessed by every person before being admitted to the Lord's table, is

* Baillie, vol. ii. p. 325.   † Whitelocke, p. 162.
‡ Rushworth, vol. vi. pp. 210-212.   See Appendix.

very clear and explicit; and the enumeration of scandalous offences is also very full. But in one clause towards the close of the ordinance, the Erastian principle is very strongly stated : " If any person suspended from the Lord's Supper shall find himself grieved with the proceedings before the eldership of any congregation, he shall have liberty to appeal to the classical eldership (or Presbytery), and from them to the Provincial Assembly (or Synod), from thence to the National, and from thence to the Parliament. And it is further ordained, That the members of both Houses, that now are members of the Assembly of Divines, or any seven of them, be a standing committee of both Houses of Parliament to consider of causes of suspension from the Lord's Supper not contained in this ordinance ; unto which committee any eldership shall present such causes, to the end that the Parliament, if need require, may hear and determine the same." The undisguised Erastianism of this ordinance was exceedingly displeasing to the Assembly, and rendered them unwilling to put it into operation at all, even so far as it went, lest they should seem to consent to a principle which they so decidedly condemned. " This," says Baillie, " has been the only impediment why the Presbyteries and Synods have not been erected; for the ministers refuse to accept of Presbyteries without this power." Both parties, indeed, were equally resolute,—the Parliament not to grant, and the Assembly not to be satisfied without the recognition of what they regarded as of divine right,—a full liberty to keep from the holy table all scandalous persons. And although the divines were perfectly able to refute the sophistry of the Erastian lawyers in argument, they could not change their hearts, nor make them willing to submit to the purifying, though humbling precepts of the gospel ; consequently these unhappy men continued tenaciously to retain a power which they could not hold and exercise, but to the injury of religion, and to the ruin of themselves and of the kingdom.

R

Not only was the Assembly dissatisfied with the conduct of Parliament in thus attempting to retain an Erastian power in ecclesiastical affairs, but all the Presbyterians, both ministers and people throughout the kingdom, and particularly those of the city of London itself, were both grieved and displeased with conduct so grasping and unwise. A petition was addressed to Parliament from the Common Council of London, praying that Church governmˁnt might be speedily settled and observed, and that greater power might be given to the ministers and elders than was established by the Parliament, according to the warrant of the Word of God. The House answered, " That they had already taken much pains in debating of Church government ; and they conceived the city and Common Council were informed falsely of the proceedings of the House, else they would not have precipitated the judgment of the Parliament ; however, they take it as a good intention of the petitioners promoting this business." A similar petition from the city ministers received a still more uncourteous answer,—two of the members were sent to tell them, that " they need not attend any longer for an answer to their petition, but to go home, and look to the charges of their several congregations."* These ungracious answers gave rise to a feeling of alienation between the city and the Parliament, the completed effect of which was, that counterpoise, or rather paralysis of each other's energies, which laid both prostrate beneath the power of the army, by whom the Parliament was at last trampled out of existence, —so swift and sure was the blow of retributive justice. Had Parliament abandoned its Erastian principles, and granted the petitions of the Assembly, the ministers, and the people, it would have been so deeply rooted in the grateful affection of the kingdom, and its power would have been so thoroughly consolidated, that not even Cromwell's deep schemes and iron strength could have greatly shaken, much less utterly

* Whitelocke, p. 187.

overthrown it. But it sinned obstinately against the " Prince of the kings of the earth ;" and therefore He dashed it to pieces.

One very probable reason why the Parliament were at this time assuming a more haughty tone than formerly was, the depression of the king's power, who had never been able to make head against the army to any considerable extent since the battle of Naseby, on the 14th of June. Yet even in this point of view, the conduct of the Parliament was marked by something little short of infatuation ; for the power of the army had passed completely into the hands of Cromwell, though Fairfax still held, nominally, the chief command ; and a very moderate degree of penetration might have enabled them to have perceived that they had no means of counterbalancing the power of the army except by the wealth and influence of the city of London, which was thoroughly Presbyterian. The Independents in both Parliament and Assembly were delighted with the delay caused by the Erastian obstinacy ; and to these two parties, Independents and Erastians, there was added, as Baillie says, " a third party, of worldly, profane men, who were extremely affrighted to come under the yoke of ecclesiastic discipline." The very fact of such a combination against the Presbyterian system would go far to prove its truth and scriptural character ; for that can scarcely be other than a good cause, which provokes the opposition of such conflicting elements, and some of them elements essentially evil.

[1646.] Though hitherto disappointed, the Assembly and the city continued to exert themselves by plying the Parliament with petition upon petition ; and to one of these, signed by the whole magistracy of London, addressed to both Houses, 15th January 1646, the Parliament felt it necessary to return a courteous and complimentary answer, thanking them for their care and zeal for God's worship, and assuring them of their readiness to promote so good a work.* Adverting to

* Whitelocke, p. 194.

this petition, Baillie says, "No doubt, if they be constant they will obtain all their desires ; for all know that the Parliament here cannot subsist without London, so that whatsoever they desire in earnest and constantly, it must be granted." On the 20th of February it was "Resolved by the Lords and Commons in Parliament assembled, That there be forthwith a choice made of elders throughout the kingdom of England, according to such directions as have already passed both Houses, bearing date the 19th of August 1645." But on the 14th of March, a more complete ordinance passed both Houses, containing full regulations respecting the choice of elders and of every thing necessary for the organization of the Presbyterian form of Church government. Even in this ordinance the same Erastian element appeared. By one clause it was enacted, "That in every province persons shall be chosen by the Houses of Parliament, that shall be commissioners to judge of scandalous offences, not enumerated in any ordinance of Parliament, to them presented ;" and upon the decision of these commissioners it was to depend whether the eldership might suspend persons accused of such offences from the sacrament.*

Before this ordinance had passed the Lords, and as soon as its tenor was known from the deliberations of the Commons, both the Assembly and the city ministers prepared to give the most decided opposition to this Erastian clause. "I wish," says Baillie, writing to one of the city ministers, "by all means that unhappy court of commissioners in every shire may be exploded. If it must be so, let the new cases of scandal come to the Parliament by the letters of the eldership, or any other way, but not by a standing court of commissioners. This is a trick of the Independents' invention, of purpose to enervate and disgrace all our government, in which they have been assisted by the lawyers and the Erastian party. This troubles us all exceedingly,—the whole As-

* Rushworth, vol. vi. pp. 224-228. See Appendix.

sembly and ministry over the kingdom ; the body of the city is much grieved with it: but how to mend it we cannot well tell. In the meantime it mars us to set up any thing ; the anarchy continues, and the vilest sects daily increase." Such, indeed, was the inevitable consequence of allowing the kingdom to continue without any regular form of Church government and discipline, the presence of which acts by a moral constraint on even those who do not admit its authority, as the experience of all ages and countries can amply testify.

Fully aware of the extreme importance of obtaining a right adjustment of this essential point, the Presbyterians of both Scotland and England made every possible exertion to secure it. And there seemed to be one favourable opportunity, by availing themselves of which it might yet be accomplished. The unhappy king, beaten from the field by successive and ruinous defeats, had retired to Oxford, where he found himself almost driven to distraction by the wretched cabals of his selfish and unprincipled adherents. In these circumstances he proposed a new negotiation for peace, and many letters were interchanged between him and the Parliament on this subject. But the Parliament were now not only secure of triumph, but also under the influence of Cromwell and his friends, who had no wish for a peace ; and for these reasons they rose in their demands to such a degree, that all prospects of peace were greatly obscured. The Scottish Parliamentary commissioners, on the other hand, were desirous of peace on such terms as should not annihilate the regal dignity, and therefore they endeavoured so far to modify the demands of the English Parliament, that they might be such as the king could honourably grant. But the English Parliament felt that they had no longer any urgent need of assistance from a Scottish army, and therefore were not inclined to listen to the more reasonable proposals of the Scottish commissioners. Still, they could not at once dishonourably violate their

Solemn League and Covenant with Scotland, and therefore they continued to receive, with due respect, the communications of the Scottish Parliament through its commissioners. And as these commissioners were all Presbyterians, they felt deeply interested in the question of the right establishment of Presbyterian Church government in England, according to the principles of the Solemn League of both nations. For this reason they presented to the English Parliament several papers respecting the pending treaty of peace, and the various matters involved in it ; one of which necessarily was, the form of religion to be established, to which the king was to be requested to give his concurrence. On the subject of religion these papers took up the points that had so much engaged the attention of the Assembly, and gave their opinion in the following manner :—

" Having perused the several ordinances, directions, and votes of the honourable Houses concerning Church government, delivered unto us, which we conceive will be the matter of the propositions of religion, and in this sense only we speak to them, we do agree to the direction for the present election of elders, to the subordination of congregational, classical, provincial, and national assemblies, and to the direction concerning the members of which they are constitute, and the times of their meeting. Only we desire, that no godly minister be excluded from being a member of the classical presbytery ; nor any godly minister, having lawful commission, from being a member of the provincial and national Assemblies, there being the greater need of their presence and assistance in such Assemblies, that there are no ruling elders to join with and assist them. And we desire that a fixed time be appointed for the ordinary meeting of the national Assembly, with power to the Parliament to summon them when they please ; and with liberty to the Church to meet oftener, if there shall be necessary cause : the ordinary meeting thereof being most necessary for preserving truth and unity in the whole Church, against the errors that may arise and multiply in the Church, and against the divisions and differences that may distract the inferior Assemblies of the Church, and for receiving and determining appeals from provincial assemblies, which otherwise will be infinite, and lie over long without determination, and the exigence of religion sometimes being such that it will require an extraordinary meeting.

" We agree to the rules and directions concerning suspension from the sacrament of the Lord's Supper, in cases of ignorance and scandal. Only we desire that the congregational elderships may have power to judge in cases of scandal not enumerated, with liberty to the person grieved to appeal, as in other Reformed Churches. This we conceive to be a power no more arbitrary in this Church, than in them who are limited by the rules expressed in Scripture, and do exercise this their power with such moderation as is a comfort, help, and strengthening of civil authority. The appointing of provincial commissioners, such as are appointed in the ordinance, will minister occasion to such debates and disputes, in this and other Churches, as will be very unpleasant to Parliaments and civil powers, will make a great disconformity betwixt this and other Churches, and a present rent and division in this Church; is such a mixture in Church government as hath not been heard of in any Church before this time, and may prove a foundation of a new Episcopacy, or of a High Commission. And the work may be better done by the Assemblies of ministers and elders, who have this in their ecclesiastical charge, and will be no less tender of the honour of Par- liament, by whose laws they live and are protected; and as able and willing to give satisfaction to the people, whose consciences and con- versation are best known unto them, as any other persons whatsoever. Concerning the suspension of the ministers themselves, although scan- dal in them deserveth double censure, yet we conceive it to be most agreeable that they have their censure from the classical or other superior Assemblies of the Church, where there be ministers to judge them. We do also agree to the ordinance of ordination of ministers; only we desire it may be provided that it stand in force for all time to come.

" There be other matters contained in the ordinances; as, The man- ner of subordination of the Assemblies of the Church to the Parliament, so much liable to mistake; the seeming exemption of some sorts of persons from the just censures of the Church; the ministering the sacrament to some persons against the consciences of the ministry and eldership; concerning public repentance to be only before the elder- ships, and such like; which may be taken into consideration, and with small labour and alteration be determined to the great satisfaction of many. As for the remnant, concerning the perpetual officers of the Church, and their offices; the order and power of Church Assemblies;

the order of public repentance, and of proceeding to excommunication and absolution ; we desire they may be agreed upon according to the covenant, and the advice of the divines of both kingdoms, long since offered to both Houses: which being done, they may be presently drawn in a method, and formed up in a model of Church government in three days, to the quieting the minds of all the godly, concerning the particular meaning of both kingdoms in the matter of religion, to the great content of the Reformed Churches, and which will both make us distinctly to know what we demand, and the king what he doth grant."*

Within a few days after these papers had been laid before the English Parliament, and before the two Houses had returned any answer, they were printed and published with a preface, as from a private person into whose hands they had fallen by accident, purporting to state the case between the Parliament and the Scottish commissioners.† Both Houses were exceedingly indignant that such liberty should be taken with their proceedings, and on the 14th of April concurred in a vote : " That the matter contained in these printed papers was false, and scandalous against the Parliament and kingdom of England; that they should be burned by the common hangman ; that a declaration should be drawn up refuting their untruths, and showing the innocence and integrity of the Parliament; and that the author or publisher was an incendiary between the two kingdoms." And on the 21st of April the preface was burnt as had been ordered, but not the papers of the Scottish commissioners.

The Declaration published by the Parliament for their own vindication was characterised by equal intemperate heat and bitterness, and contained a very strong assertion of the Erastian theory; coloured, however, by the pretext of their dread of the consequences which might ensue from " granting an arbitrary and unlimited power and jurisdiction to near ten thousand judicatories to be erected within this kingdom ;"

* Rushworth, vol. vi. pp. 254, 255.

† Baillie informs us that David Buchanan was the person by whom they were published. Vol. ii. p. 367.

and asserting that they " had the more reason by no means
to part with this power out of the hands of the civil magistrate, since the experience of all ages will manifest that the
reformation and purity of religion, and the preservation and
protection of the people of God in this kingdom, hath under
God been by the Parliaments, and their exercise of this
power." How easy it is to make bold and general assertions;
but had the English Parliament been required to produce
proofs and instances in maintenance of their self-complacent
assertion, they would have found that they had undertaken no
easy task. And it might have occurred to them, that such
vehemence of conduct and language might be very fairly interpreted into a proof that they were aware that they had
acted wrong, and that their anger arose from the painful and
mortifying consciousness of being detected in the commission
of what was manifestly culpable. But even yet an English
Parliament can reason and act in a similar manner, untaught
by the bitter experience of their ancestors, and unable to read
the signs of the times, however close the resemblance which
these bear to a former period.

Not even this manifestation of the Parliament's stormy
temper could appal the Assembly of Divines, although the
city ministers had somewhat quailed. Mr Marshall, by no
means one of the most rash or impetuous of the brethren,
arose in his place, and after referring to the recent ordinance,
and stating that there were several things in it which pressed
heavily upon his conscience, and upon the consciences of
many others, he moved that a committee might be appointed
to examine what points in the ordinance were contrary to
their consciences, and to prepare a petition on the subject, to
be presented to the two Houses. This was accordingly done,
and presented by the whole Assembly, with Mr Marshall at
their head, on the 24th of March. The main topics of the
petition were, an assertion of the divine right of Presbyterian
Church government, and a complaint against that clause in

the recent ordinance which appointed an appeal from the censures of the Church to a committee of the Parliament. The House appears to have been somewhat staggered by this decided course adopted by the Assembly, and appointed a committee to consider what answer should be given, and what notice should be taken of the manner in which the petition had been brought forward. The report of the committee was characterised by deep policy. First, they gave it as their opinion, that the Assembly of Divines had, in their recent petition, violated the privileges of Parliament, and incurred the penalties of a *premunire*; and next, they proposed, that since the Assembly insisted on the *jus divinum* of the Presbyterian government, certain queries which they had prepared respecting that point might be sent to the Assembly, and the divines required to return answers to the satisfaction of the Parliament. The House approved of the committee's report, and on the 30th of April sent Sir John Evelyn, Mr Fiennes, and Mr Brown, to state to the Assembly the sentiments of the House, and to require answers to the prepared list of interrogations.

These questions display so clearly the captious character and petulant temper of the Erastians, even while pretending to be merely desiring satisfaction to their scruples of conscience, that we think it expedient to insert them here :—

" Questions propounded to the Assembly of Divines by the House of Commons, touching the point of *Jus Divinum* in the matter of Church government.

" Whereas it is resolved by both Houses, that all persons guilty of notorious and scandalous offences shall be suspended from the sacrament of the Lord's Supper, the House of Commons desires to be satisfied by the Assembly of Divines in the questions following:—

" 1. Whether the parochial and congregational elderships appointed by ordinance of Parliament, or any other congregational or presbyterial elderships, are *jure divino*, and by the will and appointment of Jesus Christ? And whether any particular Church government be *jure divino*? And what that government is?

" 2. Whether all the members of the said eldership, as members thereof, or which of them, are *jure divino*, and by the will and appointment of Jesus Christ ?

" 3. Whether the superior assemblies or elderships, viz., the classical, provincial, and national, whether all or any of them, and which of them, are *jure divino*, and by the will and appointment of Jesus Christ ?

" 4. Whether appeals from the congregational elderships to the classical, provincial, or national assemblies, or any of them, and to which of them, are *jure divino* ? And are their powers upon such appeals *jure divino*, and by the will and appointment of Jesus Christ ?

" 5. Whether œcumenical assemblies are *jure divino*? And whether there be appeals from any of the former assemblies to the said œcumenical, *jure divino*, and by the will and appointment of Jesus Christ ?

" 6. Whether by the Word of God the power of judging and declaring what are such notorious and scandalous offences, for which persons guilty thereof are to be kept from the sacrament of the Lord's Supper, —and of convening before them, trying, and actual suspending from the sacrament such offenders accordingly,—is either in the congregational eldership or presbytery, or in any other eldership, congregation, or persons ? And whether such powers are in them only, or in any of them, and in which of them, *jure divino*, and by the will and appointment of Jesus Christ ?

" 7. Whether there be any certain and particular rules expressed in the Word of God, to direct the elderships or presbyteries, congregations or persons, or any of them, in the exercise and execution of the powers aforesaid ? And what are those rules ?

" 8. Is there any thing contained in the Word of God, that the supreme magistracy in a Christian State may not judge and determine what are the aforesaid notorious and scandalous offences, and the manner of suspension for the same ? And in what particulars, concerning the premises, is the said supreme magistracy by the Word of God excluded ?

" 9. Whether the provision of commissioners to judge of scandals not enumerated (as they are authorised by the ordinance of Parliament) be contrary to that way of government which Christ hath appointed in his Church ? And wherein are they so contrary ?

" In answer to these particulars the House of Commons desires of the Assembly of Divines their proofs from Scripture, and to set down the several texts of Scripture in the express words of the same. And it is ordered, that every particular minister of the Assembly of Divines, that is or shall be present at the debate of any of these questions, do, upon every resolution which shall be presented to this House concerning the same, subscribe his respective name, either with the affirmative or negative, as he gives his vote. * And those that do dissent from the major part shall set down their positive opinions, with the express texts of Scripture upon which their opinions are grounded."†

It is not difficult to perceive the bitter hostility against every kind and degree of spiritual jurisdiction which pervades these questions; nor yet is it difficult to detect the sophistical fallacy which forms the basis of the whole. In these Erastian questions there is a constant endeavour to keep a variety of details prominently before the mind, so as to obscure the main principle as far as possible; and even when the proper question of principle is stated, it is done in the same manner,—" Whether any particular Church government be *jure divino?*" The very essence of the inquiry is, " Whether there be in the Word of God Church government?" and if that be affirmed, then the question arises, " What that government is?" With regard to all matters of detail, on which the parliamentary Erastians loved to dilate, these would naturally arise either from Scripture precept or Scripture practice, applied as enlightened reason might dictate and emergencies require. But the Assembly was composed of men well able to detect the sophistry of their opponents, and therefore they declined entering, in the first place, into a series of detailed and circumstantial answers. But as they had been previously led to investigate very fully the same subject, in the course of their own deliberations while framing the Confession of Faith, they proceeded to state their main proposition on the subject of Church censures, on which, as will be perceived, the whole Erastian controversy turned, with the intention of giving a clear and explicit expression of their judgment respecting

* This was evidently for the purpose of intimidation.
† Rushworth, vol. vi. pp. 260, 261.

the master-principle and essence of the question.   This they
did in the following simple yet comprehensive proposition :
—" THE LORD JESUS, AS KING AND HEAD OF HIS CHURCH,
HATH THEREIN APPOINTED A GOVERNMENT, IN THE HAND OF
CHURCH OFFICERS, DISTINCT FROM THE CIVIL MAGISTRATE."
The affirmation of this proposition was regarded both by
the Assembly and by the Erastian party as containing a complete rejection of the Erastian principle; for, in their clear
style of reasoning, they perceived, that if Church government
were admitted to be " distinct from the civil magistrate,"
then the civil magistrate could exercise no jurisdiction in
Church matters, as that would be to break down the distinction.   Against this proposition, accordingly, the two Erastians in the Assembly, especially Coleman, directed their
whole force of argument.   Baillie says, " To oppose the
Erastian heresy, we find it necessary to say, that Christ in
the New Testament had institute a Church government distinct from the civil, to be exercised by the officers of the
Church, without commission from the magistrate.   None in
the Assembly has any doubt of this truth, but one Mr Coleman, a professed Erastian ; a man reasonably learned, but
stupid and inconsiderate, half a pleasant, and of small estimation.   But the lawyers in the Parliament did blow up the
poor man with much vanity; so he is become their champion,
to bring out, the best way he can, Erastus' arguments against
the proposition.   We give him a fair and free hearing, albeit
we fear, when we have answered all he can bring, and have
confirmed with undeniable proofs our proposition, the Houses,
when it comes to them, shall scrape it out of the Confession ;
for this point is their idol.   The most of them are incredibly
zealous for it.   The pope and the king were never more
earnest for the headship of the Church than the plurality of
this Parliament." *

After the Assembly had debated this proposition for some

* Baillie, vol. ii. p. 360.

time, and were about to put it to the vote, Coleman was taken ill, and sent a request to the Assembly, that they would delay it for a few days, as he had still some arguments to bring forward. The Assembly complied; but after an illness of four or five days he expired, and the proposition was passed, with the single dissentient vote of Lightfoot. In the account of this event contained in "Neal's History of the Puritans," the names of those who subscribed this proposition, according to the injunction of the Parliament, are given, amounting to *fifty-two*, and comprising all the men of chief eminence in the Assembly, exclusive of the Scottish divines, who spoke, but did not vote on any subject. Neal contradicts himself in his account, stating, that the Independents took " the opportunity to withdraw, refusing absolutely to be concerned in the affair;"* yet in the list which he gives there are the names of Goodwin, Nye, Greenhill, and Carter, all of them Independents,—the names of Burroughs, Bridge, and Simpson, only being wanting to complete the whole of that party who signed the Reasons of Dissent, of which mention has been already made. Indeed, the whole of Neal's statement respecting the conduct of the Presbyterians is so warped and biassed by prejudice, that it presents a very unfair view, not only of their characters, but even of the facts that occurred in which they bore a leading part.

But the Assembly were not contented with thus cutting the heart out of the Erastian theory ; they appointed a committee to prepare answers to the Parliament's questions, following out the principle of their own fundamental proposition. " The work of the Assembly," says Baillie, " these bygone weeks has been to answer some very captious questions of the Parliament, about the clear scriptural warrant for all the punctilios of the government. It was thought it would be impossible for us to answer, and that in our answers there would be no unanimity; yet, by God's grace,

---

* Neal, vol. ii. p. 395.

we shall deceive them who were waiting for our halting. The committee has prepared very solid and satisfactory answers already to almost all the questions, wherein there is like to be an unanimity absolute in all things material, even with the Independents. But because of the Assembly's way, and the Independents' miserable, unamendable design to keep all things from any conclusion, it's like we shall not be able to perfect our answers for some time ; therefore, I have put some of my good friends, leading men in the House of Commons, to move the Assembly to lay aside our questions for a time, and labour that which is most necessary, and all are crying for,—the perfecting of the Confession of Faith and Catechism." * The House of Commons followed the suggestion here alluded to, which was made about the middle of July, and as the course of events rolled on, and matters of great importance occupied the attention of the Parliament, little more inquiry was made by the House respecting the Assembly's answers to these questions.

Although the answers of the Assembly to these Erastian questions were not finally called for and printed by the Parliament, there is some reason to believe that their labour was not wholly lost to the public. For after the change of affairs which induced the Parliament to change its course, several months were allowed to pass away, lest the Commons might repeat their demand ; but at length, on the 1st of December 1646, a book was published, entitled, " *Jus Divinum Regiminis Ecclesiastici;* or, The Divine Right of Church Government Asserted and Evidenced by the Holy Scriptures. By sundry Ministers of Christ within the City of London." This work is an express and direct answer to the Parliament's questions respecting divine right, following these questions in their order, and giving to them a distinct reply point by

* Baillie, vol. ii. p. 378.—This is a sufficient refutation of Neal's assertion, that the Assembly durst not present their answers to Parliament for fear of a *premunire.*

point, confirming every argument by Scripture proofs, and by quotations from the writings of learned and able ecclesiastical authors. Judging from internal evidence, in matter, manner, and style, it appears almost certain that this work at least embodies the substance of the answer prepared by the Assembly, somewhat enlarged and modified by the city ministers, in whose name it was published. This idea is not set aside by the manner in which it is noticed by Baillie, who says: "The ministers of London have put out this day a very fine book, proving from Scripture the divine right of every part of the Presbyterial government." * We do not mean to assert, that the work published by the city ministers was the identical production of the Assembly; but that so much of the one was transfused into the other as to render them to all practical intents one work, and to relieve us from any cause to regret that the Assembly's answer was not published. On the seventh day after the appearance of this book, the House of Commons requested the Assembly to give in their answers to the *jus divinum* queries, as if to intimate their suspicion with regard to the authorship of the recent publication; but this demand was not again repeated, and no direct notice was taken of the book itself. But whether the work in question was to any considerable extent the production of the Assembly Divines or not, this at least is certain, that it is the most complete and able defence of Presbyterian Church government that has yet appeared, and places its divine right on a foundation which will not easily be shaken.†

Allusion has been made to events of great public importance, which contributed not a little to change the tone of the Parliament. These may be briefly mentioned. The military affairs of the year 1645 terminated most disastrously for the king. All his armies were beaten out of the field,

* Baillie, vol. ii. p. 411.

† A reprint of this work would be a very valuable contribution to the Presbyterian cause in the present day.

and he was constrained to retreat to Oxford with the wreck of his troops, and there to try what could be gained by intrigues and negotiations, since he could no longer maintain an open war. During the course of these negotiations there arose a degree of alienation between the English Parliament and the Scottish commissioners and Parliament, which threatened an open rupture. The English Parliament, influenced by Cromwell and his friends, were not desirous of peace; while the Scottish commissioners made every effort to procure such terms as the king might accept without absolute submission. It was while their temper was in this high and heated state, that the English Parliament treated the petitions of the city ministers, and of the Assembly itself, with that scant courtesy, if not rather overbearing haughtiness, which has been already related. Elated with success, they could not brook the firm and fearless attitude assumed by the Presbyterian divines, and resented the remonstrances of the Scottish commissioners and Parliament, as an improper interference with their imperial dignity. At this very juncture the king, despairing of obtaining from the English Parliament any terms to which he could accede, left Oxford in disguise, on the 27th of April, and after wandering about for a few days, arrived at the quarters of the Scottish army, which was besieging Newark, on the 5th of May 1646. This was totally unexpected by either the army or the commissioners of Scotland; for though his majesty had attempted to induce the Scottish general and Committee of Estates to espouse his cause against the Parliament, he had received such an answer from them as rendered it, in their opinion, impossible that he would put himself into their power. No sooner was this event known in London than the tone and temper of the Parliament was very sensibly changed. They perceived that it was no longer safe to treat the remonstrances of Scotland with disrespect; and as they were well aware how much the establishment of Presbyterian Church govern-

S

ment in both kingdoms was longed for by the Scottish Church and people, they deemed it expedient to remove some of the obstacles by which this had been hitherto prevented.

Up till this time the ordinance of March 14, for the choice of ruling elders and the erection of presbyteries, had not received the full ratification of the House of Lords; and even if it had, it would have been inoperative, because the ministers were resolute not to become members of presbyteries, so long as they were subject to such Erastian interference, and so bereft of their due powers, as would have been the case under that ordinance. But on the 5th of June both Houses not only ratified the ordinance, and on the 9th issued an order that it should be immediately put into execution,* but also at the same time laid aside the clause respecting provincial commissioners to judge of new cases of scandal,—thus removing the main obstacle to its reception by the ministers. This concession having been made, the Assembly Divines and the city ministers met at Sion College, on the 19th of June, and after some conference, agreed upon a declaration, expressing approbation of what had been done, specifying what was still defective, and declaring that they now conceive it to be their duty to put in practice the present settlement, as far as they conceive it correspondent with the Word of God.†

The actual erection of Presbyteries did not immediately follow this ordinance of Parliament, and consent of the Assembly and the city ministers; for the attention of the whole community was strongly attracted to the negotiations between the king and the Parliaments of the two kingdoms, as also between the two Parliaments themselves. It scarcely falls within our province to relate even an outline of the political intrigues which distracted the kingdom for many months after his majesty's retreat to the Scottish army; yet so much

* Whitelocke, p. 213.
† Baillie, vol. ii. p. 377; Neal, vol. ii. p. 396. In this instance also the account of Neal is unfair and inaccurate, to use no harsher terms.

must be stated as is necessary to explain the bearing of these events upon the proceedings of the Assembly. There is every reason to believe that the determination of the king to seek a retreat in the Scottish army, was the result of a complication of circumstances and of intrigues,—circumstances which he could not control, and intrigues in which he and his adherents were mutually deceivers and deceived. The fortune of war had been decisively against him, so that he could no longer expect to recover his power by conquest; and the demands of the Parliament rose with their success, so that he was constrained to contemplate the necessity of submission, if he could not contrive to divide his victorious antagonists. For that purpose he carried on a series of intrigues with all parties that would listen to him, particularly with the Independents in both army and Parliament. The decided ground taken by the Scottish Parliament, Church, and nation, in behalf of their religious liberties, as stated in their Covenant, which he regarded with intense hostility, rendered him unwilling to hold intercourse with them, and at the same time made it more than doubtful whether any measure of success could be expected to follow such an attempt. But the disagreement which took place between the English Parliament and the Scottish commissioners seemed to give some reason to hope that, by skilful management, it might at last be possible to disunite the kingdoms, and through their disunion to recover his own ascendency over both. A French agent was sent to the Scottish army to sound the Committee of Estates, who were with it; and upon receiving a half-favourable report from this agent, the king resolved to go in person to the Scottish army,—hoping, by such an apparent act of confidence in their honour and loyalty, to render it impossible for them to do otherwise than espouse his cause. But his private agent deceived him,—he deceived himself,—and the Scottish generals and statesmen were not deceived.

At the very first interview which the king had with his

Scottish subjects, they gave him distinctly to know, that they neither could nor would do any thing contrary to their engagement with England in the Solemn League and Covenant, or to the spirit of that sacred document. And in a letter to the Committee of both kingdoms, written immediately after his majesty's arrival, they declared, " That they were astonished at the providence of the king's coming to their army; and desired that it might be improved to the best advantage for promoting the work of uniformity, for settling of religion and righteousness, and attaining of peace, according to the Covenant and Treaty, by advice of the Parliaments of both kingdoms, or their commissioners: And they further declare, that there hath been no treaty betwixt his majesty and them; and in so deep a business they desire the advice of the Committee of both kingdoms." * The king soon perceived that he had both overrated his own personal influence and undervalued the power of religious principle,—that he had deceived himself, and had now to do with men who were too sagacious to be deluded, and too high-principled to be turned from the path of integrity and truth. Finding that he was not likely to gain the object which he had in view, the king wrote to the English Parliament, requesting permission " to come to London with safety, freedom, and honour;" declaring, that he was resolved " to comply with the Houses in what should be most for the good of his subjects." The Parliament itself had previously resolved to demand the king's person, declaring, " That in England the disposal of him belonged to the Parliament of England, and that the Scots army were in pay of the Parliament of England; that the king ought to be near his Parliament; and that this was consonant to the Covenant." † And in order to get quit of the Scottish army as quickly as possible, they voted, a few days afterwards, " That this kingdom had no further need of the army of their brethren the Scots in this kingdom." So early was it apparent

* Whitelocke, p. 210.   † Ibid.

that the English Parliament was determined to obtain possession of their sovereign's person, and that the Scottish nation could not otherwise protect him than by friendly negotiation, so as to secure a peace including his safety; or by declaring war against England in his behalf, contrary to their obligations in the Solemn League and Covenant, and contrary to their own determination to defend religious liberty,—of which the king was the known and determined enemy. This they saw clearly; and being at the same time aware of the republican inclinations of Cromwell and his strong party, they perceived that the only way in which they could interfere to preserve his majesty, without incurring the guilt of perjury, was to persuade him, if possible, to sign the Covenant, and consent to the establishment of Presbyterian Church government. But to this no force of argument, no urgency of persuasion, no tearful earnestness of entreaty, could induce him to consent; and after spending several months in fruitless negotiations, they were constrained to abandon the impracticable attempt, and to leave him to pursue the fatal course along which he was driven by his own wilful and infatuated obstinacy, and by the pernicious advice of his narrow-minded and selfish prelatic counsellors.

It may be necessary here to state, what it would not be difficult to prove beyond the power of dispute, did our limits and the nature of this work permit, that there was no connection whatever between the payment of the arrears due to the Scottish army, and the surrendering of the king to the English Parliament. A short statement of facts is all that can here be given; but that may be enough, at least to every mind not thickly incrusted with prejudice. From the time when the victories of the English armies rendered them able to cope with the king without the assistance of the Scottish forces, the Parliament was desirous to secure the entire glory and advantage of the triumph to themselves. For this purpose they did every thing in their power to irritate and disparage the Scot-

tish army.. They withheld the payment of the troops, con-
straining them to have recourse to the ungracious procedure
of levying the means of subsistence from the inhabitants of
the country; and they listened readily to the complaints
which were made of these exactions. Thus hampered and
discouraged, the Scottish army was unable to perform any
signal exploit, while, Fairfax and Cromwell received every
aid and encouragement that Parliament could give. The
Scottish army was naturally indignant at such treatment, and
even entertained some apprehension, that if Fairfax should
take Oxford, and obtain possession of the king's person, he
would direct his force against them, and compel them to fight,
or to retire without any thing having been accomplished for
which they had entered England. Their position at Newark,
almost in the centre of the kingdom, rendered this peculiarly
hazardous; and therefore, as soon as the king came to the
army, and Newark surrendered, they began their march
northwards, and ceased not till they arrived at Newcastle,
where they took up their quarters, waiting the course of
negotiations to secure peace, if practicable, and occupying a
favourable position for war, if peace could not be obtained,
and the king should be persuaded to sign the Covenant.

Even before the negotiations for peace commenced on the
19th of May, the English Parliament voted that an hundred
thousand pounds should be paid to the Scottish army, one
half after they should have surrendered Newcastle, Carlisle,
and the other English garrisons in their possession, and the
other half after their advance into Scotland.* The Scottish
commissioners, knowing that the Parliament had not the
means of obtaining a large supply of money without the consent and support of the city of London, gladly availed themselves of the idea which this offer suggested, and demanded
a much larger sum, with the strong conviction that the
Parliament neither could nor would grant their demand, and

* Whitelocke, p. 211.

that during the delay caused by this new element of negotiation, they might persuade the king to consent to the offered
terms of peace. " It's all our skill," says Baillie, " to gain a
little time. Their first offer to us was of one hundred thousand pounds sterling, for the disbanding of our army. We,
this day (August 18th), gave them in a paper, wherein we
were peremptor for more than double that sum for the present, beside the huge sums which we crave to be paid after-
ward. They have appointed a committee to confer with us ;
we are in some hopes of agreement. The money must be
borrowed in the city, and here will be the question ; they are
our loving friends ; but before they will part with more money,
they will press hard the disbanding of their own army as well
as ours." * Again he says, " When the king's unhappy
answer to the commissioners came hither, it was our great
care to divert this Parliament from all deliberation about the
king, till he had yet some more time of advice. We cast in
the debate of our army's return, and rendering the garrisons."
On the 1st of September the House of Commons held a long
debate on the demand of the Scottish army's payment ; and
on the 5th of the same month voted the sum of two hundred
thousand pounds on their advance to Scotland, if it could be
raised, and appointed a committee to manage the matter.†
But so far from this being the price of the king's surrender
to the Parliament, the question respecting the disposal of his
person continued to be keenly debated between the two kingdoms for above four months longer, before Scotland would
consent to relinquish the desperate and hopeless task of
endeavouring to save the infatuated and uncomplying king.
During that period Charles wrote repeatedly to the English
Parliament, expressing his desire to be near them, the more
speedily and effectually to conclude the long-continued negotiations. Sadly and unwillingly at last the Scottish Committee
of Estates relinquished the care of his majesty's person to the

* Baillie, vol. ii. p. 391.   † Whitelocke, pp. 225, 226.

commissioners of the English Parliament, on the 30th of January 1647, according to the terms of the agreement to that effect which had been concluded between the two kingdoms, and published in the form of a declaration by the Scottish Parliament on the 16th of January.

The simple statement of these facts and dates ought to be enough to set aside for ever the false and calumnious assertion that Scotland sold her king. The payment of the army's arrears was voted by the English Parliament on the 5th of September; the negotiations respecting the king were not concluded till the 16th of January. It was impossible to preserve him, without a breach of the League with England, a violation of the National Covenant, and the forcible retention of their sovereign's person, against his own will, even when engaging in a perilous war against a more powerful kingdom in his defence. His own incurable dissimulation and obstinacy urged him on his fate, which Scotland foresaw and deplored, but could not avert.

To return to the subject more immediately within our province. Although the Assembly Divines and the city ministers had expressed their opinion that they could at length consent to put into practical operation the Presbyterian Church government, as sanctioned by Parliament, they still complained of its defectiveness, and were in no haste to form themselves into Presbyteries. Repeated applications were made to Parliament for the removal of the obstacles that still remained; and on the 22d of April 1647, the Houses published resolutions, entitled, " Remedies for removing some obstructions to Church government;" in which they ordered letters to be sent to the several counties of England, requiring the ministers immediately to form themselves into distinct Presbyteries; and appointing the ministers and elders of the several Presbyteries of the province of London, to hold their Provincial Assembly in the Convocation-house of St Paul's, on the first Monday of May. According to this appointment, the first meeting of the Provincial Assembly or Synod of London was held on the 3d of May 1647.* At this Synod there were about one hundred and eight persons present, and Dr Gouge was chosen prolocutor or moderator. The province of London was divided into twelve Presbyteries; and in the formation of the Synod each Presbytery chose two ministers and four elders, as their representatives or commissioners. The ministers of Lancashire were also formed into Presbyteries and a Synod ; and in many other counties they associated themselves for the management of ecclesiastical affairs, though not in the regular form of Presbyteries and Synods.

There was now no positive obstruction to the regular and final organization of Presbyterian Church government, except the still pending treaties between the king and the Parliament. Knowing the king's attachment to Prelacy and his strong dislike to Presbytery, the Parliament did not wish to make a final and permanent establishment of the latter form of Church government till they should have endeavoured to persuade his majesty to consent, so that it might be engrossed in the treaty, and thereby obtain the conclusive ratification of the royal signature. But after the army had for a time overawed the Parliament, when the Houses again recovered something like the free exercise of their legislative functions, they voted, " That the king be desired to give his sanction to such acts as shall be presented to him, for settling the Presbyterian government for three years, with a provision that no person shall be liable to any question or penalty, only for nonconformity to the said government, or to the form of divine services appointed in the ordinances. And that such as shall not voluntarily conform to the said form of government and divine service, shall have liberty to meet for the service and worship of God, and for exercise of religious duties and ordinances, in a fit and convenient place, so as nothing be done

* Rushworth, vol. vi. p. 476.

by them to the disturbance of the peace of the kingdom. And provided that this extend not to any toleration of the Popish religion, nor to any penalties imposed upon Popish recusants, nor to tolerate the practice of any thing contrary to the principles of Christian religion, contained in the Apostles' Creed, as it is expounded in the Articles of the Church of England : nor to any thing contrary to the point of faith, for the ignorance whereof men are to be kept from the Lord's supper ; nor to excuse any from the penalties for not coming to hear the Word of God on the Lord's day in any church or chapel, unless he can show a reasonable cause, or was hearing the Word of God preached or expounded elsewhere." These were the votes of the Lords ; and to these the Commons added; "That the Presbyterian government be established till the end of the next session of Parliament, which was to be a year after that date. That the tenths and maintenance belonging to any church shall be only to such as can submit to the Presbyterian government, and to none other. That liberty of conscience granted shall extend to none that shall preach, print, or publish, any thing contrary to the first fifteen of the Thirty-nine Articles, except the eighth. That it extend not to Popish recusants, or taking away any penal laws against them. That the indulgence to tender consciences shall not extend to tolerate the Common Prayer." * These votes were passed on the 13th day of October 1647, and may be regarded as the final settlement of the Presbyterian Church government, so far as that was done by the Long Parliament, in accordance with the advice of the Westminster Assembly of Divines. For before the expiration of the period named by the Parliament, the Parliament itself had sunk beneath the power of Cromwell, whose policy was to establish no form of Church government, but to keep every thing dependent upon himself, though his chief favours were bestowed upon the Independents.

* Whitelocke, pp. 275, 276.

There is but one point more connected with the Erastian controversy which requires to be stated, namely, its effect upon the formation and ratification of the Confession of Faith. For a considerable time after the Assembly commenced its deliberations, the chief subjects which occupied its attention were, the Directories for public worship, and ordination, and the form of Church government, including the power of Church censure. Till some satisfactory conclusions had been reached on these points, the Assembly abstained from entering upon the less agitating, but not less important work of framing a Confession of Faith. But having completed their task, so far as depended upon themselves, they appointed a committee to prepare and arrange the main propositions which were to be discussed and digested into a system by the Assembly. The members of this committee were, Dr Hoyle, Dr Gouge, Messrs Herle, Gataker, Tuckney, Reynolds, and Vines, with the Scottish commissioners. These learned and able divines began their labours by arranging in the most systematic order the various great and sacred truths which God has revealed to man ; and reduced these to thirty-two distinct heads or chapters, each having a title expressive of its subject. These were again subdivided into sections ; and the committee formed themselves into several sub-committees, each of whom took a specific topic, for the sake of exact and concentrated deliberation. When these sub-committees had completed their respective tasks, the whole was laid before the entire committee, and any alterations suggested and debated till all were of one mind. And when any title or chapter had been thus fully prepared by the committee, it was reported to the Assembly, and again subjected to the most minute and careful investigation, in every paragraph, sentence, and word. It is exceedingly gratifying to be able to state, that throughout the deliberations of the Assembly, when composing the Confession of Faith, there prevailed almost an entire and perfect harmony. There appear, indeed, to have been only two subjects on which any difference of opinion existed among them. The one of these was the doctrine of election, concerning which, as Baillie says, they had long and tough debates; " Yet," he adds, " thanks to God, all is gone right according to our mind."* The other was that of which mention has been already made, namely, that " the Lord Jesus, as King and Head of his Church, has therein appointed a government in the hand of Church-officers distinct from the civil magistrate ; " which appears as the fundamental proposition of the chapter entitled " Of Church censures." This proposition the Assembly manifestly intended and understood to contain a principle directly and necessarily opposed to the very essence of Erastianism ; and it was regarded in the same light by the Erastians themselves, consequently it became the subject of long and earnest discussion, and was strenuously opposed by Lightfoot and Coleman, especially the latter. But Coleman falling ill and dying before the debate was concluded, it was carried, the sole dissentient voice being that of Lightfoot. It does not appear that the Erastian lay-assessors attempted to debate the point in the Assembly, but wisely, or at least cunningly, reserved their opposition for the House of Commons, being aware that their strength lay in power, not argument. The whole influence of the Erastians did not succeed in modifying, no, not by one word, the statement of the Assembly's faith on this vital point; although some have had the hardihood to assert that they condescended to compromise the question. The conduct of the Assembly in the Erastian controversy contrasts strongly with their conduct in the Independent controversy. With the Independents there were many instances of compromise and accommodation, or at least of attempts in that direction ; with the Erastians none, no, not so much as one. They could not compel the Parliament to give its sanction to all that they proposed; but they could and did state freely and fearlessly what they believed

* Baillie, vol. ii. p. 325.

to be the truth, earnestly and urgently petitioning that it might be ratified, then leaving the legislative powers to accept or reject on their own responsibility. To the Independents, on the other hand, they showed the utmost leniency; and while they could not abandon their own conscientious convictions, they were extremely reluctant to deal harshly with the conscientious scruples of men whom they regarded as brethren.

Some discussion took place on the thirty-first chapter in the Confession, respecting Synods and Councils; but that subject also was carried in the express language of the Assembly, and without any Erastian modification. The first half of the Confession was laid before the Parliament early in October 1646, and on the 26th of November the remainder was produced to the Assembly in its completed form, when the prolocutor returned thanks to the committees, in the name of the Assembly, for their great pains in perfecting the work committed to them. It was then carefully transcribed; and on the 3d of December 1646, it was presented to Parliament, by the whole Assembly in a body, under the title of " The Humble Advice of the Assembly of Divines and others, now by the authority of Parliament sitting at Westminster, concerning a Confession of Faith." On the 7th, Parliament ordered " five hundred copies of it to be printed for the members of both Houses; and that the Assembly do bring in their marginal notes, to prove every part of it by Scripture."* There is strong reason to believe that the House of Commons demanded the insertion of the Scripture texts, for the purpose of obtaining an additional period of delay, as indeed Baillie pretty plainly intimates.

The Assembly, accordingly, resumed their task, and after encountering a number of interposing obstacles, again produced the Confession of Faith, with full scriptural proofs annexed to all its propositions, and laid it before the Parlia-

* Whitelocke, p. 233.

ment on the 29th day of April 1647. The thanks of the
House were given to the Assembly for their labours in this
important matter ; and " six hundred copies were ordered to
be printed for the use of the Houses and the Assembly ; and
no more, and that none presume to reprint the same, till
further orders."* The appointed number of copies having
been printed, they were delivered to the members of both
Houses by Mr Byfield, on the 19th of May, when it was
resolved to consider the whole production, article by article,
previous to its being published with the sanction of Parliament, as the Confession of Faith held by that Church on
which they meant to confer the benefits of a national establishment. But the deliberations of the Parliament were interrupted by the insurrection of the army, and the numerous,
protracted, and unsatisfactory negotiations in which they were
engaged with the king ; so that they had not completed their
examination of the Confession till March 1648. On the 22d
day of that month a conference was held between the two
Houses, to compare their opinions respecting the Confession
of Faith, the result of which is thus stated by Rushworth :
" The Commons this day (March 22d), at a conference, presented the Lords with the Confession of Faith passed by
them, with some alterations, viz., That they do agree with
their Lordships, and so with the Assembly, in the doctrinal
part, and desire the same may be made public, that this
kingdom, and all the Reformed Churches of Christendom,
may see the Parliament of England differ not in doctrine.
In some particulars there were some phrases altered, as in
that of *tribute* being due to the magistrate, they put *dues* : to
the degree of marriage they refer to the law established :
particulars in discipline are recommitted : and for the title,
they make it not, '*A Confession of Faith*,' because not so
running, ' *I confess*,' at the beginning of every section ; but,
'*Articles of Faith agreed upon by both Houses of Parliament*,'

* Rushworth, vol. vi. p. 473.

as most suitable to the former title of the Thirty-nine Articles." *

Such was the last positive enactment made by the English Parliament respecting the Confession of Faith ; for the subsequent mention made of it, and of other particulars in Presbyterian Church government, during the course of their negotiations with the king, were not enactments, but attempts at accommodation with his majesty, with the view of endeavouring to secure a satisfactory basis for a permanent peace to Church and State. And it will be observed, that the only material defect mentioned in this reported conference between the Houses is, that "*particulars in discipline are recommitted.*" These " particulars" are said to have been the thirtieth chapter, " Of Church censures ;" the thirty-first chapter, " Of Synods and Councils ;" and the fourth section of the twentieth chapter, " Of Christian liberty, and liberty of conscience." The enumeration of these particulars rests on the authority of Neal,† which is by no means unimpeachable, but it is in itself probable, being quite consistent with the views of the Erastians, whose chief hostility was directed against the power of Church discipline, of which the chapters specified contain an explicit statement, according to the judgment of the Assembly. It is of some importance to remark, that these " particulars in discipline" were not *rejected* by the English Parliament, as is generally asserted, but merely recommitted, or referred to a committee to be more maturely considered. But as the Parliament itself not long afterwards fell under the power of the army, and was at length forcibly dissolved by Cromwell, the committee never returned a report, and consequently these particulars were never either formally rejected or ratified by the Parliament of England. The fact of their having been recommitted is of itself enough to prove that they were not, in the estimation of such men as Selden and Whitelocke, susceptible of an

* Rushworth, vol. vii. p. 1035.   † Neal, vol. ii. p. 429.

Erastian interpretation, although such an opinion has been hazarded by men certainly not a little their inferiors in learning, legal acumen, and intellectual power.

A full account of the literature of the Erastian controversy would be an extremely interesting and highly important production ; but to attempt any thing more than a very brief outline of it here would lead to a digression far beyond our limits. We shall therefore mention almost solely those works which were either written by some of the Westminster Divines, or were closely connected with the proceedings of that venerable Assembly. A few preliminary sentences, however, may be of use to introduce the subject.

During the earliest ages of Christianity the only relationship in which the civil magistrate and the Church stood towards each other, was that which exists between persecutors and the persecuted. When at length Constantine avowed himself a Christian, persecution ceased, and the more friendly relation of granting and receiving protection became that between the State and the Church. But Christianity had already become deeply tainted with the antichristian leaven ; Prelacy had raised its haughty head, equally inclined to domineer over what it regarded as the inferior orders of the clergy, and over the people, and to arrogate to itself exemption from the control of the civil magistrate, even in civil matters. A protracted struggle ensued between the imperial and royal powers and the Bishop of Rome, the issue of which was, not merely an exemption of ecclesiastical matters, and even persons, from civil authority, but the establishment of a supremacy over civil rulers and civil matters wielded by the Romish hierarchy, and forming a complete spiritual and civil despotism. This fearful and degrading despotism was overthrown by the Reformation ; and although the great and wise Christian divines and patriots by whose instrumentality the Reformation was effected, were unable entirely to perfect their work, yet they all, more or less clearly, indicated their judgment that the two jurisdictions, civil and ecclesiastical, ought to be, and to remain co-ordinate and distinct, mutually supporting and supported, but each abstaining from interference with the other's intrinsic and inherent rights, privileges, and powers. In some countries this high and true theory was clearly developed, in others more obscurely, and in some not at all. In no part of Reformed Christendom was it so distinctly stated, and so fully realised, as in Scotland; and nowhere was it so thoroughly rejected as in England. In England, indeed, the exact counterpart of the Romish system was established, the king's ecclesiastical supremacy rendering him equally judge of ecclesiastical as of civil matters. It was soon found that in this, as in all other things, extremes meet; the king, by a slight transfer of terms, became a civil pope, and the country was oppressed by a complete civil and spiritual despotism.

In the meantime, the great principle of truth and freedom, the principle of distinct and co-ordinate civil and ecclesiastical jurisdictions, was assailed on the Continent by Erastus, and became a subject of speculative thought and controversial literature. Unfortunately for the cause of truth and freedom, the great men of the Reformation had nearly all departed from the scene of their labours and triumphs before the Erastian theory was fully brought forward, so that it was not at once met and overthrown as it would otherwise have been. And besides, it was too accordant with the views and feelings of men of secular minds not to obtain a ready credence and a hearty welcome from politicians, who can form no higher idea of a Church than an engine of State; from lawyers, who can conceive no higher rule than statutory enactments; and from irreligious and immoral men, who equally detest and fear the strict and pure severity of divinely authorised Christian discipline. In England, also, the despotism of the Prelatic hierarchy tended to produce, in the minds of all zealous assertors of freedom, an instinctive dread of ecclesiastical

T

power, and rendered many men Erastians from terror and in
self-defence, not because they had studied the theory, and
been convinced of its truth. Such men were ready to oppose
the establishment of Presbyterian Church government on the
ground of divine right, not because they were convinced that
no system of Church government can justly lay claim to an
authority so high and sacred ; but because they were apprehensive that it would produce a species of spiritual despotism
as oppressive as that which they had just been striving to
abolish. In vain did the Scottish statesmen and divines
answer and refute their objections ; their fears were not removed, and fear is a mental emotion that cannot be set aside
by argument.

But Selden, Whitelocke, Lightfoot, and Coleman, took up
the subject on other grounds, which, though difficult, were
not equally unassailable by reason. Their chief argument
was one of analogy, although, as they used it, the appearance
which it bore was that of identity. They held that the
Christian system ought to resemble, or rather to be identical
with, the system of the Mosaic Dispensation ; and they attempted to prove, that there were not two distinct and co-
ordinate courts, one civil and the other ecclesiastical, among
the Hebrews, but that there was a mixed jurisdiction, of
which the king was the supreme and ultimate head and
ruler ; and that, consequently, the civil courts determined all
matters, both civil and ecclesiastical, and inflicted all punishments, both such as affected person and property, and such
as affected a man's religious privileges, properly termed
Church censures. From this they concluded, that the civil
magistrate, in countries avowedly Christian, ought to possess
an equal, or identical authority, and ought consequently to
be the supreme and ultimate judge in all matters, both civil
and ecclesiastical, inflicting or removing the penalties of
Church censure equally with those affecting person and property. The arguments on which they most relied were drawn

from rabbinical lore, rather than from the Bible itself, although they were very willing to obtain the appearance of its support, by ingenious versions, or perversions of peculiar passages of Scripture. Selden's argument has been already stated, and need not be repeated. The value of Lightfoot's authority may be estimated somewhat lower than is usually done, if we take into consideration, not merely the amount of his learning, but the soundness, or the reverse, of his judgment. As for instance, he strenuously maintained that the Jews are utterly and finally rejected, that those of them who embraced Christianity in the time of Christ and the apostles were the "remnant to be saved," and that there neither then was, nor ever shall be, any universal calling of them.* He held also, that the expressions, "the keys of the kingdom of heaven," and "binding and loosing," had no reference to discipline, but merely to doctrine; in which opinion he differed from almost every person, both before and since his time. His opinion of the Septuagint was equally at variance with the views of the most eminently learned and judicious men. In short, whatever may be said of his extensive and minute rabbinical lore, it is impossible to regard his judgment as entitled to much deference; consequently his advocacy of Erastian principles will not avail much for their support.

Mention has already been made of Coleman's sermon, preached before the House of Commons, on the 30th of July 1645. That sermon must be noticed as part of the Erastian literature, not so much on account of its own merits, as on account of other works to the composing of which it gave occasion. Towards the end of the sermon, various advices and directions are given, as calculated to promote the peace and welfare of the kingdom; and of these, one point on which Coleman dwelt strongly was, the unity of the Church, and the best way to procure that unity. For this he gives several directions, of which the following are the chief:—" 1. Es-

* Lightfoot, vol. i. p. 165.

tablish as few things *jure divino* as can well be. Hold out
the practice, but not the ground. 2. Let all precepts held
out as divine institutions have clear scriptures; an occasional
practice, a phrase upon the by, a thing named, are too weak
grounds to uphold such a building. I could never yet see
how two co-ordinate governments, exempt from superiority
and inferiority, can be in one State; and in Scripture no
such thing is found, that I know of. 3. Lay no more burden of government upon the shoulders of ministers than
Christ hath plainly laid upon them; let them have no more
hand therein than the Holy Ghost clearly gives them. The
ministers will have other work to do, and such as will take
up the whole man. I ingenuously profess I have a heart
that knows better how to be governed than to govern. I fear
an ambitious ensnarement; and I have cause. I see what
raised Prelacy and Papacy to such a height; and what their
practices were, being so raised. Give us doctrine; take you
the government. Give me leave to make this request, in the
name of the ministry; give us two things, and we shall do
well:—give us learning, and give us a competency. 4. A
Christian magistrate, as a Christian magistrate, is a governor
in the Church. All magistrates, it is true, are not Christians;
but that is their fault: all should be; and when they are,
they are to manage their office under and for Christ. Christ
hath placed governments in his Church. Of other governments besides magistracy I find no institution; of them I do.
I find all government given to Christ, and to Christ as Mediator; and Christ, as head of these, given to the Church. To
rob the kingdom of Christ of the magistrate and his governing power, I cannot excuse, no, not from a kind of sacrilege,
if the magistrate be His." *

Sentiments such as these could not but be agreeable to the
Erastian members of Parliament; yet they seem to have
thought that Coleman had spoken with more plainness than

* Coleman's Sermon, pp. 24-28.

prudence, for while they ordered the sermon to be printed, as was customary, they did not give him the thanks of the House—an omission which was extremely unusual. But the principles stated in Coleman's sermon were not allowed to remain long unassailed. On the 27th of August George Gillespie preached a sermon before the House of Lords ; and when it was published, he appended to it a small pamphlet of nine leaves, entitled, " A Brotherly Examination of some Passages of Mr Coleman's late printed Sermon." In this short treatise, Gillespie not only answered and refuted Coleman, but also completely turned his arguments against himself ; proving, *first*, that the proper rule for human conduct in all things, but especially in religious matters, was to obtain as much of divine guidance, or to establish as much by divine right, as possible. He then proceeds to examine in succession Coleman's directions or rules in a very masterly manner, annihilating or reversing each with great strength and clearness of argument. It is proved, that Coleman's principle, that in every divine institution Scripture must speak expressly, would involve a dangerous tampering with Scripture, and would sweep away several important Christian institutions which were never doubted ; and also, that whatever, by necessary consequence, is drawn from Scripture, is a divine truth, as well as what is expressly written therein The argument of co-ordinate jurisdictions is next taken up, and thoroughly established both by argument and by illustration. And in answer to Coleman's assertion, that he can find no institution of any government except magistracy, Gillespie proves from Scripture, that obedience is directly commanded to spiritual governors, who are " over us in the Lord," and who must have been distinct from the civil magistrate at a time when there was no Christian magistracy. In a short, but very clearly stated argument, Gillespie refutes Coleman's dangerous assertion, "That all government is given to Christ as Mediator, and Christ, as head of these, given to the Church;" and states the distinction between Christ's government as God and as Mediator,—by the right under-standing of which important idea the whole Erastian contro-versy must be decided.

Coleman soon afterwards published a pamphlet, entitled, "A Brotherly Examination Re-examined;" which is distin-guished chiefly by boldness of assertion and feebleness of ar-gument. To this Gillespie replied in another, bearing the title, "Nihil Respondes," in which he somewhat sharply ex-posed the weakness of his antagonist's reasoning. Irritated by the castigation he had received, Coleman published a bitter reply, to which he gave the not very intelligible title of "Male Dicis Maledicis,"—meaning, doubtless, that Gillespie's answer was rather of a railing character, or, to use a phrase of modern times, displayed a bad spirit. This Gillespie answered in an exceedingly vigorous pamphlet, entitled, "Male Audis," in which he swept rapidly over the whole Erastian controversy, so far as Coleman and some of his friends had brought it forward, convicted him and them of numerous self-contradic-tions, of unsoundness in theology, of violating the covenant which they had sworn, and of inculcating opinions fatal to both civil and religious liberty. To this Coleman did not attempt to reply, feeling, probably, that he was overmatched.

Several of these controversial pamphlets appeared in the course of the year 1646; and towards the close of the same year, Gillespie published his celebrated work, "Aaron's Rod Blossoming; or, The Divine Ordinance of Church Govern-ment Vindicated." In this remarkably able and elaborate production, Gillespie took up the Erastian controversy as stated and defended by its ablest advocates, fairly encounter-ing their strongest arguments, and assailing their most for-midable positions, in the frank and fearless manner of a man thoroughly sincere, and thoroughly convinced of the truth and goodness of his cause. The work is divided into three books; the *first* treating "Of the Jewish Church Government;" the *second*, "Of the Christian Church Government;" and the *third*, "Of Excommunication from the Church, and of Suspension from the Lord's Table." In the first book the five following propositions are demonstrated :—" 1. That the Jewish Church was formerly distinct from the Jewish State. 2. That there was an ecclesiastical sanhedrim and government distinct from the civil. 3. That there was an ecclesiastical excommunication distinct from civil punishments. 4. That in the Jewish Church there was also a public exomologesis, or declaration of repentance, and thereupon a reception or admission again of the offender to fellowship with the Church in the holy things. 5. That there was a suspension of the profane from the temple and passover." In this part of his work Gillespie boldly met and completely overthrew the united strength of Selden, Lightfoot, and Coleman, on their own chosen field of Hebrew learning.

In the second book or part of his work, " Of the Christian Church Government," the main element of the controversy which he had to encounter is of a nature so abstract, that it requires peculiar clearness of thought and accuracy of reasoning to keep the subject intelligible, and to draw the requisite distinctions. Coleman had in his sermon said, that " a Christian magistrate, as a Christian magistrate, is a governor in the Church ; " and that " all government is given to Christ as Mediator, and Christ, as head of these, is given to the Church : " from this he drew, though not very distinctly, the inference, that the Christian magistrate is directly the vicegerent of Christ, and therefore rules in the Church ; yet when pushed on this point he recoiled, and modified his inference so as to state it in the following terms, " that magistracy is given to Christ to be serviceable in his kingdom." But this modified statement would not have answered the purposes of the Erastians; and therefore their principle was more boldly and plainly expressed by Mr Hussey, minister at Chesilhurst, in Kent. This thorough Erastian boldly maintained, both

"that all government is given to Christ as Mediator, and that
Christ, as Mediator, has placed the Christian magistrate under
him, and as his vicegerent, and has given him commission to
govern the Church." It will be at once perceived, that the
very terms of this proposition involved an inquiry into the
nature and extent of Christ's mediatorial sovereignty. To
this point, accordingly, Gillespie directed his attention, in his
answer to Hussey's argument. He draws the distinction between the power and sovereignty of Christ as the Eternal
Son of God, and as God-man and Mediator. Considered as
the Eternal Son of God, as the Word by whom the universe
was called into being, he necessarily rules over all, and magistrates derive their power from him : considered as God-man
and Mediator, his direct sovereignty is in and over the Church,
which is his body ; and all power has been given to him both
in heaven and in earth, to be wielded by him for the safety
and the extension of his spiritual kingdom. A further distinction is drawn by Gillespie betwixt *power over* and *power
in* any kingdom ; which are not necessarily identical, although
the one may be employed for the purpose of promoting and
securing the other. In this argument, some have thought
that Gillespie has drawn his distinctions too fine, more so than
was necessary for his argument, or than many would be able
to follow or willing to admit. Beyond all question, he has
overthrown the Erastian theory, "that the civil magistrate is
Christ's vicegerent, and appointed to govern the Church;"
but some have been afraid that one aspect of his argument
might seem to countenance the Voluntary theory, and to
exempt civil government from the duty and responsibility of
giving countenance and support to the Church. Certainly no
such idea was ever in Gillespie's mind, nor is it my opinion
that his reasoning, rightly understood, gives it the least
shadow of support. Besides, if there be any danger arising
from the extreme fineness with which his distinctions are
drawn in that branch of his argument, it is completely re-

moved by the succeeding chapter, in which he treats " of the power and privilege of the magistrate in things and causes ecclesiastical, what it is, and what it is not." It would be well if magistrates would study carefully the passage alluded to, that they might acquire some information respecting the proper nature and boundaries of their duties and responsibilities *circa sacra*, about religious matters, as distinguished from what they have always been so eager to usurp, power *in sacris*, in religious matters, which forms no part of their peculiar duty, and is not within their province.

The third book, " Of Excommunication from the Church, and of Suspension from the Lord's Table," has the appearance of being an answer to Prynne, who had written largely against the exercise of such power by Church-officers. But it is evident that Gillespie had more in view than merely to answer Prynne. He makes no express reference to the Parliament's *jus divinum* queries, but he meets them nevertheless, and gives to them very conclusive answers, while appearing to be merely replying to a less formidable antagonist. The very tenor of Prynne's writings gave him this opportunity, for Prynne kept as closely to the line of the parliamentary queries as he with propriety could, so that Gillespie was both enabled and fairly entitled to answer both at once, so far as they were identical or similar. The work, in short, is a very complete refutation of the whole Erastian theory, taking up its leading points systematically, clearing away all obscurities of language, reducing every argument to its elementary principles, stating these in the form of simple propositions, and in terms strictly defined, so as to preclude sophistry or mere verbal subtleties, and proceeding to refute error and demonstrate truth, in a manner singularly clear and forcible, displaying, each in a very high degree, extensive learning, sound judgment, intellectual acuteness and strength, and the pure and lofty spirit of genuine Christianity.

Another very able and elaborate work on the Erastian

controversy was written and published also in the year 1646,
by Samuel Rutherford, entitled, "The Divine Right of
Church Government and Excommunication." Although
Rutherford manifests a thorough understanding of the subject, and treats very fully of all its main elements, exhibiting
great learning and extreme minuteness in thought, argument,
and illustration, his work is not, upon the whole, so successful as that of Gillespie. It is defective in point of arrangement, and especially for want of a statement of the systematic
order which the author meant to follow, though it is perfectly
plain that in his own mind there was a system by which he
regulated his course of argument. But the very minuteness
of his learning and his reasonings is felt to obscure, or rather
to overlay the subject; and while tracing out every point of
detail, the general impression is either weakened, or fails to
be forcibly conveyed. This, however, is criticism according
to modern taste; for the style of the times when Rutherford
wrote, was to exhaust every subject under discussion, and to
leave nothing unsaid upon it that could be said. In this
respect, therefore, Rutherford merely followed the spirit of the
age in which he lived; and whosoever will carefully peruse
his very elaborate work, will obtain ample materials for the
refutation of Erastianism.

There appeared another work at that time, not indeed
written by one of the Assembly of Divines, but so intimately
connected with the controversies which were agitated among
them, that it deserves to be mentioned here. This was a
treatise written by the celebrated Apollonius of Middleburg,
entitled, "Consideratio Quarundam Controversiarum ad Regi-
men Ecclesiæ Dei Spectantium, quæ in Angliæ Regno hodie
Agitantur." When this treatise was published, a copy of it
was sent to each member of the Westminster Assembly. "It
was," says Baillie, "not only very well taken, but also, which
is singular, and so far as I remember, *absque exemplo*, it was
ordered, *nemine contradicente*, to write a letter of thanks to

Apollonius."* The spirit of this work is thoroughly Presbyterian, encountering alike the theories of the Independents and the Erastians. It consists of seven chapters, each treating of a separate topic briefly, but with great clearness and force of reasoning. They are as follow :—1. Concerning the qualification of Church members. 2. Concerning a Church covenant. 3. Concerning the Church visible and instituted. 4. Concerning power ecclesiastical. 5. Concerning ecclesiastical ministry and its exercise. 6. Concerning Classes (Presbyteries) and Synods, and their authority. 7. Concerning forms or directories of faith and worship." It will at once be seen, that in the discussion of these topics the learned author must come into direct collision with both the Independents and the Erastians; yet his work has very little of a merely controversial character, being a calm and dispassionate, but very clear and able, disquisition concerning these important theological questions. There is another very valuable work by the same author, written a short time before the meeting of the Westminster Assembly, but treating very fully of the Erastian theory. Its title is, " Jus Majestatis Circa Sacra ; sive, Tractatus Theologicus de jure Magistratus circa res Ecclesiasticas." A translation of this work, for the purpose of general circulation, would be a very valuable contribution to the cause of religious liberty, which is at present beset by so many and such formidable enemies.

But we must quit this digression, however alluring the subject, and return to what remains to be stated respecting the concluding labours of the Westminster Assembly. Enough, if the attention of the reader has been directed to some of the most important works relating to the great Erastian controversy, which he may peruse for himself. And we do not hesitate to say, that it is scarcely possible for any man, especially for any Christian, to engage in a study of deeper and more universal importance. For it directly involves the glory

* Baillie, vol. ii. p. 246.

of the Mediator, as sole Head of his body the Church, and
sole King in Zion, his spiritual kingdom,—the purity, peace,
and freedom of the Church, in its administration and in the
rights and privileges of its members,—the moral and religious
welfare of the community, as involved in, and flowing from,
the efficiency and the extension of true and living Christianity,
the divinely appointed remedy for the miseries of fallen mankind,—and even the progress of civilization, the maintenance
of peace, and the stability of kingdoms, as all depending upon
the blessing and the favour and protection of Him who is
" Prince of the kings of the earth." And it is so eminently
the great controversy of the present day, that upon its right
or wrong determination depends the continuance of peace
throughout Christendom, or the speedy commencement of
commotions and conflicts of the most portentous nature, shak-
ing the foundations of society, and ending in wide-spread
anarchy and desolation.

CHAPTER V.

CONCLUSION OF THE WESTMINSTER ASSEMBLY.

The Larger and Shorter Catechisms—Inquiry concerning their Authorship
—Departure of the Scottish Commissioners—Final Dissolution of the
Westminster Assembly—The Ratification of the Directory of Worship,
and of Church Government by the Church of Scotland—Also of the Con-
fession of Faith, with an Explanation Guarding against any Erastian
Construction—Brief View of Public Events connected with the Assem-
bly's Proceedings—Struggle between the Parliament and the Army—
Cromwell's Usurpation—Death of Charles I.—Dissolution of the Long
Parliament and the Westminster Assembly—Synod of London—The
Independents in power—Committee of Triers—The Savoy Confession—
Restoration of Charles II.—Prelacy Restored—Act of Uniformity and
Ejection of Two Thousand Presbyterian Ministers on St Bartholomew's
Day—Retrospective Review and Summary of the Westminster Assem-
bly's Proceedings—Religious Uniformity in the Three Kingdoms by
Mutual Consultation, intended to Form the Basis of a Secure and Per-
manent Peace—Erastian Element and its Consequences—Mutual Mis-
understandings—Mutual Agreement—Effect on the Universities—On
Theological Literature—On Education—State of the Kingdom and
Army—Sectarians—Toleration—Its True Nature Intimated—How Misunderstood by both Parties—Liberty of Conscience—Unlimited Toleration not Granted by the Independents when in Power—Great Idea of a
General Protestant Union entertained by the Westminster Assembly—
How yet Attainable—Theological Productions of the Westminster Assembly—Conclusion.

ALTHOUGH the chief duties for which the Assembly of Divines
were summoned to meet at Westminster, may be regarded as
having been discharged when they had prepared and laid before the Parliament Directories for Public Worship and Ordination, a Form of Government, Rules of Discipline, and a

Confession of Faith, yet there remained several matters, sub-ordinate indeed, but still important, on account of which they continued to sit and deliberate for some time longer, an outline of which we now proceed to give, before offering some concluding remarks on the whole subject.

A catechism for the instruction of children and of the comparatively ignorant in religious truth will always be regarded as a most important matter by every true Christian Church ; and as the Catechism of the Church of England was undeniably both meagre and unsound, it formed a part of the Assembly's duty to prepare a more accurate and complete catechism, as a portion of the national system to be established. The attention of the Assembly was occupied almost entirely by the discussions respecting the Directories of Ordination and Worship, till towards the end of 1644. They then began to prepare for composing a Confession of Faith and a Catechism ; and according to their usual course of procedure, committees were appointed to draw up an outline, in regular systematic order, for the consideration of the Assembly. But the progress of the Assembly in these points was retarded by the various events which have been already related, so that little was done till towards the end of May 1645. The committees from that time forward carried on their labours in preparing the Confession and the Catechism simultaneously, but, as Baillie says, " languidly, the minds of the divines being enfeebled by the delay of the House to grant the petition respecting power to exclude scandalous persons from communion." After some progress had been made with both, the Assembly resolved to finish the Confession first, and then to construct the Catechism upon its model, so far at least as to have no proposition in the one which was not in the other ; by which arrangement there would be left scarcely any ground for subsequent debate and delay.* But political movements, answers to the Independ-

---

* Baillie, vol. ii. p. 379.

ents and to the Erastians, and other disturbing influences, so
impeded the Assembly's progress, that the Catechisms were
not so speedily completed as had been expected. The Shorter
Catechism was presented to the House of Commons on the
5th of November 1647, and the Larger on the 14th of April
1648. After they had been carefully perused by the Parliament, an order was issued on the 15th of September 1648,
commanding them to be printed for public use. The king,
during his residence in the Isle of Wight, after many solicitations, consented to license the Shorter Catechism, with a
suitable preface; but as the negotiations did not end in a
treaty, that consent was never realised.

There have been many inquiries instituted in order to ascertain, if possible, by whom the original outline of the
Catechism was prepared, but hitherto without success. In
our opinion, there is no reason to think that it was done by
any one person. Committees were appointed to prepare every
thing that was to be brought before the Assembly. We find
no separate committee named expressly for the purpose of
drawing up the Catechism; and we find repeated proofs of a
very close connection between the Catechism and the Confession. It may reasonably be inferred that both subjects
were conducted by the same committee, which was composed
of Drs Gouge and Hoyle, Messrs Herle, Gataker, Tuckney, Reynolds, Vines, and the Scottish ministers. Some add
Arrowsmith and Palmer; both men of great piety, learning
and abilities, and the latter termed by Baillie "the best cate-
chist in England." Palmer, it appears, was appointed to
draw up a section in the Directory of Public Worship, on
catechising; but it did not give satisfaction, and that topic
was not inserted in the Directory.* Scarcely could it be
called an unfair inference, were we to conclude from this
fact that Palmer had no peculiar share in framing the Catechism. It may be mentioned, that Dr Arrowsmith was ap-

* Baillie, vol. ii. p. 148.

pointed Master of St John's College, Cambridge, in the year
1644, before the Catechism was begun, and that his attendance upon the Assembly after that period was only occasional,
in consequence of the new sphere of duties on which he was
called to enter. Mr Palmer was also constituted Master of
Queen's College, Cambridge, in the same year; but he continued to attend the Assembly very constantly till the time of
his death, in the year 1647,—at which time the Catechism
was still unfinished. It has been also conjectured, that the
first outline of the Catechism may have been drawn by Dr
Wallis, one of the scribes of the Assembly at that period,
and afterwards so justly celebrated as Savilian Professor of
Geometry at Oxford, and one of the first mathematicians of
the age. This conjecture may have arisen from the fact that
he wrote a short treatise, entitled, " A Brief and Easy Explanation of the Shorter Catechism;" which was so much
approved of by the Assembly that they caused it to be presented to both Houses of Parliament.* But in truth, as has
been already suggested, the framing of the Catechism appears
to have been the work of the committee, and not of any one
individual; and it was brought to its present admirable degree of nearness to perfection by the united deliberations of
the whole Assembly.

The chief matters on account of which the Assembly had
been called together being now completed, so far as depended
on that venerable body itself, the Scottish commissioners
prepared to take their departure. This, indeed, had to a
certain extent already taken place, though not formally.
The celebrated Alexander Henderson had been sent to Newcastle to converse with the king, during his majesty's residence
along with the Scottish army, for the purpose of endeavouring
to persuade him to consent to such terms as might form the
basis of a satisfactory and permanent peace. Exhausted
already with the long continuance and severity of his arduous

* Reid's Lives of the Westminster Divines, vol. ii. p. 214.

public toils, and finding it impossible to make any impression on the mind of the infatuated monarch, Henderson left New-castle and returned to Edinburgh, where he soon afterwards died, leaving behind him a reputation unsurpassed by any man since the days of the first reformers. And towards the close of the year 1646, Baillie obtained permission to leave the Assembly and return to Scotland, that he might communicate to the Commission of the Scottish General Assembly what had been done by the Westminster Divines, preparatory for the meeting of the Assembly at Edinburgh in August 1647, when it was expected that the proceedings of the Westminster Assembly would be formally considered and approved of by the General Assembly of the Church of Scotland, as the ground of the desired uniformity in religion between the two kingdoms. Gillespie and Rutherford still remained, as the Westminster Assembly had been required by the Parliament to add Scripture proofs to the Confession of Faith; but Gillespie left London in time to be present in the General Assembly, Rutherford remaining a little longer. It may be stated, that the Assembly had intentionally abstained from inserting texts of Scripture in the copy of the Confession first presented to Parliament, not because they had themselves any difficulty in doing so, but to avoid giving offence to the Parliament, whose custom had previously been, to enact nothing concerning religion on divine right, or on scriptural grounds.* This change in the procedure of the Parliament was doubtless intended to cause delay; but its effect was, the rendering of the Confession a much more perfect work than it would otherwise have been.

On the 24th of October 1647, Samuel Rutherford moved, that it might be recorded in the books of the scribes, that the Assembly had enjoyed the assistance of the honourable, reverend, and learned commissioners of the Church of Scotland, during all the time they had been debating and perfecting

* Baillie, vol. iii. p. 2.

U

these four things mentioned in the Covenant, namely, a
Directory for Public Worship, a uniform Confession of Faith,
a Form of Church Government and Discipline, and a public
Catechism. The Assembly assented unanimously to this
motion; and Mr Herle, the prolocutor, rose up, and, in the
name of the Assembly, returned thanks to the honourable
and reverend commissioners for their assistance. He went
on to explain the causes which prevented the Directory from
being so well observed as it ought to be, and lamented that
the Assembly had not power to call offenders to account.
He further adverted to the chaos of confusion in which public
affairs in England were continuing, the king having been
seized by the army, and the Parliament being overawed by
the same usurping power; acknowledging that their extraordinary successes hitherto had been granted in answer to
the prayers of their brethren of Scotland, and other Protestants
abroad, as well as to their own.*

The business of the Assembly was now virtually at an
end. The subjects brought before them by Parliament had
been all fully discussed, and the result of their long and well-
matured deliberations presented to both Houses, to be approved or rejected by the supreme civil power on its own
responsibility. But the Parliament neither fully approved
nor rejected the Assembly's productions, nor yet issued an
ordinance for a formal dissolution of that venerable body.
Negotiations were still going on with the king; and in one
of the papers which passed between his majesty and the Parliament, he signified his willingness to sanction the continuation of Presbyterian Church government for three years; and
also, that the Assembly should continue to sit and deliberate,
his majesty being allowed to nominate twenty Episcopalian
divines to be added to it, for the purpose of having the whole
subject of religion again formally debated. To this proposal
the Parliament refused to consent; but it probably tended to

* Neal, vol. ii. p. 431.

prevent them from formally dissolving the Assembly, so long as there remained any shadow of hope that a pacific arrangement might be effected with his majesty.

In the meantime many members of the Assembly, especially those from the country, returned to their own homes and ordinary duties; and those who remained in London were chiefly engaged in the examination of such ministers as presented themselves for ordination, or induction into vacant charges. They continued to maintain their formal existence till the 22d of February 1649, about three weeks after the king's decapitation, having sat five years, six months, and twenty-two days; in which time they had held one thousand one hundred and sixty-three sessions. They were then changed into a committee for conducting the trial and examination of ministers, and continued to hold meetings for this purpose every Thursday morning till the 25th of March 1652, when Oliver Cromwell having forcibly dissolved the Long Parliament, by whose authority the Assembly had been at first called together, that committee also broke up, and separated without any formal dissolution, and as a matter of necessity.

As the main object of the Westminster Assembly was, to frame such a system of Church government and public worship as might unite the kingdoms of England, Scotland, and Ireland, in religious uniformity, and as the Assembly had completed its task, the next point was to lay the result of its labours before the Church of Scotland, that its consent might be obtained. This was in perfect harmony with the whole procedure of Scotland in this great and sacred enterprise. The Church of Scotland had neither the power nor the wish to force its system upon England; as little would it have submitted to English dictation in a matter so important: and although the English Parliament had not fully ratified all the propositions of the Westminster Assembly, yet, since these were completed, the delay of England was no sufficient reason why the Church and kingdom of Scotland should also

delay, if satisfied with the system which the Assembly of
Divines had prepared. Even before the completion of the
Westminster Assembly's labours, the Church of Scotland had
shown its satisfaction and its readiness to promote the desired
uniformity; for, in the General Assembly held at Edinburgh
early in the year 1645, an act of Assembly was passed on the
3d of February, ratifying the Directory of Public Worship;
and on the 15th of February another act was passed, ratifying the Form of Church Government and Ordination, though
these had not yet received the full ratification of the English
Parliament. Again, in the General Assembly which met in
August 1647, the Confession of Faith was taken into consideration, copies having been previously distributed throughout
the Church, and was solemnly ratified by an act of Assembly
passed on the 27th of August 1647. The Larger and Shorter
Catechisms, not being ready at that time, owing to the delays which had impeded the progress of the Westminster
Divines, were not ratified till the following year, when both
of them obtained the full sanction of the General Assembly
in July 1648.

It may be necessary to mention, that so jealous was the
Church of Scotland lest her sanction should be given to any
thing which bore an Erastian taint, or might, by perverse ingenuity, be so construed, that in the act of Assembly which
ratified the Confession of Faith, an explanation was inserted,
giving the Assembly's understanding of some parts of the
second article of the thirty-first chapter, which seemed, or
might be interpreted to seem, to grant more power to the
civil magistrate in the calling of synods than the Church of
Scotland was prepared to admit. And still more completely
to guard against the very suspicion of any tincture of Erastianism, the Assembly caused to be printed a series of propositions, or "Theses against Erastianism," as Baillie terms
them, amounting to one hundred and eleven, drawn up by
George Gillespie, embodying eight of them in the act which

authorised their publication. It is impossible to peruse these hundred and eleven propositions without being thoroughly convinced, that the General Assembly never would have ratified the Confession of Faith if they had understood it to contain any such Erastian taint as some in modern times have affected to discover in it. Let the third section of the twenty-third chapter be carefully perused by any intelligent and candid person, in connection with the whole proceedings of the Assembly of Divines at Westminster, and of the General Assembly of the Church of Scotland, and with the hundred and eleven propositions, and he must conclude that it cannot possibly have an Erastian meaning, even though he should be unable to state what it really does mean; unless, indeed, he were to suppose that the Westminster Assembly and the Church of Scotland did not understand the true meaning of their own propositions. But the truth appears to be, that the learned and able men of that period had so thoroughly studied and mastered the essential elements of the Erastian controversy, that they could state the propositions respecting the duty and power of the civil magistrate *circa sacra*, about religious matters, without admitting his possession of any duty and power *in sacris*, in religious matters, in terms which, to their practised minds, marked the boundaries in sharp and narrow but clear and definite distinctions; while men who have not so deeply studied these subjects, and whose mental acumen has not been so much exercised, cannot trace, and are perpetually crossing, these boundary-lines, more, it may be, from want of perspicacity or knowledge, than in wilful perverseness. A full and clear history of the Erastian controversy, stating distinctly the great principles which it involves, and their bearing upon liberty, civil and religious, would be a work of incalculable value at the present time, —that very controversy having again begun to disturb men's minds, and threatening to shake to pieces the most valuable institutions, if not to overturn the entire structure of society.

Although the course of events has led to the statement of
the Westminster Assembly's dissolution, with which this narrative might close, yet, as its influence did not at once terminate with its actual duration, it seems expedient to give a
brief outline of some of the leading events which still retained
its impress, till they became almost indistinguishably blended
with the onward movements of the national mind and history.
It will be remembered, that a new element was introduced
into the acting powers of the body politic, when, by means of
the "self-denying ordinance," members of Parliament were
prohibited from holding any post in the army, and new general
officers were appointed, while a special permission was given to
Cromwell enabling him to retain his military command. From
that time forward there was a distinction of aims and interests
between the Parliament and the army, although they continued their mutual co-operation till the king's power was
laid prostrate. In the Parliament, the Presbyterian party
retained the ascendency; in the army, the Independents appeared to do so, although they formed but one of the many
sects of which it was almost entirely composed. For some
time after the king had taken up his residence at Holmby,
the disagreement between the Parliament and the army appeared only in the shape of negotiations in the terms of which
the two parties could not agree,—the Parliament wishing to
disband a large proportion of the troops, and to send a considerable body to Ireland, to suppress the Popish insurrection in
that country,—and the army petitioning for an act of indemnity for any illegal actions they might have committed during
the war. This petition was stigmatized by the Commons as
of a mutinous tendency, subjecting its promoters to be proceeded against as disturbers of the public peace. The army
immediately formed a council of the principal officers, to
deliberate for their own protection; and to this was added
two soldiers out of each company, to assist the officers in their
council. To these soldiers was given the designation, *adju-*

tators, or assistants; but this somewhat pedantic title very speedily degenerated into the more intelligible word, *agitators*, —by which name, accordingly, they are best known. The disagreement continuing, the army seized possession of the king's person, and marched towards London, declaring their intention to new-model the government, as the only method of securing a settled peace to the nation. Eleven of the leading Presbyterian members of the House of Commons were accused as guilty of high treason, and enemies of the army, and, with equally unwise and unmanly terror, left the House.

The city of London prepared to meet the danger,—enrolled the militia, threw up defences, and made ready to repel force by force. But the Parliament was divided. The Speakers of both Houses favoured the Independents, and the absence of the eleven impeached members discouraged their party. The two Speakers and about sixty-two of the members retired to the army. This gave to that formidable power what it wanted,—the semblance of being engaged in defence of the Legislature itself,—and with increased alacrity it advanced against the city. Strife and confusion had, in the meantime, done their work. Without men of ability and determination to direct and lead them on, the citizens were unable to encounter a veteran army, and London threw open its gates, and submitted to a power, formidable indeed, but utterly unable to have taken forcible possession of the city, had it been boldly and vigorously defended.

The army having thus manifested its power, recoiled a little and allowed the Parliament to continue to sit and deliberate, as if still the supreme authority in the nation, although the king was carefully retained under the superintendence of the military leaders. At length Charles contrived to escape from Hampton Court, with the intention of withdrawing from the kingdom, and seeking the aid of foreign powers to reinstate him on his throne; but not being able to procure a passage, he intrusted himself to Hammond, governor of the Isle of Wight, by whom he was kept in Carisbrooke Castle, in real imprisonment, though treated with respect. A series of negotiations for a treaty was resumed between the king and the Parliament, which, like every preceding attempt, proved abortive, in consequence of that strange peculiarity in his majesty's character, the union of inflexible obstinacy in one point, with boundless and incurable dissimulation in every other. At the very time that the king was treating with the English Parliament for peace, he was framing a private engagement with the Scottish Royalists, by means of which he hoped to recover his power by force of arms. This led to the march into England of another Scottish army, under the command of the Duke of Hamilton, who had obtained a temporary ascendency in the Scottish Parliament, but against the opposition, and under the protest of the true and faithful Covenanters. Cromwell marched against this army, defeated it, and returned to London determined to put an end to the struggle, by putting to death a monarch whose principles were of the most despotic character, and upon whose most solemn treaties no reliance could be placed. Again was the Parliament subjected to military force. Upwards of forty of the Presbyterian members were cast into confinement ; above one hundred and sixty were excluded from the House; and none were suffered to sit and deliberate but the most determined Sectarians, in all not exceeding sixty. This violent invasion of parliamentary rights is commonly termed " Pride's purge," from the name of Colonel Pride, the person who commanded the military detachment by which it was perpetrated ; and the parliamentary section which was allowed to remain, is known by the designation of the Rump Parliament.

The republican revolution now swept onward with great rapidity and irresistible force. It was resolved that the king should be brought to trial, as guilty of treason against the people of England, before what was termed a Court of Justice. The House of Lords refused to give their consent ; and the

Commons voted the concurrence of the Lords to be unnecessary, the people being the source of all just power. The
unfortunate king was brought before the Court of Justice,
and accused of treason. He declined their jurisdiction, and
defended himself with great dignity and courage. But all
his defences were overruled. The dread sentence was pronounced; and on the 30th of January 1649, he perished on
the scaffold, the victim of an inflexible attachment to superstitious observances and despotic principles, and of an incurable perseverance in the art of dissimulation; yet in his last
moments displaying a degree of personal intrepidity, firmness
of character, and Christian-like calmness and elevation of
mind, worthy of a better cause.

No sooner had the tidings of the ill-fated monarch's tragic
end reached Scotland, than it called forth a burst of intense
sorrow and indignation from the heart of every true Presbyterian Covenanter in the kingdom. Arrangements were
instantly made for placing the young prince on the Scottish
throne, and supporting him there by force of arms, if necessary, provided he would subscribe the Covenant. To this
Charles was unwilling to consent, if he could otherwise obtain
his purpose; and with this design held the Scottish commissioners in terms, while conducting a private treaty with Montrose, in the hope of securing the kingdom by his means
without any stipulation. But while in this he showed proofs
of hereditary dissimulation, when Montrose failed, he consented to swear the Covenant which he never intended to
keep: in this respect committing a crime darker far than any
with which his father's memory is chargeable; for though
Charles I. seems to have regarded dissimulation as allowable
in diplomacy,—which perhaps statesmen in general may be
thought also to do,—he reverenced an oath, and would not on
any account have sworn what he did not intend to perform.
But Cromwell was not disposed to permit the establishment
of the royal power in Scotland, by which his own supremacy

might be endangered. He therefore marched northwards at the head of his veteran army, invaded Scotland, and after a series of military movements, in which he was fairly matched by David Leslie, he gained a decisive victory near Dunbar. The Scottish army rallied and took up a strong position near Stirling; but their flank being turned, and their resources cut off, the young prince adopted the daring enterprise of marching into England, hoping to be joined by the Royalists in that country. His hopes were disappointed, that party being thoroughly broken and dispirited; and being over-taken by Cromwell, a final struggle took place at Worcester, which ended in the total rout and dispersion of the royal army. After encountering many perilous adventures and narrow escapes, Charles fled to the Continent, and Cromwell returned to London to consolidate that power in which he had now no rival but the degraded Rump of the Long Par-liament. As he no longer needed the services of that fac-tion, he fostered, or at least encouraged a quarrel between the army and Parliament, and taking part with the former, he hastened to the House of Commons, assailed the astonished members with a torrent of violent invectives, ordered the mace, " that bauble," to be taken away, called in the military to eject the dismayed but struggling members, and having locked the door, put the key in his pocket, and returned to Whitehall. So fell the English Parliament beneath the power of military usurpation ; and at the same moment ter-minated the Westminster Assembly.

It will be remembered, that London and its immediate vicinity had been formed into twelve Presbyteries, constitut-ing the Provincial Synod of London. This Synod continued to hold regular half-yearly meetings till the year 1655, with-out encountering any direct obstruction from Cromwell, but receiving no encouragement. They then ceased to hold regular meetings as a Synod, but continued to meet as Pres-byteries, and to maintain, as far as possible, every other point of Presbyterian Church government and discipline. It is probable, or rather certain, that their ceasing to act as a Synod was caused by the conduct of Cromwell in regard to religious matters. When, upon the death of the king, the government of England was changed to a commonwealth, an ordinance was passed appointing an engagement to be taken, first by all civil and military officers, and afterwards by all who held official situations in the universities; and at last it was further ordered that no minister be capable of enjoying any preferment in the Church, unless he should, within six months, take the engagement publicly before the congregation. The consequence of this was, that while the engagement was readily taken by all the Sectarians, and by many Episcopalians of lax principles, it was refused by great numbers of the Presbyterians, several of whom were in a short time ejected from the situations to which they had been appointed by the Parliament. Cromwell and his council, carrying into full execution this course of procedure, certainly not that of *toleration*, immediately placed Independents in the situations thus rendered vacant by the ejection of the Presbyterians, prohibited the publication of pamphlets censuring the conduct of the new government, and abolished the monthly fasts, which had continued to be regularly kept for about seven years, and whose sacred influence had often been deeply and beneficially felt by both Parliament and Assembly. The Rev. Christopher Love was beheaded for being engaged in, or cognisant of, a correspondence with Scotland for the purpose of supporting the interests of Charles II. Not long afterwards, in the year 1654, an ordinance of council was issued, appointing a new committee of thirty-eight persons, nine of whom were laymen, to examine and approve all who should be presented, nominated, chosen, or appointed to any benefice with cure of souls, or to any public settled lecture in England or Wales. Of this new committee, commonly called Triers, some were Presbyterians, a large proportion Independents, and a few were Baptists. Any five were sufficient to approve; but no number under nine had power to reject a person as unqualified. In this manner, although the Presbyterian Church government was not formally abolished by Cromwell, its power was transferred to the hands of the committee of Triers, and consequently the Synods ceased to hold meetings which could no longer exercise any authority. This committee continued to exercise its functions till the Protector's death in 1658, when it was discontinued.

Another ordinance appointed commissioners, chiefly laymen, for every county, with power to eject scandalous, ignorant, and insufficient ministers and schoolmasters. This also superseded the previous arrangements which had been made by the Long Parliament for a similar purpose, and tended to bring every ecclesiastical matter under the direct control of the civil power, and in a great measure under the superintendence of the Protector himself and his council. By this ordinance, as well as by that of the Parliament, it was appointed that ample time should be allowed to the ejected person for his removal, and the fifths of the benefice were reserved for the support of his family. When the Prelatic party silenced and deposed the Puritans and Nonconformists of other days, no such generosity was shown to them or their families; but neither the Presbyterians nor the Independents were so forgetful of the principles of Christianity as to requite evil with evil, but showed kindness to their former calumniators and oppressors.

The Independents were now raised to the enjoyment of a large measure of power and favour, though the Protector managed to reserve to himself the reality without the name of ecclesiastical supremacy. They felt, accordingly, that they might now safely adopt a course on which nothing had hitherto been able to induce them to enter,—the preparation, namely, of some public document of the nature of a Confession of Faith. To this they had been often urged by the Westminster Assembly, but in vain. They were aware that a full and explicit statement of their principles would deprive them of the support of a large proportion of the numerous sects who viewed them as the leading Sectarian party, and might thereby so reduce their influence as to render their hopes of promoting their own system exceedingly feeble. But the Presbyterians were now depressed and overborne; some of the most dangerous of the sects had been forcibly suppressed, such as the Levellers, Fifth Monarchy men, &c.; and they might now promulgate their own views without incurring the danger of losing valuable adherents. Some of the leading men among them accordingly met in London, and having agreed upon the propriety of framing a Confession of Faith, as had been done by other Churches, they requested permission from the Protector to hold an Assembly for that purpose. This was granted with some reluctance, and their Assembly was appointed to meet at the Savoy, on the 12th of October 1658.

They opened their meeting with a day of fasting and prayer; and after some deliberation, resolved to keep as near as possible to the method and order of the Westminster Assembly's Confession of Faith, in framing a similar document for themselves. A committee was chosen to prepare the outline, consisting of Drs Goodwin and Owen, Messrs Nye, Bridge, Caryl, and Greenhill. In the short period of about eleven or twelve days they finished their work, which was soon afterwards published under the title of "A Declaration of the Faith and Order owned and practised in the Congregational Churches in England, agreed upon and consented unto by their elders and messengers in their meeting at the Savoy." The speed with which they completed their task contrasts very strongly with the manner in which they contrived to retard the progress of the Westminster Assembly, but may be readily explained. They followed the Assembly's Confession very closely, to which indeed their leading men had already assented; they omitted all the chapters which relate to discipline, thus avoiding the discussion of disputed topics; and they had now no object to serve by delay, but many a motive to induce them to make haste. At the end of their work there is a chapter of discipline, consisting of five sections, and giving a brief statement and assertion of the main points in which their system differed from that of the Presbyterians, respecting the power of single congregations, the method of ordination, the administration of the sacraments, the use of Synods and Assemblies to consult and advise, but without authority, and occasional communion with other Churches.* This Savoy Confession, as it is commonly called, never acquired any importance in the community, and did not supersede the Assembly's Confession of Faith even in the estimation of a large proportion of the Independents themselves; and as Cromwell, the great supporter of the Independent party, died very soon after its production, on the 3d of September 1658, it never received his public sanction.

Upon the death of Cromwell, he was succeeded by his son Richard, a man of an amiable character, but utterly unfit to conduct the government of the country in such a time of storm and peril. A plot was formed against him by a part of the army, headed by Fleetwood and Desborough, to whom the leading Independent divines, especially Mr Nye and his party, lent their ready assistance. Richard was persuaded to dissolve the Parliament; Fleetwood and Desborough, and their party, immediately summoned the Rump of the Long Parliament to re-assemble, and Richard seeing it impossible to maintain his power without another civil war, and being destitute of military talents, resolved to abdicate his authority, and retire to private life. A new series of dark intrigues followed, in which General Monk acted a prominent part, the issue of which was, the restoration of Charles II. on the 29th of May 1660. In consequence of the mutual jealousies of the various parties, the king was restored with-

* Neal, vol. ii. pp. 690-692.

out conditions of any kind; and thus the liberties, both civil and religious, of the kingdom, in defence of which so much blood had been shed, and so many miseries endured, were laid at his feet. The Prelatic hierarchy were immediately restored to the possession of all their rank, wealth, and power, and speedily proved that the persecuting spirit of Prelacy had sustained no abatement.

For a short time the king affected to treat the Presbyterian ministers with respect and kindness; and they were encouraged to hope, that although Prelacy was restored to its former supremacy, yet some modification of it might be made to which it might be possible to conform. After some consultation among themselves, they presented to his majesty a petition expressing their desires for such alterations as might lead to an accommodation and agreement in an amended and modified Episcopacy. This petition was communicated to the Prelates, who returned such an answer as greatly to obscure all prospect of any accommodation. But as matters were not yet ripe for what was intended, the king issued a declaration concerning ecclesiastical affairs, containing so many plausible statements, that the hopes of the Presbyterians were somewhat revived. At length it was arranged that a conference should be held at the Savoy, between twelve bishops and nine assistants on the part of the Episcopalian Church, and an equal number of ministers on the part of the Presbyterians. The first meeting of this conference took place on the 15th of April 1661, and it was continued, with intermissions, till the 25th of July, when it expired without producing the slightest approximation towards an agreement, the bishops refusing to make any alterations in the Book of Common Prayer, to which their discussions were limited, or to make any concession to the conscientious scruples, or more grave and solid arguments, of the Presbyterian ministers.*

* For a full account of this Conference, see History of Nonconformity, Life of Baxter, &c.

A convocation was held soon after the termination of the
conference, in which a few alterations were made in the
Prayer-Book, not all for the better ; and the proceedings of
the convocation were ratified by both Houses of Parliament.
It now remained to enforce the Prelatic system by the strong
hand of legislative power. This was done by the Act of
Uniformity, which, after passing both Houses, by small
majorities, received the royal assent on the 19th of May
1662, and was to take effect from the 24th of August following. The terms of conformity specified by this act were :
1. Re-ordination, if they had not been episcopally ordained.
2. A declaration of unfeigned assent and consent to all and
every thing prescribed and contained in the Book of Common Prayer, and administration of sacraments and other
rites and ceremonies of the Church of England, together
with the psalter, and the form and manner of making, ordaining, and consecrating of bishops, priests, and deacons.
3. To take the oath of canonical obedience. 4. To abjure
the Solemn League and Covenant. 5. To abjure the lawfulness of taking arms against the king, or any commissioned
by him, on any pretence whatsoever. Such were the terms
of the infamous and tyrannical Act of Uniformity, which was
to come into force on what is termed the Feast of St Bartholomew ; and the penalty for any one who should refuse, was
deprivation of all his spiritual promotions. The result was,
that when the fatal St Bartholomew's day arrived, about two
thousand Presbyterians relinquished all their ecclesiastical
preferments, abandoned all their worldly means of subsistence,
left their homes, and more painful than all, their churches
and their weeping and heart-stricken flocks, and became
literally strangers and pilgrims in their native country, like
their Divine Master, not having where to lay their heads.
In their day of power, when ejecting Episcopalian ministers
convicted of scandalous offences or of ignorance, they had
allowed to these men a fifth part of their former livings; but

no similar mercy or charity was shown to them. They were at once driven and abandoned to utter poverty and homelessness; and to grievous wrong was added not less grievous insult, in the cruel and contumelious treatment which they received from their proud and pitiless oppressors. Yet in one respect the day of St Bartholomew was a glorious day. It testified to a wondering world the strength and the integrity of Presbyterian principles, in their triumph over every earthly influence; or rather, let us say, it proved that the essential spirit of the Presbyterian Church is the spirit of Christianity itself, and therefore it received divine strength in the day of sore trial, that it might finish its testimony in behalf of the sole sovereignty of Christ over his own spiritual kingdom, to the laws and institutions of which man has no right to add, and which he cannot without sin diminish. Yes, for the Presbyterian Church, and even for the Westminster Assembly, by which that Church had been introduced into England, it was a glorious day. But what was it for Prelacy? A day of everlasting infamy, stamping upon its character indelibly the charge, proved by so many repeated facts, of being essentially A PERSECUTING SYSTEM.

But it is equally unnecessary and ungracious to dwell on the detailed results of this tyrannical and persecuting act; and therefore, with a few incidental remarks of some general importance, we shall pass from the painful subject. It must have been observed, that the religious body once known by the name of Puritans, became Presbyterians both in principles and practice, partly before, and thoroughly during the time of the Westminster Assembly. Against them, accordingly, as Presbyterians, was the force of persecution directed, although the demands and the penalties of the Act of Uniformity were equally applicable to the Independents and all other sects of Dissenters; and of the whole two thousand who were ejected by that act, above nine-tenths were Presbyterians. The Independents did not, at that time, number

X

more than an hundred churches in their communion; the
Baptists were still fewer; and of the other sects, the greater
part had only those lay preachers who had sprung up during
the enthusiastic times of the civil war. Of the divines who
had constituted the Westminster Assembly, not more than
six, or, in strict propriety, only four, conformed. About
thirty of them were dead before the act came into operation,
some of them very close upon the time, and one or two
almost immediately after preaching what would have proved
by persecution, as they did by death, their farewell sermons.
The names of the six who are stated to have conformed were,
Drs Conant, Wallis, Reynolds, and Lightfoot, and Messrs
Heyrick and Hodges. · But of these Dr Conant at first
refused to conform, was ejected, and continued so for a period
of eight years, when the persuasion of relatives prevailed on
him to comply, and he was appointed to a ministerial charge
in Northampton, and subsequently obtained other preferments; and Dr Wallis, who had been one of the scribes to
the Westminster Assembly, was made Savilian Professor of
Geometry at Oxford, in the year 1649—an office which in a
great measure excluded him from ecclesiastical affairs, and
rendered the act of conformity to him little different from a
university qualification. It thus appears, that almost the
entire surviving members of the Westminster Assembly gave
to the principles which they had then declared and advocated
the strong and clear testimony of suffering in their defence.

Having now stated all the leading events connected with,
and resulting from, the Westminster Assembly, we might
here conclude; but in order to obtain as clear and comprehensive a conception of the whole subject as possible, it seems
expedient to retrace, for the purpose of combining in one
view its leading principles, characteristics, endeavours, and
intentions, offering some remarks explanatory of their nature,
showing how far they were successful, or by what and to
what extent obstructed, what actual impress they gave to the

form of society, or what vital elements they infused into its heart, and how far the great objects which they sought to attain may yet be susceptible of resuscitation and accomplishment.

It has been already shown, by a series of historical deductions, that the principle of the sovereign's supremacy in ecclesiastical matters, conjoined with the encroaching and domineering spirit of Prelacy, had so nearly subverted all liberty, civil and religious, that it became the imperative duty of every Christian and every patriot to unite in resisting the cruel and degrading thraldom with which the kingdom was threatened. To that subject it is not necessary again to direct our attention. Nor need we do more than simply refer to the important fact, that the main purpose for which the Westminster Assembly was called together, and the Solemn League and Covenant was framed, was to produce, so far as might be practicable, unity of religious belief and uniformity in Church government throughout England, Scotland, and Ireland. Even for the sake of procuring and maintaining peace among the nations composing the one British empire, such an uniformity was regarded as almost indispensable. For, as the Scottish commissioners reasoned, there is "nothing so powerful to divide the hearts of people as division in religion; nothing so strong to unite them as unity in religion." The same idea was entertained by both James VI. and his son Charles I., and both of them sought to realize it by imposing the English system on the Church and people of Scotland, the one by fraud and the other by force. As might have been expected, neither of them was successful; but the attempt to realize the idea by such methods, both showed its importance, and placed it in a clearer light, as related to the two kingdoms of England and Scotland. The people of Scotland loved their Church devotedly, not only on account of its purity of doctrine and scriptural simplicity of form, but also because by its means alone had they acquired a partial release from that feudal thraldom in which they had previously been held by their haughty and oppressive nobles. And they were compelled to see that their beloved Church would never be safe from the aggressions of Prelacy so long as the prelatic form of Church government prevailed in England. On the other hand, the oppressive, persecuting, and despotic conduct of Prelacy, in its treatment of the Puritans, and in the aid which it so willingly lent to the sovereign in his invasions of civil liberty, had at length aroused the strong and free spirit of England, which determined to shake off the prelatic yoke, and to make such alterations as should render its future re-imposition impossible. Such a concurrence of sentiment and feeling between the two nations held out the prospect that at least an approach to uniformity of religion might now be obtained, such as would form the only sure basis of a thorough and permanent national peace; and that, too, not by one of the two dictating to the other, but in the only way by which real uniformity can ever be effected,—by mutual consultation and consent.

Such were the enlarged, free, and generous views which led to the calling of the Westminster Assembly, and the framing of the Solemn League and Covenant,—such, in an especial manner, were the views entertained by the Scottish Covenanters, both statesmen and divines, as is proved by that remarkably able paper presented by them to the English Parliament in the year 1641. It is, however, a painful truth, that these elevated ideas were not received and held with equal fulness, sincerity, and perseverance, by a large proportion of the English statesmen; and this defectiveness on their part allowed the remaining existence and the subsequent growth and development of those disturbing influences, which at length prevented the grand object from being fully realized. In England the struggle was chiefly in defence of civil rights and privileges, involving also, though somewhat less directly, the still more important element of religious liberty. Hence the ordinary secular opinions and feelings, that mould the course of human action, were allowed to have almost full scope, and produced their common narrowing and self-seeking influence. Had not this been the case, Erastianism would not have characterised so strongly the conduct of the English Parliament, exercising a power so baneful in impeding the final settlement of the desired religious uniformity, involving the nation in protracted anarchy, and exposing the cause of freedom to the crushing grasp of military usurpation. There might be traced, did our limits allow it, a very close connection between the development of Erastian principles in the Parliament, and the successive disasters 'which befell them through the insubordination of the army in its growing republicanism,—so close, that the latter would almost seem like the direct infliction of retributive justice upon the former, ending in the completed guilt and the final overthrow of the Parliament being almost simultaneous.

The great advantage which would arise to Christendom from the existence of something approaching to a general religious uniformity must be apparent to every reflecting mind, both as a general homage to the certainties of revealed truth, and as itself the master element of general harmony and peace. But it is contrary alike to the nature of religion and to the constitution of the human mind, to suppose that this desirable object can be obtained by compulsion. Open, candid, brother-like consultation may do much, when Christian men fairly and honestly wish to arrive at as close a degree of uniformity, in doctrine, worship, and government, as can be attained, with due respect to liberty and integrity of conscience. It was for this very purpose that the Westminster Assembly was called, and that Scottish divines were requested to be present at and aid in its deliberations. This was right, and bore fair prospect and promise of good; but mutual jealousies and rivalries arose ; men misjudged and misinterpreted each other's intentions; and the intrigues of mere worldly politicians intermingled with, biassed, and baffled far higher and holier objects than those with which such men are usually conversant. Probably the two parties of a religious character (we speak not now of mere Erastians), of whom the Assembly was composed, the Presbyterians and the Independents, were both in error; probably they both entertained narrower conceptions of the nature of religious uniformity, and also of religious toleration and liberty, than the terms, rightly understood, imply. Uniformity is not necessarily absolute identity. Neither of these two parties held that absolute identity was necessary, as appears from their respective writings; but each of them dreaded that nothing less than absolute identity would satisfy the other, and to that neither of them could agree. And this misapprehension was enough, not only to prevent the accomplishment of the purpose for which they met, but even to act as a wedge, rending them daily more widely and hopelessly asunder.

Yet, in spite of this unpropitious misapprehension, a very considerable amount of religious uniformity was produced. The Independents expressed no dissent from the Confession of Faith and the Directory of Worship prepared by the Assembly. All the Puritan nonconformists received these documents with cordial approbation. Parliament gave to their most important principles and arrangements its legislative sanction, and England was on the very point of being favoured with the establishment of a Presbyterian Church. So far did this proceed, that at first the University of Cambridge, and afterwards that of Oxford, were new-modelled, and the professorships given to Presbyterian divines. Prelatic writers have been in the habit of representing this change as barbarising these universities. To refute such calumny, nothing more is necessary than to name the men on whom these academic appointments were conferred,—men than whom none more eminent, for learning, abilities, and true piety, ever graced the universities of any age or country. But something still more striking may be said in answer to prelatic calumny. Not only did the new professors ably sustain the reputation of the English universities, they also infused into them a spirit of freedom, originality, and energy of thought, which burst forth in the manhood of the men trained under their care, with a degree of power and splendour that has scarcely been ever equalled, much less surpassed. In proof of this, it is enough to mention the names of Locke, Boyle, Newton, Tillotson, Stillingfleet, Cave, Whitby, South, and many others. In short, the Presbyterian dynasty of the universities infused into them new life, the vigorous tone and movements of which were not exhausted till the lapse of two generations.

Closely associated with the subject of university learning, is that of eminence in theological acquirements and pulpit oratory. On this point also a very prevalent fallacy exists, and is repeated and believed without inquiry. It is very common to meet with extravagant praises bestowed upon the eminent learning and the valuable theological works produced by the Church of England; but it seems to be generally forgotten, that by far the largest and most precious portion of English theological literature was composed either by the Puritan divines, or by the Presbyterians of the Westminster Assembly, or by the generation which was trained up under them in the universities. If all the works produced by these men were carefully marked and set aside, and the works of none but the genuine Prelatists were ascribed to the Church of England, her renown for theological literature would be shorn of its beams indeed. It is not denied that the Church of England has contributed many valuable additions to the literature of Christianity; and considering the ample means at her command for bestowing on her office-bearers extensive education and literary leisure, it would have been strange if she had not. But it is not the less true, that a very large share of her reputation is derived from the writings of the Puritan and Presbyterian divines, and their immediate pupils,

—from the very men whom she calumniated and persecuted, and strove to exterminate when living, and when dead, has pillaged of their hard-won honours, which she arrogates for her own, or suffers to be ascribed to her by unwise or unblushing flatterers.

Not only was an impulse given to the universities during the short prevalence of the Presbyterian Church in England, but also throughout considerable districts of the kingdom. Strenuous exertions were made to provide an adequate remedy for the deplorable state of ignorance in which the great body of the population had been suffered to remain. The removal of scandalous and ignorant ministers was the first step taken towards this desirable object. Another was, the sequestration of the surplus wealth of the Prelatic dignitaries; a portion of which it was intended to employ in providing academies, schools, and all that was necessary for instituting a national system of education. This noble and generous scheme also was embarrassed and impeded by Erastian interference; because it would have naturally fallen under the superintendence of Presbyteries, to the erection of which throughout the kingdom, with full and due powers, they could not be persuaded to consent. Even when almost paralyzed by this unhappy Erastian interference, the Presbyterian ministers set themselves to promote education to the utmost of their power. There may still be found, in several country districts in England, where Presbyterians once abounded, schools having a right to a small salary to the schoolmaster, on condition that he shall teach the children the Assembly's Shorter Catechism.* The people of England do not yet know, and cannot easily conceive, how grievous was the loss which they sustained by the unfortunate failure of the attempt to render the Presbyterian Church the ecclesiastical establish-

---

* One of these the author was fortunate enough to assist in rescuing from the hands of Socinians, a few years ago, on the strength of that very condition.

ment of the kingdom. To them it would have been a source of almost unmingled and incalculable good, giving to them the advantage of an evangelical, pious, laborious, and regularly resident ministry in every parish, together with cheap and universally accessible education, the constant inspection of elders to watch over their moral conduct, and deacons to attend to the wants of the poor in the spirit of Christian kindness and benevolence; all regulated by the superintendence of Presbyteries and Synods, to prevent the hazard of injury from local neglect or prejudice. And surely a truly wise and paternal government ought to have rejoiced at the opportunity of attaining so easily advantages so inestimable to the nation at large, and consequently to its rulers, and to all that wished its welfare. All this was once attainable,— was very nearly attained; has it become for ever impossible? We will not think so; a time may come.

Reference has been repeatedly made to the state of the army, and of the almost innumerable varieties of sects which appeared in it, and throughout the kingdom; and it has been shown that this strange and formidable chaos of religious opinions can best be accounted for by attending to the fact, that almost the entire population had been allowed, or rather constrained, to remain in a state of deplorable ignorance, by the wretched policy of the Prelatists and of the despotic monarchs, who deemed it inexpedient to teach the people to think, lest they should turn their attention to public matters, and learn to think and act for themselves. The direct consequence of this was, that when the naturally strong mind of England was fairly roused, it put forth its strength, but, like the mighty Hebrew when fallen into the hands of his adversaries, put it forth in blindness. At the commencement of the war between the king and the Parliament, ministers were appointed to accompany the parliamentary army, to train the troops in sound religious knowledge, and guide them in the worship of God. But this was both an irksome and a dan-

gerous task; sufficient numbers could not be obtained. When
the Westminster Assembly met, some of the ablest were called
to attend its deliberations; and after the self-denying ordinance, when the army was new-modelled, it was left almost
entirely to the wildly erratic instructions of self-called and
uneducated lay-preachers. It was not strange that enthusiastic notions should be promulgated, and should be widely
received, when poured forth amidst such exciting scenes and
circumstances by the wildly eloquent fervour of strong and earnest minds. And as little was it strange that the thoroughly
learned and deep-thinking divines of the Assembly should
perceive the dangerous consequences to religion, morality, and
peace, which must inevitably follow from the unrestrained
diffusion of all the lawless and extravagant fancies by which
the fermenting public mind was agitated and borne along.
They knew what had taken place in Germany, when the
peasantry were roused to insurrectionary tumults by the licentious principles and harangues of the Anabaptists, and they
dreaded the occurrence of similar events in England. For
such reasons they were exceedingly anxious that a regular
and authoritative system of Church government and discipline should be established, and put in operation with all
convenient speed; and this wish was in itself of a truly pious
and patriotic nature, even though it could be proved that the
means by which it was sought to be realized were not the
most judicious that could have been imagined.

This course of reflection leads us to make some inquiry into
the subject of religious toleration, of which so much has been
said and written, in the present as well as in former times.
The term itself, *toleration in matters of religion*, is one which
has rarely been defined with that care and exactness which its
great importance demands; consequently, the whole subject
is liable to every sort of sophistical perversion; and very many
of the controversial writings that have appeared concerning it
start from different points, and run on either in parallel or in

diverging lines, without the possibility of ever arriving at the same conclusion.   Many thousands have been oppressed, persecuted, and put to death, for maintaining and promoting God's revealed truth; many thousands have suffered equal extremities for maintaining and promoting satanic falsehood; and many thousands have sustained all degrees of punishment for the perpetration of immorality and crime.   But who will assert that the same principle appears in all these cases?   Who will say, that because it is right to suppress and punish the commission of crime, therefore it is right to suppress and punish men for asserting religious truth?   Or, that because it is wrong to suppress truth, therefore it is wrong to suppress crime, or discountenance error?   But men try to escape from such reasoning, by asserting that truth cannot be ascertained with certainty; and that therefore it is best to give equal toleration to all opinions, lest a grievous mistake should be committed, and truth suppressed instead of error.   This is the language of scepticism, and the principle which it promulgates is not toleration, but latitudinarian laxity and licentiousness.   Such language really implies, either that God did not intend to convey saving truth in a manner intelligible to the minds of men, or that he failed in his intention.   But since few will be found reckless enough to maintain such opinions in their naked deformity, the advocates of sceptical laxity have recourse to every kind of evasion, in order to conceal alike the nature of the principle which they support and of that which they oppose.   And, unhappily, these evasions are but too consonant to the character of the fallen mind of man, which is " enmity against God, and is not subject to the law of God, neither indeed can be."   This is a truth which the sincere Christian feels and knows, but which philosophers and politicians reject, despise, and hate.

The essence of the inquiry is, " Has God revealed sacred saving truth to man, as the only sure guide and rule in all religious, moral, and social duties?"   And if this be admitted, then arises the next question,—" Can this truth be so fully ascertained and known as to become a sufficient guide and rule in all such duties?" If this too should be admitted, we then arrive at the important practical inquiry,— " In what manner may the knowledge of this sacred saving truth be most successfully diffused throughout the world?" For if such truth has been revealed, and can be known, man's first duty must be to know it himself, and his next, to communicate it to others. But he may err in this second point of duty, and may actually impede, while he is intending to promote, its progress. Few will deny that it is the duty of every man, in his station, to encourage the extension of truth by every legitimate means within his power; but it does not at once appear so clear, whether it be also his duty to engage so actively in such a removal of opposing obstacles as would involve the direct suppression of error. And it is at this stage of the inquiry that the question of religious toleration arises in its proper form and character. For it never ought to be made a question, whether truth ought to be tolerated or not,—truth ought to be encouraged and diffused; but the question is, Ought error also, and with equal directness, to be suppressed? The best method of obtaining a right answer to this inquiry is, to consult the Word of God, and to investigate the nature of conscience. The Word of God, in almost innumerable instances, commands the direct encouragement of truth, and also the suppression of certain *forms* of error,— as of idolatry and blasphemy; but gives no authority to man to judge and punish errors of the mind, so far as these amount not to violations of known and equitable laws, and disturb not the peace of society. And with regard to the nature of conscience, it is manifest to every thinking man, that conscience cannot be compelled. It may be enlightened, it may be convinced, but its very nature is the free exercise of that self-judging faculty which is the essential principle of personal responsibility. Hence it is evident, that it is alike contrary to the Word of God and to the nature of conscience, for man to attempt to promote truth by the compulsive suppression of error, when that error does not obtrude itself on public view by open violation of God's commandments and the just laws of the land.   But it by no means follows that toleration means, or ought to mean, equal favour shown to error as to truth.   Truth ought to be expressly favoured and encouraged : erring men ought to be treated with all tenderness and compassionate toleration ; but error itself ought to be condemned, and all fair means employed for its extirpation.   This could never lead to persecution ; because it would constantly preserve the distinction between the abstract error and the man whose misfortune it is to be an erring man, and to whom it would show all tenderness, while it strove to rescue him from the evil consequences of those erroneous notions by which he was blinded and misled.

There is great reason to believe that the Presbyterians and the Independents of the Westminster Assembly misapprehended each other's opinions on the subject of religious toleration.   What the Presbyterians understood their opponents to mean by that term was what they called a " boundless toleration," implying equal encouragement to all shades and kinds of religious opinions, however wild, extravagant, and pernicious in their principles, and in their evident tendency. And when they somewhat vehemently condemned such laxity and licentiousness, the Independents seem to have thought that they intended or desired the forcible suppression of all opinions that differed from their own.   Yet surely the Independents might have better understood both the principles and the practice of Presbyterian Churches.   In Holland, a Presbyterian country, they had themselves enjoyed the most complete and undisturbed toleration in religious matters. They had often witnessed the interposition of the Scottish divines on their behalf in the debates of the Assembly ; and if they experienced somewhat sharper treatment and more pointed opposition from the English Presbyterians, that might easily be explained by the difference of temper in men struggling to obtain the establishment of a system, and in men living in that system when established, and then acting according to its native spirit and character. They might have made allowance also for the feeling of excited alarm with which the Presbyterians regarded the portentous growth and multiplication of heretical sects, alike dangerous to religious truth, to moral purity, and to national peace; for it must be observed, that during Cromwell's administration, when the Independents were in the enjoyment of chief power, many of these sects (such as Levellers, the Fifth-Monarchy Men, the Socinians, the Antinomians, the Quakers, &c.) were forcibly suppressed, without any opposition being offered by them to this suppression, as an intolerant interference with liberty of conscience. The only explanation, we apprehend, which can be given of this inconsistency of the Independents, is one not very creditable to their character for integrity of principle. During their struggle with the Presbyterians, they needed the support of numbers, being but few themselves, and therefore they advocated a "boundless toleration,"—of which they did not really approve, and which, when in power themselves, they did not grant.*

It has been often confidently asserted, that the Indepen-

---

* "Some, perhaps, by a *toleration* understand an *universal, uncontrolled licence* of living as you please in things concerning religion : that every one may be *let alone*, and not so much as discountenanced in doing, speaking, acting, how, what, where, or when he pleaseth, in all such things as concerneth the worship of God, articles of belief, or generally any thing commanded in religion ; and in the meantime, the parties at variance, and litigant about differences, freely to revile, reject, and despise one another, according as their provoked genius shall dispose their minds thereunto. Now, truly, though every one of this mind pretends to cry for mercy to be extended unto poor afflicted *Truth*, yet I cannot but be persuaded that such a *toleration* would prove exceeding pernicious to all sorts of men."—*Essay by Dr Owen*, appended to a Sermon preached before the House of Commons, April 29, 1646; p. 66.

dents were the first who rightly understood and publicly advocated the great principle of religious toleration. That they did assert that principle is certain; but that they were the first who did so is not the truth. Luther declared, that "The Church ought not to force persons to believe, nor to animadvert capitally on those who follow a different religion:" "That to believe is something free, yea, divine, being the fruit of the Spirit; wherefore it cannot, and ought not, to be forced by any external violence." The language of Zuingle is not less explicit: "It is at once contrary to the Gospel and to reason, to employ violent measures to extort a confession of faith contrary to conscience. Reason and persuasion are the arms that a Christian ought to employ." Even Calvin and Knox, terrible as their very names appear to some, and associated with the very essence of intolerance, repeatedly expressed sentiments precisely similar, strenuously maintaining the liberty of the conscience, and condemning persecution. And in Scotland, where the Presbyterian Church was early established, and repeatedly enjoyed much power, often as that Church suffered persecution in every form and degree, it never, in its day of power, persecuted its enemies in return. This some will think a strange assertion, accustomed as they have been to hear so much about Presbyterian intolerance; yet it is not more strange than true. And did our space permit, we could furnish ample proof that the true principles of religious toleration were both held and practised in Scotland by the Presbyterian Church, both before Independency had come into existence, and during the very time of the struggle between the two parties in England. And even in the Westminster Assembly, at the time when the subject of toleration was under discussion, the true principles of religious liberty were avowedly held and publicly taught by the Presbyterian divines, the very men who are so vehemently accused of intolerance,—at least as distinctly and earnestly as they were by the Independents. Such sentiments as the following were

frequently expressed by them in their public sermons :—
" Fierce and furious prosecution, even of a good cause, is
rather prejudice than promotion. We must tenaciously adhere to all divine truths ourselves, and, with our wisest
moderation, plant and propagate them in others. Opposites,
indeed, must be opposed, gainsaid, reclaimed ; but all must
be done in a way, and by the means, appointed from heaven.
It is one thing to show moderation to pious, peaceable, and
tender consciences ; it is another thing to proclaim beforehand
toleration to impious, fiery, and unpeaceable opinions."

In the last sentence of this quotation a distinction is drawn
which touches the essential point of the controversy between
the Presbyterians and the Independents. The Presbyterians
wished Church government to be established in the first
instance, and then a toleration to be granted to tender
consciences: the Independents, on the other hand, strove to
obtain a legislative toleration first, and then it would have
been a matter of little moment which, or whether any, form
of Church government should be established. The Presbyterians not only apprehended that this would amount to the
establishment of the Independent system, instead of their
own, and consequently, to the frustration of the very object
for which the Assembly had met, and for which they had
sworn the Covenant, namely, the promotion of uniformity in
religious matters throughout Protestant Christendom, Independency being prevalent in no European country; but also,
they regarded it with strong alarm, as sanctioning all the
pernicious heresies with which England abounded, and
establishing the principle of universal licentiousness.   On
the other hand, the Independents knew well, that unless the
spirit of a Presbyterian Church should be different in England
from what it was in every other country, its establishment
would not prevent toleration, to the utmost extent that God's
Word warrants, and an enlightened conscience can require.
Such, indeed, was the conviction of Dr Owen, who, though

not a member of the Westminster Assembly, was thoroughly acquainted with many of the leading Presbyterians, knew their sentiments, and understood their system. "Had the Presbyterian government," says he, "been settled at the king's restoration, by the encouragement and protection of the practice of it, without a rigorous imposition of every thing supposed by any to belong thereunto, or a mixture of human institutions, if there had been any appearance of a schism or separation between the parties, I do judge they would have been both to blame; for they allowed distinct communion upon distinct apprehensions of things belonging to Church order or worship,—all ' keeping the unity of the Spirit in the bond of peace.' If it shall be asked, Then why did they not formerly agree in the Assembly? I answer, 1. I was none of them, and cannot tell. 2. They did agree, in my judgment, well enough, if they could have thought so; and further I am not concerned in the difference." *

The real cause, most probably, why they did not agree, was what has been already suggested,—that the intriguing spirit of Nye involved the Assembly Independents in the political schemes of Cromwell. But though that ambitious man made use of them to promote his designs, by retarding the settlement of any thing till his power was matured; and though he continued to bestow upon them the chief share of his favour after he had seized upon the sceptre of imperial sway; he neither granted, nor did they sue for, universal toleration. This is placed beyond doubt by the circumstances connected with some ecclesiastical arrangements proposed in his Parliament in the year 1654. The leading Independent ministers laid before the Committee of Triers, at that time formed, a series of requests, in the form of a representation, one article of which was as follows :—" That this honourable Committee be desired to propose to the Parliament, that such who do

---

* Answer to Stillingfleet's Unreasonableness of Separation. Works, vol. xv. p. 433, Johnstone & Hunter's edition.

Y

not receive those principles of religion, without acknowledgment whereof the Scriptures do clearly and plainly affirm that
salvation is not to be obtained, as those formerly complained
of by the ministers, may not be suffered to preach or promulgate any thing in opposition unto such principles." In consequence of this, a discussion arose respecting the extent to
which religious toleration was to be carried, when " it was
voted, that all should be tolerated or indulged who professed
the fundamentals of Christianity ;" and a committee was appointed to nominate certain divines to draw up a catalogue
of the fundamentals, to be presented to the House.   These
divines, chiefly Owen, Nye, and Goodwin, accordingly drew
up sixteen articles, and presented them to the Committee of
Parliament, by whom they were ordered to be printed.   A
strict interpretation and application of these sixteen fundamental principles of religion would exclude from toleration
all Deists, Papists, Socinians, Arians, Antinomians, and Quakers, and even Arminians, by no very strained construction.*

* "The Principles of Faith presented by Mr Thomas Goodwin, Mr Nye,
    Mr Simpson, and other Ministers, to the Committee of Parliament
    for Religion, &c.

" 1. That the Holy Scripture is that rule of knowing God, and living
unto him, which whoso does not believe cannot be saved.

" 2. That there is a God, who is the Creator, Governor, and Judge of
the world,—which is to be received by faith; and every other way of the
knowledge of him is insufficient.

" 3. That this God, who is the Creator, is eternally distinct from all
creatures, in his being and blessedness.

" 4. That this God is one, in three persons or subsistences.

" 5. That Jesus Christ is the only Mediator between God and man,
without the knowledge of whom there is no salvation.

" 6. That this Jesus Christ is the true God.

" 7. That this Jesus Christ is also true man.

" 8. That this Jesus Christ is God and man in one person.

" 9. That this Jesus Christ is our Redeemer, who, by paying a ransom,
and bearing our sins, has made satisfaction for them.

" 10. That this same Jesus Christ is he that was crucified at Jerusalem,
and rose again, and ascended into heaven.

From this it is evident, that whether the Presbyterians really did understand and act upon the true principles of religious liberty or not, it cannot with truth be said that the views of the Independents were in any respect more liberal and enlarged. For this we blame them not, but merely state the fact. Perhaps the exact truth is, that their opinions on the subject were nearly identical, all the difference between them being that of position and circumstance; and it may fairly be admitted, that the subject had not at that period received all the attention it deserved, and the elucidation of which it was capable. It was, however, brought so strongly before the notice of the public mind, and attention was so forcibly directed to it by the ejection of the two thousand ministers on St Bartholomew's day, and by subsequent events during that and the succeeding reign, that it became one of the essential elements which produced the Revolution of 1688, and was secured by the Toleration Act of the following year. The Toleration Act itself may therefore be fairly regarded as one of the results of the Westminster Assembly, though few have been hitherto disposed to trace it to that truly illustrious source.

There was one great, and even sublime idea, brought somewhat indefinitely before the Westminster Assembly, which

"11. That this same Jesus Christ, being the only God and man in one person, remains for ever a distinct person from all saints and angels, notwithstanding their union and communion with him.

"12. That all men by nature are dead in trespasses and sins; and no man can be saved unless he be born again, repent, and believe.

"13. That we are justified and saved by grace, and faith in Jesus Christ, and not by works.

"14. That to continue in any known sin, upon what pretence or principle soever, is damnable.

"15. That God is to be worshipped according to his own will; and whosoever shall forsake and despise all the duties of his worship cannot be saved.

"16. That the dead shall rise; and that there is a day of judgment, wherein all shall appear, some to go into everlasting life, and some into everlasting condemnation."—*Neal*, vol. ii. pp. 621, 622.

has not yet been realized,—the idea of a Protestant union throughout Christendom, not merely for the purpose of counterbalancing Popery, but in order to purify, strengthen, and unite all true Christian Churches, so that with combined energy and zeal they might go forth, in glad compliance with the Redeemer's commands, teaching all nations, and preaching the everlasting gospel to every creature under heaven. This truly magnificent, and also truly Christian idea, seems to have originated in the mind of that distinguished man, Alexander Henderson. It was suggested by him to the Scottish commissioners, and by them partially brought before the English Parliament, requesting them to direct the Assembly to write letters to the Protestant Churches in France, Holland, Switzerland, and other Reformed Churches. Henderson had too much wisdom to state the subject fully to the Parliament, lest they should be startled by a thought vast beyond their conception. They gave to the Assembly the desired direction, and the letters were prepared and sent. A hasty perusal of these letters might not suggest the idea of a great Protestant union, the greater part of them being occupied with a statement of the causes which had led to the calling of the Assembly, and in vindication of themselves against the accusations wherewith they might be assailed. But towards the conclusion the idea is dimly traced ; and along with these letters were sent copies of the Solemn League and Covenant, —a document which might itself form the basis of such a Protestant union. The deep thinking divines of the Netherlands apprehended the idea, and in their answer, not only expressed their approbation of the Covenant, but also desired to join in it with the British kingdoms. Nor did they content themselves with the mere expression of approval and willingness to join. A letter was soon afterwards sent to the Assembly from the Hague, written by Duraeus (the celebrated John Dury), offering to come to the Assembly, and containing a copy of a vow which he had prepared and tendered to the distinguished Oxenstiern, chancellor of Sweden, wherein he bound himself " to prosecute a reconciliation between Protestants in point of religion." *

That this was the real object contemplated in this remarkable correspondence is indicated with sufficient plainness by Baillie : " We are thinking of a new work over sea, if this Church were settled. The times of Antichrist's fall are approaching. The very outward providence of God seems to be disposing France, Spain, Italy, and Germany, for the receiving of the gospel. When the curtains of the Lord's tabernacle are thus far, and much farther enlarged, by the means which yet appear not, how shall our mouth be filled with laughter, our tongue with praise, and our heart with rejoicing ! " † There are several other hints of a similar character to be found in Baillie's Letters ; and on one occasion Henderson procured a passport to go to Holland, most probably for the purpose of prosecuting this grand idea. But the intrigues of politicians, the delays caused by the conduct of the Independents, and the narrow-minded Erastianism of the English Parliament, all conspired to prevent the Assembly from entering farther into that truly glorious Christian enterprise. Days of trouble and darkness came ; persecution wore out the great men of that remarkable period ; pure and vital Christianity was stricken to the earth and trampled under foot; and when the time of deliverance came at the Revolution, it found the Churches too much exhausted to resume the mighty tasks begun, but not accomplished, in the previous generation. Peace and repose were chiefly sought ; listless inactivity and spiritual deadness ensued ; and all the noble purposes and great ideas of a former age were basely forgotten or sinfully despised.

But although the Westminster Assembly and its labours seemed to have been thus consigned to oblivion, or mentioned by prelatic or infidel historians merely as a topic on which

---

* Lightfoot, p. 86.   † Baillie, vol. ii. p. 192.

they might freely pour forth their spite or their mockery, its influence in the deep undercurrent of the national mind was unseen, but was not unfelt. Even in England, where every effort was made to destroy alike its principles and their fruit, it succeeded in communicating a secret impulse of irresistible energy to the nation's heart. This was first proved by the noble testimony borne on St Bartholomew's day, in defence of religious liberty. And the feeling thus called into action showed its might when afterwards the Popish tyrant, James VII., was hurled from his throne by the indignant voice of a free Protestant people. Let it be frankly granted that the English bishops bore a considerable part in that memorable Revolution; but let it also be remembered, that in their youth they had imbibed the principles of religious and civil liberty under the instruction of Presbyterian and Independent professors and masters in the universities; and let it also be remembered that the Toleration Act was the production of the same well-trained generation : and when these things are borne in mind, it will not be said that the nation derived no advantage from the labours of the Westminster Assembly.

In Scotland its results were more directly and signally beneficial, being fully accepted by the Church, and ratified by the State. Not even twenty-eight years of ruthless persecution could extinguish the bright light of sacred truth which it had contributed to shed over our own northern hills, or trample out of existence the strong spirit of liberty which it inspired and hallowed. What can ever expel from the mind and heart of a Christian people that single sentence of the Confession of Faith : " God alone is Lord of the conscience, and hath left it free from the doctrines and commandments of men which are in any thing contrary to his Word, or beside it, in matters of faith or worship." The people who can feel and understand that sacred truth can never be enslaved. And although, after the Union, the perfidy of traitorous statesmen introduced the unconstitutional element of patronage into the external arrangements of the Church of Scotland, contrary to the express stipulations of the Act of Security, by which the Scottish nation had so anxiously sought to protect their National Church; yet it required the lapse of generations to produce a race sufficiently degenerated to allow the pernicious element to do its work. Even when a majority of the Scottish ministers had become unfaithful, the Confession of Faith and the Catechism continued to infuse their strong and living principles of Christian truth into the hearts and minds of the people, maintaining a spirit and an energy that nothing could subdue. The effect of this was seen in the Secession; and not less manifestly in the deep and steady devotedness with which the ministrations of evangelical truth were attended in the Established Church itself. A recent and still more signal manifestation of the power of these principles was displayed in the memorable Disruption of 1843, when, in vindication of their truth, and to secure the liberty of maintaining them, four hundred and seventy-four ministers gave up all connection with the State, and all the advantages thence arising, rather than surrender spiritual freedom in obedience to Christ alone. Such was the state of the Churches in both kingdoms throughout the listless length of a dreary century,—the still and heavy torpor of lethargic sluggishness above, the silent but strong current of a deep life-stream beneath.

CHAPTER VI.

THE THEOLOGICAL PRODUCTIONS OF THE WESTMINSTER ASSEMBLY.

It has been suggested repeatedly, that in order to render this work a full History of the Westminster Assembly, it ought to contain, at least, a brief sketch of its theological productions. This was not at first thought necessary, because as its chief production was the Confession of Faith, and as that was held to be almost universally known, there did not appear much need for any thing more than the mention of its name. But in deference to the opinion of others, a distinct chapter is now added to this edition, containing the suggested outline.

After having spent a few weeks in discussing the doctrines of the Thirty-nine Articles of the Church of England, the Assembly was required by the Parliament to direct its deliberations to the important topics of Discipline and a Directory of Worship and Church Government. On the 17th day of October 1643, accordingly, the Assembly took into consideration, first, the subject of Government. The whole matter was very fully argued, chiefly on scriptural grounds, during the remainder of that year, and throughout the whole of 1644, with numerous delays and interruptions; and when completed was not ratified by the English Parliament, but allowed to lie dormant in the hands of the Committee of Accommodation till June 1646. But a copy of it was transmitted to Scotland, laid before the General Assembly, and approved by that body on the 10th of February 1645. It contains a very distinct statement of the supremacy of Christ, of the Church, of its Office-bearers, of Congregations and their Office-bearers, of Church Courts and their jurisdiction through all their ascend- ing gradations,—Sessions, Presbyteries, Provincial Synods, and General Assemblies,—and of all that relates to the Ordi- nation of Ministers. These topics are all succinctly and clearly stated, and supported by proofs from Scripture. No other proof, by reasoning, or reference to tradition, or the practice of primitive Christianity, or of other Churches, is given; because the Assembly regarded nothing as having any authority in regard to the Church but the Word of God. But if any person should wish to know the reasonings of the Assembly on the subject of Church government, he may find them in their fullest form in the volume commonly designated "The Grand Debate."

The Directory of Public Worship was another of the strictly theological subjects which engaged the attention of the Westminster Assembly. As the whole Prelatic system had been abolished before the Assembly met, and as the en- forcement of its Liturgy and ceremonies had already been the cause of such prolonged contests and excessive afflictions in England, till nearly all its truly evangelical ministers had been forced to join the Puritans, and in doing so had already adopted a purely scriptural form of public worship, the As- sembly had little to do but to state, in their own well-weighed and concise terms, a Directory of Public Worship in which nearly all were already agreed. This was accordingly done during the course of 1644, its various topics being taken up from time to time, in the intervals between their discussions on more controverted matters. The Directory was trans- mitted to Scotland along with the subject of Church Govern- ment, and approved by the General Assembly on February 3, 1645. It will be found in the common editions of the volume usually designated the "Confession of Faith," from the most important portion. The topics of the Directory need not be here either enumerated or explained; but we may be permitted to recommend its very careful and repeated perusal by all ministers, and all who are preparing for the office of the ministry. They will find it both full of sound and well-expressed instruction, and eminently suggestive,—much more so, we anticipate, than they would readily expect.

When the Assembly was about to begin the important task of preparing a Catechism, it was suggested that it would be more prudent first to prepare a Confession of Faith, and then the Catechism might be so constructed as to contain no doctrinal proposition but what was in the Confession, and thereby be a preparatory training for the subsequent study of that graver work. The mode in which the Assembly carried on its work has been already described, and need not be repeated, further than by stating that a re-arrangement of the committees was made with express reference to the framing of the Confession, so that the primary committee, appointed to prepare and arrange the main propositions which were to be submitted to the Assembly, was composed entirely of its most able and learned divines. These were, Dr Hoyle, Dr Gouge, Messrs Herle, Gataker, Tuckney, Reynolds, and Vines, with the four Scottish commissioners, Henderson, Rutherford, Baillie, and Gillespie. Henderson was already well prepared for entering on this most important task, having been requested by the General Assembly of the Scottish Church, in the year 1641, to draw up a new and full Confession of Faith, which the Church might adopt; and although this had not been actually produced, yet the subject had been thereby placed definitely before his capacious mind, and must have frequently engaged his thoughts.

These learned and able divines began their labours by arranging, in the most systematic order, the various great and sacred truths which God has revealed to man; and then reduced these to thirty-two distinct heads or chapters. These were again sub-divided into sections; and the committee formed themselves into several sub-committees, each of which took a specific topic, for the sake of exact and concentrated deliberation. When these sub-committees had completed their respective tasks, the whole results were laid before the entire committee, and any alterations suggested, and debated till all were of one mind, and fully agreed as to both doctrine and expression. And when any title or chapter had been thus thoroughly prepared by the committee, it was reported to the Assembly, and again subjected to the most minute and careful investigation, in every paragraph, sentence, and even word. All that learning the most profound and extensive, intellect the most acute and searching, and piety the most sincere and earnest, could accomplish, was thus concentrated in the Westminster Assembly's Confession of Faith, which may be safely termed the most perfect statement of Systematic Theology ever framed by the Christian Church.

In the preliminary deliberations of the committee the Scottish divines took a leading part, for which they were peculiarly qualified; but no report of these deliberations either was or could be made public. The results alone appeared, when the committee, from time to time, laid its matured propositions before the Assembly. And it is gratifying to be able to add, that throughout the deliberations of the Assembly itself, when composing, or rather formally sanctioning, the Confession of Faith, there prevailed almost an entire harmony. There appear, indeed, to have been only *two* subjects on which any difference of opinion existed among them. The one of these was the doctrine of election, concerning which Baillie informs us that they had "long and tough debates;" the other was about the leading proposition of the chapter entitled, "Of Church Censures," viz., "The Lord Jesus, as King and Head of his Church, hath therein appointed a government in the hand of Church-officers, distinct from the civil magistrate." This proposition the Assembly manifestly intended and understood to contain a principle directly and necessarily opposed to the very essence of Erastianism, and it was regarded in the same light by the Erastians themselves; hence it had to encounter their most strenuous opposition. It was, however, somewhat beyond the grasp of the lay members of the Assembly, especially since their champion, Selden, had in a great measure withdrawn from the debates after his signal discomfiture by Gillespie; and consequently it was carried triumphantly, the single dissentient voice being that of Lightfoot, the other Erastian divine, Coleman, having died before the conclusion of the debate. The framing of the Confession occupied the Assembly somewhat more than a 'year. After having been carefully transcribed, it was presented to the Parliament on the 3d of December 1646. The House of Commons required the proof by Scripture texts to be added. This also was done, and a completed copy again laid before the House on the 29th day of April 1647. Finally, on the 27th of August 1647, the General Assembly of the Church of Scotland passed an act approving the Confession of Faith, with a caveat in the concluding sentence of that act, guarding against some portions of it which might be construed as yielding too much to the authority of the civil magistrate. This Act will be found in all the common editions of the Confession of Faith, and deserves to be noticed.

There have been many objections urged against the use of Creeds and Confessions of Faith; but almost the only objection which is now attempted with any degree of confidence, is that which accuses Confessions of usurping a position and authority due to divine truth alone. This objection itself has its origin in an erroneous view of what a Confession of Faith really is, and wherein the necessity of there being a Confession consists. That necessity does not lie in the nature of the truth revealed to man; but in the nature of the human mind itself. A Confession is not a revelation of divine truth,

—it is "not even a rule of faith and practice, but a help in both," to use the words of the Westminster Confession itself; but it is a declaration of the manner in which any man, or number of men—any Christian, or any Church—understands the truth which has been revealed. Its object is, therefore, not to teach divine truth; but to exhibit a clear, systematic, and intelligible declaration of our own sentiments, and to furnish the means of ascertaining the opinions of others, especially on religious doctrines.

The Christian Church, as a divine institution, takes the Word of God alone, and the whole Word of God, as her only rule of faith; but she must also frame and promulgate a statement of what she understands the Word of God to teach. This she does, not as arrogating any authority to suppress, change, or amend anything that God's Word teaches; but in discharge of the various duties which she owes to God, to the world, and to those of her own communion. Since she has been constituted the depositary of God's truth, it is her duty to him to state, in the most distinct and explicit terms, what she understands that truth to mean. In this manner she not only proclaims what God has said, but also appends her seal that God is true. Thus a Confession of Faith is not the very voice of divine truth, but the echo of that voice from souls that have heard its utterance, felt its power, and are answering to its call. And, since she has been instituted for the purpose of teaching God's truth to an erring world, her duty to the world requires that she should leave it in no doubt respecting the manner in which she understands the message which she has to deliver. Without doing so, the Church would be no teacher, and the world might remain untaught, so far as she was concerned. For when the message had been stated in God's own words, every hearer must attempt, according to the constitution of his own mind, to form some conception of what these words mean; and his conceptions may be very vague and obscure, or even

very erroneous, unless some attempt be made to define, eluci-
date, and correct them.   Nor, indeed, could either the hearers
or the teachers know that they understood the truth alike,
without mutual statements and explanations with regard to
the meaning which they respectively believe it to convey.
Still further, the Church has a duty to discharge to those of
its own communion.   To them she must produce a form of
sound words, in order both to promote and confirm their
knowledge, and also to guard them against the hazard of
being led into errors; and, as they must be regarded as all
agreed, with respect to the main outline of the truths which
they believe, they are deeply interested in obtaining some
security that those who are to become their teachers in future
generations shall continue to teach the same divine and saving
truths.   The members of any Church must know each other's
sentiments; must combine to hold them forth steadily and
consistently to the notice of all around them, as witnesses for
the same truths; and must do their utmost to secure that the
same truths shall be taught by all their ministers, and to all
candidates for admission.   For all these purposes the formation of a Creed, or Confession of Faith, is imperatively necessary; and thus it appears that a Church cannot adequately
discharge its duty to God, to the world, and to its own members, without a Confession of Faith.

There never has been a period in which the Christian
Church has been without a Confession of Faith, though these
Confessions have varied both in character and in extent. The
first and simplest Confession is that of Peter: " Thou art the
Christ, the Son of the living God." That of the Ethiopian
treasurer is similar, and almost identical: " I believe that
Jesus Christ is the Son of God." This Confession secured
admission into the Church; but without this, admission
could not have been obtained. It was not long till this simple
and brief primitive Confession was enlarged; at first, in order
to meet the perverse notions of the Judaizing teachers, and

next, to exclude those who were beginning to be tainted with the Gnostic heresies. It then became necessary, not only to confess that Jesus Christ was the Son of God, but also that Jesus Christ was come in the flesh, in order to prevent the admission, and to check the teaching, of those who held that Christ's human nature was a mere phantasm or appearance. In like manner the rise of any heresy rendered it necessary, first, to test the novel tenet by the Word of God and by the decision of the Holy Spirit, and then to add to the existing Confession of Faith a new article, containing the deliverance of the Church respecting each successive heresy. Thus, in the discharge of her duty to God, to the world, and to herself, the Church was constrained to enlarge the Confession of her Faith. But this unavoidable enlargement ought not to be censured as unnecessarily lengthened and minute; for, let it be observed, that it led to a continually increasing clearness and precision in the testimony of what the Church believes, and tended to the progressive development of sacred truth. Further, as the need of a Confession arises from the nature of the human mind, and the enlargement of the Confession was caused by the successive appearance and refutation of error, and as the human mind is still the same, and prone to the same erroneous notions, the Confession of Faith, which contains a refutation of past heresies, furnishes, at the same time, to all who understand it, a ready weapon wherewith to encounter any resuscitated heresy. The truth of this view will be most apparent to those who have most carefully studied the various Confessions of Faith framed by the Christian Church. And it must ever be regarded as a matter of no small importance by those who seek admission into any Church, that in its Confession they can obtain a full exhibition of the terms of communion to which they are required to consent. The existence of a Confession of Faith is ever a standing defence against the danger of any Church lapsing unawares into heresy. For although no Church ought to regard her Confession as a standard of faith, in any other than a subordinate sense, still it is a standard of admitted faith, which the Church may not lightly abandon, and a term of communion to its own members, till its articles are accused of being erroneous, and again brought to the final and supreme standard, the Word of God and the teaching of the Holy Spirit, sincerely, humbly, and earnestly sought in faith and prayer.

The first thing which must strike any thoughtful reader, after having carefully and studiously perused the Westminster Assembly's Confession of Faith, is the remarkable comprehensiveness and accuracy of its character, viewed as a systematic exhibition of divine truth, or what is termed a system of theology. In this respect it may be regarded as almost perfect, both in its arrangement and in its completeness. Even a single glance over its table of contents will show with what exquisite skill its arrangement proceeds, from the statement of first principles to the regular development and final consummation of the whole scheme of revealed truth. Nothing essential is omitted ; and nothing is extended to a length disproportioned to its due importance. Too little attention, perhaps, has been shown to the Confession in this respect ; and we are strongly persuaded that it might be very advantageously used in our theological halls as a textbook. This, at least, may be affirmed, that no private Christian could fail to benefit largely from a deliberate and studious perusal and re-perusal of the Confession of Faith, for the express purpose of obtaining a clear and systematic conception of sacred truth, both as a whole, and with all its parts so arranged as to display their relative importance, and their mutual bearing upon, and illustration of, each other. Such a deliberate perusal would also tend very greatly to fortify the mind against the danger of being led astray by crude notions, or induced to attribute undue importance to some favourite doctrine, to the disparagement of others not less essential, and with serious injury to the harmonious analogy of faith.

There is another characteristic of the Westminster Confession to which still less attention has been generally directed, but which is not less remarkable. Framed, as it was, by men of distinguished learning and ability, who were thoroughly conversant with the history of the Church from the earliest times till the period in which they lived, it contains the calm and settled judgment of these profound divines on all previous heresies and subjects of controversy which had in any age or country agitated the Church. This it does without expressly naming even one of these heresies,—the great Antichristian system alone excepted,—or entering into mere controversy. Each error is condemned, not by a direct statement and refutation of it, but by a clear, definite, and strong statement of the converse truth. There was, in this mode of exhibiting the truth, singular wisdom combined with equally singular modesty. Every thing of an irritating nature is suppressed, and the pure and simple truth alone displayed ; while there is not only no ostentatious parade of superior learning, but even a concealment of learning the most accurate and profound. A hasty or superficial reader of the Confession of Faith will scarcely perceive that, in some of its apparently simple propositions, he is perusing an acute and conclusive refutation of the various heresies and controversies that have corrupted and disturbed the Church. Yet, if he will turn to Church history, make himself acquainted with its details, and resume his study of the Confession, he will often be surprised to find in one place the wild theories of the Gnostics dispelled ; in another, the Arian and Socinian heresies set aside ; in another, the very essence of the Papal system annihilated ; and in another, the basis of all Pelagian and Arminian errors removed. Thus viewed, the Confession of Faith might be so connected with one aspect of Church history as to furnish, if not a text-book according to chronological arrangement, in studying the rise and refutation of heresies, yet a valuable arrangement of their relative import-

z

ance, doctrinally considered. And when we advert to the fact, that owing to the sameness of the human mind in all ages, there is a perpetually recurring tendency to reproduce an old and exploded error, as if it were a new discovery of some hitherto unknown or neglected truth, it must be obvious that were the peculiar excellence of our Confession, as a deliverance on all previously existing heresies, better known and more attended to, there would be great reason to hope that their reappearance would be rendered almost impossible, or, at least, that their growth would be very speedily and effectually checked.

Closely connected with this excellence of the Confession of Faith is its astonishing precision of thought and language. The whole mental training of the eminent divines of that period led to this result. They were accustomed to cast every argument into the syllogistic form, and to adjust all its terms with the utmost care and accuracy. Every one who has studied the propositions of the Confession must have remarked their extreme precision ; but, without peculiar attention, he may not perceive the exquisite care which these divines must have bestowed on this part of their great work. This may be best shown by an instance. Let us select one from chapter iii., "On God's Eternal Decree," sections 3 and 4: " By the decree of God, for the manifestation of his glory, some men and angels are predestinated unto everlasting life, and others foreordained to everlasting death. These angels and men thus predestinated and foreordained," &c. The expressions to which we wish to draw the reader's attention are the words *predestinated* and *foreordained.* A hasty or superficial reader might perceive no difference between these words. But if so, why are they both used ? for there is no instance of mere tautological repetition in the concise language of the Confession. But further, let it be well remarked that the word " predestinated " is used only in connection with " everlasting life," and the word " foreordained" with " everlasting death." And when the compound form of the proposition is assumed, both terms are used to represent each its respective member in the general affirmation. Why is this the case? Because the Westminster Divines did not understand the meaning of the terms *predestination* and *foreordination* to be identical, and therefore never used these words as synonymous. By *predestination* they meant *a positive decree determining to confer everlasting life;* and this they regarded as the basis of the whole *doctrine of free grace,* arising from nothing in man, but having for its divine origin the character and sovereignty of God. By *foreordination,* on the other hand, they meant *a decree of order, or arrangement, determining that the guilty should be condemned to everlasting death;* and this they regarded as the basis of *judicial procedure,* according to which God "ordains men to dishonour and wrath for their sin," and having respect to man's own character and conduct. Let it be further remarked, that while, according to this view, the term *predestination* could never with propriety be applied to the *lost,* the term *foreordination* might be applied to the *saved,* since they also are the subjects, in one sense, of judicial procedure. Accordingly there is no instance in the Confession of Faith where the term *predestination* is applied to the *lost,* though there are several instances where the term *foreordination,* or a kindred term, is applied to the *saved.* And let this also be marked, that the term *reprobation,* which is so liable to be misunderstood and applied in an offensive sense to the doctrine of predestination, is not even once used in the Confession of Faith and the Larger and Shorter Catechisms. Later writers on that doctrine have indeed employed that word, as older writers had done, and had thereby furnished occasion to the opponents of the doctrine to misrepresent it; but the Westminster Divines cautiously avoided the use of an offensive term, carefully selected such words as were best fitted to convey their meaning, and in every instance used them with the most strict and definite precision. Many other examples might be given of the remarkable accuracy of thought and language which forms a distinguished characteristic of the Confession of Faith; but we must content ourselves with suggesting the line of investigation, leaving it to every reader to prosecute it for himself.

Another decided and great merit of the Confession consists in the clear and well-defined statement which it makes of the principles on which alone can securely rest the great idea of the co-ordination, yet mutual support, of the civil and the ecclesiastical jurisdictions. It is but too usual for people to misunderstand those parts of the Confession which treat of these jurisdictions,—some accusing them of containing Erastian concessions, and others charging them with being either lawless or intolerant. The truth is, they favour no extreme. Proceeding upon the sacred rule, to render to Cæsar what is Cæsar's, and to God what is God's, they willingly ascribe to the civil magistrate a supreme power in the State,—all that belongs to his province, not merely with regard to his due authority over the persons and property of men, but also with regard to what pertains to his own official mode of rendering homage to the King of kings. It is in this latter department of magisterial duty that what is called the power of the civil magistrate *circa sacra—about* religious matters—consists. But there his province ends, and he has no power *in sacris— in* religious matters. This is most carefully guarded in the leading proposition of chapter xxx. :—"THE LORD JESUS, AS KING AND HEAD OF HIS CHURCH, HATH THEREIN APPOINTED A GOVERNMENT IN THE HAND OF CHURCH OFFICERS, DISTINCT FROM THE CIVIL MAGISTRATE." The leading Erastians of that period, learned and subtle as they were, felt it impossible to evade the force of that proposition, and could but refuse to give to it the sanction of the Legislature. They could not, however, prevail upon the Assembly either to modify or suppress it; and there it remains, and must remain, as the unanswered and unanswerable refutation of the Erastian heresy by the Westminster Assembly of Divines. In modern times it has been too much the custom of the opponents of Erastianism tacitly to grant the Erastian argument,—or, at least, the principle on which it rests,—by admitting, or even asserting, that if a Church be established, it must cease to have a separate and independent jurisdiction, and must obey the laws of the State, even in spiritual matters; but then declaring, that as this is evidently wrong, there ought to be no Established Church. There is more peril to both civil and religious liberty in this mode of evading Erastianism than is commonly perceived; for if it were generally admitted that an Established Church ought to be subject, even in spiritual matters, to the civil jurisdiction of the State, then would civil rulers have a direct and admitted interest in establishing a Church, not for the sake of promoting Christianity, nor with the view of rendering homage to the Prince of the kings of the earth, but for the purpose of employing the Church as a powerful engine of State policy. That they would avail themselves of such an admission is certain; and this would necessarily tend to produce a perilous contest between the defenders of religious liberty and the supporters of arbitrary power; and if the issue should be the triumph of Erastianism, that issue would inevitably involve the loss of both civil and religious liberty in the blending of the two jurisdictions,—which is the very essence of absolute despotism. Of this the framers of our Confession were well aware; and therefore they strove to procure the well-adjusted and mutual counterpoise and co-operation of the two jurisdictions, as the best safeguards of both civil and religious liberty, and as founded on the express authority of the Word of God. It never yet has been proved, from either Scripture or reason, that they were wrong, although their views have been much misunderstood and grievously misrepresented.

The Confession of Faith has often been accused of advocating intolerant and persecuting principles. It is, however,

in truth, equally free from latitudinarian laxity on the one
hand, and intolerance on the other. An intelligent and candid
perusal of chapter xx., " On Christian Liberty, and Liberty
of Conscience," ought of itself to refute all such calumnies.
The mind of man never produced a truer or nobler proposition than the following :—" God alone is lord of the conscience, and hath left it free from the doctrines and commandments of men, which are in anything contrary to his Word,
or beside it, in matters of faith or worship." The man who
can comprehend, entertain, and act upon that principle, can
never arrogate an overbearing and intolerant authority over
the conscience of his fellow-man, much less wield against him
the weapons of remorseless persecution. But there is a very
prevalent, and yet very false, method of thinking, or pretending to think, respecting toleration and liberty of conscience.
Many seem to be of opinion that toleration consists in making
no distinction between truth and error, but regarding them
with equal favour; which was precisely the theory of Nye
and his brethren, and also of Cromwell—till they were in
possession of power, but no longer. This opinion, if carefully
analyzed, would be found to be essentially of an infidel character. Many seem to think that by liberty of conscience is
meant, that every man should be at liberty to act in every
thing according to his own inclination, without regard to the
feelings, convictions, and rights of other men. This would,
indeed, be to convert liberty into lawlessness, and to make
conscience of licentiousness. But the Confession proceeds
upon the principle that truth can be distinguished from error,
right from wrong; that though conscience cannot be compelled, it may be enlightened; and that when sinful, corrupt,
and prone to licentiousness, men may be lawfully restrained
from the commission of such excesses as are offensive to public feeling, and injurious to the moral welfare of the community. If this be intolerance, it is a kind of intolerance of
which none will complain but those who wish to be free from

all restraint of law, human and divine. Nothing, in our opinion, but a wilful determination to misrepresent the sentiments expressed in the Confession of Faith, or a culpable degree of wilful ignorance respecting the true meaning of these sentiments, could induce any man to accuse it of favouring intolerant and persecuting principles. Certainly the conduct of those who framed it gave no ground for such an accusation, though that calumny has been often and most pertinaciously asserted. On this point also it would be well if people would take the trouble to ascertain what precise meaning the framers of the Confession gave to the words which they employed; for it is not doing justice to them and their work to adopt some modern acceptation of a term used by them in a different sense, and then to charge them with holding the sentiment conveyed by the modern use or misuse of that term. Yet this is the method almost invariably employed by the assailants of the Confession of Faith. It may be readily admitted that the Westminster Divines used expressions in reference to what was called "unlimited toleration," which were not only strong and severe, but harsh, and susceptible of being so construed as to have a persecuting aspect,—expressions which would not now be used. But let it be also remembered, that these expressions were not employed against the principle of toleration itself, rightly understood. They were aimed against that licentiousness which was claimed as a cover to immoralities too horrible to be named, and to civil misdemeanours, perpetrated in the name of religion, fatal to the very existence of society. The avowed toleration of such atrocities by an Assembly of Divines would have amounted to nothing less than a proclaimed dissolution of all law, civil, moral, and religious, human and divine.

A few remarks may be made with regard to the plan according to which the Confession is constructed. A Confession of Faith is simply a declaration of belief in religious truths, not scientifically discovered by man, but divinely revealed to man. While, therefore, there may fairly be a question whether a course of Systematic Theology should begin with disquisitions relative to the being and character of God, as revealed, or with an inquiry what Natural Theology can teach, proceeding thence to the doctrines of Revelation, there can be no question that a Confession of Faith in revealed religion ought to begin with that revelation itself. This is the plan adopted by the Westminster Confession. It begins with a chapter on the Holy Scriptures; then follow four chapters on the nature, decrees, and works of God in creation and providence: and these five chapters form a distinct division, systematically viewed, of the Confession. The next division relates to the Fall and consequent miserable condition of man, the Remedy divinely provided, its nature, mode of application, and results as effectually applied: and this division, beginning with the sixth chapter, ends with the eighteenth. The next two chapters, relating to subjects of such deep and comprehensive importance as the Law of God and the Liberty of Conscience, may well be regarded as themselves constituting a third division. The fourth, beginning with the chapter on Religious Worship, and proceeding with the various relations between the visible church and the world, contains eleven chapters, from the twenty-first to the thirty-first, inclusive of both. The two remaining chapters, looking forward to the future so far as that has been revealed, conclude the Confession. This plan, when rightly understood, appears, as we venture to think, as perfect as any uninspired production can' well be, and it is so because it closely follows the course and language of inspiration.

Some captious objections may be made to a few expressions which have either become obsolete, or have undergone a change of meaning by the modifications incident to every living language in the lapse of time, and by the progress of cultivation. But any slight obscurity thus occasioned may be easily removed, either by referring to the writings of that age, or by the insertion in modern editions of two or three glossarial notes. In one instance there may seem to be a collision between the statement of the Confession on the subject of Creation, and the discoveries and deductions of Geology; but as this is not greater than the apparent disagreement between the Bible and Geology, it will of course be removed whenever the Mosaic record and Geology have been reconciled; till then, those who subscribe the Confession of Faith are in no worse condition than those who believe the Bible, and may safely allow science to prosecute its investigations without anxiety and alarm, confident in this, that when these apparently conflicting inquiries have been fully elucidated, it will be found that the truth of God's works has but confirmed the truth of God's Word.

A plan similar to that already described was also employed in preparing those admirable digests of Christian doctrine, the Larger and Shorter Catechisms, and so far as can be ascertained, by the same committee. For a time, indeed, they attempted to prosecute the framing of both Confession and Catechisms at once; but after some progress had been made with both, the Assembly resolved to finish the Confession first, for reasons already stated. By this arrangement they wisely avoided the danger of subsequent debate and delay. Various obstacles, however, interposed, and so greatly impeded the progress of the Assembly, that the Catechisms were not so speedily completed as had been expected. They were at length presented to the House of Commons, the Shorter on the 5th of November 1647, and the Larger on the 14th of April 1648. Both were transmitted to Scotland, carefully examined by the General Assembly, and approved, —the Larger by an Act passed on the 2d July 1648, and the Shorter, on the 28th July 1648.

It is not necessary to state the systematic method of the Catechisms, as that has been done with regard to the Confession, which they closely followed, with one very important exception,—the Catechisms contain nothing relative to Church government, but are purely doctrinal. This might arise very naturally from the consideration, that as a catechism is intended chiefly for the use of children, it ought not to contain any thing unsuited to their period of life and stage of mental development. This very prudent omission has already been productive of the most beneficial results, from the ready access which it secured to all parties who agreed in doctrine, but contended fiercely on the subjects of form and government. Results, even more beneficial than ever, may be hoped for as likely to arise from the same happy omission. Scottish Presbyterianism, split asunder as it is into three great sections, yet all retaining their hereditary regard for the Shorter Catechism, so long used as the very basis of Scottish education, may yet combine in determining that it shall not cease to be universally employed in conveying religious instruction to the minds of their children, and their children's children through all succeeding generations. Such a result would itself secure that the labours of the Westminster Assembly had not been in vain.

There is one anecdote connected with the formation of the Shorter Catechism, both full of interest and so very beautiful that it must not be omitted. In one of the earliest meetings of the committee, the subject of deliberation was to frame an answer to the question, " What is God ? " Each man felt the unapproachable sublimity of the divine idea suggested by these words ; but who could venture to give it expression in human language ! All shrunk from the too sacred task in awe-struck, reverential fear. At length it was resolved, as an expression of the committee's deep humility, that the youngest member should make the attempt. He modestly declined, then reluctantly consented ; but begged that the brethren would first unite with him in prayer for divine enlightenment. Then in slow and solemn accents he thus began his prayer :—
" O God, thou art a spirit, infinite, eternal, and unchange-

able, in thy being, wisdom, power, holiness, justice, goodness, and truth." When he ceased, the first sentence of his prayer was immediately written by one of the brethren, read, and adopted, as the most perfect answer that could be conceived, —as, indeed, in a very sacred sense, God's own answer, given to prayer and in prayer, descriptive of himself. Who, then, was the youngest member of the committee? When we compare the birth-dates of the respective members of the committee, we find that George Gillespie was the youngest by more than a dozen years. We may, therefore, safely conclude that George Gillespie was the man who was thus spiritually guided to frame almost unconsciously this marvellous answer.

The only other productions of the Westminster Assembly were controversial rather than theological, although much directly religious truth is contained and earnestly enforced in those productions. They have been already mentioned, namely, "The Reasons of Dissent, together with the Answers of the Assembly;" which work is also known by the title of "The Grand Debate." Closely connected with this is another but much smaller work, entitled, "Answer to a Copy of a Remonstrance," &c. This production is now very rarely to be met with, and deserves to be republished, as a complete vindication of the Assembly against the insinuations of their opponents then and detractors since. I have already stated my strong conviction that the work entitled "Jus Divinum Regiminis Ecclesiastici; or, The Divine Right of Church Government," although bearing to be "By sundry Ministers of Christ within the City of London," if not directly the production of the Assembly, at least contains the answer prepared by them to the queries concerning the *jus divinum* proposed by the Parliament. A subsequent examination and comparison of this work with other kindred works by members of the Assembly, strongly confirms that opinion, which I would thus express:—The *Jus Divinum* of the city ministers

appears to me to be both virtually and substantially the
Assembly's Answer to the Parliament, containing actually
that very Answer as prepared by them ; but with such additional amplifications in statement and illustrations, by the
city ministers themselves, as might both render it more complete and fit for publication as a distinct work on the subject,
and at the same time entitle them to publish it on their own
responsibility.   This work well deserves to be republished,
with such explanatory notes as might adapt it to the present
age ; for the principles which it states and advocates have
not yet been received as they ought,—as they must and will,
before there can be a reign of righteousness and peace.

We have already made some remarks on the necessity for
the existence of Creeds and Confessions, and the important
purposes subserved by these subordinate standards ; and we
resume that view for the purpose of stating the inference to
which it ought to lead.   Since a Church cannot exist without some Confession, or mode of ascertaining that its members are agreed in their general conception of what they
understand divine truth to mean ; and since the successive
rise of heretical opinions, and their successive refutation,
necessarily tend to an enlargement of the Confession, and at
the same time to an increasing development of the knowledge
of divine truth, ought it not to follow that the various Confessions of separate Churches would have a constant tendency
to approximate, till they should all blend in one harmonious
Confession of one Church general ?   No one who has studied
a Harmony of Protestant Confessions can hesitate to admit
that this is a very possible, as it is a most desirable result.
When, further, we rise to that spiritual element to which also
our attention has been directed, we may anticipate an increasing degree of enlightenment in the Christian Church, bestowed by the Holy Spirit, in answer to the earnest prayers
of sincere and humble faith, which will greatly tend to hasten
forward and secure an amount of Christian unity in faith and

love far beyond what has existed since the times of the apostles. Entertaining this pleasing idea, we might expect both that the latest Confession of Faith framed by a Protestant Church would be the most perfect, and also that it might form a basis of evangelical union to the whole Church. To some this may seem a startling, or even an extravagant idea. But let it be remembered, that, owing to a peculiar series of unpropitious circumstances, the Westminster Assembly's Confession of Faith has never yet been adequately known to the Christian Churches. By the Scottish Church alone was it fully received; and in consequence of the various events which have since befallen that Church, comparatively little attention has been paid to the Confession of Faith till recent times. It is now, we trust, in the process of becoming more known and better understood than formerly; and we feel assured that the more it is known and the better it is understood, the more highly will its great and varied excellences be estimated. This will tend, at the same time, to direct to it the attention of other Churches; and we cannot help anticipating the degree of surprise which will be felt by many ingenuous minds, that they had remained so long unacquainted with a production of such remarkable value.

Such a result would be the realization of the great idea entertained by the leading members of the Westminster Assembly, and especially by the Scottish commissioners,—with whom, indeed, it originated. No narrow and limited object could satisfy the desires and anticipations of these enlightened and large-hearted men. With one comprehensive glance they surveyed the condition of Christendom and the world,—marked its necessities, and contemplated the remedy. Thus they formed the great, and even sublime idea of a Protestant union throughout Christendom; not merely for the purpose of counterbalancing Popery, but in order to purify, strengthen, and unite all true Christian Churches; so that, with combined energy and zeal, they might go forth, in glad compliance with the Redeemer's command, teaching all nations, and preaching the everlasting gospel to every creature under heaven. Such was the magnificent conception of men whom it has been too much the fashion to stigmatize as narrow-minded bigots. It is not in the heart of a bigot that a love able to embrace Christendom could be cherished,—it is not in the mind of a bigot that an idea of such moral sublimity could be conceived. It may be said, no doubt, that this idea was premature. Premature it was in one sense, for it could not be then realized; but the statement of it was not premature, for it was the statement of the grand result which ought to have been produced by the Reformation. In still another sense it was not premature, any more than it is premature to sow the seed in spring from which we expect to reap the autumnal harvest. The seed must be sown before the harvest can be produced,—the idea must be stated before it can be realized. It must then be left to work its way into the mind of man,—to grow, and strengthen, and enlarge, till in due time it shall produce its fruit in its season.

May it not be hoped that the fruit-bearing season is at hand? A time of refreshing and revival has come; the lethargic sleep of a century has passed away; the awakening throb of Christian life is high and warm; and again, snapping her benumbing bands asunder, the Church is going forth on her heavenly mission with renewed energy and power. All things seem hastening forward to some mighty change or development. On all sides the elements of evil are mustering with almost preternatural rapidity and strength. Popery has, to an unexpected degree, recovered from its deadly wound and its exhausted weakness, and is putting forth its destructive energies in every quarter of the world, especially in the high regions of political intrigue and diplomatic management. Numerous and startling are the coincidences which are appearing between the period of the Westminster Assembly and the present time. So strong are these, that they force upon a reflecting mind the thought that all human events move in revolving cycles, one age but producing a renewed aspect of the past. In England the dread aspect of Laudean Prelacy has re-appeared—called, indeed, by a new name, but displaying all the formidable characteristics of its predecessor—the same in its lofty pretensions, in its Popish tendencies, in its supercilious contempt of every other Church, and in its persecuting spirit. The civil government appears to be impelled by something like infatuation, and is introducing, or giving countenance to, measures that are darkly ominous to both civil and religious liberty, as if hastening onward to a crisis which all may shudder to contemplate. The masses of the community are in a state ripe for any convulsion, however terrible, having been left for generations uneducated and uninstructed in religious truth. The Scottish Ecclesiastical Establishment has been rent asunder; its constitution has been changed, or rather subverted; and those who firmly maintained the principles of the Westminster Assembly have been constrained to separate from the State, in order to preserve these principles unimpaired. The true Presbyterian Church of Scotland is again disestablished, as she has been in former times; but she is Free—free to maintain all those sacred principles bequeathed to her by reformers, and divines, and martyrs— free to offer to all other evangelical Churches the right hand of brotherly love and fellowship—free to engage with them in the formation of a great evangelical union, on the firm basis of sacred and eternal truth. Surely these concurring events are enough to constrain all who are able to comprehend them, to long for some sure rallying ground on which the defenders of religious truth and liberty may plant their standard. Such a rallying ground we think the Confession of Faith would afford, were its principles carefully considered and fully understood.

But revolving cycles, though similar, are not identical.

Each has in itself some characteristics of a peculiar nature, and to that extent part of its characteristics may terminate in its own period, and part may survive and expand into the new revolving movement. Thus, while the course of human events is one of revolving cycles, one tends to produce another, and that to expand and perfect what it received, and also to transmit its own new influences to its successor,—all combining to carry on the ripening and widening movements that make the world's history. The truth of this view may be seen by closely marking the characteristics of the conflict which shook the nations two hundred years ago, and that which has begun to shake them now. At the Reformation, the idea of separate and co-ordinate jurisdictions, civil and ecclesiastical, was introduced; but the supreme civil power wished to combine and possess both, and this gave rise to what has been called Erastianism. At first, however, the conflict was waged chiefly respecting uniformity in matters external, and submission to all civil decrees concerning rites, ceremonies, vestments, and common prayer. Subsequently, it related to a still more important point—discipline. On all these matters the unscriptural encroachments of the civil power were resisted,—not so much, in some instances, because of their importance, as because of the principle which they involved. But the recent, and still present and pending struggle, regards the actual assumption of supremacy by civil courts over spiritual courts as such; and is therefore of a much more formidable character than that in which our ancestors were engaged. The ancient contest was founded ostensibly on the desirableness of national uniformity in public worship; the modern is founded ostensibly on the fact of endowments, and on the civil rights which such endowments are said to involve or confer. The ancient contest was waged on the ground of the royal prerogative; the modern, on the ground of abstract law. In the ancient struggle the two kingdoms of England and Scotland strove to preserve both civil and religious liberty; and though or a time both seemed lost, yet the result was, the complete gaining and establishing of the former by the Revolution of 1688, and the full settlement of the British Constitution: in the modern struggle religious liberty has yet to be asserted, defended, and secured, and that, too, against a power in many respects more formidable than any that has hitherto been encountered by the Christian Church—the power of abstract law, in what is assumed to be a free country, and in which religious toleration is understood to be maintained. Hence it is, that whatever even seems to oppose the decisions of courts of law, must expect to be overwhelmed with reproach and contumely; as if human law were infallible, and whatever opposed it were necessarily wildly and intolerably wrong. The Erastianism of human law is Erastianism in its most pernicious and terrible aspect; and if triumphant, can end in nothing but the entire destruction of religious liberty, and consequently of true religion itself. Its direct aim is the abolition of spiritual courts; and so far as Establishments are concerned, it has succeeded; for that is no true spiritual court which either cannot meet without the permission of the civil authority, or where not merely its decisions can be reviewed and reversed by one of a different character, but where the judges themselves can be punished for their conscientious judgments. And since the Lord Jesus Christ instituted a government in his Church, the loss of spiritual courts is the loss of that government, and necessarily the loss of direct union with the Head and King of the Church,—which is, in other and plainer words, the loss of spiritual life and true religion.

The cycle in which we live displays much of the impress of its predecessor, and has also duties, advantages, and perils of its own. It may not be now either premature or too late to cherish the hope of at length accomplishing the Christian enterprise for which the Westminster Assembly met together; and of realising the great idea which filled the minds of its

most eminent Christian patriots.   The wide diffusion of
knowledge, the rapid communication of thought and action
from clime to clime, and the very progress of events in the
world's history, have rendered many a mighty undertaking of
easy achievement now, which, two centuries ago, was utterly
impossible.   And what was gained then furnishes now a van-
tage-ground on which the struggle may be more propitiously
waged.   Civil liberty and religious toleration are citadels not
certainly impregnable, but not easily to be reduced.   It is
equally the duty and the interest of all who value these to
unite in their defence ; for the loss of them to one class of
British citizens, or to one Church in Britain, would issue in
the loss of them to all.   Let but the attempt be made, in the
spirit of faith, and prayer, and sincerity, and love unfeigned,
and there may now be realised a religious union embracing
all true Christians.

The errors which prevented the success of the Westminster Assembly may be to us beacons, both warning from
danger and guiding on to safety.   In their case, political
influence and intrigue formed one baneful element of deadly
power.   Let all political influence be distrusted and avoided,
and let political intrigue be utterly unknown in all our
religious deliberations.   In times of trouble and alarm,
"Trust not in princes, nor in the sons of men," with its divine
counterpart, "Trust in the Lord, and stay yourselves upon
your God," should be the watchword and reply of all true
Christian Churches.   Dissensions among brethren, groundless
jealousies, and misconstructions, and want of openness and
candour, were grievously pernicious to the Westminster
Assembly.   If the Presbyterians and the Independents could
have banished the spirit of dissension, expelled all petty
jealousy, and laid their hearts open to each other in godly
simplicity and sincerity, all the uniformity that was really
necessary might have been easily obtained.   And if all
truly evangelical Christians, whether they be Presbyterians,

or Independents, or Baptists, or Methodists, or Episcopalians, such as some that could be named, would but give full scope to their already existing and strong principles and feelings of faith and hope and love, there could be little difficulty in framing such a Christian union,—term it Presbyterian or Evangelical, so that it be truly scriptural,—as might be able, by the blessing and the help of God, to stem and bear back the growing and portentous tide of Popery and infidelity, that threaten, with their proud waves, once more to overwhelm the world.

Has not the time for this great evangelical and scriptural union come? It is impossible for any one to look abroad upon the general aspect of the world with even a hasty glance, without perceiving indications of an almost universal preparation for some great event. The nations of the earth are again still—not in peace, but, like wearied combatants, resting on their arms a brief breathing space, that, with recovered strength and quickened animosity, they may spring anew to the mortal struggle. During this fallacious repose there has been, and there is, an exertion of the most intense and restless activity, by principles the most fiercely hostile, for the acquisition of partisans. Despotism and democracy, superstition and infidelity, have alike been mustering their powers and calling forth their energies, less, apparently, for mutual destruction, according to their wont and nature, than in order to form an unnatural coalition and conspiracy against the very existence of free, pure, and spiritual Christianity. Nor, in one point of view, has Christianity been recently lying supine and dormant. Many a noble enterprise for the extension of the gospel at home and abroad has been planned and executed; and the great doctrines of saving truth have been clearly explained and boldly proclaimed, with earnest warmth and uncompromising faithfulness. A time of refreshing also has come from the presence of the Lord,—a spirit of revival has been poured forth upon the thirsty Church, and the hearts of Christian brethren have learned to melt and blend with a generous and rejoicing sympathy, to which they had too long been strangers. Can all these things be beheld and passed lightly over, as leading to nothing, and portending nothing? That were little short of blind infatuation. What they do fully portend it were presumptuous to say; but it is not difficult to say for what they form an unprecedented preparation. What now prevents a world-wide evangelical and scriptural union? "All things are prepared; come to the marriage." "If ye love ME, love one another." "Because HE laid down his life for us, we also ought to lay down our lives for the brethren." Had these been fully the principles and rules of conduct of the Westminster Assembly, its great idea might have been realised. Let them be those that animate and guide all Christian Churches now. They have been felt in our great unions for prayer; they should be felt by all who venerate and can understand the standards of the Westminster Assembly. And if they be, then may we not only accomplish the object of its Solemn League and Covenant, concur in its Confession of Faith, and realise its great idea of a general evangelical union; but we may also, if such be the will of our Divine Head and King, be mightily instrumental in promoting the universal propagation of the gospel, and drawing down from above the fulfilled answer of that sacred prayer in which we all unite,—"THY KINGDOM COME: THY WILL BE DONE IN EARTH, AS IT IS IN HEAVEN."

APPENDIX.

I.

(See page 125.)

EVERY person must be aware, that one of the charges most frequently and vehemently urged against the Presbyterian Church of Scotland, is that of its being possessed by such a bigoted and proselytizing spirit as led it to attempt, by undue means, to force its own system upon England during the troubled period of the civil war. In the hope of showing the utter groundlessness of that accusation, and of repelling it at once and for ever, I have resolved to append to this work the following important document, which contains a distinct statement, by the Scottish commissioners, of the views and desires entertained by the Church and State of Scotland before the civil war had begun. The paper was written by Alexander Henderson, towards the close of the year 1640, and given in by the Scottish commissioners to the Lords of the Treaty, as they were termed, in the beginning of 1641, when the business of negotiation had been transferred from Ripon to London. It was printed and published about the same time, that it might be so fairly before the community as to enable all whom it concerned to know precisely what it was that Scotland wished and recommended, and to prevent, if possible, all calumnious misrepresentation. Certainly the publication of such a document tended, of itself, to bind the Scottish commissioners, and consequently the Scottish Church and kingdom, which they represented, from making any attempt to force their own system upon England, even if they had been afterwards inclined; since it put it in the power of the English Church and Parliament to appeal immediately to this public declaration. There is no doubt that it both prepared the mind of England for the calling of the Westminster Assembly, about two years and a-half afterwards, and contributed to prevent, for a time, the rise of any considerable degree of jealousy in the ecclesiastical proceedings that followed, till the harmony that had prevailed was destroyed by the Independent and Erastian controversies. Prelatic writers make no mention of this important document, and consequently indulge in the most violent accusations against the Church of Scotland for presuming to endeavour to enforce its system upon England. Let the truth be known; from that the Church of Scotland has nothing to fear :—

"Our Desires concerning Unity in Religion, and Uniformity of Church Government, as a special Mean to Conserve Peace in his Majesty's Dominions.

As we shall not make any proposition about this last article, of establishing a firm and happy peace, but that which we conceive to be both expedient and just; so will your lordships, we doubt not, in your wisdom consider, that since that which is sought is not a cessation of arms for a time, but peace for ever, and not peace only, but perfect amity and a more near union than before,—which is of greater consequence than all the former articles,—it is no marvel that a composition so excellent, and so powerful to preserve the whole island in health against all inward distempers, and in strength against all contagion and wounds from without, require many ingredients, of which, if any one be wanting, we may on both sides please ourselves for the present with the sweet name of peace, and yet for no long time enjoy peace itself, which hath not only sweetness and pleasure, but also much more profit and true honour than all the triumphs on earth.

As we account it no less than usurpation and presumption for one kingdom or Church, were it never so mighty and glorious, to give laws and rules of reformation to another free and independent Church and kingdom, were it never so mean,—civil liberty and conscience being so tender and delicate, that they cannot endure to be touched but by such as they are wedded unto, and have lawful authority over them; so have we not been so forgetful of ourselves, who are the lesser, and of England, which is the greater kingdom, as to suffer any such arrogant and presumptuous thoughts to enter into our minds,—our ways also are witnesses of the contrary against the malicious, who do not express what we are or have been, but do still devise what may be fuel for a common combustion. Yet charity is no presumption, and the common duty of charity bindeth all Christians at all times, both to pray and profess their desire that all others were not only almost but altogether such as themselves, except their afflictions and distresses; and, beside common charity, we are bound, as commissioners in a special duty, to propound the best and readiest means for settling of a firm peace. As we love not to be curious in another commonwealth, nor to play the bishop in another diocese, so may we not be careless and negligent in that which concerneth both nations.

We do all know and profess, that religion is not only the mean to serve God, and to save our own souls, but that it is also the base and foundation of kingdoms and estates, and the strongest band to tie subjects and their prince in true loyalty, and to knit their hearts one to another in true unity. Nothing so powerful to divide the hearts of people as division in religion; nothing so strong to unite them as unity in religion: and the greater zeal in different religions the greater division; but the more zeal in one religion the more firm union. In the paradise of nature the diversity of flowers and herbs is pleasant and useful; but in the paradise of the Church different and contrary religions are unpleasant and hurtful. It is therefore to be wished that there were one Confession of Faith, one form of Catechism, one Directory for all the parts of the public worship of God, and for prayer, preaching, administration of sacraments, &c., and one form of Church government, in all the Churches of his majesty's dominions.

This would,—

1. Be acceptable to God Almighty, who delighteth to see his people walking in truth and unity, and who would look upon this island with the greater complacency that we were all of one heart and one soul in matters of religion.

2. This unity in religion will preserve our peace, and prevent many divisions and troubles. Of old (as Beda recordeth) the difference about the time of observing of Easter, although no great matter in religion, and although in divers independent kingdoms,

had troubled their peace, if the wiser sort had not brought them to a uniformity; wherein they were so zealous that they would not suffer so much as one small island, which differed from the rest, to be unconform.

3. His majesty and his successors in their government shall be eased of much trouble which ariseth from differences of religion, and hath been very grievous unto kings and emperors, as Eusebius witnesseth in his 3d book, chap, 12, of the Life of Constantine. *Sedition begotten in the Church of God* (saith Constantine) *seemeth to me to contain in itself more trouble and bitterness than any war or battle.*

4. Since, by Divine Providence, his majesty is king of divers kingdoms, it shall be much content both to himself, to his nobles and court, and to all his people, when his majesty shall in person visit any of his kingdoms, that king, court, and people may, without all scruple of conscience, be partakers of one and the same form of divine worship, and his majesty with his court may come to the public assembly of the people, and serve God with them, according to the practice of the good kings of Judah; as, on the other part, difference in forms of divine worship divideth between the king and the people.

5. This shall be a great comfort to all his majesty's subjects, when they travel abroad from their own country to any other place in his majesty's dominions, whether for commerce or whatsoever negotiation and affairs, that they may with confidence resort to the public worship as if they were at home, and in their own parish church, and shall satisfy many doubts, and remove many exceptions, jealousy, and scandals, which arise upon resorting to different forms of worship.

6. The names of heresies and sects, of Puritans, Conformists, Separatists, which rend the bowels both of Church and kingdom, are a matter of much stumbling to the people, and diminish the glory of his majesty's reign, shall no more be heard; but as the Lord is one, his name shall be one, and the name of the people one, in all his majesty's dominions.

7. Papists and recusants shall despair of success to have their religion set up again, and shall either conform themselves or get them hence; and irreligious men shall have a great scandal removed out of their way, which shall be a mean of great safety and security, and of 'many blessings both to king and people. ' I am persuaded,' (saith Constantine, as Eusebius recordeth in his Life, lib. ii. c. 63,) ' were I able, as it is in my desires, to bind all the true worshippers of God by the common bond of concord, all the subjects of my empire would quickly turn themselves to their pious ordinances.'

8. This unity of religion shall make ministers to build the Church with both their hands, whilst now the one hand is holden out in opposition against the other party, and shall turn the many and unpleasant labours of writing and reading of unprofitable controversies into treatises of mortification, and studies of devotion and practical divinity.

This unity of religion is a thing so desirable, that all sound divines and politicians are for it, where it may be easily obtained and brought about. And as we conceive so pious and profitable a work to be worthy of the best consideration, so are we earnest in recommending it to your lordships, that it may be brought before his majesty and the Parliament, as that which doth highly concern his majesty's honour and the weal of all his dominions, and which, without forcing of consciences, seemeth not only to be possible, but an easy work. But because the matter is of great weight, and of a large extent, and therefore will require a large time, our desire is, that for the present some course may be taken for an uniformity in government.

1. Because there can be small hope of unity in religion, which is the chief bond of peace and human society, unless first there be one form of ecclesiastical government.

2. Because difference in this point hath been the main cause of all other differences between the two nations, since the reformation of religion.

3. Because (although it ought not to be so) we find it true in experience, that Churchmen, through their corruption, are more hot and greater zealots about government than about matters more substantial,—their worldly dignities and wealth being herein concerned; as Erasmus rendered this reason of the animosity of the Church of Rome against Luther, seeking after reformation, that he meddled with the Pope's crown and the monks' bellies.

4. It is observed by politicians, and we have found it in experience, that Churchmen do not only bear with different religions, and suffer divisions both in Church and policy to rise and grow;

but do also foment and cherish the contrary factions, that they themselves may grow big, and swell in greatness, while both sides have their dependence upon them, and have their thoughts busied about other matters than about Church government, and the ambition, pomp, and other corruptions, of Church governors.

5. None of all the Reformed Churches, although in nations far distant one from another, and under divers princes and magistrates, are at so great a difference in Church government as these two kingdoms be, which are in one island, and under one monarch,—which made King James, of happy memory, to labour to bring them under one form of government.

But since all the question is, Whether of the two Church governments shall have place in both nations? (for we know no third form of government of a National Church distinct from these two) we do not presume to propound the form of government of the Church of Scotland as a pattern for the Church of England, but do only represent, in all modesty, these few considerations, according to the trust committed unto us.

1. The government of the Church of Scotland is the same with the government of all the Reformed Churches, and hath been by them universally received and practised, with the reformation of doctrine and worship; from which so far as we depart, we disjoin ourselves as far from them, and do lose so much of our harmony with them. Whence it is that from other Reformed Churches it hath been written to the Church of Scotland, ' *That it was a great gift of God that they had brought together into Scotland the purity of religion, and discipline whereby the doctrine is safely kept; praying and beseeching them so to keep these two together, as being assured that if the one fall the other cannot long stand.*' Upon the other part, the government of the Church of England was not changed with the doctrine at the time of Reformation. The Pope was rejected, but his hierarchy was retained; which hath been a ground of jealousy and suspicion to the Reformed Churches, of continual contention in the Church of England these eighty years past (since the beginning of Queen Elizabeth, her reign), and of hopes and expectation to the Church of Rome; for, saith Contzen, in his Politicks, lib. ii. cap. 18, ' *Were all England once brought to approve of bishops, it were easy to reduce it to the Church of Rome.*' But what one prince hath begun, and by reason of the times, or of

other hinderances, could not promote or perfect, another, raised up by the mercy of God, may bring to pass; according to the example of good Josiah, like unto whom there was no king before him,— which we heartily wish may be verified of King Charles.

2. The Church of Scotland hath been continually, and many sundry ways, vexed and disquieted by the bishops of England.

(1.) By the continual and restless negotiation of the prime prelates in England with some of that faction in Scotland, both before the coming of King James into England, (which we are ready to make manifest,) and since his coming; till at last a kind of Episcopacy was erected there by the power of the prelates of England, against the Confession of Faith, the Covenant, and Acts of the National Assemblies, of the Church of Scotland.

(2.) The prelates of England, without the consent or knowledge of the Church of Scotland, gave episcopal consecration to some corrupt ministers of the Church of Scotland, and sent them home to consecrate others like unto themselves; and when some great men have been, for their obstinacy in Papistry, excommunicated by the Church of Scotland, they have been absolved from the sentence by the prelates of England: so that they have usurped the power of that which, in their own opinion, is the highest ordination, and of that which is indeed the highest point of jurisdiction.

(3.) They rested not here, but proceeded to change the form of divine worship; and for many years bred a great disturbance, both to pastors and people, by five articles of conformity with the Church of England.

(4.) Having in the former prevailed, and finding their opportunity, and rare concourse of many powerful hands and heads ready to co-operate, they made strong assaults upon the whole external worship and doctrine of our Church, by enforcing upon us a Popish Book of Common Prayer, for making Scotland first, as the weaker, and thereafter England, conform to Rome; and upon the consciences, liberties, and goods of the people, by a Book of Canons and Constitutions Ecclesiastical, establishing a tyrannical power in the persons of our prelates, and abolishing the whole discipline and government of our Church, without so much as consulting with any Presbytery, Synod, or Assembly, in all the land.

(5.) They procured subsidies to be lifted for war against us, under pain of deprivation to all of the clergy that should refuse.

(6.) They commanded both preaching and imprecations against us, as enemies to God and the king.

(7.) They have received into the ministry, and provided places for such of our ministers as, for their disobedience to the voice of the Assembly, and their other faults and scandals, were deposed in Scotland. And finally, they have left nothing undone which might tend to the overthrow of our Church, not only of late, by the occasion of these troubles whereof they have been the authors, but of old, from that opposition which is between Episcopal government and the government of the Reformed Churches by Assemblies. Upon the contrary, the Church of Scotland never had molested them, either in the doctrine, worship, ceremonies, or discipline of their Church, but have lived quietly by them, kept themselves within their line, and would have been glad to enjoy their own liberties in peace; which yet is, and by the help of God shall be, our constant desire. Yet can we not conceal our minds, but in our consciences, and before God, must declare,—not from any sauciness, or presumptuous intention to reform England, but from our just fears and apprehensions, that our reformation, which hath cost us so dear, and is all our wealth and glory, shall again be spoiled and defaced from England,—that whatsoever peace shall be agreed upon, we cannot see nor conceive the way how our peace shall be firm and durable, but our fear is, that all will run into a confusion again, ere it be long, if Episcopacy shall be retained in England; for the same causes will not fail to produce the same effects. Their opposition against, and hatred of, the government of the Reformed Churches,—their credit at Court, and nearness to the king, living in England,—the opinion they have of their own great learning, and of the glory of their prelatical Church, joined with the small esteem and disdain of our Christian simplicity,—the consanguinity of their hierarchy with the Church of Rome, and their fear to fall before us at last,—will still be working, especially now, when they are made operative, and shall be set on work at the first advantage, by their vindictive disposition to be avenged upon us for the present quarrel, which can never be changed by any limitations. As, on the contrary, the cause being taken away, the effects will cease, and the peace shall be firm. It would seem that limitations, cautions, and triennial Parliaments, may do much; but we know that fear of perjury, infamy, excommunication, and the power of a National Assembly,—which was in Scotland as terrible to a bishop as a Parliament,—could not keep our men from rising to be prelates; and after they had risen to their greatness, their apology was,— ' *These other cautions or conditions were rather accepted of for the time, to prevent all occasion of jangling with the contentious, than out of any purpose to observe them for ever.*' Much is spoken and written for the limitations of bishops; but what good can their limitation do to the Church, if ordination and ecclesiastical jurisdiction shall depend upon them, and shall not be absolutely into the hands of the Assemblies of the Church? and if it shall not depend upon them, what shall their office be above other pastors? or how shall their labours be worthy so large wages? What service can they do to King, Church, or State? Rome and Spain may be glad at the retaining of the name of Bishops, more than the Reformed Churches, which expect from us at this time some matter of rejoicing.

3. The Reformed Churches do hold without doubting, their Church-officers, Pastors, Doctors, Elders, and Deacons, and their Church government by Assemblies, to be *jure divino,* and perpetual, as is manifest in all their writings. And on the other hand, Episcopacy, as it differeth from the office of Pastor, is almost universally acknowledged, even by the bishops themselves, and their adherents, to be but a human ordinance, established by law and custom for conveniency, without warrant of Scripture; which, therefore, by human authority may be altered and abolished, upon so great a conveniency as is the hearty conjunction with all the Reformed Churches, and a durable peace of the two kingdoms, which have been formerly divided by this partition-wall. We therefore desire, that *jus divinum* and *humanum,* conscience and convenience, yea, the greater conveniency with the lesser, and, we may add, a conveniency and an inconveniency, may be compared, and equally weighed in the balance, without adding any weight of prejudice.

4. The Church of Scotland, warranted by authority, hath abjured Episcopal government, as having no warrant in Scripture, and by solemn oath and covenant divers times before, and now again of late, hath established the government of the Church by Assemblies; but England, neither having abjured the one nor sworn the other, hath liberty from all bands of this kind to make choice of that

which is most warrantable by the Word of God. And, lest it be thought that we have wilfully bound ourselves of late by oath that we be not pressed with a change, we desire it to be considered, that our late oath was nothing but the renovation of our former oath and Covenant, which did bind our Church before, but was transgressed of many by means of the prelates.

5. If it shall please the Lord to move the king's heart to choose this course, he shall, in a better way than was projected, accomplish the great and glorious design which King James had before his eyes all his time, of the unity of religion and Church government in all his dominions,—his crowns and kingdoms shall be free of all assaults and policies of Churchmen. Which, whether in the way of ecclesiastical jurisdiction and Church censure, or by complying with the Pope, the greatest enemy of monarchy, or by bringing civil governments into a confusion, or by taking the fat of the sacrifice to themselves, when the people are pleased with the government, and when they are displeased, by transferring the hatred upon authority,—which was never wont to be done by any good statesmen: all which, all these ways, have proceeded from bishops seeking their own greatness, never from Assemblies, which, unless overruled by bishops, have been a strong guard to monarchy and magistracy,—both the one and the other being the ordinances of God. The Church shall be peaceably governed, by common consent of Churchmen, in Assemblies,—in which the king's majesty hath always that eminency which is due unto the supreme magistrate, and by which all heresies, errors, and schisms, abounding under Episcopal government, shall be suppressed; and the State, and all civil matters, in Parliament, Council, and other inferior judicatures, governed by civil men, and not by Churchmen,—who, being out of their own element, must needs stir and make trouble to themselves and the whole State, as woful experience hath taught. The work shall be better done, and the means which did uphold their unprofitable pomp and greatness may supply the wants of many preaching ministers to be provided to places; and, without the smallest loss or damage to the subjects, may be a great increase of his majesty's revenues. His royal authority shall be more deeply rooted in the united hearts, and more strongly guarded by the joint forces, of his subjects, as if they were all of one kingdom; and his greatness shall be enlarged abroad, by becoming the head of all the

Protestants in Europe, to the greater horror of his enemies, and to the sowing of greatness to his posterity and royal succession. All which we entreat may be represented unto his majesty and the Houses of Parliament, as the expression of our desires and fears, and as a testimony of our faithfulness in acquitting ourselves in the trust committed unto us; but no ways forgetting our distance, or intending to pass our bounds, in prescribing or setting down rules to their wisdom and authority, which we do highly reverence and honour, and from which only, as the proper fountain, the laws and order of reformation in this Church and Policy must proceed, for the nearer union and greater happiness of his majesty's dominions."

Let the thoughtful reader ponder well the deep meaning of this remarkable document; and while he will perceive in it a complete vindication of the Church of Scotland, he will also be constrained, when he contemplates the present sufferings of that Church, to admire the almost prophetic foresight of that great man by whom it was written, who saw clearly that the Prelatic spirit would never cease to strive for the overthrow of the Presbyterian Church.

II.

(See pages 201, 202; 238–240.)

So much reference has been made by a certain class of writers to the name and reputation of the learned Selden, and the influence which he is said to have exercised in the Westminster Assembly, that I have thought it expedient to state his arguments more fully in the body of the Work than their own merit seems to me to deserve. I have given them also as reported by Lightfoot, who, being likewise an Erastian, cannot be suspected of doing them injustice. But as the same discussion is reported in Gillespie's own notes of the Assembly's proceedings, I am persuaded that the general reader will peruse the following extract with considerable curiosity and interest :—

"DEBATE RESPECTING MATTHEW XVIII.

"Mr Selden said, There is nothing in Matthew xviii. of excommunication or jurisdiction; which could not be exercised by the ancient Church, till the Church of Rome got their power from the emperor., That some late men—as Dominicus Solo,. and Sayrus, and Henriquez—say that there is some power given to the Church, which the Church afterwards did specificate to be a power of excommunication. He said, Matthew's Gospel was the first that was written, about eight years after Christ's ascension, the first year of Claudius: that it was written in Hebrew, and translated into Greek by John: that though the Hebrew that Matthew wrote be not extant, yet two editions of the Gospel (are) in Hebrew, one by Munster, another by Tilius: that we find in Tilius' edition *Kahal*, Matt. xviii., and *Guedah*, Matt. xviii., though in Munster's *Kahal* be in both places. Now, there being no place of the New Testament written when this was written, we must expound it by the custom of the Jews, which, according to the law (Lev. xix. 17), was, that when one offended his brother, the offended brother required satisfaction; and if he get it not, speak to him before two or three witnesses; and if he hear them not, to tell it to a greater number (for which he offered to show many Hebrew authors and Talmudists.) That they had in Jerusalem, beside the great sanhedrim, two courts of 23, and in every city one court of 23. That the casting out of the synagogue was only the putting of a man in that condition that he might not come within four cubits of another; that any man being twelve years of age might excommunicate another; not that he was altogether cast off from having any thing to do with the synagogue. He said the convocation was called Clerus Anglicanus, and the parliament Populus Anglicanus. So here *Guedah* and Ἐκκλησια signify only a select number; that the word is used in one place for woman; Deut. xxiii., 'shall not enter into the congregation.' That Christ, when he said 'Dic Ecclesiæ,' was in Capernaum, where there was a court of 23; that the meaning is, tell the sanhedrim, which can redress the wrong. That if the Jewish State had been Christian, their civil government might have continued, though the ceremonies were gone; so that *Ecclesia* here would have been a civil court."

Gillespie's answer, as given by himself, is as follows:—

"It is a spiritual, not a civil court, which is meant by 'the Church,' Matt. xviii. ; for, 1. *Subjecta materia* is spiritual. 'If thy brother trespass against thee,' is not meant of personal or civil injuries, but of any scandal given to our brother, whereby we trespass against him, inasmuch as we trespass against the law of charity. Augustine and Testatus expound it of any scandal, and the coherence confirmeth it ; for scandals were spoken of before in that chapter. 2. The end is spiritual—the gaining of the offender's soul, which is not the end of a civil court. 3. The persons are spiritual, for Christ speaks to his apostles. 4. The manner of proceeding is spiritual (verses 19, 20),—prayer, and doing all in the name of Christ ; which places, not only our divines, but Testatus and Hugo Cardinalis, expound of meetings for Church censures, not of meetings for worship. 5. The censure is spiritual —binding of the soul, or retaining of sins.—(Verse 18, compared with Matt. xvi. 19 ; John xx. 23.) 6. Christ would not have sent his disciples for private injuries to a civil court, especially those who were living among heathens.—(1 Cor. vi. 1.) 7. If we look even to the Jewish customs, they had spiritual censures. To be held 'as a heathen man and a publican,' imports a restraint *a sacris;* for heathens were not admitted into the temple.—(Ezek. xliv. 7–9 ; Acts xxi. 28.) So the profane were debarred from the temple. Josephus (Antiq., lib. xix. cap. 17) tells us that one Simon, a doctor of the law of Moses, in Jerusalem, did accuse King Agrippa as a wicked man, that should not be admitted into the temple. Philo (Lib. de Sacrificantibus) writeth, it was the custom in his own time that a manslayer was not admitted into the temple. The Scripture also giveth light in this ; for if they that were ceremonially unclean might not enter into the temple, how shall we think that they which were morally unclean might enter ?"

The close coincidence of the debate, as here given, with the account of it in Lightfoot's journal, will at once be perceived, confirming the authenticity of both; the chief difference between them being, that Gillespie's is the more clear and succinct of the two, as might have been expected from his intellectual pre-eminence.

While giving some fragmentary records of the opinions of the

2 B

leading men among the Westminster Divines on peculiar points, it may not be inexpedient to show what were the sentiments of Gillespie on the subject of the election of ministers, and how far these were entertained by the Church of Scotland at that period, and are identical with those held by the evangelical majority of the present time. The arguments of Henderson, Gillespie, and Rutherford, have been already stated, as used by them in the debate on the subject, an account of which will be found in page 175 of this work. On a subsequent occasion, when Gillespie, in his " Male Audis," was answering the Erastian arguments of Coleman and Hussey, the subject came again under discussion, and drew forth from Gillespie a re-statement of his opinion. Hussey had boldly affirmed, that the Parliament may require such as they receive for preachers of truth, " *to send out able men to supply the places, and that without any regard to the allowance or disallowance of the people.*" This truly tyrannical theory Gillespie strongly condemns; reminds his opponent that one, and not the least, of the controversies between the Papists and the Protestants is, what right the Church hath in the vocation of ministers; refers to the Helvetic Confession, which says, that the right choosing of ministers is by the consent of the Church; and to the Belgic Confession, which says, " We believe that the ministers, seniors, and deacons, ought to be called to these their functions, and by the lawful election of the Church to be advanced into these rooms;" adding, " I might here, if it were requisite, bring a heap of testimonies from the Protestant writers,—the least thing which they can admit of is, that a minister be not obtruded *renitente ecclesia.* It may be helped when it is done, without making null or void the ministry, but in a well constituted Church there ought to be no intrusion into the ministry."—(Male Audis, p. 27.)

In his " Miscellany Questions," the last work that came from his pen, published after his death, Gillespie discusses the question, " Of the Election of Pastors with the Congregation's Consent," in a chapter of 24 pages, stating the various opinions held by Prelatists, Sectarians, and others, explaining what he regarded to be the system of the Church of Scotland, and answering objections. He cites with approbation the opinions of the Reformers Luther, Calvin, Zanchius, Beza, and many others, all of whom maintained, *ut sine populi consensu et suffragio nemo legittime electus,*—" that without the consent and suffrage of the people no person was lawfully elected:" also the strong language of the First and Second Books of Discipline,— " This liberty with all care must be preserved to every several kirk to have their votes and suffrages in election of their ministers;" and, " It is to be eschewed that any person be intruded in any offices of the Kirk, contrary to the will of the congregation to which they are appointed; " adding several acts of Assembly to the same effect. In answering objections, his own opinion comes very clearly into view. As, for instance, " Objection—This liberty granted to congregations prejudgeth the right of patrons. Answer—If it were so, yet the argument is not pungent in divinity, for why should not human right give place to divine right ? The states of Zealand did abolish patronages, and give to each congregation the free election of their own minister; which I take to be one cause why religion flourisheth better there than in any other of the United Provinces." Again, it is objected, " That the Church's liberty of consenting or not consenting must ever be understood to be rational, so that the Church may not disassent without objecting somewhat against the doctrine or life of the person presented." (There is nothing new, it seems, even in the objections of Law Lords, and Moderates.) In answer to this, Gillespie first cites authorities to prove that this argument is the very one used by Popish and Prelatic writers, in defence of their systems, which allowed no shadow of liberty to the people ; and then exclaims, " Now, then, if this be all that people may object, it is no more than Prelates, yea, Papists, have yielded. This objection cannot strike against the election of a pastor by the judgment and vote of the particular eldership of that church where he is to serve. Men vote in elderships, as in all courts and consistories, freely according to the judgment of their conscience, and are not called to an account for a reason of their votes. As the vote of the eldership is a free vote, so is the congregation's consent a free consent. Any man, though not a member of the congregation, hath place to object against the admission of him that is presented, if he know such an impediment as may make him incapable, either at all of the ministry, or of the ministry of that church to which he is presented. So that unless the congregation have somewhat more than liberty of objecting, they shall have no privilege or liberty, but that which is common to strangers as well as to them. Though nothing be objected against the man's doctrine or life, yet if the people desire another better, or as well qualified, by whom they find themselves more edified than by the other, that is a reason sufficient, if a reason must be given at all."

But we cannot afford space for more quotations, nor can it be necessary to do so, as those already produced must convince every unprejudiced person, that the Church of Scotland held then, as in the days of Knox, and always, down to the present time, that congregations possess the inherent right of choosing their own pastors; and that when patronage interfered with this right, the very least privilege to which they were entitled was, the expression of their free consent, or equally free dissent, without being obliged to assign reasons for either, and that no man should be intruded contrary to that free expression of their mind and will. And these opinions of Gillespie, according to Baillie, were held by the majority of the Assembly of 1649, when preparing a new Directory for the election of ministers, after the abolition of patronage by the Parliament. Yet the Church of Scotland has been disestablished, on the strength of the utterly false assertion, that the principle that "No pastor be intruded into a parish contrary to the will of the congregation," was never heard of till the year 1834!

III.

(See page 254.)

"An Ordinance of theLords and Commons assembled in Parliament, about Suspension from the Lord's Supper." —20th October 1645.

It was my intention to have inserted the whole of this important ordinance in the Appendix, for the purpose of showing the exact point on which the Westminster Assembly and the Parliament disagreed, as well as the extent to which they were of one mind. But as that has been done with considerable distinctness in the body of the work, and as I am desirous to avoid all unnecessary expansion, it seems to me expedient for the present to suppress that rather prolix document, reserving to myself the power of inserting it in a future edition, should it be then thought desirable, or should I prosecute the intention of enlarging the work.

IV.

(*See page* 258.)

" AN ORDINANCE OF THE LORDS AND COMMONS ASSEMBLED IN PARLIAMENT, CONCERNING THE CHOICE OF ELDERS."—14th March 1646.

For the reasons above stated, and with still greater reluctance, I have resolved to abstain from inserting this ordinance also. And I may add, that had the plan of the present work, and the dimensions within which it was judged necessary to confine it permitted , there are a number of very important documents, little known or regarded, which might have been inserted in the Appendix, and would have formed a very valuable addition to the means by which the general reader may acquire some adequate knowledge of the true history and character of the Westminster Assembly of Divines.

V.

THE SCOTTISH COMMISSIONERS.

A BRIEF notice of the Scottish Commissioners to the Westminster Assembly may be interesting to those who have not ready access to the biographical memoirs of those eminent men.

1.—ALEXANDER HENDERSON.

THIS very distinguished man, the leader of the Second Reformation in Scotland, was born in the year 1583, in the parish of Creich, in Fifeshire. Of his direct parentage nothing is known, except that his father was a cadet of the family of Henderson of Fordel, an ancient and honourable family in the same county. He entered the University of St Andrews in the year 1599, and took the degree of Master of Arts in 1603; and a few years afterwards was appointed to a Professorship in the same University. He continued to retain his class of philosophy and rhetoric, which he taught with great applause, till about the year 1613, when he was presented to the parish of Leuchars, through the influence, it is said, of Archbishop Gladstanes. As he at that time favoured Prelacy, which King James was imposing upon the Church of Scotland, his settlement was strenuously opposed by the people. They fastened the church door on the day of his induction, and kept it so securely, that he and the ministers who accompanied him were obliged to make their entrance by a window. He does not appear to have paid any attention to the wishes or the welfare of the people, but merely to have viewed Leuchars as a position from which to commence a course of ambition and of clerical preferment.

But a change was at hand, which affected the whole of his future life and conduct. The venerable and heavenly-minded Robert Bruce had about that time been permitted to return from his banishment to the Highlands, and took advantage of his recovered liberty to preach in those parts of the country to which he obtained access. Mr Henderson, having learned that Bruce was to preach in the neighbourhood, felt a strong desire to hear a man so celebrated. He went secretly to the church—tradition names Dairsie as the place—and took a position in a dark corner, where he could remain concealed. Bruce entered the pulpit, and, after a solemn pause, gave out as his text the following words: "Verily, verily, I say unto you, He that entereth not by the door, but climbeth up some other way, the same is a THIEF AND A ROBBER." Every word, uttered with the grave emphasis of Bruce's deep voice, went to the heart of Henderson, as it described and condemned his mode of entrance into Leuchars. He returned with the arrow in his heart, and the result was his conversion. From that time forward he was a changed man. Hitherto he had been a favourer of the Prelatic system, but without having studied it, or tried it by Scripture. He now felt it his duty to study the difference between the Prelatic and Presbyterian systems; and arrived at the clear conviction that Episcopacy was equally unauthorised by the Word of God and inconsistent with the constitution of the Church of Scotland.

The progress of events soon constrained him to bear his testimony to the truth publicly. He opposed the Articles of Perth, at the Assembly held in that town in the year 1618. From that time forward, for a considerable number of years, Henderson remained in comparative obscurity, prosecuting his pastoral duties earnestly, maintaining correspondence with the most pious ministers throughout the country, and jealously watched by the Prelatic party. A remarkable revival of vital godliness was during that period spreading extensively throughout the kingdom, preparatory, no doubt, for the coming struggle; and in that revival Henderson was deeply interested. But the very stillness of that religious revival, appearing to the Prelatic party to be something like gloomy acquiescence in their innovations, led them to anticipate a complete triumph, and they roused themselves to make a final effort.

Then came the crisis. In the year 1636, a book of ecclesiastical canons was sent down from England; and in the course of the same year a book of ordination. In the following year a liturgy appeared, and was ordered to be read in all the churches. Henderson and other ministers presented a petition to the Privy Council, praying to be relieved from constrained compliance with these injunctions. This was the commencement of a regular and lawful mode of opposition; but the rash pride of the prelates compelled the resistance to assume a more stormy aspect. The attempt to enforce the reading of the liturgy in Edinburgh, on the 23d of July 1637, caused a tumult, in which a woman's hand dashed to the earth all the anticipations of that tyrannical party. That tumult was soon allayed, but not the deep and strong spirit of resistance which had taken possession of the energetic mind of Scotland. Grave, earnest, and thoughtful men, now resolved to combine for the restoration and defence of their religious and civil liberties, and of these Henderson became at once the acknowledged leader. The union thus begun was knit into sacred strength by the NATIONAL COVENANT, framed chiefly by Henderson and John-ston of Warriston, and subscribed by thousands in the Greyfriars' Church, on the 28th day of February 1638.

This solemn and sacred document was subscribed with great cordiality throughout the entire kingdom, and gave to the COVE-NANTED REFORMATION a name and a power which can never perish while spiritual freedom is dear to those whom the truth has made free indeed. The union of Scottish Presbyterians thus con-firmed was too strong to be put down by force, or set at defiance. The king consented that a General Assembly should be held, in which all religious matters might be considered. This Assembly, the first which had been held since that of Perth, in 1618, met at Glasgow on the 21st of November 1638, and Henderson was unanimously chosen to be the moderator. The position was one of great difficulty, and demanded a man not only of high principle and calm courage, but of the most consummate prudence. Henderson was equal to the position and its duties, as he fully proved by his firmness and decision when the royal commissioner at-tempted to dissolve the Assembly; his grave dignity, when he pronounced sentence on the bishops; and his prophet-like solemnity when he summed up the proceedings at the close, and sealed them with the awful reference to the curse of Hiel the Bethelite.   Henderson was at this time translated from Leuchars to Edinburgh, contrary to his declared love of retirement, on the condition that he should be allowed to retreat to some quiet rural parish when overtaken by the infirmities of age,—a quiet retreat which the public necessities of the period never permitted him to realise.

From that time forward he was constrained to take a prominent part in all public duties.   Papers on public affairs, which would now be called State Papers, were written by him, though issued in the name of the nobility; he was constrained to aid in conducting negotiations for peace with the king; he was made Rector of the University of Edinburgh ; and when the English Parliament began to entertain the idea of seeking a reformation of church government in their own country, and of seeking an alliance with Scotland and its Church, they anxiously sought the concurrence and aid of Alexander Henderson.   The correspondence with England was almost entirely conducted by him, till it issued in the English Parliament summoning the Westminster Assembly, and requiring ministers from Scotland to be present at and aid in its deliberations.

During the discussions of the Westminster Assembly, Henderson continued to retain his high influence with all parties, and to exercise it wisely, as the history of its proceedings amply proves.   When the king went to the Scottish army, and withdrew with it to Newcastle, Henderson was sent thither, as a last attempt to induce his majesty to consent to the terms proposed by the Parliament.   But as the Parliament had abolished Episcopacy, which Charles had determined to support, he drew Henderson into a discussion by exchange of letters on the Episcopalian controversy, and the binding force of the coronation oath.   This epistolary controversy extended to five letters on the part of the king, and three on that of Henderson.   At length Henderson, worn out in constitution with his numerous, weighty, and incessant labours, and sick at heart with the obstinate infatuation of the despotic and deceitful monarch, abandoned his hopeless enterprise to save a king, whom no reasoning could convince, and no treaties could bind, resolved to return to Scotland, that he might at last die in peace.   He arrived in Edinburgh on the 11th of August, and died on the 19th of the same month, in a state of calm serenity, holy hope, and deep gratitude to God for having called him to believe and preach the glorious gospel.

A brief outline of the mental character and abilities of Alexander Henderson has been already given in the preceding pages of this work, and need not be here repeated. Yet, if our space had permitted, we should have liked to have directed attention to those remarkable papers on public affairs which were written by him. They display statesmanship of the very highest order, surpassed in splendour of diction by those of Milton, but not surpassed even by Milton in comprehensiveness of thought, loftiness of principle, and dignity of expression, while they are perfectly free from the proud scorn and fierce denunciations in which the stern republican indulged. They are every way worthy of a truly Christian statesman,—a character which the world has rarely seen, and for want of which the suffering nations are convulsed and miserable.

Episcopalian writers have assigned the victory to the king, in the controversial correspondence between him and Henderson. For such a preference nothing but the most blinding prejudice can account, as it would be very easy to prove, had we space to give even a brief analysis of the respective arguments. We may add, that not only in learning and reasoning are Henderson's papers immeasurably superior to those of the king, but even in calm and graceful dignity of style, in which a sovereign might have been expected to excel, from the habitual influence of his high station. But Henderson was by nature a king of men, and his whole bearing and language were always kingly. He was one of those great men whom God gives to elevate a nation, and work a mighty work; and whose departure leaves that age dark, feeble, and deploring.

2.—SAMUEL RUTHERFORD.

THERE is some difficulty in ascertaining either the birth-place of Samuel Rutherford or the year in which he was born; but the most probable account is, that he was born about the year 1600, and that Nisbet, a village close to the river Teviot, in the parish of Crailing, Roxburghshire, was his birth-place. He appears to have received his early education at Jedburgh. In the year 1617, he became a student in the University of Edinburgh, where he took his degree of Master of Arts in 1621. In 1623 he was elected one of the Regents of the College; which office he relinquished in 1625, and devoted himself to the study of divinity. In the year 1627 he was settled pastor at Anwoth, in the stewartry of Kirkcudbright, without having been constrained to come under any engagement to the bishop.

Rutherford continued to discharge the duties of the ministry in this small and remote parish, with great zeal, unwearied diligence, and remarkable success, during a period of nine years. But that period was not without its troubles. First, he lost his two children, and then his wife died, after a severe illness of above a year, by which his gentle and affectionate heart was very deeply afflicted. He was himself laid aside from his public labours for thirteen weeks by a fever, which reduced him to extreme debility for a time. After his recovery, he continued to prosecute his labours with increased earnestness and activity, and became very dear, not only to all the people of his own charge, but to the entire district around. Many anecdotes are preserved by tradition of the influence which he acquired, and the way in which he used it for the reformation of evil customs, and the promotion of vital godliness. There is a traditionary account, also, of a private visit paid to him by Archbishop Ussher, at first as an unknown stranger, till a discovery took place; and the archbishop at Rutherford's request, preached in the pulpit of the Presbyterian minister, and stayed another day to enjoy his heavenly conversation.

But the quiet and holy life which Rutherford had hitherto led was not permitted to continue. The death of Bishop Lamb having made the see of Galloway vacant, Sydserff, bishop of Brechin, was translated to Galloway, and immediately began a course of oppressive domination over his new diocese. Rutherford had published an elaborate work against Arminianism, written in Latin; and Sydserff, who held Arminian tenets, directed his persecuting power against the author. Rutherford was summoned to appear before the bishop's High Commission Court, and deprived of his office, in 1636. The Court of High Commission in Edinburgh ratified the sentence of deposition, and banished him to Aberdeen, in which Prelacy reigned supreme. The Aberdeen doctors at first engaged him in controversial disputations; but three of these discussions

were enough for them, and they prudently ceased from a controversy in which they were overmatched. In a short time, the influence of Rutherford began to be felt in Aberdeen, among the
people; and the baffled doctors petitioned the court that he
might be sent farther north, or banished from the kingdom. The
king had actually granted a warrant to that effect, when the power
of Prelacy was overthrown by the commotion of 1637; in consequence of which, Rutherford ventured to return to Anwoth,
which he reached in February 1638. He was sent by his presbytery to attend the Assembly of Glasgow, and by that Assembly
was appointed to be one of the professors of divinity at the University of St Andrews, to his own grief and that of his beloved and
attached flock at Anwoth.

In the year 1643, he was sent to London, as one of the commissioners from the Church of Scotland, to the Westminster Assembly. While he attended that Assembly, he greatly distinguished
himself by his skill in debate, his eloquence in preaching, and his
great learning and ability as an author. Few works of that age
surpass, or even equal, those which were produced by Rutherford,
during that intensely laborious period of his life. The first of
these was entitled "The Due Right of Presbytery." Next appeared "Lex Rex," a profound work on constitutional law,
which has not yet found its superior. Soon afterwards he published a work on "The Divine Right of Church Government," in
opposition to the Erastians. Three very excellent works on practical theology were produced in the same toilful and prolific period,
"The Trial and Triumph of Faith," "Christ's Dying and Drawing Sinners," and "Survey of the Spiritual Antichrist." In 1649
he published a "Free Disputation against Pretended Liberty of Conscience," chiefly directed against the claims of the English Sectarians for an unlimited licence to utter every opinion, and engage in
every practice which any man might choose, without regard to
the peace or welfare of the community,—a degree of licentiousness
which Cromwell was at last constrained to put down by the strong
hand of armed power, when it threatened danger to even his iron
sway.

Not long after his return from London, he was elevated to the
Principalship of the New College in St Andrews; and while discharging his professorial duties with all his former zeal, resumed

also his practice of preaching, in which he so much delighted, as often as opportunity and time permitted. When the contests between the Resolutioners and the Protesters arose, Rutherford joined the Protesters, and advocated their views with great and even impassioned eagerness. This led to alienation between him and friends with whom he had been formerly accustomed to hold intimate and cordial intercourse, and greatly distressed all the remainder of his life, while it exposed him to the fierce hostility of those traitors and tyrants who were plotting for the restoration of Prelacy. Sharp, in particular, treated him with the utmost contumely, procuring an order from the Committee of Estates to burn his " Lex Rex" at the market cross in Edinburgh, and presiding at the repetition of the same mean act beneath Rutherford's own windows in St Andrews. Rutherford was at the time sinking under toil, grief, and bodily sickness, yet his persecutors procured a sentence against him, depriving him of his situation in the college, confiscating his salary, confining him to his own house, and citing him to appear before the ensuing Parliament, on a charge of high treason. On hearing of this summons, he calmly remarked, that he had got another summons before a superior Judge and judicatory, and sent back the following message : " I behove to answer my first summons ; and ere your day arrive, I shall be where few kings and great folks come."

He then prepared a dying testimony in behalf of the covenanted Reformation ; and having thus finished his work on earth, looked rapturously forward to the hour of his release. During his few remaining days he enjoyed remarkable happiness and elevation of spirit in the near prospect of death, or rather of departure to be with Christ. His language to those friends who came to see him, was full of holy joy. His last words were, " Glory, glory dwelleth in Emmanuel's land ; " and having uttered these words, he expired, on the morning of the 20th of March 1661, in the sixty-first year of his age. The threatening sound of the coming storm, so soon to burst in a tempest of persecuting fury on Scotland, had been but faintly heard by him, when the hand of his Saviour snatched him from its violence, and took him to his home in heaven.

3.—ROBERT BAILLIE.

ROBERT BAILLIE was born in Glasgow on the 30th of April 1602. His father, a merchant in that city, was a younger son of Robert Baillie of Jerviston, near Hamilton, and thus connected with several families of distinction in the west of Scotland. He was educated at the public school, at that time taught by Robert Blair, who afterwards became eminent as a divine. He entered the University of Glasgow in 1617, and took his degree of Master of Arts in 1620, with considerable distinction. Being fond of learning, and desirous to acquire as much of it as possible before entering on the duties of the ministry, to which he had devoted himself, Baillie continued to attend the college, under Boyd of Trochrig, and Cameron, who had previously been professor of divinity at Saumur. Cameron was accustomed to inculcate the slavish tenet, " That all resistance to the supreme magistrate in any case was unlawful;" and the effect of this was never entirely banished from the mind of Baillie. He became one of the regents in the college in the year 1625, about which time he received orders from Law, archbishop of Glasgow. In the year 1631 he was appointed minister of Kilwinning, through the influence of the Eglinton family, and was soon afterwards married. Up till this period, and for some years longer, Baillie had been disposed to conform to many of the Prelatic ceremonies recently introduced; but was strongly opposed to all Arminian and Popish doctrines.

But the despotic proceedings of the king and the Prelatic party, in their attempt to impose their canons and liturgy on the Church and people of Scotland, roused the somewhat compromising and timid spirit of Baillie, and impelled him to study, more carefully than he had previously done, the real nature and tendency of such arbitrary men and measures. With some hesitation he joined those who petitioned against the violent imposition of these books; and at length joined in the subscription of the National Covenant. From that time forward his conduct became more decided than before, though he continued to cherish some scruples in regard to the total abolition of diocesan Episcopacy, as he showed by his modified vote in the Glasgow Assembly, when that point was decided. When the king attempted to subdue the Covenanters by force, and they raised an army in defence of their civil and religious liberties, Baillie accompanied a regiment of men raised in Ayrshire, as their chaplain, when the free Scottish nation met the king in arms at Dunse Law.

Baillie's strong literary tendency led him to employ his ready and prolific pen in writing against the innovations of the Prelatic faction ; and the extensive and exact learning displayed in his writings induced the men of greater action to employ him in literary labours. He was in consequence summoned to Newcastle in 1640, and sent to London soon afterwards as one of the commissioners for conducting the treaty with the king. After his return to Scotland he was, contrary to his inclination, appointed one of the professors of divinity in the University of Glasgow. To this office he was admitted in July 1642.

This important position, however, he was not long allowed to occupy undisturbed. He was appointed by the Assembly of 1643 as one of the Scottish commissioners to attend the Westminster Assembly of Divines, and arrived at London on the 18th of November the same year. He continued at the post of duty and labour till December 1646, with the exception of one short journey to Scotland, to report to the Scottish Assembly what progress had been made by the Westminster divines. During the period of his residence in London, the restless pen of Baillie was incessantly engaged, both in the production of elaborate controversial treatises and in the writing of those numerous "Letters and Journals" which give such full, minute, and graphic accounts of the Westminster Assembly.

On resuming his duties in the university, Baillie employed all his influence for the important object of carrying into effect various overtures passed by previous Assemblies " for the advancement of learning and good order in grammar schools and colleges." But this most laudable attempt was frustrated by the recurrence of fresh troubles in the Church and kingdom. When the king fell into the hands of the English army and Parliament, a secret treaty, termed " the Engagement," was framed between the Royalists of the two kingdoms, for the purpose of attempting to rescue the infatuated monarch from the danger into which his open despotism and known disregard for the faith of treaties had led him. This unhappy attempt introduced the most deplorable disunion into

Scotland, both in Church and State. In a short time the Church was split into two parties, known by the names of Resolutioners and Protesters; of which it may be fairly said, that the Resolutioners were too ready to adopt the base course of compromise and expediency in which mere politicians delight, while the Protesters not only maintained a stern and uncomplying attitude, but allowed themselves to use the language of keen asperity, and showed somewhat of a vindictive spirit. Alexander Henderson was dead before these disastrous contentions began. Gillespie, too, was no more; and the men of less commanding talents and inferior judgment were unable to sway the public mind, as had been done during the great period of the Covenant. Baillie joined the Resolutioners, as was to be expected from his early training and his constitutional timidity. He continued to hold his position and discharge his duties as professor,—often with great grief and vexation, in consequence of the increasing confusion in Church and State. Soon after the restoration of Charles II. Baillie was elevated to the Principalship of the University; but did not long enjoy his well-earned honours, and not for one moment in peace. His remaining days were imbittered by the perfidious and treacherous conduct of nearly all those whom he had most trusted,—of the king, of Lauderdale, and chiefly of Mr James Sharp, better known as Archbishop Sharp,—a man whose memory is more deeply stained with the base and cruel crimes of treachery and persecution than almost any other that ever disgraced the country which gave him birth.

But the time of Robert Baillie's relief from all earthly troubles was at hand. He lived to see the re-imposition of Episcopacy in Scotland, and the entry of Archbishop Fairfoull into Glasgow in April 1662, and died, weary and heart-broken, toward the end of August in the same year, in the sixty-first year of his age, in time to be spared from witnessing the storm of bloody persecution then breaking out, by which Scotland was devasted for twenty-eight dark and terrible years of crime and suffering.

4.—GEORGE GILLESPIE.

FEW men have gained so much renown within so short a period as George Gillespie,—few have been more beloved when living, more bewailed when dead. He was the son of the Rev. John Gillespie, minister at Kirkcaldy, and was born on the 21st of January 1613. In the year 1629 he commenced his academic studies at the University of St Andrews, where he is said to have early distinguished himself. But when he had completed his course and was ready to enter the ministry, he was constrained to pause for a period. Being convinced that Prelatic church government is of human invention, he would not submit to receive ordination from a bishop, and could not, at that juncture, obtain admission to the ministry without it. But Lord Kenmure took him into his household as domestic chaplain, where he resided till the death of that pious nobleman in 1634. Soon afterwards he occupied a similar position in the family of the Earl of Cassilis, and at the same time acted as tutor to Lord Kennedy, the Earl's eldest son. He had thus both leisure and inducement to prosecute his studies; which subsequent events prove him to have done with equal assiduity and success.

When, in 1637, the king and the Prelatic party had formed the desperate resolution of forcibly imposing the Book of Canons and the Liturgy upon the Church and people of Scotland, George Gillespie, in the early part of the summer of that year, published his work entitled, "A Dispute against the English Popish Ceremonies." Nothing could have been more suited to the emergency. It encountered systematically, and point by point, all the arguments of the Prelatic party, with such an extensive array of learning, and such acuteness and power of reasoning, as to excite universal astonishment. At that time Gillespie was only in his twenty-fifth year, and both friends and foes marvelled at the appearance of a work so elaborate from the pen of such a youth. The only answer attempted by the Prelatic party was their procuring an order from the Privy Council that the book should be called in and burned. It is not, however, by such a process that a true and able book can be destroyed. Gillespie's work still exists, and may yet be of service.

The power of the bishops departed; and, as George Gillespie had become known and admired, he was not allowed to remain much longer in a private position. Having received a call from the church and parish of Wemyss, he was ordained to the pastoral charge thereof by the Presbytery of Kirkcaldy, on the 26th of April 1638; and was the first who was admitted by a presbytery, at that period, without the authority of the bishops. From that time forward Gillespie, notwithstanding his youth, occupied a prominent position. He was a member of the famous Glasgow Assembly of 1638; and he was also sent as one of the commissioners to London in 1640. He was translated to Edinburgh in 1642, and continued to be one of the ministers of that city during the remainder of his life.

George Gillespie was one of the commissioners sent by the Scottish General Assembly to take part in the deliberations of the Westminster Assembly. He arrived at London, along with Alexander Henderson, on the 15th of September 1643, and almost immediately became one of the most prominent members of that august assembly, although the youngest man and minister of the whole, being only in the thirtieth year of his age and the fifth of his ministry. "That is an excellent youth," says Baillie; "my heart blesses God in his behalf. There is no man whose parts in a public dispute I do so admire. He has studied so accurately all the points that are yet come to our Assembly; he has got so ready, so assured, so solid a way of public debating; that however there be in the Assembly divers very excellent men, yet, in my poor judgmen, there is not one who speaks more rationally, and to the point, than that brave youth has done ever." Great, unquestionably, must have been the learning and the ability of the man who met and defeated, each on his own peculiar ground, such antagonists as Goodwin and Nye, on the Independent controversy; and Coleman, Lightfoot, and "the learned Selden," on the side of Erastianism; as the accounts of contemporaries prove Gillespie to have done.

In addition to his constant attendance in the Assembly, and his arduous exertions in the course of its debates, Gillespie employed his acute and powerful mind in written controversy with the ablest advocates of Erastianism. In two or three vigorous pamphlets he completely silenced Coleman, whose reputation for Hebrew learning had procured him the name of Rabbi Coleman. But he had also planned, and was all the while prosecuting, a much larger work. That work appeared about the close of the year 1646, under the title of "Aaron's Rod Blossoming; or, the Divine Ordinance of Church Government Vindicated." This remarkably able and elaborate work was conclusive on the subject of the Erastian controversy. Not one of the learned and able Erastians of that age even made the attempt to answer it, although they did not relinquish their sullen grasp of unscriptural power. It has not been answered yet; and although it may not be suited to the forms of modern thought and expression, yet if its reasonings were recast in a modern mould it would still be found triumphantly conclusive.

Nor was it in the field of controversy alone that Gillespie employed his pre-eminent mental qualifications. He took an equally active and influential part in the framing of the Confession of Faith and the Catechisms, which embodied the doctrinal decisions of the Assembly; and some memorable anecdotes have been preserved relating to his special eminence in connection with these more strictly theological productions.

When the public labours of the Westminster Assembly drew near a close, the Scottish commissioners returned to their native country. Gillespie, along with Baillie, appeared at the General Assembly which met in August 1647, and laid before it the result of their protracted labours. The Confession of Faith was ratified by that Assembly, and so became the doctrinal standard of the Church of Scotland, subordinate only to the Bible, on which all of its doctrines were avowedly founded. The same Assembly caused to be printed a series of propositions, or " Theses against Erastianism," as Baillie terms them, amounting to one hundred and eleven, drawn up by Gillespie. The perusal of these propositions would enable any person of unprejudiced and intelligent mind to master and refute the whole Erastian theory, and could not fail, at the same time, to call forth sentiments of admiration towards the clear and strong mind by which they were framed.

George Gillespie was appointed moderator of the General Assembly of 1648, although worn out with the great and incessant toils in which he had been engaged, and suffering under a severe illness which already displayed the symptoms of consumption. His influence was sufficient to preserve the Assembly from consenting to give any countenance to the weak and wicked intrigues already begun by worldly politicians; but the renewed anxiety and labour incurred by these exertions completely exhausted his remaining strength. He left Edinburgh, and retired to Kirkcaldy, his birth-place, in the faint hope of obtaining, by change of scene and air, some renovation to his health. But continuing to sink, and being no longer able to attend Church courts, he addressed a letter to the Commission of Assembly in September, stating his opinions concerning the duties and the dangers of the time. Feeling death at hand, he partly wrote and partly dictated what may be termed his dying " Testimony against association with malignant enemies of the truth and godliness." At length, on the 17th of December 1648, his toils and sorrows ceased, and he fell asleep in Jesus. So passed away from this world one of those bright and powerful spirits which are sent in troublous times to carry forward God's work among mankind, and recalled to heaven when that work is done.

5.—WARRISTON.

ARCHIBALD JOHNSTON of Warriston, was one of the elders appointed by the General Assembly to act as commissioners to the Westminster Assembly. Previous to this he had distinguished himself in the struggle between the Church of Scotland and its Prelatic oppressors. He was rapidly becoming eminent as an advocate at the Scottish bar, when the outraged Church roused itself to resist the imposition of the Canons and Liturgy. Immediately he joined the assertors of religious liberty, and took an active part in all their public procedure ; in which his great legal knowledge, acuteness of intellect, soundness of judgment, and promptitude in action, proved signally beneficial to the cause of truth and righteousness. When the General Assembly met at Glasgow in 1638, Mr Johnston was unanimously chosen to be clerk of the Assembly ; for which office he was peculiarly qualified, being as well acquainted with ecclesiastical as with civil law. A very remarkable congeniality of mental endowments and moral qualities, soon rendered Johnston and Henderson almost inseparable companions and fellow-counsellors. The great National Covenant was framed by their conjoint powers of knowledge and thought ; they were the leading men of the commissioners appointed to treat for peace with the king ; by them the Solemn League and Covenant between England and Scotland was written ; and their labours were again conjoined when they were sent together to the Westminster Assembly.

Two years before that period, the king having come to Scotland with a view of conciliating or deceiving the Covenanters, showed great favour to Mr Johnston, raised him to the order of knighthood, and made him one of the judges in the Court of Session, by the title of Lord Warriston. But these preferments and honours did not induce him to swerve a hair's breadth from his fidelity to the Covenanted Church of Scotland, which was dearer to him than rank and wealth, and the smiles of a monarch.

In the Westminster Assembly Warriston attended very constantly, and frequently engaged in the discussions and debates of that grave and learned body, fully maintaining his high reputation. Even the English Parliament requested him to sit among them and aid in their deliberations, although he was not, and could not become, a member of that high court.

After the decapitation of Charles I. by the English Parliament, against the strong and earnest protestations of both State and Church in Scotland, the outraged and indignant feeling of the community enabled the Scottish Royalists to gain the ascendency in public affairs, and they determined to place his son on the throne of Scotland, and framed an engagement with the English Royalists to aid them in the attempt to recover that of England also. Warriston did his utmost to prevent the nation from entering upon a course which could only lead to ruin; and when he could not prevail, he joined the Protesters, and aided their counsels. Cromwell easily triumphed over the divided power of Scotland; but Warriston, though he strove to avert a war with England, refused to hold office under the Protector, whom he regarded as a usurper of regal power. Some years afterwards he was induced to accept the office of clerk-register under the administration of Cromwell.

On the restoration of Charles II. the Marquis of Argyle was thrown into prison, and orders were issued for the seizure of others, including Warriston, but he escaped and fled to the continent. While there, he was attacked by a severe illness, and reduced almost to death by that and the unskilfulness—some say the treachery— of a physician. From the prostration of all bodily and even mental power, caused by this illness and treatment, he never wholly recovered. The cold, revengeful eye of Charles was still upon him; and in 1663 he was seized in France, brought to Scotland, tried, condemned, and executed, when so enfeebled by age and disease that he could scarcely either stand or speak. Yet with the calm tranquillity and spiritual elevation of a martyr, he gave the relics of his wasted life to the cause in which he had strenuously expended his strength.

6.—LAUDERDALE.

JOHN MAITLAND, afterwards Earl and Duke of Lauderdale, was descended from the Maitlands of Lethington, a family which was first raised to distinction by the great abilities of that very acute and unscrupulous statesman, the secretary of Queen Mary, and political antagonist of John Knox. Lethington, the family seat, was the birth-place of John Maitland, in the year 1616. In his youth he manifested considerable ability, and became distinguished for his classical acquirements. His first public appearance was at the period of the conflict between the Prelatic party and the Covenanters, when he keenly espoused the cause of Covenanted Reformation. He was at that time known as Lord Maitland, his father, the Earl of Lauderdale, being still alive. His rank and talents caused him to be regarded as a valuable acquisition, and his apparent zeal made him to be trusted and employed by the Scottish Church and Parliament. After having been engaged in various important negotiations, in some of which his violent temper and language injured the cause which he advocated so harshly, he was nominated one of the commissioners to the Westminster Assembly; but his attendance was neither very regular nor of much importance, and before its deliberations closed, the death of his father caused his return to Scotland.

Not long after this period the Earl of Lauderdale became a decided Royalist, was one of the framers of the Engagement, or secret treaty with the king, and after the decapitation of that unhappy monarch, attached himself to the fortunes of his son. He was taken prisoner at the battle of Worcester, and remained in confinement till the overthrow of the Commonwealth by Monk. He then hastened to the Hague, where the young king was residing, and was received with open arms, and trusted with almost unlimited power in regard to Scottish affairs. His influence was exerted for a time through the medium of the Earl of Middleton and the Privy Council at Edinburgh; and its first manifestation was the overthrow of the Presbyterian Church, the establishment of Prelacy, and the commencement of remorseless persecution. But Middleton, proving unmanageable, was set aside in 1662; Rothes, who succeeded him, was also set aside in 1667; and from that time Lauderdale resided in Scotland, and conducted the persecution himself with grim and horrible delight.

Nothing more savagely ferocious,—more base, brutal, and bloody, —than the conduct of Lauderdale was ever recorded, to stain the annals of history and disgrace human nature. On this point we have neither space nor inclination to dwell, but must leave him to the unutterable infamy which will for ever blacken his name and memory. But a time of retribution came at last. In 1672 the king degraded the title of a duke by bestowing it on Lauderdale, and the English peerage by elevating him into its rank. But his treachery had made him universally distrusted, and his arrogance had become intolerable. In the beginning of 1682 he was deprived of all his offices and pensions, and cast aside as a worn-out political tool. He did not long survive his disgrace, but died in the summer of the same year, leaving behind him no son to inherit either his titles or his shame; and without one friend to lament his fall.

VI.

PHILIP NYE AND RELIGIOUS LIBERTY.

REFERENCE has been so frequently made to the conduct of Philip Nye, in the Westminster Assembly, and his suspected intercourse with Cromwell, that it seems necessary to investigate these topics somewhat more fully than could be done in the limits of a footnote. Mr Nye was one of those Puritan divines who fled to Holland to escape from the severe and tyrannical proceedings of Laud. During his residence in Holland, at Arnheim, he adopted the views of the Independents. About the beginning of the Long Parliament he returned to England, and obtained a charge at Kimbolton, in Huntingdonshire, through the influence of Lord Kimbolton, also called Lord Mandeville, and afterwards Earl of Manchester. That nobleman was an intimate friend of Oliver Cromwell, and by his means Nye and Cromwell became also friends.

When the Parliament summoned the Assembly of Divines to meet at Westminster, Philip Nye was one of those so summoned; and the rectory of Acton near London was conferred upon him, as conveniently securing his constant attendance. No man was more urgent in recommending the signing of the Solemn League and Covenant than Nye; and for a time it seemed as though he would have been one of the most earnest in procuring the desired uniformity in religion between the two kingdoms. But there is reason to believe that Nye and Cromwell had, at a very early period, resolved that the Independent, or Congregational system, should be the only one to which they would consent. This became apparent early in 1644, by the publication of the " Apologetical Narrative," written by Nye.

The state of public affairs must be carefully marked, in order to perceive the bearing of events upon each other. For some time after the commencement of the war the king appeared likely to be successful. Neither Essex nor Waller displayed any military skill. There appeared more energy in the Earl of Manchester; but that energy may be fairly attributed to Cromwell, who was now his lieutenant-general, and had already begun to raise and train that body of troops who were afterwards known as Cromwell's " Ironsides," and who were never beaten. The Parliament had urged the approach of the Scottish army. They had rapidly advanced towards York, and being joined by Fairfax, Manchester, and Cromwell, laid siege to that city. Prince Rupert hastened to its relief; and the battle of Marston was fought on the 2d July 1644, in which the Royalists were totally defeated. But in the autumn of the same year, the two armies of Waller and Essex were lost in the west counties, and the success of the war continued doubtful. In October, Manchester and Cromwell encountered and worsted the king at Newbury; but Manchester refused to prosecute their success, and an open rupture ensued between him and Cromwell. In the latter part of November, Cromwell complained in his place in Parliament of this dilatory and ineffectual prosecution of the war, and moved that members of Parliament should cease to remain also commanders in the army. This proposal, called the Self-denying Ordinance, passed in the Commons on the 19th December 1644, but was not accepted by the Lords. The treaty of Uxbridge engaged the attention of all parties during the month of January and the early part of February 1645. But this treaty was broken off on the 20th or 21st of February, and the Self-denying Ordinance was soon afterwards re-introduced, and finally passed on the 3d of April 1645. By this ordinance Cromwell also, as a member of Parliament, should have laid down his command; but he could not be spared from the army. On the 9th of April he was again at the head of his men, actively and successfully engaged cutting off convoys and hemming in the king, with a degree of energy which promised a speedy termination of the war. On the 14th of June the battle of Naseby was fought, where Cromwell, at the head of his " new-modelled" army, routed the king, and destroyed all his prospects of success.

Let it be observed, that throughout the whole of this period the proceedings of the Assembly were prevented from making almost any progress by Nye and his friends. Their opposition, by means of protracted debates on every minute point, began early in 1644. On the 20th of February in that year, Nye attempted to gain the favour of the Parliament by arguing that the setting up of presbyteries would be dangerous to liberty. Failing in this attempt, which the parliamentary members themselves repelled, he prosecuted the safer method of retarding the progress of the Assembly by protracted delays. This course was rendered safe and successful by an order which Cromwell induced the Parliament to pass on the 13th of September 1644, when the battle of Marston had removed urgent danger, to refer to the committee of both kingdoms the matters in dispute between Presbyterians and Independents. This committee received all statements but decided nothing, and ceased to exist in March 1646; but, before it ceased to exist, the army had been remodelled, and, with Cromwell at its head, had reduced the king to despair, and made itself master of both Parliament and kingdom. During all this time it was believed that Nye managed to keep up a constant intercourse with Cromwell and the army. Of this the Scottish commissioners entertained no doubt; but as they still cherished the hope that a satisfactory conclusion might at last be obtained, they kept themselves within the limits of honourable and fair discussion, leaving intrigues to be defeated by the course of providence, and refuting sophistry by clear reasoning.

When the king, on the 6th of May 1646, betook himself to the Scottish army, a slight change seemed to come over the Parliament. The ordinance for the erection of presbyteries, which had lain in abeyance since November 1644, was issued by the Parliament 9th June 1646, but hampered by unsuitable conditions and limitations. But when it was found that the obstinacy of the infatuated king was absolutely invincible, and that to retain him any longer in the Scottish army would at once involve a war with England, and frustrate all the proceedings of the Westminster Assembly, the Scottish commissioners felt it to be their duty to abandon all further contests in England, allow the king to return to the Parliament as he desired, and leave the English nation to settle the affairs of their own State and Church as they might determine, taking with them to Scotland the doctrinal productions of the Westminster Assembly, to be ratified and established in their own country.

The Scottish Royalists, indeed, attempted to frustrate these prudent and peaceful designs, and were but too successful. Their ill-omened engagement involved Scotland in a war with England, and laid the divided kingdom prostrate beneath England's mighty Protector. This sagacious and high-principled man did not, however, prevent the Scottish people from continuing to enjoy the religious worship of their choice, though he deprived church government of all power, and balanced party against party so as greatly to paralyze both, as he had done in England.

But the career of Nye was not yet at an end. When both Parliament and Assembly had been dissolved by Cromwell, it was still found necessary to have some method of providing religious instruction for the nation. A committee of divines, called the Committee of Triers, was appointed; and in this committee Nye continued to wield great power. The two parties, the Presbyterians of the old Puritan race, and the more modern Independents, were still opposed to each other. Various attempts, by conferences and otherwise, were made to frame some agreement between them. In these attempts such men as Owen, and Baxter, and Howe took part; but all their attempts were frustrated, and chiefly by Philip Nye. This I can confidently state, on the authority of the mild, gracious, and tolerant John Howe. In a letter to Baxter, dated 25th May 1658, he says, " I cannot yet meet with an opportunity for further discourse with Mr Nye; nor do I hope for much success in any further treaty with him, I perceive so steady a resolution to measure all endeavours of this kind by their subservience to the advantage of one party. I resolve, therefore, to make trial what his Highness will do, as speedily as I can.'"—(*Life of Howe*, by Rogers, p. 92.)

Baxter himself, writing to the Independents in their time of power, says: " It was the toleration of all sects unlimitedly that I wrote and preached against, and not (that I remember) of mere Independents. Those that did oppose the toleration of Independents, of my acquaintance, did not deny them the liberty of Independency, but opposed *separation,* or their gathering of other churches out of parish churches that had faithful ministers. If they would have taken parish churches on Independent principles, without separation, neither I nor my acquaintance did oppose them, no, nor their endeavour to reform such churches. The case greatly differed: For an Independent to refuse parish churches when no ceremony, no liturgy, no oath or subscription is required of him, which he scrupleth, is not like his refusing oaths, subscriptions, liturgy, ceremonies, &c. But, in a word, *grant us but as much, and take us but in, as we granted to, and took in, the Independents, and we are content.* Make this agreement, and all is ended; we desire no more of you. We never denied the Independents the liberty of preaching lectures, as often as they would, nor yet the liberty of taking parish churches. They commonly had presentations, and the public maintenance; and no subscription, declaration, liturgy, or ceremonies, were imposed on them. Again, I say, I ask from you no more liberty than was given the Independents by their brethren, called Presbyterians.—(*Baxter's Life*, by Sylvester, p. 131.)

Such statements as these, and more might easily be adduced, prove clearly enough what the men who knew Nye thought of his character and conduct, and of the manner in which he used power when it was in his grasp. And, it may be added, that he held that grasp very tenaciously. Throughout the whole period of Cromwell's sway Nye retained great influence. Not only was he one of the triers, but he was also one of the commissioners for ejecting ministers and schoolmasters,—a task in which he manifested no reluctance to take an active share. He aided in framing the Declaration of the Faith, Order, and Practice of the Congregational Churches in 1658; but it was rendered ineffectual by the death of Cromwell in the same year. On the restoration of Charles II., it was debated in Council for several hours, whether the deep and incessant political intrigues in which Nye had been so long engaged did not render it necessary to include him in the act of attainder. The result was, that he was ejected from his benefice; and it was declared, that if he should accept of, or exercise any office, ecclesiastical or civil, he should stand as if he had been totally exempted from the act of indemnity. To him alone, of all the Westminster divines, was such severity shown; and as his papers had been seized, the Council were in possession of information which seemed to them to justify such procedure. The act of attainder included only three men who were not of those who had acted as judges when the late king was sentenced to die. These three were, Colonel Lambert, Sir Harry Vane, and the notorious Hugh Peters. That it was seriously debated whether Philip Nye should not be included in such a class of men, the actual regicides, or their most intimate associates, sufficiently indicates how deeply involved he was believed, and even well known to be, in all the intrigues of the period, and especially in all those political measures that led to the decapitation of Charles I.

There is one incident in Nye's conduct, at an early stage of the Westminster Assembly's proceedings, already recorded in the pages of this work (pp. 202, 203), relative to which some brief remarks are still necessary. Congregational writers are in the habit of boasting of his position and speech on that occasion, as the first public, open, and full assertion of the great principle of religious liberty. Nothing can be more inconsistent with historical truth. The occasion already referred to is the only one which at all resembles the boasted traditionary anecdote. But the avowed object of Nye on that occasion was not the assertion of religious liberty, but an attempt to excite the jealousy of the Parliament against the Presbyterian system, by asserting that such a system, rising court above court, with successive right of appeal from the lower to the higher, till it should reach a General Assembly, representing the whole Church in a kingdom, was inconsistent with *civil liberty.* This attempt was both censured by the Assembly and repelled by the most of the leading members of Parliament who were present. Its manifest and total failure mortified Nye so much that he did not again repeat it in the Assembly; but from that day his efforts were incessant to cause and prolong delay, while his secret intercourse with the army and with Cromwell was carried on with greater activity than ever. His interposed retardations and incessant intrigues were successful. Nothing was settled till Cromwell abolished Parliament, and turned the remnant of the Assembly into a Committee of Triers, in which Nye's influence was predominant, and continued to be, till the Restoration laid Britain prostrate beneath the basest and most profligate of all her kings, to the extreme danger and well nigh the utter ruin of all liberty, both civil and religious. And yet this intriguing man, whose conduct was so largely instrumental in producing such a disastrous result, is still held up and applauded by some as the great assertor of religious liberty!

It is with great reluctance that I have directed so much attention to the conduct of Nye. But I felt myself compelled to take some notice of the claim so pertinaciously raised on his behalf, as the first true assertor of religious liberty, to the disparagement equally of Scottish Presbyterians and English Puritans, and very specially to the discredit of the Westminster Assembly. Men have a strange power of persuading themselves that they are in the right, and that their course is the only right and safe one. I have no doubt that Philip Nye fully believed that the Independent system, as he understood and practised it, was the best for the interests of civil and religious liberty, and that he thought himself justifiable in using every method to secure its triumph; and even succeeded in persuading himself that those methods were right, although they involved a violation of the Solemn League and Covenant, which he had sworn to maintain. "He was a great politician," says Neal; and there is scarcely any thing which a great politician cannot persuade himself to believe,—scarcely any course which he cannot persuade himself to adopt,—if they seem fitted to promote his political designs. But it is not by great politicians that religious liberty has ever been promoted, nor by their deep schemes that its maintenance has been secured. Had Nye been less of a politician, there is reason to believe that neither a revived Laudean Prelacy nor a resuscitated Popery would ever again have endangered the liberties, both civil and religious, of Britain; and it will be well if, in the conflict which must still be waged against both of these hostile powers, the defenders of these priceless blessings avoid all courses that "great politicians" may recommend, and act openly, boldly, and firmly, without intrigue or compromise, in accordance only with the strong principles of the Word of God.

It may be thought by some that we have applied the term Presbyterian in several instances, when the term Independent or Congregational would have been more appropriate. We do not wish to dispute about a mere word; but a brief statement of the reason why the word Presbyterian has been used in relation to events which others ascribe to the Independent party, may here be given. Before the Long Parliament had resolved to abolish Prelacy, and summon an Assembly of Divines to deliberate on the system to be adopted in its stead, the Puritan ministers had begun to form themselves into presbyteries. Numbers more of them looked not to Scotland only, but also very specially to Holland, where the Presbyterian form was in full order, for a model into some conformity with which the English Church might be advantageously moulded. When the Assembly met there were only five of its members avowedly Independents, and they never amounted to more than ten or eleven. During the deliberations of the Assembly, Nye and Goodwin almost alone maintained the strictly distinctive element of Congregationalism,—in some instances Nye alone. That distinctive and even separatist, or individualizing element, while the defending of it kept Nye at the head of all the innumerable forms of Sectarianism in the army and throughout the kingdom, and rendered him so useful to Cromwell, was never adopted and maintained in the same manner by even those men who came to be regarded as the leading Independents. Neither Owen nor Howe were ever Independents according to Nye's system, but approached indefinitely near to the Presbyterian system, as it existed in Scotland and Holland, and could readily have joined with these Churches. We therefore include them, and all such liberal-minded men, in the general designation of Presbyterians. For the same reason we regard the noble band of Nonconformist Puritan divines who were ejected on St Bartholomew's Day as Presbyterian Puritans, or rather as Puritan Presbyterians; that is, we regard them as a noble band of sincere, self-denying Christian ministers, whose scriptural tenets were those which have been designated Puritan, and who were not only prepared to adopt the Presbyterian system of church government, but preferred it, as both founded upon and most agreeable to the Word of God, and as most conducive to a nation's welfare. Ample evidence might easily be procured from the writings of an overwhelming majority of these high-principled men, to prove that we have not misrepresented their sentiments, and that we have given them the designation which most correctly describes them, and by which they ought to be known—the Nonconformist Puritan Presbyterians. To them, to the Churches of Scotland and Holland, and, above all, to the sacred truths and principles which they all drew from the Holy Scriptures, we ascribe the glory of the declaration and defence of religious liberty; and neither to the Long Parliament, to the army Sectarians, to Cromwell, to Philip Nye, nor to any or all of those who, in proclaiming a "boundless toleration," did their utmost to break down all distinctions between truth and error, and thereby to plunge the human mind into the wild whirlpool of mental, moral, and religious anarchy. I have no wish to disparage either the Dissenting Brethren of the Westminster Assembly, or the Independent ministers or systems of any period; but I feel it to be my duty to assert historical truth, and to vindicate the character of the Westminster Assembly, and of the true Presbyterian divines, Church, and system, in doctrine, government, and discipline, as most successfully embodying and defending the principles of Religious Freedom.

THE END.

Related publications from Still Waters Revival Books

The Harmony of Protestant Confessions
Revised and considerably enlarged by Peter Hall
Twelve major Confessions, beginning with Augsburg (1530) through to The Confession of Scotland (1560), are catalogued according to topics in this unique and massive volume. The Westminster Confession (1647), The Synod of Dort (1619), The Thirty-nine Articles of the Church of England (1571), and the Irish Articles of 1615, have all been appended to this work, increasing its value and making it the most comprehensive compilation and topically indexed reference tool available to creedal Christians today!

Commentary on the Shorter Catechism (2 Vol.) by Thomas Boston
In this set on the *Shorter Catechism* we see a marriage of Boston's esteemed abilities of exposition with what has been called by many "the most useful teaching aid in Christianity,"— the Westminster Assembly's magnificent *Shorter Catechism.* Not only is this the most comprehensive and extensive commentary available on the *Shorter Catechism* (over 1300 pages), but its pages breathe with the fragrance of singlehearted devotion to Christ and His jealousness for truth, *in that special way that only these old Puritan writings can*!

Commentary on the Larger Catechism (2 Vol.) by Thomas Ridgeley
Consisting of over 1300 pages, this massive commentary on the Larger Catechism is unrivaled in scope or extensiveness. It is designed to be read in families and has been called *"the best book of its class."* John Wilson, the editor, notes, *"Upon the whole, it is probable that the English language does not furnish a work of this nature that, for perspicuity of language, extent of research, accuracy of judgement, and judicious description of the numerous subjects that fall under examination, any way equals this work of Dr. Ridgeley...*he was accounted one of the most considerable divines of his age."

The Works of George Gillespie (2 vol.)
One of the great theologians of all time — almost singlehandedly steering the Westminster Assembly at certain points. This rare work contains Gillespie's personal notes during that Assembly, *A Dispute Against English Popish Ceremonies* (a classic on Reformed worship) and much more. It also includes a memoir of Gillespie's life and writings, written by William M. Hetherington.

The Westminster Assembly: Its History and Standards by Alexander F. Mitchell
The author has given a *succinct account of English Puritanism* from its origin up to and including the meeting of the Westminster Assembly. Mitchell has endeavored to give prominence to aspects of this period in Puritan history which have hitherto been generally overlooked. Mitchell's account of this age of brilliance is a veritable information cornucopia, in which all lovers of Puritanism, the Westminster Assembly, and *especially the truth of Christ* (which these our forefathers in the faith so boldly proclaimed), can readily take delight!

Minutes of the Sessions of the Westminster Assembly of Divines Edited by A. F. Mitchell & John Struthers

The Westminster Assembly and Its Work by B. B. Warfield
Dealing with some of the most important aspects of the Assembly's work, this volume is extremely pertinent for today, particularly in the chapters dealing with inspiration, God's decree (absolute sovereignty) and the Holy Spirit.

History of the Westminster Assembly by William M. Hetherington
900 *hardcover* copies also available in our *Numbered Collectors Edition* series.